MULTICULTURAL EDUCATION SERIES

James A. Banks, Series Editor

Education Research in the Public Interest:
Social Justice, Action, and Policy
GLORIA LADSON-BILLINGS AND
WILLIAM F. TATE, EDS.

Multicultural Strategies for Education and
Social Change: Carriers of the Torch in
the United States and South Africa
ARNETHA F. BALL

We Can't Teach What We Don't Know:
White Teachers, Multiracial Schools,
SECOND EDITION
GARY R. HOWARD

Un-Standardizing Curriculum:
Multicultural Teaching in the Standards-
Based Classroom
CHRISTINE E. SLEETER

Beyond the Big House: African American
Educators on Teacher Education
GLORIA LADSON-BILLINGS

Teaching and Learning in Two Languages:
Bilingualism and Schooling in the United
States
EUGENE E. GARCÍA

Improving Multicultural Education:
Lessons from the Intergroup
Education Movement
CHERRY A. MCGEE BANKS

Education Programs for Improving
Intergroup Relations: Theory, Research,
and Practice
WALTER G. STEPHAN AND
W. PAUL VOGT, EDS.

Walking the Road: Race, Diversity, and
Social Justice in Teacher Education
MARILYN COCHRAN-SMITH

City Schools and the American Dream:
Reclaiming the Promise of Public
Education
PEDRO A. NOGUERA

Thriving in the Multicultural Classroom:
Principles and Practices for Effective
Teaching
MARY DILG

Educating Teachers for Diversity: Seeing
with a Cultural Eye
JACQUELINE JORDAN IRVINE

Teaching Democracy: Unity and Diversity
in Public Life
WALTER C. PARKER

The Making—and Remaking—of a
Multiculturalist
CARLOS E. CORTÉS

Transforming the Multicultural Education
of Teachers: Theory, Research, and Practice
MICHAEL VAVRUS

Learning to Teach for Social Justice
LINDA DARLING-HAMMOND, JENNIFER FRENCH, AND
SILVIA PALOMA GARCIA-LOPEZ, EDS.

Culture, Difference, and Power
CHRISTINE E. SLEETER

Learning and Not Learning English:
Latino Students in American Schools
GUADALUPE VALDÉS

Culturally Responsive Teaching:
Theory, Research, and Practice
GENEVA GAY

The Children Are Watching: How the
Media Teach About Diversity
CARLOS E. CORTÉS

Race and Culture in the Classroom:
Teaching and Learning Through
Multicultural Education
MARY DILG

The Light in Their Eyes: Creating
Multicultural Learning Communities
SONIA NIETO

Reducing Prejudice and Stereotyping
in Schools
WALTER STEPHAN

Educating Citizens in a Multicultural
Society
JAMES A. BANKS

Multicultural Education, Transformative
Knowledge, and Action: Historical and
Contemporary Perspectives
JAMES A. BANKS, ED.

Education Research in the Public Interest

Social Justice, Action, and Policy

EDITED BY

GLORIA LADSON-BILLINGS
AND WILLIAM F. TATE

Teachers College, Columbia University
New York and London

Published by Teachers College Press, 1234 Amsterdam Avenue, New York, NY 10027

Copyright © 2006 by Teachers College, Columbia University
Chapter 8 Copyright © 2006 by James A. Banks

The poem "Gwendolyn Brooks (1917–2000)" that appears at the beginning of Chapter 5 is reprinted by the permission of its author, Anthony Walton.

Library of Congress Cataloging-in-Publication Data

Education research in the public interest : social justice, action, and policy /
    edited by Gloria Ladson-Billings and William F. Tate.
        p. cm. — (Multicultural education series)
    Includes bibliographical references and index.
    ISBN-13: 978-0-8077-4705-6 (alk. paper)
    ISBN-10: 0-8077-4705-X (alk. paper)
    ISBN-13: 978-0-8077-4704-9 (pbk. : alk. paper)
    ISBN-10: 0-8077-4704-1 (pbk. : alk. paper)
        1. Multicultural education—United States. 2. Education—Research—
    United States. 3. Education—Political aspects—United States.
    I. Ladson-Billings, Gloria. II. Tate, William F. III. Series.
    LC1099.3+ 2006   2006040434

ISBN-13:   ISBN-10:
978-0-8077-4704-9 (paper)   0-8077-4704-1 (paper)
978-0-8077-4705-6 (cloth)   0-8077-4705-X (cloth)

Printed on acid-free paper
Manufactured in the United States of America

13 12 11 10 09 08 07 06   8 7 6 5 4 3 2 1

For Marlena, Markela, & Martin,
Our Next Generation of Public Trustees

—G. L-B.

For Kim, Quentin, and Cameron
Who Support and Inspire Me Daily

—W. F. T.

Proceeds from this volume will be donated to the
American Educational Research Association (AERA)

Contents

Series Foreword   ix

    JAMES A. BANKS, *University of Washington, Seattle*

Introduction   1

    GLORIA LADSON-BILLINGS, *University of Wisconsin–Madison*

PART I: POLICY AND POLITICS

1. What Should Count as Educational Research:
   Notes Toward a New Paradigm   17

       JEAN ANYON, *City University of New York*

2. Interrupting the Right:
   On Doing Critical Educational Work in Conservative Times   27

       MICHAEL W. APPLE, *University of Wisconsin–Madison*

3. Carry It On:
   Fighting for Progressive Education in Neoliberal Times   46

       DAVID HURSH, *University of Rochester*

4 Public Intellectuals and the University   64

       ALEX MOLNAR, *Arizona State University*

5. Trudge Toward Freedom:
   Educational Research in the Public Interest   81

       WILLIAM AYERS, *University of Illinois, Chicago*

6: "This *Is* America" 2005: The Political Economy of
   Education Reform Against the Public Interest   98

       PAULINE LIPMAN, *DePaul University*

PART II: THE MAKING OF THE PUBLIC SUBJECT

7. Hopes of Progress and Fears of the Dangerous: Research,
    Cultural Theses, and Planning Different Human Kinds   119

    THOMAS S. POPKEWITZ, *University of Wisconsin–Madison*

8. Democracy, Diversity, and Social Justice:
    Educating Citizens for the Public Interest in a Global Age   141

    JAMES A. BANKS, *University of Washington, Seattle*

9. Multiculturalism, Race, and the Public Interest:
    Hanging on to Great-Great-Granddaddy's Legacy   158

    CARL A. GRANT, *University of Wisconsin–Madison*

10. Public Interest and the Interests of White People Are Not
    the Same: Assessment, Education Policy, and Racism   173

    DAVID GILLBORN, *Institute of Education, University of London*

PART III: THE SCHOOL AND CURRICULUM AS SITES OF EDUCATION RESEARCH IN THE PUBLIC INTEREST

11. Curriculum and Students: Diverting the Public Interest   199

    CATHERINE CORNBLETH, *University of Buffalo*

12. Making Educational History:
    Qualitative Inquiry, Artistry, and the Public Interest   213

    TOM BARONE, *Arizona State University*

13. The Art of Renewing Curriculum Research   231

    DONALD BLUMENFELD-JONES, *Arizona State University*

Afterword: In the Public Interest   247

    WILLIAM F. TATE, *Washington University*

About the Editors and the Contributors   261

Name Index   264

Subject Index   268

Series Foreword

THE NATION'S DEEPENING ETHNIC TEXTURE, interracial tension and conflict, and the increasing percentage of students who speak a first language other than English make multicultural education imperative in the 21st century. The U.S. Census Bureau (2000) estimates that people of color made up 28% of the nation's population in 2000, and predicts that they will make up 38% in 2025 and 50% in 2050 (El Nasser, 2004).

American classrooms are experiencing the largest influx of immigrant students since the beginning of the 20th century. About a million immigrants are making the United States their home each year (Martin & Midgley, 1999). More than seven and one-half million legal immigrants settled in the United States between 1991 and 1998, most of whom came from nations in Latin America and Asia (Riche, 2000). A significant number also come from the West Indies and Africa. A large but undetermined number of undocumented immigrants also enter the United States each year. The influence of an increasingly ethnically diverse population on the nation's schools, colleges, and universities is, and will continue to be, enormous.

Forty percent of the students enrolled in the nation's schools in 2001 were students of color. This percentage is increasing each year, primarily because of the growth in the percentage of Latino students (Martinez & Curry, 1999). In some of the nation's largest cities and metropolitan areas, such as Chicago, Los Angeles, Washington, DC, New York, Seattle, and San Francisco, half or more of the public school students are students of color. During the 1998–1999 school year, students of color made up 63.1% of the student population in the public schools of California, the nation's most-populous state (California State Department of Education, 2000).

Language and religious diversity is also increasing among the nation's student population. In 2000, about 20% of the school-age population spoke a language at home other than English (U.S. Census Bureau, 2000). Harvard professor Diana L. Eck (2001) calls the United States the "most religiously diverse nation on earth" (p. 4). Islam is now the fastest-growing religion in the United States. Most teachers now in the classroom and in teacher education programs are likely to have students from diverse ethnic, racial, language, and religious groups in their classrooms during their careers. This is true for both inner-city and suburban teachers.

An important goal of multicultural education is to improve race relations and to help all students acquire the knowledge, attitudes, and skills needed to participate in cross-cultural interactions and in personal, social, and civic action that will help make our nation more democratic and just. Multicultural education is consequently as important for middle-class White suburban students as it is for students of color who live in the inner-city. Multicultural education fosters the public good and the overarching goals of the commonwealth.

The major purpose of the *Multicultural Education Series* is to provide preservice educators, practicing educators, graduate students, scholars, and policymakers with an interrelated and comprehensive set of books that summarizes and analyzes important research, theory, and practice related to the education of ethnic, racial, cultural, and language groups in the United States, and to the education of mainstream students about diversity. The books in the *Series* provide research, theoretical, and practical knowledge about the behaviors and learning characteristics of students of color, language minority students, and low-income students. They also provide knowledge about ways to improve academic achievement and race relations in educational settings.

The definition of multicultural education in the *Handbook of Research on Multicultural Education* (Banks & Banks, 2004) is used in the *Series*: Multicultural education is "a field of study designed to increase educational equity for all students that incorporates, for this purpose, content, concepts, principles, theories, and paradigms from history, the social and behavioral sciences, and particularly from ethnic studies and women's studies" (p. xii). In the *Series*, as in the *Handbook*, multicultural education is considered a "metadiscipline."

The dimensions of multicultural education, developed by Banks (2004) and described in the *Handbook of Research on Multicultural Education*, provide the conceptual framework for the development of the books in the *Series*. They are: *content integration, the knowledge construction process, prejudice reduction, an equity pedagogy,* and *an empowering school culture and social structure.* To implement multicultural education effectively, teachers and administrators must attend to each of its five dimensions. They should use content from diverse groups when teaching concepts and skills, help students to understand how knowledge in the various disciplines is constructed, help students to develop positive intergroup attitudes and behaviors, and modify their teaching strategies so that students from different racial, cultural, language, and social-class groups will experience equal educational opportunities. The total environment and culture of the school must also be transformed so that students from diverse groups will experience equal status in the culture and life of the school.

Although the five dimensions of multicultural education are highly interrelated, each requires deliberate attention and focus. Each book in the series focuses on one or more of the dimensions, although each book deals with all of them to some extent because of the highly interrelated characteristics of the dimensions.

.

This engaging and timely book explores a topic that is especially appropriate for the challenging and divisive times in which we live: How can educational researchers serve and promote the public interest? This is a complex and contentious question because individuals and groups within a democratic and pluralistic society such as the United States hold divergent views about which policies and practices will best serve the public interest. An essential tenet of a democratic society is that individuals and groups with diverse points of view will participate in dialogues in public spaces in order to find common ground.

Individuals and groups define the "public interest" differently. Neoconservatives, who are now exercising a significant influence on educational policy and practice in the United States, would argue that their policies and goals serve the public interest (Finn, 1991; Stotsky, 1999). Neoconservatives have appropriated some of the language and phrases of progressives, such as "Leave No Child Behind," which is the copyrighted motto of the Children's Defense Fund (CDF) (Franklin, 2005, p. 333) that was coined by Marian Wright Edelman, CDF's founder and President (Edelman, 1987).

The other problematic aspect of using research to serve the public interest is that the dominant and mainstream research paradigm that is institutionalized in U.S. colleges and universities maintains that rigorous and objective research should not be influenced by human interests, values, and the life experiences of researchers (Kaplan, 1964). However, as scholars of color and feminist scholars have described in a series of pioneering and trenchant studies, mainstream "objective" research has often depicted marginalized racial, social-class, and gender groups in stereotypical ways that contributed to their victimization and the denial of democracy and social justice. Mainstream researchers have also frequently reinforced institutionalized race, class, and gender stratification. As Code (1991) has stated, the claim of objectivity can enable researchers to avoid epistemic responsibility to the communities they study.

The claim of objectivity has often resulted in research that was detrimental to social justice and the broad public interest, and was later proven to be scientifically invalid. The science of phrenology—which involved studying the shape of the human skull to make inferences about mental and behavioral characteristics (Chernow & Vallasi, 1993)—became a major weapon in the scientific quest to prove that some races were inferior to others. The phrenologists gained substantial influence during the 1820s and 1830s in part because of their use of scientific methods and assumptions to establish the superiority of some races. Horsman (1981) notes that the phrenologists "found in skulls and heads what they wanted to find: a physical confirmation of supposedly observed cultural traits" (p. 145).

In more recent years, scientific research that has claimed to be objective has also been detrimental to democracy and social justice. Among the most salient examples are the research paradigm of the 1960s that described the culture of low-income youth as deprived (Riessman, 1962), and the descriptions of the in-

tellectual abilities of African Americans that were constructed by Arthur Jensen
(1969) and Richard R. Herrnstein and Charles R. Murray (1994). These researchers argued that African Americans are genetically inferior to Whites. As I stated
in an earlier publication (Banks, 1998), the alternative is not to give up the quest
for objectivity in social science and educational research. Rather, the goal should
be to reformulate and reconstruct objectivity so that its formulation will involve
the participation of scholars from diverse racial, ethnic, and gender groups. Harding (1991) states that this kind of reconstruction of objectivity results in "strong
objectivity."

The group of progressive scholars who penned this book are in the tradition
of earlier transformative scholars who attained respect and recognition from the
mainstream scholarly and research community and yet who have—through their
research and actions—promoted the public interest, democracy, and social justice
(Banks, 1996). Kenneth B. Clark (1993) and John Hope Franklin (1989, 2005),
who were important mentors for me, epitomized transformative scholars who were
highly respected within their academic disciplines. Both Clark and Franklin did
work that supported the plaintiffs in the *Brown v. Brown of Education of Topeka*
Supreme Court case. Clark (1993) testified in the case and described research he
conducted that was later cited in the *Brown* decision. Franklin helped Thurgood
Marshall and the other lawyers for the plaintiffs research the historical arguments
for *Brown*. Writes Franklin (2005):

> While I set out to advance my professional career on the basis of the highest standards
> of scholarship, I also used that scholarship to expose the hypocrisy underlying so much
> of American social and race relations. It never ceased being a risky feat of tightrope
> walking, but I always believed that if I could use my knowledge and training to im-
> prove society it was incumbent on me to make the attempt. (p. 376)

Clark and Franklin also took many other actions to support civil rights. However, as their lives and several of the skillfully crafted essays in this book make
clear, scholars who become involved in action are subject to criticism from their
academic colleagues, as well as to the vagaries, whims, and contradictions of
political battles and struggles in the real world beyond the academy. Clark spent
most of his career working to advance school desegregation. However, he was
harshly criticized in the late 1960s and early 1970s by Black Power advocates after many African Americans had become disillusioned with school desegregation
because of the high price that Blacks were paying for it.

Franklin, who testified against Robert Bork—the controversial nominee for
the Supreme Court who had a questionable record on civil rights—was deeply
disappointed and chagrined when President Ronald Reagan said that individuals who opposed Bork's nomination were a "lynch mob" (quoted in Franklin,
1989, p. 364). Writes Franklin, "One must be prepared for any eventuality when
he makes any effort to promote legislation or to shape the direction of public

policy or to affect the choice of those in public service" (pp. 363–364). The consequences and reactions that followed Derek Bell's (1994) unsuccessful efforts to convince his colleagues at the Harvard Law School to hire women of color are other indications of the risks and possibilities involved when scholars participate in social action within the academy or the civic community.

Scholars and researchers who view social justice as a key goal of their research and who interpret social justice as promoting educational equality for marginalized groups are highly vulnerable to being perceived pejoratively as "advocates," rather than as scholars. Researchers whose work focuses on mainstream groups or whose research on marginalized groups reinforces mainstream concepts, paradigms, and theories are more likely to be perceived as "objective" scholars, not as advocates.

Pursuing *transformative* research—which I define as research that challenges mainstream and institutionalized findings, interpretations, and paradigms (Banks, 2006)—is professionally risky but, as the chapters in this book indicate, is personally enriching because it makes a difference and helps to humanize our troubled and divided society. The informative and heartfelt essays in this book should stimulate a needed and important discourse about ways in which scholars can conduct educational research that enhances democracy and social justice while advancing the kind of scientific knowledge that will make a difference in the lives of students.

—James A. Banks
Series Editor

REFERENCES

Banks, J. A. (Ed.). (1996). *Multicultural education, transformative knowledge, and action.* New York: Teachers College Press.

Banks, J. A. (1998). The lives and values of researchers: Implications for educating citizens in a multicultural society (AERA Presidential Address). *Educational Researcher,* *27*(7), 4–17.

Banks, J. A. (2004). Multicultural education: Historical development, dimensions, and practice. In J. A. Banks & C. A. M. Banks (Eds.), *Handbook of research on multicultural education* (2nd ed., pp. 3–29). San Francisco: Jossey-Bass.

Banks, J. A. (2006). *Race, culture, and education: The selected works of James A. Banks.* New York & London: Routledge.

Banks, J. A., & Banks, C. A. M. (Eds.). (2004). *Handbook of research on multicultural education* (2nd ed.). San Francisco: Jossey-Bass.

Bell, D. A. (1994). *Confronting authority: Reflections of an ardent protester.* Boston: Beacon.

California State Department of Education. (2000). Available online at http://data1.cde.ca.gov/dataquest

Chernow, B. A., & Vallasi, C. A. (Eds.). (1993). *The Columbia encyclopedia* (5th ed.). New York: Columbia University Press.

Clark, K. B. (1993). Racial progress and retreat: A personal memoir. In H. Hill & J. E. Jones Jr. (Eds.), *Race in America: The struggle for equality* (pp. 3–18). Madison: The University of Wisconsin Press.

Code, L. (1991). *What can she know? Feminist theory and the construction of knowledge.* Ithaca, NY: Cornell University Press.

Eck, D. L. (2001). *A new religious America: How a "Christian country" has become the world's most religiously diverse nation.* New York: HarperSanFrancisco.

Edelman, M. W. (1987). *Families in peril: An agenda for social change.* Cambridge, MA: Harvard University Press.

El Nasser, H. (2004, March 18). Census projects growing diversity: By 2050: Population burst, societal shifts. *USA Today,* p. 1A.

Finn, C. E. (1991). *We must take charge: Our schools and our future.* New York: Free Press.

Franklin, J. H. (1989). *Race and history: Selected essays, 1938–1988.* Baton Rouge: Louisiana State University Press.

Franklin, J. H. (2005). *Mirror to America: The autobiography of John Hope Franklin.* New York: Farrar, Straus & Giroux.

Harding, S. (1991). *Whose science? Whose knowledge? Thinking from women's lives.* Ithaca, NY: Cornell University Press.

Herrnstein, R. J., & Murray, C. (1994). *The bell curve: Intelligence and class structure in American life.* New York: The Free Press.

Horsman, R. (1981). *Race and manifest destiny: The origins of American racial Anglo-Saxonism.* Cambridge, MA: Harvard University Press.

Jensen, A. R. (1969). How much can we boost IQ and scholastic achievement? *Harvard Educational Review, 39,* 1–123.

Kaplan, A. (1964). *The conduct of inquiry: Methodology for behavioral science.* San Francisco: Chandler.

Martin, P., & Midgley, E. (1999). Immigration to the United States. *Population Bulletin, 54*(2), 1–44. Washington, DC: Population Reference Bureau.

Martinez, G. M., & Curry, A. E. (1999, September). *Current population reports: School enrollment-social and economic characteristics of students* (update). Washington, DC: U.S. Census Bureau.

Riche, M. F. (2000). America's diversity and growth: Signposts for the 21st century. *Population Bulletin, 55*(2), 1–43. Washington, DC: Population Reference Bureau.

Riessman, F. (1962). *The culturally deprived child.* New York: Harper & Row.

Stotsky, S. (1999). *Losing our language: How multicultural classroom instruction is undermining our children's ability to read, write, and reason.* New York: Free Press.

U.S. Census Bureau. (2000). *Statistical abstract of the United States* (120th ed.). Washington, DC: U.S. Government Printing Office.

Introduction

GLORIA LADSON-BILLINGS

I BEGAN THIS PROJECT with some feelings of energy and optimism. There
is increasing public interest in the work of education at all levels—teaching,
curriculum, assessment, and policy. That interest translates into inquiry for
those of us whose lives are in education research. I was amazed at how quickly
I was able to assemble a top-flight group of scholars to write chapters for this
volume. The book began taking shape in record time, and I am challenged by my
colleagues, who have written in strong, straightforward voices about the work of
education researchers as they engage with the public. And then the rains came—
the hurricane rains of Katrina came.

I watched Katrina from the other side of the Atlantic Ocean. I, along with two
of the contributors to this volume, was attending a conference in London when
news from the BBC and CNN World arrived about the strength of the hurricane;
the devastation of an area the size of the United Kingdom; and the utter despair
of the poor, elderly, and Black citizens of the Gulf Coast region. What could we
say about the public interest when it appeared that the public institutions most
responsible for responding to the most needy segments of the public had almost
no interest in them?

The strange contrast between the response to September 11th and Hurricane
Katrina left a sickening feeling in the pit of my stomach. Let me be clear: These
are not equivalent events. September 11th was an attack of foreign terrorists that
made us all feel confused and vulnerable. The nation mourned the death of so
many Americans and lifted up the heroism of hundreds of brave first responders. We rallied around a president whose competence (and legitimacy) many of
us questioned. New York, the city that never sleeps, became a place that was
home to us all. I worried about whether my family members who live in New
York were safe. I heard scores of stories about New Yorkers exhibiting their best
selves. There were reports of merchants who handed out sneakers to women who
were walking through Manhattan in high-heeled shoes because the transportation
system was impacted. There were other reports of children passing out bottles of
water to the stunned commuters. Help for victims of 9/11 came in many forms
from around the country and throughout the world.

Education Research in the Public Interest, edited by Gloria Ladson-Billings and William F. Tate. Copyright © 2006 by Teachers
College, Columbia University. All rights reserved. Prior to photocopying items for classroom use, please contact the Copyright
Clearance Center, Customer Service, 222 Rosewood Dr., Danvers, MA 01923, USA, tel. (978) 750-8400, www.copyright.com.

1

Hurricane Katrina was a natural disaster. It was not contained to a few buildings in New York and Washington, D.C., and to a field in Pennsylvania. The storm could not be prevented. Indeed, the last few years have seen a number of devastating tropical storms and hurricanes. The state of Florida alone was battered by three to four major storms in the 2004 hurricane season. The shock of Katrina was the way so many U.S. citizens were left to fend for themselves. In an administration that claimed to leave no child behind, large numbers of poor, elderly, and Black citizens were left behind. Our horror was not over the path of destruction the storm left but rather the gaping hole in the safety net left by 25 years of public neglect.

The spectacle that became the Hurricane Katrina crisis forces me to ask the question, "Which public(s) command(s) our interest and what, if anything, can we say about those publics that we regularly and systematically ignore?" More than 40 years ago Michael Harrington (1962) published the book, *The Other America*, that is credited with launching the War on Poverty. In it he described the social and economic isolation that millions of poor urban and rural citizens experience in America. He also described their relatively invisible status in the American psyche. During the 2004 presidential campaign, Democratic vice-presidential candidate John Edwards tried to bring an awareness of the persistence of two Americas to the consciousness of the American electorate:

> Today, under George W. Bush, there are two Americas, not one: One America that does the work, another that reaps the reward. One America that pays the taxes, another America that gets the tax breaks. One America—middle-class America—whose needs Washington has long forgotten, another America—narrow-interest America—whose every wish is Washington's command. One America that is struggling to get by, another America that can buy anything it wants, even a Congress and a president. (Retrieved October 6, 2005, from http://en.wikiquote.org/wiki/John_Edwards)

But even Edwards was not referencing the poorest of the poor. His appeal was to the middle class, who were slowly but surely feeling the impact of stagnant wages and increasing health care costs. The desperately poor who emerged across our media or were perhaps "washed up" after Katrina represent an entirely new magnitude of poverty to which too many had become insensitive and unaware. Katrina's gift was its in-your-face confrontation of how we are going to define the public and its interests.

Some might question the relevance of Hurricane Katrina to a volume on education research and the public interest. However, in the aftermath of the hurricane, where cities and small towns are attempting to pull their lives back together, we can see examples of how the inequities continue to be manifest. The hurricane was an equal opportunity destroyer. Million-dollar beachfront homes and casinos were destroyed along with housing projects, tenements, and shotgun houses. But the process of reconstruction has very different patterns. Evacuees from the wealthier communities have been able to place their children in private schools or attend public schools outside of the urban community of New Orleans. Evacuees from the infamous lower 9th ward and most of New Orleans proper were told that their public schools might not reopen for the 2005–2006 academic year.

The public interest aspect of education research is linked to the increasing public involvement in education. Since the *Brown v. Board of Education* decisions (in 1954 and 1955), it has been clear that there is a national interest in education. The contour of that interest has shifted with the political winds. There have been times when education barely registered on the national agenda. Ronald Reagan was determined to dismantle the Education Department. His disdain for what he termed "big government" forced him to urge policies such as vouchers, character education, and an emphasis on back-to-basics curricula such as reading, mathematics, and history. However, we must recall that it was during Reagan's administration that the agenda for federal intervention in education was re-set. The release of *A Nation at Risk* in 1983 set the direction for education reform. This report was followed by a spate of documents and initiatives decrying the terrible state of the nation's educational system.

The response to the alarm that education was failing on all fronts was to raise the bar and depend primarily on standardized assessments to measure academic progress. During the first term of the George W. Bush administration, the Elementary and Secondary Education Act was due for reauthorization. Instead of focusing the reauthorization solely on the compensatory aspects of Title I, the Bush White House made it an omnibus act that affected all public schools. Their program, called No Child Left Behind (NCLB), required schools to test students regularly, hire what were termed "highly qualified" teachers, and use "scientifically proven" teaching methods. Unfortunately these grand plans were not matched with adequate funding from the federal government.

As shortsighted as I think NCLB is, there are aspects of it that do exactly what education needs. For example, it forces schools to disaggregate their data by racial/ethnic group. This is particularly important in suburban and metropolitan districts where so-called good schools were guilty of masking the poor academic performance of students of color by the much greater numbers of their White middle-class students. However, the real genius of NCLB was to include all students—not just Title I students—in the reauthorization. This approach forced many educators off the sidelines and into the fray. We were no longer talking simply about "other people's children" (Delpit, 1995)—we now had to think about our own children. But those points do not outweigh the serious flaws in the legislation or its unfunded mandates.

NEW ORLEANS AND THE PERFECT STORM

I reflect back on New Orleans and the aftermath of the hurricane because New Orleans provides a perfect example of what happens when *everything* goes wrong. Before Katrina the statistics on Orleans Parish painted a grim picture of life for many of its citizens. According to the U.S. Census Bureau (2000), New Orleans had a population of 484,674 before the hurricane. Sixty-seven percent of that population was African American, with 23.7% of the total population living below the poverty line and 35% of the African American population living below the poverty line. More than 40,000 New Orleans residents had less than a ninth-grade education and 56,804 residents had between ninth- and twelfth-grade educations without diplomas. A telling statistic is that 96.1% of the public school population was African American, which means that most of the White families with school-age children sent their children to private schools. Thirteen percent of the public school teachers in the state were uncertified.

Education clearly was not working for those in New Orleans who depended on public schools. It was not working long before the streets were flooded and the roofs were blown away. A well-known Norman Rockwell painting shows a little African American walking between federal marshals on her way to school. That depiction represents a little girl named Ruby Bridges, who was the first African American to integrate New Orleans schools. Wells (2004) details the history of resistance by White communities bordering New Orleans to allowing African American students to enter their schools. Bridges's story, while compelling, is even more extraordinary in light of the context of school desegregation in New Orleans. Out of 137 African American students who applied to attend formerly all-White schools, only 4 were selected. One of the 4 students was Ruby Bridges. She attended the William Frantz Elementary School, and all the White students boycotted the school. Only one teacher, a White woman from New York, was willing to teach Ruby. As a consequence of her attending the previously all-White school, Ruby's father was fired from his job and her grandparents were evicted from their tenant farm. For most of us, the story of Ruby Bridges is a story of courage and heroism—and it is that. But the deeper story is the story of how America's fatal flaw—racism—continues to distort and destroy the promise on which the nation claims to be founded. The same mentality that allowed White citizens to oppose school desegregation in the 1960s was present among White citizens who armed themselves to prevent desperate Black citizens of New Orleans from seeking refuge from the floodwaters in the midst of the hurricane disaster. Which public are we referencing when, in 2005, a public official (a sheriff) points a gun at destitute evacuees, says, "You're not coming in here," and leaves them to wither on a freeway overpass? (Glass, 2005).

This history of New Orleans school desegregation is a part of a larger history of not just educational access denied but also of citizenship denied. Limiting education is but one of the ways to create second-class citizenship. However, it is one of the more effective ways, because once a people are miseducated and/or undereducated, the society can claim the need to use "merit" as the standard according to which postsecondary decisions (e.g., college admission, job placement) will be made. New Orleans is a municipality where people were *systematically* excluded from social benefits—housing, health, employment, and education. Hurricane

Katrina brought to the surface the horror that had existed in New Orleans for more than a century. The horror of Hurricane Katrina is made more frustrating by the history of flooding in the Gulf Coast region. In the great Mississippi flood of 1927, Louisiana officials deliberately flooded African American neighborhoods, allegedly to prevent greater flooding in other parts of the city. Officials dynamited the Poydras levee, and ultimately 700,000 people, half of them African Americans, were displaced. More horrific than the flood (which killed about 246 people) were the conditions that existed in the evacuation camps.

Now, almost 80 years later, we see an eerily similar situation. The poor are abandoned and displaced, and we seem to have learned little from the lessons of history. What, if anything, can education research tell us about what we should do to ensure that the rebuilding process in New Orleans does not reproduce the substandard education that had become emblematic of the city?

In many ways New Orleans has the opportunity to do exactly what Anyon (2005) argues must be done to improve urban schools. The schools must be reformed in tandem with improvements to the entire city. In the case of New Orleans, everything has to be rebuilt and the schools have an opportunity to emerge anew. Unfortunately, some disturbing rumblings have already emerged. The city's power elite, civic leaders, developers, and speculators plan to build a "different" New Orleans—one with fewer poor people and presumably fewer African Americans. Because so many of the city's displaced residents are poor, it is unlikely that they will be able to quickly pick up and return to the city. If they have been fortunate enough to find housing, employment, and decent schooling in another city, we cannot expect them to return to New Orleans. With fewer residents returning to the city, the school population will be smaller. The smaller school population can provide an opportunity for smaller schools (and hopefully smaller classrooms).

With a smaller school population, New Orleans has an opportunity to be more selective in the hiring of teachers and other school personnel. It even has the opportunity to create a new school district that is not limited to the geographic confines of Orleans Parish. Orfield and Eaton (1996) point out that one of the major problems that school desegregation addresses is the concentration of poverty. A new school district configuration can address that. Foster (1997), Irvine (2002), Delpit (1995), Siddle-Walker (1996), and Hilliard (2000) all address the point that African Americans do know how to educate themselves. Anderson (1988) and Willis (2002) detail the historical pattern of African Americans creating, building, maintaining, and sustaining educational institutions. A new New Orleans school district has the opportunity to build on this legacy of success.

It is important to acknowledge that schools are not the sole site of community and individual development. Rothstein (2004a) has consistently argued that in addition to school improvement, policymakers and educators must pursue expanded notions of schooling that include out-of-school experiences and "social and economic policies that will enable children to attend school more equally ready to learn" (p. 109). The policies that Rothstein references, similar to Anyon (2005), include expanded and affordable health services and housing along with jobs that allow people to make a true living wage. Rubinowitz and Rosenbaum (2000) documented the ability of low-income African Americans to "move to opportunity" by integrating into suburban communities. Comparisons between the people who moved to suburban communities and those who moved within the city show significant differences. Forty percent of the students who attended schools in the suburbs were enrolled in college-track curricula compared to the 24% enrolled in college tracks in the city. Fifty-four percent of the African American students who moved to the suburbs enrolled in some type of postsecondary education, 27% of them in a 4-year college. Their city counterparts enrolled in postsecondary programs at the rate of 21%, with only 4% enrolled in a 4-year college. On the economic front, 75% of the mothers who moved to the suburbs were working compared to just 41% of their counterparts who remained in the city.

But all was not positive in the suburbs. African American students had higher rates of special education placement in the suburbs, with 19% of them placed in special-needs categories versus 7% in the city. This special education disproportionality is consistent with Skiba, Michael, Nardo, and Peterson's (2002) findings on Black students regarding special education placement and discipline referrals.

I recount these figures to point toward the troubling attitudes and behaviors that are likely to emerge even if New Orleans has the opportunity to start over and create a new city that truly provides equal opportunities for all its residents. Unfortunately, as a critical race theorist, I am not optimistic about the likelihood of a just resolution to the reconstruction of New Orleans. If I were forced to predict the outcome of the reconstruction, it would resemble the following scenario:[1]

> The year is 2008 and with my eyes closed and ears wide open I can tell I am in New Orleans. The aroma is a mix of savory and sweet—hot and languid. I can smell the down-home gumbo, the tangy jambalaya, and a wonderful shrimp etouffee simmering on the collective stoves of French Quarter restaurants. My sweet tooth is tickled by the prospect of luscious hot bread pudding and bananas foster. Yes, my nose tells me I am in New Orleans. My ears also tell me that I am in the Big Easy. I hear the strains of Dixieland coming from one street corner and Zydeco coming from another. There is no other town where this music is so prominent and evident in everyday living. However, it is when I open my eyes that I begin to doubt myself. Some aspects of the city are immediately recognizable. I see Jackson Square with the lovely Cathedral of St Louis on one side and the Mississippi River on the other. The shops of the French Quarter are humming with activity. Tourists are browsing the many souvenir shops. Every now and then I see someone with a T-shirt attesting to their experience of having survived Katrina.
>
> As I look down Poydras I can see that the horror of the Superdome and the New Orleans Convention Center have been replaced by a new sports

and convention center complex. A gleaming new Hyatt Hotel sits between the two. I decide to grab the trolley on Canal Street and head out toward the zoo. I recognize the grandeur of the Garden District. Organizations like National Historic Preservation have worked hard to make sure the stately mansions were brought back to their timeless beauty. Looking at this community, you would never guess that a hurricane and flooding had ever occurred. I step off the trolley at Tulane University, where I see a bustling campus, beautifully appointed and clearly a center of academic activity. It looks like the new New Orleans is better than ever.

I return downtown so that I can head toward the places I know best, I want to check out Congo Square in Louis Armstrong Park. I want to see if someone dusted off Marie Laveaux's tomb. I want to see how Xavier, Dillard, and Southern Universities came through the disaster. I am buoyed by what I have seen at both Tulane and Loyola. When I get hungry, I will probably sneak into Dooky Chase to eat some things that have not been on my diet for years, but Leah Chase is an institution, having cooked at that location since 1946, that has earned a special place in my heart. One year when my family and I were in New Orleans for the Sugar Bowl game, we had dinner at Dooky Chase. It was late on a Sunday evening and there wasn't much foot traffic. The food was not particularly outstanding, but I wanted my teenage daughter to go to a Black New Orleans institution. Some days after we returned home, I noticed that my credit card was missing. In attempting to retrace my steps, I realized that the last time I had used the card was at the restaurant. A quick phone call to New Orleans got me in touch with the maître'd, who informed me that he had found the card but did not know how to get in touch with me. In a matter of minutes, the card was destroyed and canceled.

Louis Armstrong Park is just where it was. It has been cleaned up and the marker for Congo Square remains. This is the place where former enslaved Africans spent their Sunday afternoons. Their stories of resistance and survival were formulated here. To me, it is sacred ground. I breathe a sigh of relief, but my relief is short-lived. My visits to Dillard, Xavier, and Southern Universities are much less satisfying. Both Dillard and Xavier have had to merge with two of the city's predominately White institutions—Xavier with Loyola and Dillard with Tulane. Southern (SUNO) has closed and moved its operation to Baton Rouge. The state has decided it can no longer afford to have two branches of the Southern campus.

I decide to pick up my spirits with a shrimp po'boy at Dooky Chase's, but when I turn down Orleans Street I barely recognize it. Gone are the ramshackle public housing units and in their place there is nothing. Just as it is in North Philadelphia, Detroit, South Central Los Angeles, East Oakland, East St. Louis, and countless other U.S. cities, there has been no attempt to rebuild in this area. The infamous 9th ward that was home to a large number of the city's poor and African American community lays fallow. It is caught between the greedy land developers from the East Coast and the holier-than-thou environmentalists from the West Coast. The two groups are mired in litigation, while squeezed in the middle are the poorest of the poor who would like to return but have nowhere to live.

Without a 9th ward Orleans Parish schools were a very different place.

Instead of 60,000 students, they now have less than half that number, with about 28,000 students. When the first residents returned to repopulate the city, those with school-age children were offered vouchers to take to private schools because the public system was not yet fully online. By the time the city was up and running, the damage done by the diversion of students from the public system had taken its toll. The failure to bring all segments of the community back into the city means that there was a smaller tax base on which to build a school system.

The booming downtown area was deceptive. Yes, there were gleaming new hotels and department stores. In fact, several corporate headquarters had relocated to the newly reconstructed New Orleans. These companies were able to make sweet deals with the city fathers. They were promised tax credits and a variety of workplace waivers that allowed them to hire people for their low-level jobs (e.g., janitors, cafeteria workers, clerks) without providing full benefits. Housing was at a premium in the new city. Condos and town-houses dominated the downtown area. The stately mansions remained in the hands of the city's old-money families. The poor were locked out. A few of the poor were able to find some housing across the river in the Algiers section of the city, but there is not much in the rebuilt city that can accommodate people of modest means.

For many months New Orleans was known as the "childless city" ("New Orleans Faces Months," 2005). Those poor families with children did not return because they did not want to risk moving their children out of the somewhat stable school environments they had found in other communities. Others worried that the level of contamination caused by the sewage, standing water, and lack of sanitation had created a toxic environment that they could not risk with their children. Still others recognized that the limited social services—day care, after-school programs, community centers—meant that there was not enough community infrastructure in which their children could flourish.

New Orleans had become a city of odd demographics. It reminded me of the District of Columbia. It was a place where almost no families sent their children to public schools. Private schools were springing up all over the place. In a nod to its French heritage, the city became home to several lyceums attended by the wealthiest residents. The public schools, although smaller, were not much better than before the disaster. Few "highly qualified" teachers had returned to the system. Most of the newer teachers had found jobs in other communities. Large numbers of veteran teachers had retired. This smaller school system had its share of "competent" teachers, but a better assessment was that most of the system's teachers were mediocre.

The pattern of racism seemed clear to me, but I was assured that race had nothing to do with how the city had been reconstructed. I was shown how a variety of old-line (read, Creole) families had been an integral part of the rebuilding. Indeed, the mayor was Black. No, racism had no place in New Orleans. The city was just adamant about not allowing an unsavory element to repopulate the new city. I had been in this place before. Every time someone said the words *urban renewal*, I witnessed the dissolution of poor African American communities, the loss of community control, the influx of high-end homes, and the disappearance of strong public schools.

The new New Orleans is an adult city—a kind of Las Vegas south. The needs of low- to moderate-income families are not taken into consideration. There is a need for some low-income people to do service work in the hotels and growing number of casinos that jump-started the economy after the hurricane. Many of these workers are migrant and undocumented. They rarely demand social services for fear of being harassed by government officials regarding their immigration status. Many of these workers work two (and sometimes three) jobs.

The strange thing about this new New Orleans is that so many people are so positive about the reconstruction. The newspapers are filled with good-news stories about new hotels, restaurants, and businesses opening. The bureau of tourism is thriving, and conventions and meetings are at an all-time high. As a part of the redevelopment, the city provides huge discounts for organizations to book their conferences and conventions in New Orleans. The voices of the suffering poor are muted and their advocates are regularly dismissed. The only thing they can hope for is another devastating hurricane. Then the nation will be forced to gaze upon them once again.

CODA

Some might argue that the chronicle I detailed is far-fetched and has no basis in reality. However, the story has a basis in the historical reality of generations of New Orleans families. In both the flood of 1927 and Hurricane Betsy, the African American community was the most vulnerable. Rumors of deliberate levee breaches and slow responses (or responses primarily motivated by the possibility of political gain) have kept African Americans suspicious and distrustful of their governments at all levels—local, state, and federal.

The one thing that many planners and reconstruction gurus have not understood is the incredible pull of family in the New Orleans African American community. Many of the residents of the 9th ward have not lived anywhere other than New Orleans. With family members deceased and dispersed because of Hurricane Katrina, many African Americans have lost their moorings. Their extended families provided the safety net that kept them from starvation and homelessness. The complex and vital social networks of mothers, grandmothers, aunts, uncles, and cousins are what kept people connected to and functioning in the city, no matter how marginal those existences were.

I am reminded, as I consider the case of New Orleans, about the national trauma brought on by the attacks of September 11, 2001. Cornel West (2004) points out that 9/11 provided an opportunity for the entire nation to feel exactly what the disenfranchised and poor feel all of the time—unsafe, hated, and despised. Indeed, West argues that for the first time America had the collective "blues." Since African Americans are a blues people, one might ask what a blues nation can learn from a blues people. In spite of the despair of Katrina, there were some stories of leadership, heroism, and courage. And much of this virtue was exhibited not by first responders (who were cut off from the ability to respond) but by the very people whose lives were placed in jeopardy by the hurricane and flood. Americans met 9/11 with the full force of the government—attacks on Afghanistan, creation of a Department of Homeland Security, increased airport security, more stringent rules for immigration, and an all-around heightening of our fears. What will be the full force of the government for the victims of Katrina?

What, then, can education research offer to a place of such utter devastation and despair? My initial response is: Nothing. But, as I think about our work, I am convinced that the hurricane also gave us an opportunity to recapture our humanity. It was John Dewey (1927) who wrote that democracy and education are intertwined in their responsibilities to help the public solve its problems. Our work is not merely about data points and effect sizes. It is also about what difference our work can make in the lives of real people. Hurricane Katrina brings shame upon us all. We have no excuse for our ignorance about poverty. We cannot keep writing about schools as some idyllic, romantic places where a few students are failing. The work we have to do must be done in the public interest. We cannot hide behind notions of neutrality or objectivity when people are suffering so desperately. The questions we pursue, the projects we choose, the agenda we champion have to be about more than career advancement. If education research is going to matter, then we have to make it matter in the lives of real people around real issues. It is just too bad that we have had to have a disaster to make this clear to us.

The contributors to this volume have taken an expansive view of the notion of public interest and the relationship that education and education research have to that notion. As editors, we have organized this volume to reflect what we see as a thematically coherent whole. Part One—Policy and Politics—includes works from Jean Anyon, Michael W. Apple, David Hursh, Alex Molnar, William Ayers, and Pauline Lipman.

Jean Anyon begins by looking at the macro-social policies that limit real school reform in urban schools. Social policies such as thwarting minimum wage hikes or moving decent paying jobs to the suburbs work to limit home ownership and shrink the urban tax base. Ultimately, city schools have fewer resources than their suburban counterparts. Anyon argues that, despite these challenges, poor communities—particularly poor communities of color—can and do have agency that can be activated through coalition building and social movements.

Michael Apple tackles what he terms the "conservative restoration" with a series of action-oriented steps that critical education researchers must take if they are to convince a cynical public that progressive ideas are more than mere pipe dreams. His chapter challenges those on the left of the political spectrum to *not* assume that the many people who have joined with conservative politics are blindly following conservative power-brokers. Rather, the new conservative discourse resonates with the hopes, fears, and dreams of a great many people.

David Hursh addresses the spate of neoliberal policies that are dismantling and discrediting progressive education strategies. Hursh's analysis looks at both

U.S. and British school reform efforts and pays specific attention to the U.S. federal legislation No Child Left Behind, to Chicago School Reform, and to the New York State Regents' mandates. His chapter concludes with the civic engagement he and other scholars engage in to fight reactionary school reform policies.

Alex Molnar looks at the role of public intellectuals in the academy. His chapter details his own work examining commercialism and education. Molnar's documentation of the increased marketization in schools includes a range of commercial efforts from product advertising to privatization of the entire schooling enterprise.

William Ayers' chapter suggests that education researchers can and should broadened their perspectives by drawing on the humanities to more fully develop their knowledge and understanding of social and educational phenomena. By pulling on themes of enlightenment, emancipation, human knowledge, and human freedom, Ayers outlines an approach to educational inquiry that points toward an expansive view of humanity. This view looks at broad questions such as: What interests does our research serve? What forms of inquiry might encourage people to be more creative and to become active problem solvers? How can we do this work?

Pauline Lipman's chapter explores the connection between current education reforms and the political economy, and looks more directly at the implication of these factors for economic and social justice and democracy. Her chapter draws parallels between the push for accountability, standards, and choice on the school reform side, and economic redistribution, markets, and labor stratification on the political economy side.

Part Two—The Making of the Public Subject—includes chapters that raise fundamental questions about who gets to be a citizen and how civic participation is circumscribed by one's status. The authors in this section include Thomas Popkewitz, James A. Banks, Carl A. Grant, and David Gillborn.

Thomas Popkewitz's chapter examines the ways discourses about "evidence" and "scientifically based inquiry" are tied to a particular form of reasoning that ultimately leads to the censorship of research and scholarship. He links his argument to the way urban families became serviceable to the schooling project and the tableau on which our notions of morality and civility are counterposed.

James Banks's chapter confronts directly our notions of citizenship by asserting the rights of ethnic and cultural groups to advocate for cultural democracy in their nation states. This chapter examines trends in a range of multicultural and multiethnic nation states and argues for the challenges and opportunities that diversity presents. Banks concludes his chapter by pointing to the global public interests (e.g., HIV/AIDS, environmental concerns, war and peace) and the need for a deeper understanding of diversity and citizenship.

Carl Grant's chapter directly attacks the way race is subsumed in much of our public policy—from No Child Left Behind to the state and federal responses to Hurricane Katrina victims. More specifically, Grant looks at the way ostensibly democratic documents (such as the U.S. Constitution) and principles (e.g., equality, justice, liberty, and freedom) fail to find their way into the everyday lived experiences of racial and ethnic minority group members. Grant raises questions about who and what we mean by the "public" and "public interest" and why we continue to resist the imperative for a multicultural future.

David Gillborn's chapter wraps up this section by directly confronting the marginalization of Black children in the United Kingdom. Gillborn uses the case of high-stakes testing in the UK and its adverse impact on non-White students in schools. Gillborn uses a critical race theory counterstory to situate assessment policy in the United Kingdom. He points out that when the schools used an assessment system that demonstrated the competency of Black children it declared those assessments invalid. A new assessment, where Black children were poor performers, was deemed more legitimate. Again, the issue of who are citizens and who is the public emerges.

Part Three—The School and Curriculum as Sites of Education Research in the Public Interest—looks at some of the practical implications of education research in the public interest. It includes chapters from Catherine Cornbleth, Tom Barone, and Donald Blumenfeld-Jones.

Catherine Cornbleth returns to Popkewitz's concerns about the current cries for scientifically based educational inquiry and "what works" research. Cornbleth then looks at some of the national curriculum standards efforts in New York and California that precipitated a series of controversies and public debates about what can and should legitimately be taught in public schools.

Tom Barone's chapter addresses the challenges education researchers face in this era of retrenchment and retreat from progressive education reform, as well as strategies for qualitative researchers for confronting these challenges. Barone provides an extensive description of a socially engaged drama, "Street Rat," that focuses on homelessness in a major urban city, as an example of new ways researchers can speak to multiple publics. Barone also supplies a caution to researchers about the ways publics (in the form of research consumers/readers) create their own meaning when using these new forms of research.

Donald Blumenfeld-Jones's chapter concludes the third part of the volume. In it, he takes researchers to task for their failure to seriously engage with decision-makers. He also uses a variety of theorists—Buber, Marcuse, Schwab—to look at the work of curriculum theorizing. Blumenfeld-Jones challenges readers to look to art and hermeneutics as vehicles for a more engaged curriculum research.

This volume ends with an Afterword by co-editor William F. Tate that ties together the threads of this book with our overall theme of education research in the public interest. His final words remind us that social science researchers can scarcely avoid public engagement, even if inadvertently. Tate argues that, rather than shrink from that engagement, education researchers have an obligation to take more courageous and bold steps in the face of retreats from all things public. Ultimately, our work must always ask the larger questions of whose interests are served by our inquiry.

NOTE

1. Critical race theory relies heavily on storytelling and counter-storytelling. Here I am using Derrick Bell's (1987) notion of the chronicle to set this scenario.

REFERENCES

Anderson, J. D. (1988). *The education of Blacks in the south, 1860–1935.* Chapel Hill: University of North Carolina Press.

Anyon, J. (2005). *Radical possibilities: Public policy, urban education and a new social movement.* New York: Routledge.

Bell, D. (1987). *And we are not saved: The elusive quest for justice.* New York: Basic Books.

Delpit, L. (1995). *Other people's children: Cultural conflict in the classroom.* New York: Free Press.

Dewey, J. (1927). *The public and its problems.* New York: Henry Holt.

Foster, M. (1997). *Black teachers on teaching.* New York: The New Press.

Glass, I. (Ed.). (2005). After the flood. *This American Life* (National Public Radio Broadcast). Retrieved October 15, 2005, from http://www.thislife.org/pdf/296.pdf

Harrington, M. (1962). *The other America: Poverty in the United States.* New York: MacMillan.

Hilliard, A. G. (2000). Excellence in education versus high stakes testing. *Journal of Teacher Education, 51,* 293–304.

Irvine, J. J. (2002). *In search of wholeness: African American teachers and their culturally specific classroom practices.* New York: Palgrave/St. Martin's Press.

New Orleans faces months without children. (2005). Retrieved October 16, 2005, from http://msnbc.msn.com/id/9480718/

Orfield, G. & Eaton, S. (1996). *Dismantling desegregation: The quiet repeal of Brown v. Board of Education.* New York: The New Press.

Rothstein, R. (2004a). A wider lens on the Black–White achievement gap. *Phi Delta Kappan, 86,* 105–110.

Rothstein, R. (2004b). *Class and schools: Using social, economic, and educational reform to close the Black–White achievement gap.* New York: Teachers College Press.

Rubinowitz, L., & Rosenbaum, J. (2000). *Crossing the class and color lines: From public housing to white suburbia.* Chicago: University of Chicago Press.

Siddle-Walker, V. (1996). *Their highest potential: An African American community in the segregated south.* Chapel Hill: University of North Carolina Press.

Skiba, R. J., Michael, R. S., Nardo, A. C., & Peterson, R. (2002). The color of discipline: Sources of racial and gender disproportionality in school punishment. *The Urban Review, 34*(4), 317–342.

U.S. Census Bureau. (2000). New Orleans City, Louisiana Fact Sheet. Retrieved November 24, 2005, from http://factfinder.census.gov

Wells, A. (2004). Good neighbors? Distance, resistance, and desegregation in metropolitan New Orleans. *Urban Education, 39,* 408–427.

West, C. (2004). *Democracy matters.* New York: Penguin.

Willis, A. I. (2002). Literacy at Calhoun Colored School, 1892–1943. *Reading Research Quarterly, 37,* 8–44.

PART I

Policy and Politics

What Should Count
as Educational Research:
Notes Toward a New Paradigm

JEAN ANYON

IN *RADICAL POSSIBILITIES: Public Policy, Urban Education, and a New Social Movement* (Anyon, 2005), I argued that federal and metropolitan policies—such as those regulating the minimum wage, job and housing availability, tax rates, and public transportation—maintain large poverty populations in U.S. cities and therefore create conditions that make systemic, sustainable reform of schools in low-income urban communities unlikely, if not impossible. On this basis, I argued that even when current school reforms succeed, they fail the students—because there are neither decent jobs nor sufficient resources for college completion available to most low-income urban high school graduates. Therefore, I concluded, economic reform is an important prerequisite to urban school improvement projects having positive life consequences for students. I recommended more equitable public policies—ones that would create the economic and social conditions in poor communities to sustain school improvement and provide graduates economic and social opportunities to utilize improved educational outcomes.

I also made the case that subaltern groups in the United States (e.g., the working class, African Americans, Latinos) rarely achieve equity without social power and that the surest way to such power is through public contestation and the social movements this activity can lead to.

In this chapter I summarize central economic and social movement theory propositions offered in *Radical Possibilities* and argue as their consequence that what should count as educational research is investigation into ways of developing power and resource in low-income urban communities.

PUBLIC POLICIES THAT MAINTAIN URBAN POVERTY

Scholars typically do not link federal policies to the maintenance of poverty, to the lack of jobs that haunts American workers, or to the increasingly large portion of employment that pays poverty and near-poverty wages. Yet federal policy is determinative. The minimum wage, for example, stood at $5.15 in 2005—a mere $2 more than in 1938 (calculated in 2000 dollars). Yearly income at this wage is $10,712, ensuring that full-time, year-round minimum-wage work will not raise people out of poverty (Mishel, Bernstein, & Boushey, 2001). Analysis in 2004 found that minimum-wage standards directly affect the wages of 8.9% of the workforce (9.9 million workers); and when we include those making $1 more an hour than the minimum wage, this legislation affects the wages of as much as 18% of the workforce (Economic Policy Institute, 2004). Contrary to the claims of those who oppose raising the minimum wage (that an increase will force employers to fire or hire fewer of those affected by the increase), studies of the 1990–1991 and 1996–1997 minimum-wage increases failed to find any systematic, significant job losses associated with the increases and found no evidence of negative employment effects on small businesses (Economic Policy Institute, 2004). Federal minimum-wage legislation is a political policy that maintains poverty for many millions of U.S. families.

Radical Possibilities describes other macroeconomic policies that produce hardship. These especially penalize low-income Blacks and Latinos, the majority of whom live in low-income urban or segregated suburban neighborhoods that are fiscally stressed. These policies include job training as a predominant federal antipoverty policy when there have been too few jobs for graduates; ineffective federal implementation of policies that outlaw racial discrimination in hiring and housing; regressive income taxes that charge wealthy individuals less than half the rate charged the rich during the most of the first 60 years of the 20th century, yet substantially raise the payroll taxes paid by the working poor and middle class; and corporate tax policies in recent years that allow 60% of large U.S. corporations to pay no federal taxes at all (and in some cases to obtain millions in rebates) (see also Citizens for Tax Justice, 2002; Lafer, 2002; Orfield, 2002; Rusk, 1999).

These federal policies and practices contribute to personal, neighborhood, and educational poverty because they lead to the following problems: There are not enough jobs for poor families who need them; low-income families of color are concentrated in low-resourced urban neighborhoods; and when the wealthy do not contribute equitably to public expenses, funding for services like education declines and the quality of the services tends to be low (Anyon, 2005; Citizens for Tax Justice, 2002; Galbraith, 1998; Lafer, 2002; Mishel, Bernstein, & Schmitt, 2003).

Like federal policies, there are metro-area (regional) policies and practices that increase the problems of low-income urban residents and neighborhoods. Today, metropolitan regions are places of population growth, extensive economic inequality, and racial segregation (Orfield, 2002; Rusk, 1999). The percentage of racial minorities in large metro areas who live in the suburbs jumped from 19% to 27% during the 1990s. However, a growing share of these families live in fiscally stressed suburbs, with an increasing number of neighborhoods at poverty levels over 30% (Orfield, 2002). As in areas of concentrated poverty in the central city, low levels of taxable resources in these urbanized segregated suburbs leave services like education lacking in funds.

U.S. metropolitan areas are characterized by the following problems, all of which disadvantage urban minority families and communities: Most entry-level jobs for which adults with low to moderate education levels are qualified are increasingly located in suburbs, rather than in central cities, but public transit systems do not connect these suburban job centers to urban areas, where most low-income minorities live—thus preventing them from access to jobs there. State-allowed local zoning on the basis of income prevents affordable housing in most suburbs where entry-level jobs are located, which means there is little if any housing for low-income families near the suburban job centers. Finally, even though federal and state taxes are paid by residents throughout metro regions (including inner cities), most tax-supported development takes place in the affluent suburbs rather than in low-income areas. Thus, few jobs exist in most low-income urban neighborhoods (for development of these arguments, see Anyon, 2005; Dreir, Swanstrom, & Mollenkopf, 2001; Orfield, 2002; Rusk, 1999).

These inequitable regional arrangements and policies exacerbate federal wage and job mandates; they also contribute in important ways to joblessness and poverty in cities and urbanized suburbs and to the low quality of investment in services such as education there.

Radical Possibilities notes that federal and metro-area policies and practices are important causes of poverty—and U.S. poverty is much higher than federal guidelines suggest. Realistic poverty-threshold criteria developed by the National Research Council, and accepted by a wide range of scholars, reveal that a full 38% of American children are identified as poor—27 million who lived in families with income up to 200% of the official poverty line (Citro & Robert, 1995; Lu, 2003; see also Cauthen & Lu, 2001). By this measure—200 percent of the official poverty cutoff—a full 57% of African American children, 64% of Latino children, and 34% of White children were poor in the U.S. in 2001 (Lu, 2003; see also Mishel et al., 2003). And, as I have noted, the majority of Black and Latino children who are poor live in the inner city or in fiscally distressed, segregated suburbs (Anyon, 2005).

THE POLICIES WE NEED

We could create federal policies that would lower poverty by important margins—and support an environment that would sustain and give consequence to urban school reform. These policies include a significantly raised minimum wage, comparable-worth laws, and policies to enforce existing regulations that outlaw discrimination in hiring. A raise in the minimum wage that brought workers above poverty would improve the lives of at least a fifth of U.S. workers (Economic Policy Institute, 2004). Paying women the same that men are paid for comparable work would, according to one analysis, reduce poverty by 40%, since such a large percentage of poor people are women in low-wage jobs (Lafer, 2002). And requiring employers to hire without discriminating against Blacks and Latinos would further open opportunities currently denied.

In addition, policies that worked against U.S. poverty in the past could be reinstated: U.S. government regulation of the minimum wage that kept low-paid workers' income at the median of highly paid, unionized workers in the decades after World War II; federal support for union organizing; a federal program of job creation in cities such as during the Great Depression of the 1930s; and federal programs for urban youth that would support college completion, as such policies did for 8 million men and women after World War II (Anyon, 2005; Galbraith, 1998). These national policies were important supports of the widespread prosperity of the U.S. working and middle classes in the quarter century following World War II (Galbraith, 1998).

Metro-area policies to substantially reduce poverty by buttressing federal ones include entry-level/career-ladder job development in central cities, public transit that connects cities to outlying job centers, zoning regulations that support affordable housing in places where jobs exist, enforcement of existing anti-housing-discrimination laws, and tax-supported development in low-income areas instead of affluent suburbs, as is typically the case (see Anyon, 2005; Dreier, Mollenkopf, & Swanstrom, 2001; Orfield, 2002; Rusk 1999).

OBTAINING GOOD POLICY

I argued in *Radical Possibilities* and want to emphasize here that social movements have been the most efficacious—if not the only—method of obtaining public policies that offer basic U.S. civil and economic rights to, for example, African Americans, Latinos, the working class, and women. More than a century of active political struggle has been necessary to obtain the most fundamental civil rights for Black Americans. Five decades of labor battles were necessary before legislation in 1938 finally provided an 8-hour day, a 40-hour week, a minimum wage, and the legal end to child labor. This decades-long, vociferous advocacy culminated in the 1930s in the right to overtime pay, unemployment insurance, Social Security, and the freedom to organize unions. At least 20 years of activism were required before (White) women were permitted to vote in 1920.

And social movements have changed education. The radical tumult of the Progressive Era opened public schools to the community in many cities and increased educational opportunities for immigrant families in the form of kindergartens, vacation schools, night schools, social settlement programs, and libraries. As a result of the civil rights movement, Head Start, a radical innovation by political activists in Jackson, Mississippi, moved to center stage in federal educational policy and segregation of Blacks in public schools was made illegal. Despite later setbacks, integration victories have been significant. Gary Orfield (2001) has shown, for example, that "despite the re-segregation of many school districts in the U.S., a Southern black student is 32,700 times more likely to be in a white majority school than a black student in 1954 and fourteen times more likely than his counterpart in 1964" (p. 35). Indeed, the South is presently the only region of the country where Whites typically attend schools with significant numbers of Blacks (Orfield, 2001).

In the 1970s and 1980s, the women's, disabilities, and bilingual education movements also had significant impacts on schooling, opening up opportunities previously denied great numbers of students. Finally, in recent years, a movement of an invigorated and federally expressed political right has pushed both America and its schools in conservative directions: Education, economic opportunity, and civil rights have all been weakened by the rise of an organized, well-funded political right (see, e.g., Apple, 2001; McGirr, 2002; Phillips, 2002).

This history suggests that in order to obtain equitable policy in low-income communities, a social movement that builds economic and educational power there is required. I argue below that educational research can be a pivotal activity in this process.

TOWARD A NEW PARADIGM OF EDUCATIONAL RESEARCH

The paradigm within which almost all educational research has occurred places the investigative focus on characteristics of schools (e.g., students, teachers, administrators, curriculum, pedagogy) or on district, state, and federal education policy (and sometimes the relations among these). While this standard framework has explained a good deal about middle-class American schools, it is not equipped to capture the external social structures and public policy decisions that plague urban schools and systems and render them impotent to fundamentally improve the education—and life chances—of the vast majority of their students.

Based on the data and analysis in *Radical Possibilities,* some of which is presented above, I want to offer the outlines of a new paradigm for educational research that has as a goal to further the systemic, sustainable reform of urban education. This paradigm moves the focus of research to opportunity structures and policies existing outside of schools and educational arenas that severely circumscribe the potential in urban districts. This external lens highlights the contribution of public policy and social structure to urban educational failures, to the economic limitations facing graduates, and to the processes by which these external forces affect what happens inside urban schools and districts. Such research would investigate ways in which we could replace public policies that contradict and circumvent school reform with policies that will support and complement the efforts of educators and school reformers. Most important, research in this paradigm would attempt to understand the processes by which we might vastly increase the power and resources of urban communities and families. In this latter pursuit, I envision several types of research activities.

Document and Describe Oppression

In order to know how to work against the social forces that impinge on educational equity, we need to identify oppressive policies and practices and document their effects. For example, in *Ghetto Schooling* (Anyon, 1997) I traced how, over the course of a century, an urban school district was stripped of its resources by political and economic decisions and policies made by governing elites at the federal, state, corporate, and local levels. This political and economic denuding eventually devastated the public schools, rendering them destitute, chaotic, and dysfunctional. Once we know the power of exclusionary and oppressive social forces like these to affect the quality and extent of educational offerings, we can more successfully aim our efforts at dislodging those determinants.

Study the Powerful

In order to transform policies and practices that undermine urban communities and schools, we need to understand how those with the power to make the decisions think, act, and organize themselves: Power analyses of public policy decision making that impacts education are called for. A model of this type of work at the national level is the work of sociologist William Domhoff (2001). He has carried out network analyses of institutions and organizations to which national policymakers belong—linked corporation boards, government groups, private clubs, foundations, think tanks, elite school trusteeships, and so on. By assessing the actions and interactions of overlapping members of these groups, Domhoff identifies what he calls a policy elite. It is the functioning of this elite that needs to be examined—and their actions interrupted. When we know who the powerful decision makers are and what they do, we are more likely to be able to know how and where to intervene. Power analyses of policy elites would be useful at the state and city levels as well.

Assess Efforts of Urban Communities
to Create Power and Opportunity

Poor, minority, and working-class families who have fought for opportunity and rights have had to build their own collaborative power in order to obtain these goals. An important focus of the new research paradigm would be to assess "best practice" in power-building by communities.

Numerous questions arise: How do African American and Latino families and communities make sense of and "imagine" educational, economic, and political prospects for change (Dumas, in progress)? What are successful methods of organizing and building power in communities? How can the synergy resulting from cross-metro-area collaborations be measured and utilized? How can community education reform groups link with efforts to obtain power and justice in jobs, housing, and immigrant rights? How can local economic and educational victories be "scaled up"?

The research paradigm I am proposing here could provide answer to these questions, thereby providing direction for future strategic action.

Study Social Movements

In *Radical Possibilities* I theorized how people might be brought into the social issue campaigns that are percolating in cities nationwide and how these disparate struggles might be brought together in a strong, unified movement for economic and educational change. Such theorizing has not been tested. This is fertile ground for research. Important questions require answers:

- How can we assess and promote understanding of connections between political-economic forces and issues of culture, identity, and psychology? What social and psychological processes encourage people to become involved in social protest? For example, what encourages low-income parents—who may both be working in minimum-wage jobs—to join and engage with local community/school organizing groups? What supports assist these efforts, and what forces constrain them?
- How do parent and other social issue groups collaborate to build social movements? What have been the barriers to collaboration, and what has sustained it? What attempts have been made to specifically connect economic and educational issue campaigns, and what have been the results?
- What should we count as "success" in social movements, and what makes some social movements more productive than others?

The resolution of such questions could inform our daily work as educators and scholars.

Study Student Activists

Increasing numbers of low-income urban high school students are organizing for college-readiness programs in high school; for gay and lesbian, immigrant, and prisoner rights; and for job opportunities. What, if anything, distinguishes these activist youth from those who, say, are incarcerated or otherwise caught up in the juvenile justice system? What can we learn from any differences in background, experience, education, and support that may exist? How can urban educators grasp the perspicacity and anger of their students and channel it into informed resistance and political agency? Documenting "resistance" is not enough; we must discover and practice ways to make student rebellion work in productive ways for the students and their schools and communities.

Investigate Ways to Make Schools Movement-Building Spaces

Of huge import is this final example of research in the proposed paradigm: are studies that would investigate how and under what conditions school personnel are willing and able to connect classrooms and schools to the swirl of social justice organizing in urban neighborhoods.

In *Radical Possibilities* I gave examples of ways in which school-based personnel could engage in movement-building activities: working with community-based organizing groups as part of various curriculum topics; developing their own organizing skills; and involving their students in issue organizing, by assisting them as they map community assets, carry out power analyses of their neighborhood and city, and create a campaign in the school and community to encourage support for a problem they feel passionate about solving.

As a former inner-city teacher Brooklyn, New York, and Washington, D.C., I understand how difficult political work in schools can be. Almost everything seems to conspire against activism by teachers and other school personnel who might want to get involved. I do not think research has ever systematically studied teachers or other school-based personnel who engage politically inside the school and connect this work to ongoing community struggle. Do we know what conditions and strategies would assist them? Do we know how such teachers navigate the constraints and the possibilities?

A radical research paradigm would investigate ways in which teachers and other personnel could be encouraged and supported in this kind of work. There are exemplars in many schools and districts, often described in the journal *Rethinking Schools*. The new paradigm of research would (as an example) assess these exemplars, to determine ways to replicate and increase their range and effectiveness.

THE PROMISE OF RESEARCH

What can we expect from a research program that aims to find ways to build power in low-income urban communities strong enough to change policies and practices governing economic and educational resource distributions?

On one level, this question is simply rhetorical: *Most* educational research seeks to provide guidance into how to alter existing policies or practices deemed problematic, but the extent to which research findings effect change is small. The impotence of most research to alter established policy and practice is well recognized. On another level, the question of what promises this new paradigm can offer is strategic and exhortatory. Whether in central-city neighborhoods or segregated low-income suburbs, economic and educational tragedy and pain are gut-wrenching daily constants. It seems to me that if we do *not* take up the task of trying to increase power in poor neighborhoods, if we do *not* take up the task of assisting educators, youth, parents, and communities struggling for opportunity, we are at risk of a strategic failure of enormous proportions. For U.S. history demonstrates that the primary route to transformative equity is through concerted public protest and organization. One way to increase the likelihood of such progress is through our daily work as educators and scholars. Civil rights leader Ella Baker used to say that people could assist the movement by "casting down their buckets" wherever they lived and worked. I want to add that by moving to a politically radical research paradigm like the one described here, we have nothing to lose but our political timidity and despair.

REFERENCES

Anyon, J. (1997). *Ghetto schooling: A political economy of urban educational reform.* New York: Teachers College Press.

Anyon, J. (2005). *Radical possibilities: Public policy, urban education, and a new social movement.* New York: Routledge.

Apple, M. (2001). *Educating the "right" way: Markets, standards, God, and inequality.* New York: Routledge Falmer.

Cauthen, N., & Lu, H-H. (2001). *Living on the edge: Employment alone is not enough for America's low-income children and families* (Research Brief No. 1). Mailman School of Public Health, National Center for Children in Poverty, Columbia University, New York.

Citizens for Tax Justice. (2002). *Surge in corporate tax welfare drives corporate tax payments down to near record low.* Washington, DC: Author.

Citro, C., & Robert, M. (1995). *Measuring poverty: A new approach.* Washington, DC: National Academy Press.

Domhoff, G. W. (2001). *Who rules America? Power and politics* (4th ed.). New York: McGraw Hill.

Dreier, P., Mollenkopf, J., & Swanstrom, T. (2001). *Place matters: Metropolitics for the 21st century.* Lawrence: University Press of Kansas.

Dumas, M. (in progress). *The cultural production of the Black educational imagination in the post-civil rights era: Toward an historical ethnography of the meaning of education in an urban Black community.* Doctoral dissertation, Graduate Center, City University of New York.

Economic Policy Institute. (2004). *EPI issue guide: Minimum wage.* Washington, DC: Author.

Galbraith, J. K. (1998). *Created unequal: The crisis in American pay.* New York: The Free Press, Simon & Schuster.

Lafer, G. (2002). *The job training charade*. Ithaca, New York: Cornell University Press.

Lu, H-H. (2003). *Low-income children in the United States*. National Center for Children in Poverty, Mailman School of Public Health, Columbia University, New York.

McGirr, L. (2002). *Suburban warriors: The origins of the new American right*. Princeton, NJ: Princeton University Press.

Mishel, L., Bernstein, J., & Boushey, H. (2001). *The state of working America: 2000/2001*. Ithaca, NY: Cornell University Press.

Mishel, L., Bernstein, J., & Schmitt, J. (2003). *The state of working America: 2002/2003*. Ithaca, NY: Cornell University Press.

Orfield, G. (2001). *Schools more separate: Consequences of a decade of resegregation*. Cambridge, MA: The Civil Rights Project at Harvard University.

Orfield, M. (2002). *American metropolitics: The new suburban reality*. Washington, DC: Brookings Institution Press.

Phillips, K. (2002). *Wealth and democracy: A political history of the American rich*. New York: Broadway Books, Random House.

Rusk, D. (1999). *Inside game/outside game: Winning strategies for saving urban America*. Washington, DC: Brookings Institution Press.

CHAPTER 2

Interrupting the Right: On Doing Critical Educational Work in Conservative Times

MICHAEL W. APPLE

CULTURE COUNTS

OVER THE PAST DECADE, I have been engaged in a concerted effort to analyze the reasons behind the rightist resurgence—what I call "conservative modernization"—in education and to try to find spaces for interrupting it (see Apple, 2000, 2006). My aim has not simply been to castigate the right, although there is a bit of fun in doing so. Rather, I have also sought to illuminate the dangers, and the elements of good sense, not only bad sense, that are found within what is an identifiable and powerful new hegemonic bloc—the various factions of the rightist alliance of neoliberals, neoconservatives, authoritarian populist religious conservatives, and some members of the managerial new middle class.

I have a number of reasons for doing so. First, people who find certain elements of conservative modernization relevant to their lives are not puppets. They are not dupes who have little understanding of the "real" relations of this society. This smacks of earlier reductive analyses that were based in ideas of "false consciousness." My position is very different. I maintain that the reason that some of the arguments coming from the various factions of this new hegemonic bloc are listened to is because they *are* connected to aspects of the realities that people experience. The tense alliance of neoliberals, neoconservatives, authoritarian populist religious activists, and the professional and managerial new middle class only works because there has been a very creative articulation of themes that resonate deeply with the experiences, fears, hopes, and dreams of people as they go about their daily lives. The right has often been more than a little manipulative in its articulation of these themes. It has integrated them within racist nativist discourses, within economically dominant forms of understanding, and within a problematic sense of "tradition." But this integration could only occur if they were organized around people's understanding of their real material and cultural lives.

The second reason I have stressed the tension between good and bad sense—aside from my profound respect for Antonio Gramsci's writings about this—has to do with my belief that we have witnessed a major educational accomplishment over the past three decades in many countries. All too often, we assume that educational and cultural struggles are epiphenomenal. The real battles occur in the paid workplace—the "economy." Not only is this a strikingly reductive sense of what the economy is (its focus on paid, not unpaid, work; its neglect of the fact that, say, cultural institutions such as schools are also places where paid work goes on, etc.) (Apple, 1988), it also ignores what the right has actually done. Conservative modernization has radically reshaped the common sense of society. It has worked in every sphere—the economic, the political, and the cultural—to alter the basic categories we use to evaluate our institutions and our public and private lives. It has established new identities. It has recognized that to win in the state, you must win in civil society. The accomplishment of such a vast educational project has many implications. It shows how important cultural struggles are. And, oddly enough, it gives reason for hope. It forces us to ask a significant question. *If the right can do this, why can't we?*

I do not mean this as a rhetorical question. As I have argued repeatedly in my own work, the right has shown how powerful the struggle over meaning and identity can be. While we should not want to emulate their often cynical and manipulative processes, the fact that they have had such success in pulling people under their ideological umbrella has much to teach us. Granted there are real differences in money and power between the forces of conservative modernization and those whose lives are being tragically altered by the policies and practices coming from the alliance. But the right wasn't as powerful 30 years ago as it is now. It collectively organized. It created a decentered unity, one where each element sacrificed some of its particular agenda to push forward on those areas that bound them together. Can't we do the same?

I believe that we can, but only if we face up to the realities and dynamics of power in unromantic ways. As I argued in *Educating the "Right" Way* (Apple, 2006), the romantic possibilitarian rhetoric of some of the writers on critical pedagogy is not sufficiently based on a tactical or strategic analysis of the current situation, nor is it sufficiently grounded in its understanding of the reconstructions of discourse and movements that are occurring in all too many places (see also Apple & Buras, 2006). Here I follow Cameron McCarthy (2000), who wisely reminds us, "We must think possibility within constraint; that is the condition of our time."

We need to remember that cultural struggles are not epiphenomenal. They *count*, and they count in institutions throughout society. In order for dominant groups to exercise leadership, large numbers of people must be convinced that the maps of reality circulated by those with the most economic, political, and cultural power are indeed wiser than other alternatives. Dominant groups do this by attaching these maps to the elements of good sense that people have and by changing the very meaning of the key concepts and their accompanying structures of feeling that provide the centers of gravity for our hopes, fears, and dreams about this society. (Think, for example, of the ways in which No Child Left Behind has appropriated the concerns and language surrounding progressive critiques of schools for their race and class inequalities [see Apple, 2006].) The right has been much more successful in doing this than the left, in part because it has been able to craft—through hard and lengthy economic, political, and cultural efforts—a tense but still successful alliance that has shifted the major debates over education and economic and social policy onto its own terrain.

Evidence of this is all around us in the terms we use, in the arguments in which we engage, indeed even in many of the cultural resources we employ to imagine alternative futures. For example, as I completed the writing of one of my latest books, one of the top-selling books on *The New York Times* fiction list is Tim La-Haye (yes, the Tim LaHaye of extremely conservative evangelical leadership) and Jerry Jenkins's *The Indwelling* (LaHaye & Jenkins, 2000), the seventh of a series of books about "true believers" who confront the "Antichrist." The imagined future is a time of "rapture" when the good are taken up to heaven and the bad are condemned to eternal damnation. Who each of these groups are is predictable. In a number of ways, then, the authoritarian populist "outside" has moved to become the inside. It has creatively learned how to use the codes of popular adventure and science fiction novels to build an imaginative space of possibility, and a "muscular" yet sensitive conservative Christianity, that gives meaning to people's daily lives and hopes.[1]

Just as these spaces create imagined futures, so, too, do they help create identities. Neoliberalism creates policies and practices that embody the enterprising and constantly strategizing entrepreneur out of the possessive individualism it establishes as the ideal citizen. Neoconservatism creates imagined pasts as the framework for imagined and stable futures, futures in which identities are based on people knowing the knowledge and values that neoconservatives themselves have decided "have stood the test of time." Authoritarian populist religious conservatives also have an imagined past where a society, based on God's knowledge and values, has pre-given identities that enable women and men to rearticulate the neoliberal ideology of "choice" and to act in what are seen as godly ways toward bringing society to God. And managerialism, with its insistent focus on auditing and reductive models of accountability, establishes new identities for the professional and managerial middle class, identities that give new meaning to their lives and enable them to recapture their feelings of worthiness and efficacy (Apple, 2006). Out of all of these multiple spaces and identities, and the conflicts, tensions, and compromises that their interactions generate, policies evolve. These policies are almost never purely from only one of these elements within this bloc. Rather, they often embody a rich mix that somehow must accommodate as many themes as possible from within the multiple forces of conservative modernization—without at the same time alienating those groups believed to be significant who are not yet integrated under the hegemonic umbrella of the right but whom the right would like to bring under its leadership in the future.

This is a truly difficult task, and it is filled with contradictory impulses. Yet, even with its contradictions and tensions, it has moved the balance of forces significantly to the right. Educational policies have been part of that move. In fact, education has not only been drawn along by the pressure of these rightist waves, it has actually played a major role in building these waves. The conservative alliance has paid attention to education—both formal and informal—and it has paid off for them. Indeed, in most of the critical discussions in the academic and popular literature of the effects of neoliberal, neoconservative, and managerial policies and practices in education in a number of countries, it is *their* policies that have provided the outlines of the debates in which we engage—vouchers, markets, national standards, high-stakes testing, and so on.

CONTRADICTORY REFORMS

As I have demonstrated elsewhere, policies often have strikingly unforeseen consequences. Reforms that are instituted with good intentions may have hidden effects that are more than a little problematic. I have shown that the effects of some of the favorite reforms of neoliberals and neoconservatives—for instance, voucher plans, national or statewide curricula, and national or statewide testing are examples—quite often reproduce or even worsen inequalities (Apple, 2006; see also Lipman, 2004). Thus, we should be very cautious about accepting what may seem to be meritorious intentions at face value. Intentions are too often contradicted by how reforms may function in practice. This is true not only for large-scale transformations of educational policies and governance but also for moves to change the ways curriculum and teaching go on in schools.

The framework I have employed to understand this is grounded in what in cultural theory calls the act of repositioning. In essence, it says that the best way to understand what any set of institutions, policies, and practices does is to see it from the standpoint of those who have the least power (see Harding, 1991; Lukacs, 1971). That is, every institution, policy, and practice—and especially those that now dominate education and the larger society—establishes relations of power in which some voices are heard and some are not. While it is not preordained that those voices that will be heard most clearly are also those that have the most economic, cultural, and social capital, it is most likely that this will be the case. After all, we do not exist on a level playing field. Many economic, social, and educational policies when actually put in place tend to benefit those who already have advantages.

These points may seem overly rhetorical and too abstract, but unfortunately there is no small amount of truth in them. For example, in a time when all too much of the discourse around educational reform is focused on vouchers and choice plans on the one hand and on proposals for national or state curricula, standards, and testing on the other, there is a good deal of international evidence that such policies may actually reproduce or even worsen class, gender, and race inequalities (Apple, 2006). Thus, existing structures of economic and cultural power often lead to a situation in which what may have started out in some educators' or legislators' minds as an attempt to make things better, in the end is all too usually transformed into another set of mechanisms for social stratification. While much of this is due to the ways in which race, gender, class, and "ability" act as structural realities in this society, some of it is related to the hesitancy of policymakers to take seriously enough the complicated ways in which education is itself a political act.

Near the end of the introductory section of a recent volume on the politics of educational policies and practices, *Learning as a Political Act*, the editors state that as progressives they are committed to an "intellectual solidarity that seeks to lay bare the ideas and histories of groups that have been silenced in mainstream educational arenas" (Segarra & Dobles, 1999, p. xiii). There are a number of key concepts in this quote—intellectual solidarity, laying bare, silencing. Each speaks to a complicated history, and each phrase again says something about our understanding of democracy. They are "keywords." They come from a very different tradition from that provided by the linguistic mapping of markets. They also speak to a different politics of official knowledge.

Over the past decade, it has become increasingly clear that the school curriculum has become a battleground. Stimulated in large part by neoliberal complaints about "economically useless" knowledge, by neoconservative laments about the supposed loss of discipline and lack of "real knowledge," and by religious authoritarian populists' relentless attacks on schools for their supposed loss of God-given "traditional" values, discussions of what should be taught in schools and how it should be taught are now as contentious as at any time in our history.

Evidence of this is not hard to find. In his repeated call for a return to a curriculum of "facts," E. D. Hirsch Jr. argues that schools have been taken over by progressive educators from Rousseau to Dewey (Hirsch, 1996), a claim that has almost no empirical warrant at all and largely demonstrates how disconnected he is from the daily life of schools (Apple, 2005; Buras, 1999). Most schooling in the United States is already fact-driven. In addition, school districts throughout the country are constantly looking over their shoulders, worried that their reading, social studies, or mathematics programs will be challenged by the forces of the authoritarian religious right—although as I demonstrate *Cultural Politics and Education*, sometimes school systems themselves create the conditions for the growth of rightist antischool movements in their own communities by being less than democratic in their involvement of the community (Apple, 1996). Other evidence of such contentiousness is visible in the fact that the content of the mathematics curriculum was even recently debated in the editorial pages of *The New York Times*, where spokespersons for constructivist and traditional curricula went head to head. Many more instances might be cited. But it is clear that the debate over "what knowledge is of most worth" has taken on more than a few political overtones.[2]

Much of the debate over this goes on with little empirical substance. For example, the argument that we must "return" to teaching, say, mathematics in "traditional" ways is obviously partly an ideological one. (We need to restore discipline; students have too much freedom; "bad" knowledge has pushed "good" knowledge to the sidelines.) Yet it is also based on a claim that such a return will lead to higher achievement and ultimately to a more competitive economy. Here, neoliberal and neoconservative emphases are joined with authoritarian populist mistrust of child-centeredness. This is where Jo Boaler's (1998) richly detailed qualitative and quantitative comparison of mathematics curricula and teaching enters.

Boaler engages in a fine-grained analysis of two secondary schools with decidedly different emphases. While her book is based on data from England, its implications are profound for debates over curriculum and teaching in the United States and elsewhere. Both schools are largely working class, with some minority and middle-class populations as well. Both sets of students had attended our equivalent of middle schools that were dominated by more traditional academic methods. And both had similar achievement profiles. One school overtly focused on preparing its students for national tests. Its program was almost totally teacher directed, organized around textbooks that were geared to the national tests, ability grouped, and run in such a way that speed and accuracy of computations and the learning of procedural rules for dealing with mathematical problems were highly valued—all those things that traditionalists here say are currently missing in mathematics instruction. Furthermore, the boundary between mathematics and both the real world and other subjects was strong (see also Bernstein, 1977). The other school did not group by ability. It was decidedly more "progressive" both in its attitude toward students (there was a more relaxed communication style between teachers and students; student input was sought on the curriculum) and in its mathematics program. In this second school, the instruction was project based, with a minimum of textbook-based teaching and a maximum of cooperative work among the students. The boundary between mathematics and "real-world" problems was weak.

The first school was quiet, on-task, well organized–the very embodiment of the dream of nearly all elements of conservative modernization. The second was more noisy; students were not always fully on-task and had very flexible time schedules. Both schools had dedicated and hardworking teachers. Yet the differences in the results were striking, in terms of both overall achievement and the differential effects of each orientation on the students themselves.

The more traditional school, with its driving concern for covering material that would be on the test, stressed textbook knowledge and moved relatively rapidly from topic to topic. The more student-centered approach of the second school sacrificed some coverage, but it also enabled students to more fully understand the material. By and large, students in the first school actually did less well on the standardized tests than those in the second, especially but not only on those parts of the tests that needed them to actually think mathematically, in large part because they could not generalize to new contexts as well as did those students who had used their mathematics in more varied (though more time-consuming) projects. Further—and of great importance for equity—young women in the second school did consistently better in a more cooperative atmosphere that stressed understanding and use rather than coverage. The same held true for social class. Working-class students were consistently disadvantaged in the more pressured and text- and test-based agenda of traditional mathematics instruction.

This is a complex situation, and Boaler is talking about general tendencies here. But her overall conclusions are clear and are supported by a very nice combination of data. In sum, a return to (actually, given the fact that most mathematics instruction is still chalk and talk and textbook based, it would be much more honest to say the *continuation of*) the traditional mathematics programs that the critics are demanding increases neither students' mathematical competence nor their ability to use their mathematical knowledge in productive ways. While it may keep classrooms quiet and students under control, it may also systematically disadvantage young women—including, as Boaler shows, the brightest young women—and economically disadvantaged students.[3] Finally, it may have one other effect—a strengthening of students' dislike of mathematics and their feeling that it is simply irrelevant for their future. If this is true for mathematics, it is worth considering the hidden negative effects of the more general policies being proposed by neoconservative reformers who wish to return to what they have constructed, rather romantically, as "the tradition" in all subjects.

If Boaler's conclusions are even partly generalizable, as I think they may very well be (see Gutstein, 2006), the hidden effects of certain reform movements may not be what we had in mind. Tighter control over the curriculum, the tail of the test wagging the dog of the teacher and the curriculum, more pressure, more reductive accountability plans—all of this may lead to less equitable results, not more. Boredom, alienation, and increased inequalities are not the ideal results of schooling. Once again, looking outside of our usual all-too-limited and parochial boundaries can be more than a little beneficial. The careful research underpinning Boaler's volume needs to be taken seriously by anyone who assumes that in our unequal society there is a direct relationship between policy intentions and policy results. There isn't.

One of the most important tasks of critical education, therefore, is an empirical one. Just as Boaler did, we need to make research public not only on the negative effects of the policies of conservative modernization, but just as importantly on the positive effects of more socially and educationally critical alternatives. A good example of this is the SAGE program in Wisconsin, where significantly reducing class size within schools that historically have served a larger portion of dispossessed people has had much more robust results than, say, marketization and voucher plans (Molnar et al., 1999). This is one form of interrupting dominant discourses and policies, and much more of it needs to be done (Apple & Buras, 2005). However, in doing this we cannot simply rely on the dominant forms of what counts as evidence. In Linda Tuhiwai Smith's (1999) words, we need "decolonizing methodologies" (see also Gitlin, 1994).

MAKING CHALLENGES PUBLIC

My arguments in the previous section of this chapter have been at a relatively general level because I did not want us to lose sight of the larger picture. How else can these retrogressive movements be interrupted? Let me now get more specific and tactical, since I am convinced that it is important to interrupt rightist claims immediately—in the media, in academic and professional publications, and in daily life.

One crucial example of such interruption is found in the Educational Policy Project formed under the auspices of the Center for Education Research, Analysis, and Innovation. This involves the ongoing construction of an organized group of people who are committed to responding very rapidly to material published by the right. This group includes a number of well-known educators and activists who are deeply concerned that the right has successfully used the media to foster its own ideological agenda, just as it has devoted a considerable amount of resources to getting its message to the public. For example, a number of conservative foundations have full-time staff members whose responsibility it is, for example, to fax synopses of reports to national media, to newspapers, and to widely read journals of opinion and to keep conservative positions in the public eye. Progressives have been much less successful in comparison, in part because they have not devoted themselves to the task as rigorously or because they have not learned to work at many levels, from the academic to the popular, simultaneously. In recognition of this, a group of socially and educationally critical educators met first in Milwaukee and has been continuously meeting to generate an organized response to conservative reports, articles, research, and media presentations.

A full-time staff member was hired by the Center to focus on conservative material, to identify what needs to be responded to, and to help edit responses written by individual members of the group. A website has been developed that publishes these responses and/or original publications of more progressive research and arguments. The project also focuses on writing op-ed pieces, letters to the editor, and other similar material and on making all of this available to the media. This requires establishing contacts with journals, newspapers, radio, television, and so on. This is exactly what the right did. We can and must do similar things. It requires hard work, but the Educational Policy Project is the beginning of what we hope will be a larger effort involving many more people. The reader can see the kinds of things that have been done by going to the following website for the Educational Policy Project, now housed at Arizona State University: http://www.asu.edu/educ/epsl/

This is just one example of one strategy for bringing what we know to parts of the public in more popular forms. There are many other examples posted on the website and published as reports, responses in journals, letters to the editor, and op-ed pieces. While this project is relatively new, it shows considerable promise. In combination with the use of talk radio, call-in shows, and similar media strategies in *multiple* languages,[4] these kinds of activities are part of a larger strategy to bring both more public attention to what the dangers are in the "solutions" proposed by the right and to what the workable alternatives to them might be. Integrating the educational interventions within a larger focus on the media is absolutely crucial (Bourdieu, 1998; Kellner, 1995; McChesney, Wood, & Foster, 1998; Ratner, 1997).

LEARNING FROM OTHER NATIONS

During one of the times I was working in Brazil with Paulo Freire, I remember him repeatedly saying to me that education must begin in critical dialogue. Both of these last two words were crucial to him. Education must hold our dominant institutions in education and the larger society up to rigorous questioning; at the same time, this questioning must deeply involve those who benefit least from the ways in which these institutions now function. Both conditions are necessary, since the first without the second is simply insufficient to the task of democratizing education.

Of course, many committed educators already know that the transformation of educational policies and practices—or the defense of democratic gains in our schools and local communities—is inherently political. Indeed, this is constantly registered in the fact that rightist movements have made teaching and curricula the targets of concerted attacks for years. One of the claims of these rightist forces is that schools are "out of touch" with parents and communities. While there are elements of insight in such criticisms, we need to find ways of connecting our educational efforts to local communities—especially those members of these communities with less power—that are more truly democratic than those envisioned by the right.

There is a good deal of efficacy in turning to the experiences of other nations to learn about what the effects of neoliberal and neoconservative policies and practices actually are. Yet there are many more things that we can learn from other nations' struggles. For example, currently in Porto Alegre, Brazil, the policies of participatory budgeting are helping to build support for more progressive and democratic policies there in the face of the growing power of neoliberal movements at a national level. The Workers Party has been able to increase its majority even among people who had previously voted in favor of parties with much more conservative educational and social programs *because* it has been committed to enabling even the poorest of its citizens to participate in deliberations over the policies themselves and over where and how money should be spent. By paying attention to more substantive forms of collective participation and, just as importantly, by devoting resources to encourage such participation, Porto Alegre has demonstrated that it is possible to have a "thicker" democracy, even in times of both economic crisis and ideological attacks from neoliberal parties and the conservative press. Programs such as the "Citizen School" and the sharing of real power with those who live in *favelas* (slums) provide ample evidence that thick democracy offers realistic alternatives to the eviscerated version of thin democracy found under neo-liberalism (Apple et al., 2003). Just as important is the pedagogic function of these programs. They develop the collective capacities among people to enable them to continue to engage in the democratic administration and control of their lives (Elson, 1999). This is time-consuming; but time spent in such things now has proven to pay off dramatically later on.

A similar story can be told about another part of Brazil. In Belem, a "Youth Participatory Budget" process was instituted. It provided resources and space for the participation of many thousands of youth in the deliberations over what programs for youth needed to be developed, over how money should be spent, and over creating a set of political forums that could be used by youth to make public their needs and desires. This is very different from most of the ways youth are dealt with in all too many countries, where they are seen as a "problem," not as a resource (Lesko, 2001). A similar instance is found in New Zealand, where, under the original leadership of the International Research Institute on Maori and Indigenous Education at the University of Auckland, multiracial groups of youth are formed in communities to publicly discuss the ways in which youth see their realities and advance proposals for dealing with these realities. In this way, alliances that begin to cut across race, class, and age are being built. There are models, then, of real participation that we can learn from and that challenge the eviscerated vision of democracy advanced by neoliberals by putting in place more substantive and active models of actually "living our freedoms." The issue is not the existence of such models; it is ensuring that they are made widely visible.

THINKING HERETICALLY

In order to build counterhegemonic alliances, we may have to think more creatively than before—and, in fact, may have to engage in some nearly heretical rethinking. Let me give an example. I would like us to engage in a thought-experiment. I believe that the right has been able to take certain elements that many people hold dear and connect them to other issues in ways that might not often occur "naturally" if these issues were less politicized. Thus, for instance, one of the reasons populist religious groups are pulled into an alliance with the right is because such groups believe that the state is totally against the values that give meaning to their lives. They are sutured into an alliance in which other elements of rightist discourse are then able to slowly connect with their own. Thus, they believe that the state is antireligious. Others also say that the state seeks to impose its will on White working-class parents by giving "special treatment" to people of color and ignoring poor White people. These two elements do *not* necessarily have to combine. But they slowly begin to be seen as homologous.

Is it possible, for example, that by taking religion out of the mix that some parts of the religious community that currently find collective identities on the right would be less susceptible to such a call if more religious content was found in school? If religious studies had a more central place in the curriculum, is it less likely that people who find in religion the ultimate answers to why they are here would be less mistrustful of the state, less apt to be attracted to a position that public is bad and private is good? I am uncertain whether this would be the case. But I strongly believe that we need to entertain this possibility.

Do not misunderstand me. I am decidedly not taking the position that we should use vouchers to fund private religious schools, nor am I saying that the authoritarian populist religious right should be pandered to. Rather, I am taking a position similar to that espoused by Warren Nord: Our failure to provide a clear place for the study of religion in the curriculum makes us "illiberal" (Nord, 1995). Yet I do not want to end with Nord's position. Rather, I see it as a starting point. In earlier books, I have argued that at times people "become right" because of the lack of responsiveness of public institutions to meanings and concerns that are central to their lives. Teaching more *about*, not for, religion doesn't just make us more "liberal" in Nord's words. It may also help interrupt the formation of antipublic identities. While I say much more about this elsewhere (Apple, 2006), these points have important implications because they can point to strategic moves that can be made to counter the integration of large numbers of people under the umbrella of conservative modernization.

As I have demonstrated elsewhere, people often become right at a local level not through plots by rightist groups but because of local issues and sentiments (Apple, 1996). Making schools more responsive to religious sentiments may seem like a simple step, but it can have echoes that are profound since it may undercut one of the major reasons some populist groups who are also religious find their way under the umbrella of rightist attacks on schools and on the public sphere.

I am not a romantic about this. I do think that it could be dangerous and could be exploited by the religious right. After all, some of them do have little interest in "teaching about" and may hold positions on Christianity and other religions that both construct and leave little room for the "Other." Yet the centrality of religious sentiments need not get pushed toward neoliberalism. It need not be connected to a belief that public schools and teachers are so totally against them that marketization and privatization are the only answers. Thus, I'd like us to think seriously—and very cautiously—about the possible ways members of some of the groups currently found under the umbrella of the conservative alliance might actually be pried loose from it and might work off the elements of good sense they possess. In saying this, I am guided by a serious question: In what ways can religious commitments be mobilized for socially progressive ends? Our (often justifiable) worries about religious influences in the public sphere may have the latent effect of preventing such a mobilization by alienating many people who have deep religious commitments and who might otherwise be involved in such struggles (Apple, 2006; Wallis, 2005). If many evangelicals do commit themselves to helping the poor (Smith, 1998), for example, in what ways can these sentiments be disarticulated from seeing capitalism as "God's economy" and from only helping the "deserving poor" and rearticulated toward greater social and economic transformation. It would seem well worth studying the recent histories of religious involvement in, say, the anti-WTO struggles to understand this better. At the very least, we cannot act as if religious beliefs about social and educational justice are outside the pale of progressive action, as too many critical educators do. A combination of caution, openness, and creativity is required here.

Yet another example is to take advantage of the shared elements of good sense among groups that usually have very different agendas in order to work against specific policies and programs that are being instituted by other elements within the new hegemonic alliance. That is, there *are* real tensions within conservative modernization that provide important spaces for joint action.

This possibility is already being recognized. Because of this, for example, there are some truly odd political couplings emerging today. Both the populist right and the populist left are occasionally joining forces to make strategic alliances against some neoliberal incursions into the school. For instance, Ralph Nader's group Commercial Alert and Phyllis Schlafly's organization the Eagle Forum are building an alliance against Channel One (Coniff, 2000). Both are deeply committed to fighting the selling of children in schools as a captive audience for commercials. They are not alone. The Southern Baptist Convention has passed a resolution opposing Channel One. Groups such as Donald Wildmon's American Family Association and, even more importantly, James Dobson's powerful conservative organization, Focus on the Family, have been working with Nader's groups to remove Channel One from schools and to keep it out of schools where it is not already established. This tactical alliance has also joined together to support antigambling initiatives in a number of states and to oppose what was one of the fastest-growing commercial technology initiatives in education—ZapMe! Corp. Though now financially troubled because of overexpansion, ZapMe! provided free computers to schools in exchange for being able to collect demographic data on students, which it then uses to target advertising specifically at these children.

The tactical agreement is often based on different ideological positions. While the progressive positions are strongly anticorporate, the conservative positions are grounded in a distaste for the subversion of traditional values, "the exploiting of children for profit," and a growing rightist populist tension over the decisions that corporations make that do not take into consideration the "real folks" in America. This latter sentiment is what the rightist populist and nativist Pat Buchanan has worked off of for years. In the words of Ron Reno, a researcher at Focus on the Family, we need to fight "a handful of individuals exploiting the populace of America to make a buck" (quoted in Coniff, 2000, p. 13).

This teaming up on specific causes is approached more than a little cautiously on both sides, as you would imagine. As Ralph Nader says, "You have to be very careful because you can start tempering your positions. You can be too solicitous. You have to enter and leave on your own terms. You tell them, 'Here's what we're doing, if you want to join us fine. If not, fine.'" Phyllis Schlafly portrays her own reasons this way. "[Nader and I] agree that the public schools should not be used for commercial purposes. A captive audience of students should not be sold for profit. I agree with that. I don't recall his objection to the content of the news, which is what stirs up a lot of conservatives" (quoted in Coniff, 2000, p. 13).

Schlafly's comments show the differences as well as similarities in the right–left division here. While for many people across the divide there is a strong distaste for selling our children as commodities, divisions reappear in other areas. For one group, the problem is a "handful of individuals" who lack proper moral values. For the other, the structural forces driving our economy create pressures to buy and sell children as a captive audience. For conservatives, the content of the news on Channel One is too "liberal;" it deals with issues such as drugs, sexuality, and similar topics. Yet, as I have shown in my own analysis of what counts as news in the major media and on Channel One, even though there is some cautious treatment of controversial issues, the content and coding of what counts as news is more than a little conservative and predominantly reinforces dominant interpretations (Apple, 2000).

These differences should not detract from my basic point. Tactical alliances are still possible, especially where populist impulses and anticorporate sentiments overlap. These must be approached extremely carefully, however, since the grounding of much of the populism of the right is also in a racist nativism, a very dangerous tendency that has had murderous consequences. A recognition, though, of the anticorporate tendencies that do exist here is significant, since it also points to cracks in the alliance supporting some aspects of conservative modernization in general and to similar fissures within the ranks of authoritarian populism itself. For example, the fact that Ralph Reed was hired as a consultant to burnish Channel One's image has also created a number of tensions within the authoritarian populist ranks (Coniff, 2000).

Another area that is ripe for such coalitions is that of national and state curricula and testing. Neither the populist right nor the populist left believes that such policies leave room for the cultures, histories, or visions of legitimate knowledge that they are so deeply committed to. While the specific content of such knowledge is decidedly dissimilar for each of these groups, the fact that there is agreement both on a generally anti-elitist position and on the fact that the very processes involved are antidemocratic provides room for tactical alliances not only against these processes but also against even further incursions of managerialism into schools (Apple, 2006). In addition, given the ideological segregation that currently exists in society, working (carefully) with such groups has the advantage of reducing stereotypes that they may hold (and perhaps that we might also hold?). It increases the possibility that the populist right will see that progressives may in fact be able to provide solutions to serious issues that are so distressing in populist movements of multiple orientations. This benefit should not be minimized.

My position, then, embodies a dual strategy. We can and must build tactical alliances where this is possible and where there is mutual benefit—and where such an alliance does not jeopardize the core of progressive beliefs and values. At the same time, we need to continue to build on more progressive alliances between our core constituencies around issues such as class, race, gender, sexuality, ability, globalization and economic exploitation, and the environment. That such a dual strategy can be used both to organize within already existing alliances and to work across differences is made clear in the anti-WTO mobilizations in Seattle, Washington, Philadelphia, Genoa, and a number of other cities throughout the world.

Once the issue of tactical alliances is raised, however, it is nearly impossible to ignore charter schools. For a number of people on both the left and the right, charter schools have been seen as a compromise that can satisfy some of the demands of each group. Here, though, I would urge even more caution. Much of the discussion of these schools has been more than a little romantic. It has accepted the rhetoric of "de-bureaucratization," experimentation, and diversity as the reality. Yet, as Amy Stuart Wells and her colleagues have demonstrated, charter schools often can and do serve less meritorious ends. They can be manipulated to provide public funding for ideologically and educationally problematic programs, with little public accountability. Beneath the statistics of racial equality they supposedly produce, they can exacerbate White flight and be captured by groups that actually have little interest in the cultures and futures of those whom they assume are the "Other." They are used as the "constitutive outside" in attacks on public schooling for the majority of children in schools throughout the United States, by deflecting attention to what must be done there. Thus, they often can and do act to deflect attention from our lack of commitment to provide sufficient resources and support for schools in urban and rural areas. And in a number of ways they threaten to become an opening wedge for voucher plans (Wells, Lopez, Scott, & Holme, 1999).

Having said this, however, I do not believe that charter schools will go away. Indeed, during the many periods of time when I have lectured and engaged in educational and political work in countries in, say, Latin America and Asia, it has become ever more clear to me that there is considerable interest in the charter school movement. This is especially the case in those nations that have a history of strong states and strong central control over the curriculum, teaching, and evaluation and where the state has been inflexible, highly bureaucratic, and unresponsive. Given this situation, it is absolutely crucial that the terrain of charter schools *not* be occupied by the forces within the conservative alliance. If charter schools become, as they threaten to, primarily a site where their function is to deflect attention from schools where the vast majority of students go, if they are allowed to be used as vouchers "incognito," if they serve to legitimate concerted attacks on teachers and other educators, then the effects will not be limited to the United States. This will be a worldwide tragedy. For these very reasons, it is crucial that some of our empirical, educational, and political energy go into guaranteeing that charter schools are a much more progressively inclined set of possibilities than they are today. We need to work so that the elements of good sense in the movement are not lost by its being integrated under the umbrella of conservative modernization.

MAKING CRITICAL EDUCATIONAL PRACTICES PRACTICAL

You will notice that I said "some" of our energy in the previous paragraph. Once again, we need to be extremely cautious that by focusing our energies on "alternatives" such as charter schools we are not tacitly enhancing the very real possibility that progressives will devote so much of their attention to them that action in the vast majority of schools will take a back seat. While all of the tactical and strategic foci I have mentioned are important, there is one area that I believe should be at the center of our concerns as educators—providing real answers to real practical problems in education. By showing successful struggles to build a critical and democratic education in real schools and real communities with real teachers and students today, attention can be refocused on action not only in charter schools but on local elementary, middle, and secondary schools in communities much like those in which most of us spend our lives. Thus, publicizing such "stories" makes critical education seem actually "doable," not merely a utopian vision dreamed up by "critical theorists" in education. For this very reason, political/educational interventions such as the popular and widely translated book *Democratic Schools* (Apple & Beane, 1995) and the increasingly influential journal *Rethinking Schools* become even more important. This is crucial if we are indeed to interrupt the right. Since the right does have an advantage of speaking in "common sense" and in "plain-folks Americanism" (Kintz, 1997; Watson, 1997)—and peoples' common sense *does* have elements of good and bad sense within it—we can also use these progressively inclined elements to show that it is not only the right that has answers to what are real and important issues of educational practice.

For example, the specific vocational and academic programs in which curricula and teaching are linked to paid work and to the economy in socially progressive ways—which were originally built in the Rindge School of Technical Arts in the Boston area—have powerfully demonstrated that those students and parents who are (justifiably) deeply concerned about their economic futures do *not* have to turn to neo-liberal policies to find practical answers to their questions (Rosenstock & Steinberg, 1995). I can think of little that is more important than this. The forces of conservative modernization have colonized the space of practice and of providing answers to the question of "What do I do on Monday?" in part not because the right has all the answers but because the left has too often evacuated that space.

Here again, we have much to learn from the right. While we do not need progressive imitators of, say, E. D. Hirsch, we do need to be much more active in actually attempting to convince teachers, community members, and an increasingly skeptical public that questions such as *what* will I teach, *how* will I teach it, *how* will I evaluate its success—in essence, all those practical questions that people have a right to ask and to which they are entitled to get sensible answers—will be taken very seriously. In the absence of this, we are left standing on the sidelines while the right reconstructs not only common sense but the schools that help produce it.

This is where the work of a number of critically inclined practicing educators has proven to be so important. Critical models of answering these day-to-day questions have been provided by Debbie Meier and her colleagues at Central Park East School in New York and then at Mission Hill School in Boston; Bob Peterson, Rita Tenorio, and their colleagues at Fratney Street School in Milwaukee; the staff at Rindge School; and many other educators in similar schools throughout the country. They also directly respond to the arguments that are made by neoliberals, neoconservatives, and authoritarian populists. They do this not only by defending the very idea of a truly public school—although they are very good at marshaling such a defense (Lowe & Miner, 1992, 1996; Meier, Sizer, Nathan, & Thernstrom, 2000)—but also by demonstrating workable alternatives that are based both on high expectations for their diverse students and on a deep-seated respect for the cultures, histories, and experiences of these students and their parents and local communities (Apple & Beane, 1995; Dance, 2002; Ladson-Billings, 1994). These methods need to be combined with the ways in which educational actions can be connected to social movements that are pressing for change in other areas (Anyon, 2005). Only then can the neoliberal, neoconservative, and managerial factions of the new alliance be undercut at the level of the school.

HOPE AS A RESOURCE

Much more could be said about interrupting the right and about building workable alternatives. I have written this chapter and the book on which it is based—*Educating the "Right" Way*—to contribute to an ongoing set of crucial debates about the means and ends of our educational institutions and about their connections to larger institutions and power relations. Keeping such debates alive and vibrant is one of the best ways of challenging "the curriculum of the dead." Building and defending a truly democratic and critical education is a collective project (Apple et al., 2003). We have much to learn from each other.

Let me end with something that I always want to keep in the forefront of my own consciousness when times are difficult. Sustained political and cultural transformations are impossible "without the hope of a better society that we can, in principle and in outline, imagine" (Panitch & Leys, 1999, p. vii). All of us hope that our work will contribute to the larger movement that is struggling to loosen the grip of the narrow concepts of "reality" and "democracy" that have been circulated by neoliberals and neoconservatives in education and so much else over the past decades. Historically, there have been alternatives to the limited and increasingly hypocritical conception of democracy that even social demo-cratic parties (under the label of the "third way") in many nations have come to accept. In the words of Panitch and Leys (1999), we need "to insist on a far fuller and richer democracy than anything now available. It is time to reject the prevail-ing disparagement of anything collective as 'unrealistic' and to insist on the moral and practical rightness, as well as the necessity, of egalitarian social and economic arrangements" (p. viii). As they go on to say, this requires "the development of popular democratic capacities and the structures that nurture rather than stifle or trivialize them" (p. viii). The movements surrounding conservative moderniza-tion may be "wrong," not "right." They may in fact "stifle or trivialize" a vision of democracy that is based on the common good. But they certainly don't have trivial effects on millions of people all over the world. Our children, our teachers, and our communities deserve something better.

NOTES

1. Of course, people read all kinds of fiction and are not compelled to follow its pre-cepts. Thus, people can read hard-boiled detective novels in which women and men detec-tives often engage in violent acts of retribution. This does not necessarily mean that the readers are in favor of such acts. The politics of pleasure follows its own relatively autono-mous logic. Most people engage in what have been called "guilty pleasures," and reading books like *The Indwelling* may fall under that category for many readers. However, the fact that it is a national best-seller still has considerable importance.

2. Of course, in actuality the content and form of curricula and teaching have always been political issues. See Apple (2005). On some of the recent curriculum struggles in England and Wales, see Hatcher and Jones (1996).

3. The focus on keeping youth "under control" is connected to a long history of the fear of youth and of seeing them as constantly in need of regulation. For an insightful discus-sion of this history, see Lesko (2001).

4. For example, in one of the "teach-ins" in which I participated in preparation for the anti-WTO mobilizations in Seattle and Washington, D.C., very few people had thought about the integration of Spanish-language newspapers, television, radio, and websites in building support for the movement. Yet these are among the fastest-growing media in the United States, and they reach an audience that is suffering deeply from the effects of globalization and economic exploitation.

REFERENCES

Anyon, J. (2005). *Radical possibilities*. New York: Routledge.

Apple, M. W. (1988). *Teachers and texts*. New York: Routledge.

Apple, M. W. (1996). *Cultural politics and education*. New York: Teachers College Press.

Apple, M. W. (2000). *Official knowledge* (2nd ed.). New York: Routledge.

Apple, M. W. (2004). *Ideology and curriculum* (3rd ed.). New York: Routledge.

Apple, M. W. (2005). Comment on E. D. Hirsch, Jr., In D. Ravitch (Ed.), *Brookings papers on education policy*. Washington, DC: Brookings Institution Press.

Apple, M. W. (2006). *Educating the "right" way: Markets, standards, God, and inequality* (2nd ed.). New York: Routledge.

Apple, M. W., & Beane, J. A. (Eds.). (1995). *Democratic schools*. Alexandria, VA: Association for Supervision and Curriculum Development.

Apple, M. W., & Buras, K. L. (2005). School choice, neoliberal promises, and unpromising evidence. *Educational Policy, 19*, 550–564.

Apple, M. W., & Buras, K. L. (Eds.). (2006). *The subaltern speak: Curriculum, power, and educational struggles*. New York: Routledge.

Apple, M. W., Cho, M. K., Gandin, L. A., Oliver, A., Sung, Y.-K., Tavares, H., & Wong, T.-H. (2003). *The state and the politics of knowledge*. New York: Routledge Falmer.

Bernstein, B. (1977). *Class, codes, and control* (2nd ed.; Vol. 3). London: Routledge & Kegan Paul.

Boaler, J. (1998). *Experiencing school mathematics*. Philadelphia: Open University Press.

Bourdieu, P. (1998). *Acts of Resistance*. Cambridge, MA: Polity Press.

Buras, K. (1999). Questioning core assumptions. *Harvard Educational Review, 69*, 67–93.

Coniff, R. (2000, May). Left–right romance. *The Progressive*, pp. 12–15.

Dance, L. J. (2002). *Tough fronts*. New York: Routledge.

Elson, D. (1999). Socializing markets, not market socialism. In L. Panitch & C. Leys (Eds.), *Necessary and unnecessary utopias* (pp. 67–85). New York: Monthly Review Press.

Gitlin, A. (Ed.). (1994). *Power and method*. New York: Routledge.

Gutstein, R. (2006). *Reading the world through mathematics*. New York: Routledge.

Hirsch, E. D., Jr. (1996). *The schools we need and why we don't have them*. New York: Doubleday.

Harding, S. (1991). *Whose science, whose knowledge?* Ithaca, NY: Cornell University Press.

Hatcher, R., & Jones, K. (Eds.). (1996). *Education after the conservatives*. Stoke-on-Trent, UK: Trentham Books.

Kellner, D. (1995). *Media culture*. New York: Routledge.

Kintz, L. (1997). *Between Jesus and the market*. Durham, NC: Duke University Press.

Ladson-Billings, G. (1994). *The dreamkeepers*. San Francisco: Jossey-Bass.
LaHaye, T., & Jenkins, J. (2000). *The indwelling*. New York: Tyndale.
Lesko, N. (2001). *Act your age!* New York: Routledge.
Lipman, P. (2004). *High stakes education*. New York: Routledge.
Lowe, R., & Miner, B. (Eds.). (1992). *False choices*. Milwaukee: Rethinking Schools.
Lowe, R., & Miner, B. (Eds.). (1996). *Selling out our schools*. Milwaukee: Rethinking Schools.
Lukacs, G. (1971). *History and class consciousness*. Cambridge, MA: MIT Press.
McCarthy, C. (2000, January). Unpublished lecture. International Sociology of Education Conference, University of Sheffield, England.
McChesney, R., Wood, E. M., & Foster, J. (Eds.). (1998). *Capitalism and the information age*. New York: Monthly Review Press.
Meier, D., Sizer, T., Nathan, L., & Thernstrom, A. (2000). *Will standards save public education?* Boston: Beacon.
Molnar, A., Smith, P., Zahorik, J., Palmer, A., Halbach, A., & Ehrle, K. (1999). Evaluating the SAGE program. *Education Evaluation and Policy Analysis, 21*, 165–177.
Nord, W. (1995). *Religion and American education*. Chapel Hill: University of North Carolina Press.
Panitch, L. & Leys, C. (Eds.). (1999). *Necessary and unnecessary utopias*. New York: Monthly Review Press.
Ratner, E. (1997). *101 ways to get your progressive issues on talk radio*. Washington, DC: National Press Books.
Rosenstock, L., & Steinberg, A. (1995). Beyond the Shop. In M. W. Apple & J. A. Beane (Eds.), *Democratic schools* (pp. 41–57). Alexandria, VA: Association for Supervision and Curriculum Development.
Segarra, J., & Dobles, R. (Eds.). (1999). *Learning as a political act* (*Harvard Educational Review* Reprint Series No. 33). Cambridge, MA: Harvard University Press.
Smith, C. (1998). *American evangelicalism*. Chicago: University of Chicago Press.
Smith, L. T. (1999). *Decolonizing methodologies*. New York: Zed Books.
Wallis, J. (2005). *God's politics*. San Francisco: Harper.
Watson, J. (1997). *The Christian coalition*. New York: St. Martin's Press.
Wells, A., Lopez, A., Scott, J., & Holme, J. (1999). Charter schools as postmodern paradox. *Harvard Educational Review, 69*, 172–204.

CHAPTER 3

Carry It On: Fighting for Progressive Education in Neoliberal Times

DAVID HURSH

FOR OVER A CENTURY progressives and conservatives have opposed one another over educational goals and methods (Kliebard, 2004). For example, at the turn of the previous century, sociologists began debating whether inequality resulted from "deficient" individuals or unequal social structures. In 1901, sociologist Edward Ross (1901), out of fear of the non-English-speaking immigrants arriving in the later 1800s, welcomed education as the means of assimilating and controlling the immigrants, whom he saw as "the enemy" of society. In contrast, Lester Frank Ward (1883) attributed social inequality not to the "deficiencies" of individuals but to the social structures that reproduce inequality.

Likewise, in the early 1900s David Snedden and John Dewey quarreled over whether education was primarily preparation for work or for democratic citizenship. Snedden perceived the task of education as aiding "the economy to function as efficiently as possible," (Wirth, 1977, p. 163) basically stating that what was good for industry was good for America. Dewey responded to Snedden by stating that he was not "interested in preparing workers for the existing industrial regime" (Dewey, 1915, p. 42) but, rather, that schools and industry, like all social institutions, were to be judged based on the "contribution they make to the all-around growth of every member of society" (Dewey, 1950, p. 147).

Snedden's views reflected those of the social efficiency movement, sparked by Frederick Winslow Taylor (1911, see also Kanigel, 2005), whose publications on "scientific management" promoted standardization, accountability, and reward and punishment in the workplace. Looking at our schools today, it is not hard to figure out whose ideas prevailed. While progressive ideas have sometimes influenced education—Rugg's socially critical textbooks in the 1930s, African American Freedom Schools,[1] and Deweyan alternative schools in the 1960s (Miller,

2002), and constructivism over the past decade—policies exacerbating inequality and promoting cultural assimilation and social efficiency have prevailed. The last decade has been especially unkind to progressive ideals. The corporate and politically powerful have pushed through reforms focusing on standards, accountability, and consequences. These reforms include the rise of state and federal policies that require the use of standardized tests to assess and reward or punish students, teachers, schools and districts; the increasing privatization of education as public funds are diverted to private corporations to develop standardized tests and administer both public schools (Bracey, 2005), and charter schools; and the expanding influence of a few publishing and testing companies over schools' curriculum and pedagogy. These reforms have increased educational inequality, eroded democratic participation in school governance, and diminished teachers' and other educators' control over their profession.

Progressive educators cannot sit on the sidelines hoping that this attack on students, teachers, and public schools will pass. If we care about democracy and social justice, then we must respond and work to replace these reforms with educational policies and practices that promote a democratic society. In this chapter I begin by suggesting that while it has always been difficult to successfully realize progressive policies, we face more significant barriers today. The attack on the right to free, quality public elementary and secondary education, low-cost higher education, and Social Security is being fueled by a neoliberal ideology that calls into question the social democratic principles that evolved over the last century. Further, the last decade of educational reforms has created as assessment system of standards, standardized tests, markets, and accountability that makes returning control to educators and parents any part of the curriculum and pedagogy exceedingly difficult. Lastly, progressives have lost control over the public discourse, enabling proponents of policies harmful to the public good and equality to win debates and elections. In response, I suggest that progressive educators need to engage in research that illuminates the neoliberal political interests behind the recent reforms and in activities that connect progressive educational reforms to other social reforms that promote democratic decision making and social and economic equality.

THE POLITICS OF REVERSING NEOLIBERAL POLICIES

As progressive educators, we confront several obstacles in reversing the educational reforms of the last decade. First, we should not be surprised at the dominance of educational policies perpetuating inequality, assimilation, and social efficiency given that our social policies do little to protect the rights and welfare of the poor and middle class. What rights and protections that exist have been won only through sustained struggle, often during times when it was difficult for those in power to resist the demands. For example, Social Security and unemployment insurance were won during the Depression era, when such policies became necessary to avoid a wider revolt (Skocpol, 1980). The post–World War II civil rights movement began and achieved success in part because the United States could not claim to lead the free world against the Soviet Union while denying the vote to a large number of its own citizens.

Even these victories were only partial. Social Security passed with a provision excluding those working as domestic household workers and in agriculture, two significant sources of jobs for African Americans, especially in the South. Similarly, benefits for World War II veterans under the Servicemen's Readjustment Act, known as the G.I. Bill, were applied unfairly, denying African Americans assistance to attend college, receive job training, start businesses, and purchase new homes (Katznelson, 2005). And separate and unequal schooling, which was found unconstitutional under *Brown v. Board of Education*, has been largely reinstated as policies that would alleviate segregation have been either abandoned or determined themselves to be unconstitutional (Kozol, 2005; Orfield & Eaton, 1996).

Moreover, these meager gains—especially as compared to those in other industrialized countries—are increasingly under attack as both Republicans and Democrats endorse neoliberal policies to reduce, eliminate or privatize social services such as social security, public education, and welfare, and to support corporate growth by reducing corporate regulations and taxes and removing trade barriers. Neoliberals, then, want to make education more efficient and less expensive by introducing competition through markets, by requiring standardized tests so schools can be compared to one another and judged for efficiency, and, as much as possible, by handing education over to corporations that are supposedly more efficient that government bureaucracies.

These neoliberal policies have become so dominant that they seem to many to be necessary, inevitable, and unquestionable. "Everywhere we hear it said, all day long—and this is what gives the dominant discourse its strength—that there is nothing to put forward in opposition to the neoliberal view, that it has presented itself as self evident" (Bourdieu, 1998, p. 29). Therefore, reversing the recent reforms will require challenging the prevalent neoliberal discourses used by corporate and political leaders by developing policy discourses and practices in which public schools promote democratic decision making, responsibility, and equality. For example, small schools, including the Urban Academy in New York and Deborah Meier's Missions Hills public charter school, have instituted governance structures in which students, parents, teachers, and community members have more input into the purposes and processes of the school.

Second, the nature of recent education reforms makes them more difficult to reverse. Previously, most education decisions were made at the local level, with schools or districts reforming their own curriculum and pedagogy. However, state and federal governments have implemented most of the recent reforms, shifting control away from the local districts. Moreover, most of the recent reforms include standards that regulate curriculum and pedagogy and assessments that are used to hold students and teachers accountable. When the assessments are used to determine whether students are promoted from either a particular grade or from high school, the tests become high stakes for students. And because under No Child Left Behind (NCLB) the assessments are used to determine whether a school or district is achieving adequate yearly progress (AYP), the tests are high stakes for schools and districts. Schools and teachers, therefore, face significant pressure to teach what will be tested. Consequently, reversing the reforms will require returning significant control over assessment, curriculum, and pedagogy to local schools and districts and implementing assessment practices that allow flexibility in curriculum and pedagogy.

Lastly, we are losing the battle against these antidemocratic reforms even though many of us have published research demonstrating the negative consequences of high-stakes standardized testing, educational markets, and privatization on student learning, educational equality, and democracy (e.g., Amrein & Berliner, 2002; Gillborn & Youdell, 2000; Haney, 2000; Hursh, 2004, 2005; Hursh & Martina, 2003; Lipman, 2004, 2005; McNeil & Valenzuela, 2001; Meier, 2005; Robertson, 2000). As Thomas Frank argues in *What's the Matter with Kansas? How Conservatives Won the Heart of America* (2005), we need to do more than provide data. While most Americans were worse off economically after the first four years of the George Bush administration, a majority voted to re-elect Bush to continue policies that take from the poor and the middle class and give to the rich. Frank observes that Bush administration policies either have repealed or aim to repeal most of the progressive policies implemented since the early 1900s, including policies protecting the environment and providing Social Security, social welfare, and public education. "Bush may," Frank warns, "well repeal the entire twentieth century" (2005, p. 8).

Therefore, in this chapter I suggest first that we continue researching the recent reforms promoting standardized testing, accountability, and consequences, paying particular attention not only to how they are instantiated in practice and their effects on students, teachers, schools, and communities, but also to the political and ideological forces driving the reforms. As I will describe briefly below, many of the reforms arise from collaboration between the corporate and political elite, who aim to increase efficiency by introducing competition, markets, and quantitative assessments. Further, I will show how they have adopted neoliberal economic and political theory that aims to privatize "the public provision of goods and services . . . along with deregulating how private producers can behave, giving greater scope to the single-minded pursuit of profit and showing significantly less regard for the need to limit social costs" (Tabb, 2002, p. 7). Because the same neoliberal policies that guide education also guide current social polices, this analysis of educational policies can aid in critiquing social and economic policies as well. As I will describe, both Chicago's and the federal government's educational policies promote privatizing educational services with little concern that they exacerbate educational and social inequality.

Moreover, we need not only to reveal the impact neoliberalism has had on educational policy but also to promote a contrasting vision for democracy and education.

Iris Young (2000) builds on many of Dewey's ideas regarding our social institutions as places that contribute to democratic participation and abilities. In *Inclusion and Democracy*, she presents "a normative ideal of democracy as a process of communication among citizens and public officials, where they make proposals and criticize one another, and aim to persuade one another of the best solution to collective problems" (p. 52). One characteristic of her normative ideal is an alternative to the current market-based, aggregative model of democratic decision making that supports the notion that schools will improve because families will leave so-called failing schools for successful ones. She promotes, instead, a deliberative model in which families deliberate with educators and the community over the purpose and processes of schooling. Her vision also includes inclusive political communication, which gives all members of the community a chance to participate in and affect community decision, and differentiated solidarity, which attempts to be inclusive while respecting difference through "respect and mutual obligation" (p. 221). It is precisely because our federal government lacks respect and mutual obligation for others—in particular the urban African American poor—that Hurricane Katrina resulted in thousands of unnecessary injuries and deaths.

Our analysis can be useful to community members, activists, and academics working to understand and change social policies. We need to present our research in venues other than education conferences and in publications other than education journals. While we cannot engage in research that is less than rigorous, we also need to write for a more general audience. At a time when educators are increasingly derided by the political right as elitist and concerned with only their own careers (Johnson & Salle, 2004), we need to appear in more accessible publications, including but going beyond the opinion pages of newspapers. While tenure and promotion depend in large part on publishing in peer-reviewed journals, promotion committees should examine the quality of the work even when it is published in less academically prestigious but more accessible publications.

Because education is only one of the ways in which social inequality is produced and reproduced, we need to work with others locally, regionally, and nationally who are resisting policies producing an economically and spatially segregated society: one group primarily composed of the poor, urban, and people of color and the other primarily upper-middle to upper class, suburban, and White. Together we need to develop a better understanding of how policy is generated and applied as well as who are the political and corporate leaders constructing the policy; we also need to develop a counternarrative to the current individualist and materialist view of democracy. We need, writes Jean Anyon (2005) in *Radical Possibilities: Public Policy, Urban Education, and a New Social Movement*, to organize better to better protect and improve education, housing, health care, and other social services. Anyon describes how over the last three decades, the "organized, well funded political Right" has pushed through macroeconomic policies that promote their own class position and weaken education, economic opportunity, and civil rights for the people of color and the urban poor (p. 10). In response, Anyon calls for a new well-organized social movement composed of educators, parents, and other activists who demand that economic, housing, health, and educational policies promote social justice.

STANDARDIZED EXAMS, ACCOUNTABILITY, MARKETS, AND PRIVATIZATION

After the publication of *A Nation at Risk* (National Commission on Excellence in Education, 1983), corporate and governmental leaders began to call for standards, assessment, and efficiency in public education. Soon thereafter, states began implementing standardized testing requirements as a way not only to assess students, teachers, and schools, but in some states as a requirement for students' promotion from particular grades or from high school. Most notably, Texas in 1984 mandated the Texas Achievement Assessment System (TAAS) requiring students to pass tenth-grade exams in English and math to graduate from high school (Haney, 2000). In Florida students must now pass a test to be promoted from third grade and to graduate from high school. Florida also provides students in low-scoring schools with vouchers towards tuition for private and parochial schools in the state. In New York, the Regents began requiring students pass five subject-area tests to graduate from high school, and in New York City the chancellor for the district began requiring that students pass standardized tests to be promoted from third, fifth and seventh grade (Herzenhorn, 2005).

However, with the passage of NCLB in 2002, the federal government initiated its own testing requirements and increased the high-stakes ante. Not only has the federal government required all states to implement an assessment system with standardized tests in multiple subjects and grades, it uses the tests to divert funding away from public education and toward for-profit and nonprofit corporations to tutor students, administer schools, or convert public schools to charter schools.

Because NCLB's testing requirements result in a large number of failing districts and schools and, eventually, because it calls for every student to achieve proficiency on every test, which will result in the failure of every school,[2] it is likely that the real aim of neoliberal supporters of NCLB is not to improve public education but to replace public schools with publicly funded charter schools and voucher programs. In fact, the Bush administration policies and public statements provide evidence that this is the goal. Early drafts of NCLB provided vouchers to attend private schools. President Bush has authorized federal funds for a $50 million experimental voucher program in Washington, D.C., and for organizations that promote voucher and charter school programs. Former secretary of education Rodney Paige would often use public meeting to promote charter schools. Others, such as Howard Fuller, founder of the pro-voucher organization Black Alliance for Educational Options, has stated: "Hopefully, in years to come the [NCLB] law will be amended to allow families to choose private schools as well as public schools" (quoted in Miner, 2004, p. 11).

The Bush administration and their allies are not the only policymakers supporting privatizing public education. Pauline Lipman (2003), in *High Stakes Education: Inequality, Globalization, and Urban School Reform*, describes how the Chicago public schools (CPS) have come under the increasing control of corporate and governmental interests that make educational decisions based not on what will promote educational equality but what will enable Chicago to compete internationally in the tourism and financial markets when local industries close or move away. Consequently, those in power are developing a two-tier educational system that prepares the children of the professional and managerial class for higher education and children of the poor for jobs in the retail and service industry.

Lipman shows how the mayoral-appointed head of trustees Gery Chico and his budget director Paul Vallas, as chief executive officer, "installed a corporate, regulatory regime centered on high stakes tests, standards, and remediation" (p. 36). Since 1995, she writes, " the CPS has initiated a variety of differentiated programs, schools and instructional approaches with significant implications in Chicago's current economic context" (p. 48). Over the last decade the CPS has created two sets of schools: one for the children of the professional and managerial class and a second for the working poor. Programs and schools for the middle and upper class include international baccalaureate (IB) programs and college prep regional magnet high schools. In contrast, schools for the working poor focus on vocational education, restricted (basic skills) curricula, and intensified regimentation of instruction and/or control of students, including schools that employ "teacher-read scripts and mastery of a fixed sequence of skills" (p. 49) based on a deficit model of "economically disadvantaged students."

The district, as a means of accountability, introduced standardized tests with the publication of results by school. The test scores are used not only to reward and punish schools but also to legitimate allowing those schools with high test scores to retain flexibility in achieving their goals, while those schools with low test scores (principally those composed primarily of students of color and students living in poverty) are required to use regimented methods of instruction. Schools that failed to perform at minimum levels on the required tests, Lipman writes (2004),

> Were put on a warning list, on probation, or their leadership and staff were reconstituted by the central office. Low test scores also carried severe consequences for students, including retention at benchmark grades three, six, and eight and mandatory summer school. . . . Accountability measures were backed up by new after-school and summer remedial programs. . . . In 1997, it [the CPS] established academic standards and curriculum frameworks to standardize the knowledge and skills to be taught in each grade. (p. 36)

Consequently, those students most in need of an invigorating curriculum that builds on their culture (Ladson-Billings, 1994; Valenzuela, 1999) receive an impoverished curriculum focused on raising the students' test scores.

Chicago's new Renaissance 2010 plan promises to exacerbate an already unequal system. Lipman (2005) details how the plan essentially privatizes the public schools and turns control over to the corporate and political elite. She writes that Renaissance 2010 "calls for closing 60 public schools and opening 100 small schools, two-thirds of which will be charter or contract schools run by private organizations and staffed by" (p. 54) non-union teachers and school employees. Renaissance 2010 is only part of the ongoing effort by Chicago's elite to "reshape education in the image of the market by creating school choice, privatizing schools, weakening unions, and eliminating democratic participation in school decision making" (p. 54). Schools will not be governed by the local school councils, to which teachers, parents, and community members are elected, but rather by New Schools for Chicago, a board comprised of corporate and CPS leaders chosen by the Commercial Club for Chicago, an organization representing the city's corporate and political elite. New Schools for Chicago will use current corporate models to evaluate the schools by developing "performance contracts" that focus on student test scores. By undermining democratic control of schools, further deprofessionalizing teachers, and transferring public funds to private for-profit corporations, Renaissance 2010 is a renaissance only for some.

Lipman (2004) concludes her analysis of the Chicago schools:

> The policy regime that I have described is producing stratified knowledge, skills, dispositions, and identities for a deeply stratified society. Under the rubric of standards, the policies impose standardization and enforce language and cultural assimilation to mold the children of the increasingly linguistically and culturally diverse workforce into a most malleable and governable source of future labor. This is a system that treats people as a means to an end. The "economizing of education" and the discourse of accounting reduce people to potential sources of capital accumulation, manipulators of knowledge for global economic expansion, or providers of the services and accessories of leisure and pleasure for the rich. Students are reduced to test scores, future slots in the labor market, prison numbers, and possible cannon fodder in military conquests. Teachers are reduced to technicians and supervisors in the education assembly line—"objects" rather than "subjects" of history. This system is fundamentally about the negation of human agency, despite the good intentions of individuals at all levels. (p. 179)

Chicago's education policies, as Lipman shows, are guided by neoliberal principles emphasizing economic efficiency, employability, privatization, and markets. The CPS ostensibly offers choice through a variety of programs, but the programs that prepare students for university are located in the high-income residential areas and provide only a few slots for students from low-income neighborhoods. While appearing to be egalitarian, in reality the schools, as Snedden desired almost a century before, are preparing students for their "probable destinies"—preparing economically privileged students to be leaders as professionals and managers and economically underprivileged students to be followers as military recruits and service and retail workers. The same principles are evident in the policies proposed by the federal and state governments.

U.S. educational policy changes, write Whitty, Power, and Halpin (1998), in *Devolution and Choice in Education: The School, the State and the Market*, are "dominated by neoliberalism, along with a particular emphasis on market mechanisms" (p 35). Proponents of markets and choice argue that they will result in more efficient and effective schools. "Much of the choice/markets agenda," Robertson (2000) notes, "has been shaped by the criticism of schools as inefficient bureaucracies that are unresponsive either to community or individual interests" (p. 174). Schools, and particularly teachers, are unresponsive, write the critics, because they know parents cannot take their children elsewhere. Therefore, "efficiency and equity in education can only be addressed through 'choice' and where family or individuals are constructed as customers of educational services" (p. 174). Increasing the range of parents' choice over their children's schools and funding schools based on the number of students that they attract introduce a competitive market to the allocation of resources.

Competition and choice, neoliberals argue, are necessary in an increasingly global society that requires more efficient schools and will result in increased educational equality. Bush's former secretary of education, Rodney Paige, often linked education efficiency with increasing the nation's economic competitiveness and with decreasing educational inequality. Paige, in response to an Organization of Economic and Cooperative Development report, stated:

> This report documents how little we receive in return for our national investment. This report also reminds us that we are battling two achievement gaps. One is between those being served well by our system and those being left behind. The other is between the U.S. and many of our higher achieving friends around the world. By closing the first gap, we will close the second. (International report, 2003)

Similarly, education policymakers in New York justified the new testing and accountability regime (including requiring students pass five state Regents exams to graduate from high school) on the grounds that standardized testing is the only way to ensure that all students, including students of color and those living in poverty, have an opportunity to learn. They argue that it is these same students who, because of the end of industrialization and the rise of globalization, can no longer be permitted to fail. All students must succeed educationally in order to ensure that the individual and the nation succeed economically. These ideas are reflected in a recent statement by the New York State chancellor of education:

> The requirement that *every* child be brought to a Regents level of performance is revolutionary. It is a powerful lever for equity. It is changing for the better the life prospects of millions of young people, particularly poor and minority children who in the past

would have been relegated to a low standards path. Too often, these children emerged from school without the skills and knowledge needed for success in an increasingly complex economy. (Hayden, 2001, p. 1; emphasis in original)

The recent reforms, then, have been promoted, in part, as being more efficient, as increasing equity, and as ensuring that every student will learn. However, research, such as Lipman's and others that I cited above (Gillborn & Youdell, 2000; Haney, 2000; McNeil, 2000), provide evidence that the reforms are creating a more unequal system with a stratified curriculum in which some students are presented with a challenging curriculum and others are not.

The quantitative data from two large states, New York and Texas, indicate that the achievement gap has increased between advantaged and disadvantaged students, White students and students of color, students with and without disabilities, and students for whom English is a first and second language. In New York, fewer students, especially students of color and students with disabilities, are completing high school. From 1998 to 2000, the number of students dropping out increased by 17%. A recent report from the Harvard Center for Civil Rights concluded that New York State now has the lowest graduation rate of any state for African-American (35%) and Latino/a (31%) students (Orfield, Losen, Wald, & Swanson, 2004). In New York City only 38% of all students graduate on time, the fifth worst of the 100 largest cities in the nation (Winter, 2004). According to another recent study, New York's graduation rate ranks 45th in the nation (Haney, 2003). The tests have also negatively affected English language learners, who were the highest diploma-earning minority in 1996 and the highest dropout minority in 2002 (Monk, Sipple, & Kileen, 2001). Lastly, dropouts among students with disabilities increased from 7,200 in 1996 to 9,200 in 2001.

McNeil (2000) documents how the emphasis on tests and test scores undermined exemplary schools and teachers in Houston, Texas. In her study of several Houston schools that successfully educated low-income students of color, McNeil aimed to understand what made the schools successful. However, during her research TAAS was implemented and, as a result, she documented how previously successful schools began to expect less of their students as they prepared them to pass the more basic skills required on the tests. For example, rather than teaching students to write well, teachers taught students to write the five-paragraph essay with five sentences in each paragraph that would receive passing grades on the standardized tests. Because culturally advantaged middle- and upper-class students are likely to rely on their cultural capital to pass the exams, it is disadvantaged students who receive the additional drilling. Unfortunately, learning to write five-sentence five-paragraph essays does not transfer well to literacy required beyond the test and outside of school. Because less is expected of disadvantaged students, they fall further behind.

Moreover, rather than ensuring that more students do well, the pressure to raise test scores encourages schools to force weak students out of school before they take the required exam. In Texas, urban students are more likely to be retained in school, especially in ninth grade, the year before the required TAAS exam is first given. Students who are repeatedly retained are likely to give up and drop out of school. Haney (2000), in his study of the Texas education reforms, concludes that in 1996–1997 17.8% of students were being retained in ninth grade (24.2% of African American and 25.9% of Hispanic students) and that only 57.57% of African-American and 52.11% of Hispanic ninth-grade students were in twelfth grade 4 years later.

Moreover, schools in Texas face a double-edged sword: They need to raise test scores but face possible sanctions for high dropout rates. Paige, as superintendent of the Houston School District, resolved this dilemma by ordering principals to list students not as having dropped out but as having left for another school or for some other reason. Such creative bookkeeping resulted in the district claiming a greatly reduced dropout rate to 1.5% in 2001–2002 and winning awards for excellence.

Eventually critics claimed that the dropout rate was covered up, and research has revealed the rate to be much higher. Robert Kimball, assistant principal at one of the Houston high schools, raised questions when his school amazingly reported no dropouts even though its freshman class of 1,000 had dwindled to 300 by senior year. A subsequent state investigation into 16 high schools revealed that of 5,000 students who left school, 2,999 students should have been reported as dropouts but were not (Winerip, 2003). Significantly, Kimball adds, "Almost all of the students that were being pushed out were at-risk students and minorities" (Capellaro, 2004).

FORGING THE FUTURE:
PROMOTING PROGRESSIVE ECONOMIC AND EDUCATION POLICY

David Berliner (2005) began his 2004 American Educational Research Association Presidential Invited Speech by stating that in his three co-authored reports on the effects of high-stakes testing programs on curricula, instruction, school personnel, and student achievement, he concluded that the programs "are ineffective in achieving their intended purposes" and cause "severe unintended negative effects, as well." Yet his reports, plus the ones I cited above and many others, have been insufficient in repealing failing policy.

As Frank (2005) reminds us, data are not enough; we need to understand why it is that failing policies are promoted and accepted by the public, develop an alternative to the current high-stakes testing and accountability system, and work with community members to propose meaningful democratic policies not only in education but also in health, housing, employment, and elsewhere.

The reform emphasis on high-stakes testing, accountability, privatization, and markets reflects three decades of neoliberal economic thought as the implicit and explicit foundation for public policies. Neoliberalism privileges corporations, markets, and profit over communities, social services, and meaningful, well-paying work. As stated earlier, neoliberal assumptions have become so dominant that they are rarely questioned. Sociologist Pierre Bourdieu (1998) noted:

> A whole set of propositions is being imposed as self-evident: it is taken for granted that maximum growth, and therefore productivity and competitiveness, are the ultimate and sole goal of human actions; or that economic forces cannot be resisted. Or again—a presupposition which is the basis of all the presuppositions in economics—a radical separation is made between the economic and the social, which is left to one side . . . as a kind of reject. (p. 31)

Neoliberalism forms the foundation for policies at the city (Chicago), state (New York), and federal levels. Policymakers have successfully promoted their policies in part because they assert that we have no choice if we are to remain competitive in a global economy and to provide equal educational opportunity. However, the discourse of equality is disingenuous. We need to respond by revealing that the real purpose of high-stakes testing regimes includes shifting the blame for economic problems to schools (Apple, 1996), reducing or privatizing educational costs and services, and serving corporate interests in a global economy.

We cannot only be critics. We need to develop conceptually and practically a democracy that provides the jobs, health care, and transportation necessary for a community to flourish. This will require elaborating on a conception of inclusive, differentiated deliberative democracy and developing both the public space and structures in which such processes can occur. For example, we need to develop school governance structures where parents, students, educators, and the community are accountable to one another in providing a quality education to all students. The 28 schools that make up the New York Performance Standards Consortium (PSC) and Deborah Meier's Mission Hill School in Boston are examples of public schools that require all the members of the community to be accountable to one another and share responsibility for the school's success. Such governance models require, as Meier reminds us, that we put in the hard work of listening to and learning from one another to develop a school that reflects the interests of the community (Meier, 2005).

Furthermore, when possible, we need to collaborate with the community on educational, political, and social issues. As a founding member of Chicago Teachers for Social Justice (http://www.teachersforjustice.org/html), Pauline Lipman not only writes about the policies affecting Chicago schools, teachers, students, and community members but also has immersed herself in the politics of Chicago school reform and works alongside teachers and community members to combat Chicago's reforms, including Renaissance 2010.

Angela Valenzuela's academic research gradually immersed her in Houston's inner-city Latino community and then Texas education politics. She is active in the League of United Latin American Citizens (LULAC), testified in the Mexican American Legal Defense of Education Fund (MALDEF) federal suit against the Texas Education Agency and the State Board of Education, and works with members of the Texas legislature to craft and promote legislation regarding assessment, limited English proficient youth, bilingual education, school vouchers, and school finance (Foley & Valenzuela, 2004). (See her website at: http://texasedequity.blogspot.com/)

In 1999 I helped start the Coalition for Common Sense in Education (CCSE), a group of educators, parents, and students working primarily to combat high-stakes testing in New York. We focused initially on working to preserve the right of the schools that comprise the Performance Standards Consortium (PSC), all but two of which are in New York City and one of which is Rochester's School Without Walls, to use portfolios and projects and other more authentic methods of assessment in place of Regents exams. The previous commissioner of education had granted the schools a waiver from the Regents exams, but the current commissioner, Richard Mills, was considering revoking the waiver. We met and planned strategy with parents, teachers, administrators, and students from the schools, and with Performance Assessment Review Board members (who assessed the schools), which included Ted Sizer, Deborah Meier, Michelle Fine, myself, and others. Initially, our political strategy focused on convincing the commissioner to continue the waiver. After it quickly became clear that the commissioner intended to revoke the waiver no matter what evidence we presented—the PSC students achieved significantly greater academic success than their peers in comparable public schools—we began lobbying members of the Regents. Later the commissioner appointed a blue ribbon panel to review the PSC's assessment materials, and the panel recommended that the waiver be extended. However, the commissioner rejected the panel's recommendation and revoked the waiver. That decision led the PSC, along with Time Out from Testing (www.timeoutfromtesting.org) and CCSE, to file a lawsuit arguing that the commissioner did not follow due process. After losing at every court level, we returned to lobbying first the Regents and then the legislature. On several occasions we transported busloads of teachers, parents, students, and administrators to Albany for the day to rally and lobby legislators. In Albany we had dozens of teams lobby legislators; my lobbying team consisted of three passionate and knowledgeable ninth graders and myself. Over time, our lobbying efforts began to include some of the information presented earlier on the negative effects the Regents exams has on student graduation rates and on problems with the tests themselves, described more fully elsewhere (Hursh, 2003; Hursh & Martina, 2003, 2004).

Our lobbying contributed to the New York Senate's decision to hold hearings on the exams in fall of 2003. At those hearings, numerous educators who have been involved in the issue of high-stakes testing in New York testified, including Walter Haney (2003), Michele Fine (2003), Bill Cala (2003), Dan Drmacich, and Richard Ryan. Bill Cala, Fairport Central School District superintendent, has actively fought against the Regents and NCLB mandates, including resisting NCLB's requirement that high school students' names be turned over to the military without explicit parental permission. Dan Drmacich, School Without Walls principal, has led CCSE since the beginning. Richard Ryan, University of Rochester professor, is an internationally renowned researcher on student motivation.

While we were putting political pressure on legislators, we also continued to educate the public. We have brought to Rochester numerous speakers, including Angela Valenzuela, Alfie Kohn, and Peter Sacks (2001). In the spring of 2005 we organized a speaker series that included Deborah Meier, Peter McWalters (Rhode Island commissioner of education), Douglas Christiansen (Nebraska commissioner of education), and myself.

After 6 years of political organizing, our efforts paid off with a limited political victory. While the legislature was hesitant to intervene in policy decisions made by the Regents (a system intended to "remove education from politics"), in the summer of 2005 the Republican-controlled state assembly passed a bill that would not only have reinstated the waiver for the 28 schools but permitted school districts to develop alternatives to the standardized Regents exams. The bill then went to the Democratic-controlled Senate, which appoints the members of the Regents and the commissioner. Because the Democrats were not interested in embarrassing those they had appointed and knew that the Republican governor was likely to veto the bill, members of the Senate approached the commissioner to reach a compromise: They would not pass the bill if the Regents would reinstate the waiver. A compromise was reached, and the schools have to give a Regents exam only in math and English until 2010, at which time the Regents can then reimpose the testing requirements (Herzenhorn, 2005).

However, for CCSE, reinstating the waiver was necessary but not sufficient. CCSE also aims to reduce the impact of the Regents exams so that it is only one of the multiple measures used to assess students (see, e.g., Valenzuela, 2002); therefore, it continues to lobby the legislature and Regents to increase assessment flexibility for all schools and to educate the public regarding educational issues. In the fall of 2005 we began to work with Leonard Salle (Johnson & Salle, 2004; Salle & Forrest, 2005) of the Commonweal Institute on developing a progressive movement that encompasses not only educational issues but also issues of poverty, health, and other problems exacerbating inequality.

Over the past years we have become more adept at organizing: sending out press releases, setting up appointments with legislators, drafting legislation, writing editorials, and arranging and publicizing speakers. However, our success has been limited. Most of the educational reforms we have resisted have, unfortunately, been implemented. In Chicago, Texas, and New York we still have high-stakes testing and are still governed by NCLB. If we are going to succeed, the recent reforms need to be understood as part of a larger effort by neoliberal governments to reduce and privatize social services. We need other community activists to understand that the battle over education is central to equality and democracy, and we need to understand that the same is true for housing, transportation, employment, health, and other policies that will enable urban communities to thrive.

While our recent political success has been limited, Jean Anyon (2005) reminds us that some progressive victories came in times when the nation was most conservative. The civil rights movement began in earnest in the 1950s, following the apex of McCarthyism. Other movements—such as the welfare rights, women's rights, antiwar, and the environmental movements—were either rekindled or ignited during the 1960s after the supposedly quiet and conservative 1950s. Moreover, while not as visible as the civil rights and antiwar demonstrations of the 1960s and 1970s, over the last several decades many progressive groups have been working actively for reform. We need to learn from and connect with other activists and theorists to develop strategies and tactics to replace the last decade of neoliberal reforms with progressive, socially democratic ones. Democracy and equality require that we do not fail.

Education not only has been and will continue to be contested, but it is central to the larger struggle over what kind of society and government we desire. Our fight for education that promotes democratic citizenship and equality requires that we engage with the broader political and economic struggles. We cannot afford to lose.

NOTES

1. Beginning in the 1963 and expanding during Freedom Summer in 1964, Freedom Schools were set up by the African American community as alternatives to the public schools where they could learn about their heritage and rights as citizens (Miller, 2002).

2. Numerous critics have exposed the inconsistencies and impossibilities underlying NCLB. Linn (2003), Hursh (2004, 2005), Hursh & Martina (2003) and others (Bracey, 2005) have described the way in which NCLB measures of AYP sometimes results in schools with rising test scores being labeled as failing and schools with falling test scores being labeled as succeeding. Further, the AYP requirement that all students achieve proficiency by 2014 has been revealed as a pedagogical impossibility.

REFERENCES

Amrein, A. L., & Berliner, D. C. (2002, March 28). High-stakes testing, uncertainty, and student learning, *Education Policy Analysis Archives*. Retrieved May 15, 2004, from http://epass.asu.edu/epaa/v10n18/

Anyon, J. (2005). *Radical possibilities: Public policy, urban education, and a new social movement.* New York: Routledge.

Apple, M. (1996). *Cultural politics and education.* Buckingham, UK: Open University Press.

Berliner, D. C. (2005, August 2). Our impoverished view of educational reform. *Teachers*

College Record. Retrieved September 10, 2005, from http://www.tcrecord.org/Content.asp?ContentID=12106

Bourdieu, P. (1998). *Acts of resistance: Against the tyranny of the market.* New York: The New Press.

Bracey, G. W. (2005, June). No Child Left Behind: Where does the money go? *Education Policy Studies Laboratory.* Retrieved September 10, 2005, from http://edpolicylab.org

Cala, W. (2003). Testimony before the New York Senate Standing Committee on Education. Retrieved September 15, 2005, from http://www.timeoutfromtesting.org/testimonies.php

Cala, W. (2004). The mismeasure and abuse of our children: Why school officials must resist state and national testing reforms. In S. Mathison & E. W. Ross (Eds.), *Defending public schools: The nature and limits of standards-based reform and assessment* (Vol. 4; pp. 149–165). Westport, CT: Praeger.

Capellero, C. (2004). Blowing the whistle on the Texas Miracle: An interview with Robert Kimball. *Rethinking Schools, 19*(1). Retrieved December 2004 from: http://rethinkingschools.org/archive/1901/tex191.shtml

Dewey, J. (1915, May 5). Education vs. trade-training—Dr. Dewey's reply. *The New Republic, 3*(28), 42–43.

Dewey, J. (1950). *Reconstruction in philosophy.* New York: New American Library, Mentor Books.

Fine, M. (2003). Testimony before the New York Senate Standing Committee on Education. Retrieved September 15, 2005, from http://www.timeoutfromtesting.org/testimonies.php

Foley, D., & Valenzuela, A. (2004). Critical ethnography: The politics of collaboration. In N. K. Denzin & Y. S. Lincoln (Eds.), *The Sage handbook of qualitative research* (3rd ed.). Thousand Oaks, CA: Sage Publications.

Frank, T. (2005). *What's the matter with Kansas? How conservatives won the heart of America.* New York: Metropolitan Books.

Gillborn, D., & Youdell, D. (2000). *Rationing education: Policy, practice, reform and equity.* Philadelphia: Open University Press.

Haney, W. (2000, August 19). The myth of the Texas miracle in education, *Education Policy Analysis Archives.* Retrieved May 15, 2005, from http://epaa.asu.edu/v8n1

Haney, W. (2003). Testimony before the New York Senate Standing Committee on Education. Retrieved October 5, 2003, from http://www.timeoutfromtesting.org/testimonies/923_Testimony_Haney.pdf

Hayden, C. (2001, May 7). Letter to the Hon. Richard Brodsky and the Hon. Richard Green, New York State Assembly.

Herzenhorn, D. M. (2005, July 19). Mayor plans new standards for 7th graders. *New York Times.* Retrieved July 21, 2005, from http://www.nytimes.org

Hursh, D. (2003). Imagining the future: Growing up working class, teaching in the university. *Educational Foundations, 17*(3), 55–68.

Hursh, D. (2004). Undermining democratic education in the USA: The consequences of global capitalism and neo-liberal policies for education policies at the local, state, and federal levels. *Policy Futures in Education, 2*(3/4), 601–614.

Hursh, D. (2005). The growth of high-stakes testing in the USA: Accountability, markets and the decline of educational inequality. *British Educational Research Journal, 31*(4), 605–622.

Hursh, D., & Martina, C. A. (2002, November). *The rise of testing and accountability and the decline of teacher professionalism and local control: A critical analysis of the changing forms of governmentality in New York.* Paper presented at the annual meeting of the American Educational Studies Association Conference, Pittsburgh.

Hursh, D., & Martina, C. A. (2003, October). Neoliberalism and schooling in the U.S.: How state and federal government education policies perpetuate inequality. *Journal for critical education policy studies, 1*(2). Retrieved October 22, 2003, from: http://www.jceps.com

Hursh, D., & Martina, C. A. (2004). Neoliberalism and schooling in the United States: How state and federal government education policies perpetuate inequality. In D. A. Grabbard & E. W. Ross (Eds.), *Defending public schools: Education under the security state* (Vol. 1). Westport, CT: Praeger.

International report. (2003, September 26). *Education Review.* Retrieved October 1, 2003, from http://www.ed.gov/news/newsletters/index.html

Johnson, D. C., & Salle, L. M. (2004, November). *Responding to the attack on public education and teacher unions: A Commonweal Institute Report.* Retrieved November 25, 2004, from http://www.commonwealinstitute.org/IssuesEducation.htm

Kanigel, R. (2005). *The one best way: Frederick Winslow Taylor and the enigma of efficiency (Sloan technology).* Cambridge, MA: MIT Press.

Katznelson, I. (2005). When affirmative action was White: An untold history of racial inequality in twentieth-century America. New York: Norton.

Kliebard, H. (2004). *The struggle for the American curriculum: 1893–1958* (3rd ed.). New York: Routledge Press.

Kozol, J. (2005, September). Still separate, still unequal: America's educational apartheid. *Harpers, 311*(1864), 41–54.

Ladson-Billings, G. (1994). *Dreamkeepers: Successful teachers of African-American children.* San Francisco: Jossey-Bass.

Linn, R. (2003). Accountability: Responsibility and reasonable expectations. *Educational Researcher, 32*(7), 3–13.

Lipman, P. (2004). *High stakes education: Inequality, globalization and urban school reform.* New York: Routledge.

Lipman, P. (2005). We're not blind. Just follow the dollar sign. *Rethinking Schools, 19*(4), 54–58.

McNeil, L. (2000). *Contradictions of school reform: Educational costs of standardized testing.* New York: Routledge.

McNeil, L., & Valenzuela, A. (2001) The harmful impact of the TAAS system of testing in Texas: Benath the accountability rhetoric. In G. Orfield & M. L. Kornhaber (Eds.), *Raising standards or raising barriers? Inequality and high stakes testing in public education* (pp. 127–150). New York: Century Foundation Press.

Meier, D. (2005). No Child Left Behind and democracy. In D. Meier, A. Kohn, L. Darling-Hammond, T. R. Sizer, & G. Wood (Eds.), *Many children left behind: How the No Child Left Behind Act is damaging our children* (pp. 66–78). Boston: Beacon.

Miller, R. (2002). *Free schools, free people: Education and democracy after the 1960s.* Albany: State University of New York Press.

Miner, B. (2004, Summer). Seed money for conservatives. *Rethinking Schools, 18*(4), 9–11.

Monk, D., Sipple, J., & Killeen, K. (2001, September 10). Adoption and adaptation: New York State school districts' responses to state imposed high school graduation requirements: An eight-year retrospective. Retrieved November 8, 2001, from http://www. albany,edu/edfin/CR01_MSK_Report.pdf

National Commission on Excellence in Education. (1983). *A nation at risk: A report to the nation and the secretary of education*, Washington, DC: U.S. Department of Education.

Orfield. G., & Eaton, S. (1996). *Dismantling desegregation: The quiet reversal of* Brown v. Board of Education. New York: The New Press.

Orfield, G., Losen, D., Wald, J. & Swanson, C. (2004). *Losing our future: How minority youth are being left behind by the graduation-rate crisis*. Cambridge, MA: The Civil Rights Project at Harvard University.

Robertson, S. (2000). *A class act: Changing teachers' work, the state, and globalizaton.* New York: Falmer Press.

Ross, E. (1901). *Social control: A survey of the foundation of order.* New York: Macmillan.

Sacks, P. (2001). *Standardized minds: The high price of America's testing culture and what we can do to change it.* New York: Perseus.

Salle, L. & Forrest, K. A. (2005). *Creating progressive infrastructure now: An action plan for reclaiming America's heart and soul.* Retrieved February 5, 2005, from http://www. commonwealinstitute.org/IssuesPI.htm

Skocpol, T. (1980). Political response to capitalist crisis: Neo-Marxist theories of the state and the case of the New Deal. In T. Skocpol & J. Campbell (Eds.), *American society and politics: Institutional, historical, and theoretical perspectives* (pp. 48–73). New York: McGraw-Hill.

Tabb, W. (2002). *Unequal partners: A primer on globalization.* New York: The New Press.

Taylor, F. W. (1911). *The principles of scientific management.* New York: Harper & Brothers.

Valenzuela, A. (1999). *Subtractive schooling: U.S.-Mexican youth and the politics of caring.* Albany: State University of New York Press.

Valenzuela, A. (2002). High-stakes testing and U.S.-Mexican youth in Texas: The case for multiple compensatory criteria in assessment. *Harvard Journal of Hispanic Policy, 14,* 97–112.

Ward, L. F. (1883). *Dynamic sociology, or applied social science as based upon statistical sociology and the less complex sciences* (Vol. 2). New York: Appleton.

Whitty, G., Power, S., & Halpin, D. (1998). *Devolution and choice in education: The school, the state and the market.* Philadelphia: Open University Press.

Winerip, M. (2003, August 13). The "zero dropout" miracle: Alas! alack! A Texas tall tale. *New York Times,* p. B7.

Winter, G. (2004, February 26). Worst Rates of Graduation are in New York. *New York Times,* p. B3.

Wirth, A. (1977). Philosophical issues in the vocational-liberal studies controversy (1900–1917): John Dewey vs. the social efficiency philosophers. In A. A. Bellack & H. M. Kliebard (Eds.), *Curriculum and evaluation* (pp. 161–172). Berkeley: McCutchan.

Young, I. M. (2000). *Inclusion and democracy.* New York: Oxford University Press.

CHAPTER 4

Public Intellectuals
and the University

Alex Molnar

INTRODUCTION

THE ROLE OF PUBLIC INTELLECTUAL has been much discussed over the past decade. Most often the discussion has centered on how academics working in a university setting can meaningfully bring their expertise to bear in shaping politics and policies without at the same time sacrificing their academic integrity. There are enough examples of dishonest work by "scholars" and "fellows" associated with private think tanks to give this concern currency. On the whole, I think we can rely on the integrity of most university-based academics.

A more general problem with the idea of public intellectuals working in a university context is that the structure of the university reward system does not favor public engagement. Assistant and associate professors are kept busy teaching, advising, and serving on committees. Mostly, however, they write and hope to publish. Anyone who has even a casual acquaintance with the promotion regime in most universities realizes how all-consuming it has become. Even in professional schools and colleges such as colleges of education, professors are pushed to focus on refereed academic journals and to shy away from the less prestigious professional publications in order to secure tenure and with it an academic career. Engagement with politicians and policymakers is similarly discouraged by the reward system. That sort of involvement is risky because it may lead to controversy, and controversy may lead to the charge that the work of the academic is tainted. Few assistant or associate professors are willing to take that risk. Not surprisingly, therefore, there are lots of courses with social justice themes (perhaps in the hope students will change the world) and lots of papers and presentations at academic gatherings (where promotion credit accrues), but not much political or practical policy engagement within the context of the academic life of most untenured professors.

Education Research in the Public Interest, edited by Gloria Ladson-Billings and William F. Tate. Copyright © 2006 by Teachers College, Columbia University. All rights reserved. Prior to photocopying items for classroom use, please contact the Copyright Clearance Center, Customer Service, 222 Rosewood Dr., Danvers, MA 01923, USA, tel. (978) 750-8400, www.copyright.com.

For tenured professors the issues are somewhat different. Referred publication is, to be sure, still the coin of the realm; however, with tenure comes the opportunity and the temptation to become a "player," to whisper in the ear of power. Controversy is the terror that stalks the untenured ranks. Lack of access is what many tenured professors fear. Unfortunately, wanting to be heard by important policymakers, I suspect, has encouraged many tenured professors to trim their views to better tack into the prevailing winds. Since social science findings are never without nuance, there is plenty of trimming to be done under the guise of cautiously interpreting results or describing rather than interpreting phenomena. Moreover, praise in academic culture tends to go to the cautious and the descriptive. And, indeed, there is an important place for both caution and description in academic work.

Of course, there are many professors for whom being a "player" outside of the academy of little interest. Their careers may be built on a solid foundation of disciplinary inquiry or even of "speaking truth to power." Alas, those with power have little interest in disciplinary knowledge, and most often take no notice of their academic critics. And for their part, many professors of this inclination tend to view relevance to the rough-and-tumble world of practical policymaking as a sign of corruption.

For myself I have come to believe that a public intellectual in a university setting must inevitably hover uncomfortably between being an outsider with academically sound ideas that challenge the received wisdom of policy and practice and being someone who maintains durable long-term relationships with the policymaking world beyond the boundaries of the academy.

I was hired as an assistant professor in 1972 at a time when publishing was important, but nowhere near as important as it is today in establishing an academic career and achieving tenure. Perhaps for this reason I have had more opportunities to function as a "public intellectual" (or at the very least be involved with my practitioner colleagues) than my junior colleagues are afforded today. Along the way I have had experiences that may provide some guidance for others who want to succeed as academics and who want as part of their academic work to be engaged in the relevant politics and policymaking. What follows is a description of the development and content of my research and civic agenda in relation school commercialism as well as a consideration of the institutional contexts that have furthered it.

Twenty-two years ago I attended a meeting of the Association for Supervision and Curriculum Development (ASCD) that launched my study of and public engagement with the issue of school commercialism. In 1983 as I was walking through the exhibitor's hall at the ASCD convention, surveying the customary canvas bags and other giveaway goodies, the overhead projectors, the booths for textbooks and office equipment, I noticed a booth for McDonald's. Struck by this unexpected sight, I stopped at the booth and saw, among other handouts, a McDonald's education catalogue. The catalogue cover was mottled black and white and looked much like a traditional composition book used in schools. As I paged through it, I was astonished to see that McDonald's was offering free curriculum materials for teachers on topics such as nutrition and the environment. Of all of the places one might go for guidance on sound nutrition advice and environmental information, McDonald's would surely be at the bottom of most people's lists. I was appalled and intrigued.

I was teaching a course in curriculum planning at the time and certainly nowhere in my syllabus was there anything about the McDonald's curricula. Here I was teaching curriculum planning, and yet I knew nothing about the sort of supplemental materials McDonald's and other corporations were placing in schools. Most of my students were school principals or teachers, people who were preparing to be curriculum directors or otherwise sought to play a larger role in their schools as shapers of curriculum. When I returned to my campus, I showed my students the McDonald's catalogue and asked them about it. Was this sort of material in their schools? Could they bring me examples of such sponsored materials from their schools?

It took just two class sessions for me to accumulate four boxes of materials. Obviously there was a lot of this stuff in my students' schools. If such material was as pervasive in other schools as it appeared to be in schools in which my students worked, I realized that in my course I would have to analyze the content and implications of using corporate-sponsored materials.

In the two decades since my epiphany, I have learned that not just McDonald's, but the pork farmers, the plastic bag manufacturers, the Dairy Council, the timber industry, the oil industry, financial services companies, and many, many more all have a curriculum to offer. Schools now sell advertising on the sides of school buses, establish exclusive contracts with soda-bottling companies to sell only their wares, and name buildings after commercial enterprises. They send children on field trips to stores for lessons in "nutrition" (grocery chains), "animal care" (pet stores), and more.

It is as if the school curriculum has become a kind of souk into which one can wander, and whoever has the money to pay for admission gets to set up a booth. The metaphor does not stop with in-school advertising. Since the early 1990s public education has itself become increasingly being framed as a "product" that can be in sold in an educational marketplace. For-profit management companies are now an accepted feature on the American educational landscape.

CACE/CERU:
CREATING A CONTEXT FOR PUBLIC INTELLECTUALS

By the early 1990s limning the parallel trends of selling in schools and the selling of schools themselves had become my academic focus. As a result of my writing on the subject, Consumers Union approached me to create a research unit that focused on schoolhouse commercialism. The result was the creation in 1998 of the Center for the Analysis of Commercialism in Education (CACE) at the University of Wisconsin–Milwaukee. Since 2001 I have directed the Education Policy Studies Laboratory at Arizona State University (ASU) and CACE has become the Commercialism in Education Research Unit (CERU). Although I did not completely understand how in 1998 when CACE was formed, I have since learned that the existence of an institutional unit—with a website, an ongoing research agenda, and an interest in communicating in and outside the academic community—is an important vehicle for supporting high-quality academic work and public engagement.

As the director of ASU's Education Policy Studies Lab I am, in addition to CERU, also responsible for the Education Policy Research Unit (EPRU) and the Arizona Education Policy Initiative (AEPI). The lab also houses the Language Policy Research Unit (LPRU) directed by Terry Wiley and Wayne Wright. The bulk of my discussion here, however, primarily focuses on CERU and research conducted under its aegis.

The research I direct at CERU is guided by the belief that mixing commercial activities with public education raises fundamental issues of public policy, curriculum content, the proper relationship of educators to the students entrusted to them, and the values that the schools embody. CERU has allowed me to pursue two broad lines of investigation that build on my work prior to the creation of CACE/CERU. The first is advertising to children in schools. This line of investigation is primarily focused on the production the Annual Report on Trends in Schoolhouse Commercialism (Molnar, 2004; see also Molnar 1996, 1998, 1999, 2002, 2003; Molnar & Morales, 2000; Molnar & Reaves, 2001). The second is school privatization, which is primarily focused on the production of the annual *Profiles of For-Profit School Management Organizations* (Molnar, Garcia, Sullivan, McEvoy, & Joanou, 2005; see also Molnar, Morales, & Vander Wyst, 1999, 2000, 2001; Molnar, Wilson, & Allen, 2003, 2004; Molnar, Wilson, Restori, & Hutchison, 2002). While non-university-based advocacy organizations such as Commercial Alert examine and organize opposition to commercialism of all forms, including schoolhouse commercialism, so far as I know CERU is the only academic unit in the world dedicated to research on the topic.

With the aid of Consumer Union's ongoing financial support, and with the institutional structure provided by the Education Policy Studies Laboratory, CERU has enabled me to develop and sustain a research agenda focused on schoolhouse commercialism and to keep it in the public eye.

CERU'S FINDINGS:
SCHOOLHOUSE COMMERCIALISM TRENDING UPWARD

Commercialism in schools and classrooms isn't new. Over the last two decades, however, corporations have dramatically increased their involvement in public education. Today, almost every large corporation sponsors some type of in-school or school-related marketing program. Such programs range from advertising on school buses, on scoreboards, and in lunchrooms to the creation of curriculum materials for science, government, history, math, and current events classes.

There is no simple way to measure the extent, depth, and breath of corporate money-making activities in schools. Firms engaged in school-based commercial activities may, at different times, have an interest in making exaggerated claims about the number of children reached (in order to attract clients), remaining silent (to shield market research and product introduction information from competitors), or minimizing the size of their efforts (to lessen the possibility of a negative public reaction). In addition, the varied and particular purposes for which organizations gather data on school-focused commercializing activities result in information that is fragmentary and often not comparable, and, therefore, not reliable as a basis for identifying overall trends.

One industry group favoring corporate involvement in schools reported in 2002 that schools receive $2.4 billion a year from what the organization, the Council on Corporate and School Partnerships (2002), calls "business relationships" with corporations. The council calculated that nearly 70% of school districts engaged in so-called business partnerships, and nearly all educators in a survey planned to continue those relationships. A council news release containing those figures asserted that, from the vantage point of business leaders, "school partnerships benefit business and educators in four key areas: human capital development, community development, student achievement, and financial impact in terms of earning revenue for the business and providing needed funding for schools." How those numbers should be interpreted, however, is not entirely clear in the absence of a generally agreed-upon set of definitions.

It is clear, however, that the range of commercial activities in public education is increasingly broad. In Indianapolis, students at risk for dropping out are enrolled in an alternative school based on the premises of Lafayette Square Mall. There they attend classes, work at part-time jobs for credit, walk the mall to fulfill a mandatory gym requirement, and get their meals at the food court. Since 1998, America's largest mall developer, the Simon Property Group, has been opening alternative public schools in malls through its nonprofit Simon Youth Foundation in partnership with local public school systems. By 2004, Simon had opened 19 such "Education Resource Centers" (ERCs) in 11 states (Berdik, 2004). The stated goal was to reengage students who might be lost entirely to the public school system, in part by teaching them job skills. Yet as psychologist Susan Linn has pointed out, a mall-based school poses an inherent conflict. "Schools are supposed to be good for kids," says Linn, author of *Consuming Kids: The Hostile Takeover of Childhood*. She adds: "If a school embraces a commercial enterprise or commercial values, the school is sanctioning them. . . . A mall is full of businesses that want to sell things, and sell things to kids" (quoted in Berdik, 2004, p. D2).

Schools in shopping malls are only one example. Commercialism takes a host of other forms in schools. The challenge is how to meaningfully measure it. Lacking data sources that allow the direct tracking of developments in schoolhouse commercialism, I developed a method of indirectly tracking the phenomenon. The research on schoolhouse commercializing trends that I conduct at CERU provides annual counts of media references to eight categories of commercialism.

The data used in the CERU research derives from searches of four media databases: the popular press, the business press, and the marketing press through Lexis-Nexis, and the education press through Education Index. In 2003–2004, CERU added the Google News database to account for popular publications not included in the Lexis-Nexis "all news" database.

From 1900 to 2004, CERU's annual studies have found increases in references to each of eight categories of schoolhouse commercialism. Examples abound in each category:[1]

1. **Sponsorship of Programs and Activities.** Corporations paying for or subsidizing school events or one-time activities in return for the right to associate their name with the events and activities. This may also include school contests.
    Percent change (range is 1990–2003/2004 for all): +146
    Example: Giant Cement Holding Co. sponsors "Charleston's Promise," an in-school program in that South Carolina city that includes mentoring, workshops, parental involvement efforts, career planning, and children's visits to the company's quarry. Terry Kinder, an executive for the company, told a trade publication that the resulting goodwill helped assuage concerns about the company's foreign ownership during public permit hearings for a plant expansion ("A Conversation," 2003).

2. **Exclusive Agreements.** Agreements between schools and corporations that give corporations the exclusive right to sell and promote their goods or services in the school district—for example, exclusive pouring rights for Pepsi-Cola or Coca-Cola. In return, the district or school receives a percentage of the profits derived from the arrangement.
    Percent change: +858
    Example: Perhaps the largest contract between a school and a marketer was signed in 2003 by the Hillsborough County (Florida) school district: a $50 million, 12-year pact with Pepsi Bottling Group, ensuring that vending machines in the county's 62 middle and high schools would sell only Pepsi products. A school board member dismissed criticism that schools shouldn't abet the marketing of nutritionally harmful soft drinks. "I don't think the schools have the responsibility of being the food police," Candy Olson told the *St. Petersburg Times*. "And I don't think schools should be expected to turn up their noses" at $4 million annually (quoted in Mabe, 2003).

3. **Incentive Programs.** Corporate programs that provide money, goods, or services to a student, school, or school district when its students, parents, or staff engage in a specified activity. Among the best-known such programs is the fast-food company Pizza Hut's Book-It program, which rewards to children who complete quotas of reading with free pizzas. *Percent change: +75*

   Example: Reading, attendance, good behavior—name an outcome, and some program rewards it with commercial products. The end result contributes to a shifting view of education from a collective, public good that engages the next generation in American civic life to an individual, private good that becomes another consumer product and thereby helps reinforce a consumerist ideology. Thus a suggestion in *Forbes* that students should be awarded cash for scoring high on standardized tests becomes completely unsurprising (Miguel, 2003).

4. **Appropriation of Space.** The allocation of school space such as scoreboards, rooftops, bulletin boards, walls, and textbooks on which corporations may place corporate logos or advertising messages for a wide range of products, including soft drinks and snack foods. *Percent change: +394*

   Example: From naming rights to school bus advertisements, our institutions of public education are being turned into billboards, our children into eyeballs that marketers covet. The need for funds led Hampshire High School in Illinois to scrap a long-standing rule forbidding advertising on school property (Patterson, 2003), replacing it with a policy allowing corporate ads on scoreboards and outside auditoriums and other common areas, while asserting the board's right to vet all ads (Gaunt, 2004).

5. **Sponsored Educational Materials (SEMs).** Materials supplied by corporations or trade associations that claim to have an instructional content. *Percent change: +1038*

   Example: Chicago-based Field Trip Factory offers schools free field trips to stores: Petco to learn about animal welfare, Toys 'R' Us to learn about party planning (Mohl, 2004), and grocery stores to learn about nutrition (Pitts, 2003). The stores, in turn, pay Field Trip Factory for the exposure and for coordinating the visits (Mohl, 2004). "We are getting kids in at a young age so we can educate them and hopefully turn them into customers," said Indrani Mukherjee, general manager of a Buffalo, NY, Petco (quoted in "Reading, Writing," 2004).

6. **Electronic Marketing.** The provision of electronic programming, equipment or both in return for the right to advertise to students or their families and community members in the school or when they contact the school or district. *Percent change: +9*

Example: Cable in the Classroom and various Internet marketing schemes fall under this category, but the biggest is still Channel One Network, owned by Primedia Corp. The firm distributes thousands of dollars worth of television equipment to schools under the condition that students be required to watch a daily 12-minute news program, including two minutes of commercials. Channel One currently claims to reach about 8 million students in 370,000 classrooms in 12,000 schools (Kaufman, 2003).

7. **Privatization.** Management of schools or school programs by private, for-profit corporations or other nonpublic entities.
Percent change: +2,213
Example: The privatized public education industry is maturing and evolving. Mounting criticism of for-profit school management led six leaders in the industry to form their own trade group, the National Council of Education Providers (http://www.educationproviders.org), to lobby for more public money and for more favorable regulation. Day-to-day operations are coordinated by a professional lobbying firm, The Allen Company, operated by Jeanne Allen (Archer, 2004). Allen, it should be noted, also founded and runs the Center for Education Reform, an advocate for charter schools and defender of for-profit companies who manage them. Now that she has taken on the task of official lobbyist for the for-profit sector, Allen and the center must be seen as serving the interests of her lobbying clients rather than as disinterested education advocates.

8. **Fundraising.** Commercial programs marketed to schools to raise funds for school programs and activities, including door-to-door sales, affinity marketing programs, and similar ventures.
Percent change: not available (CERU began tracking fundraising in 1999–2000)
Example: Fundraising increasingly is no longer just for extracurricular activities.[2] A poll of parents for the National Parent Teacher Association found that in fully 68% of schools that conducted fundraising used proceeds to pay for "such basic needs as classroom equipment, textbooks, and school supplies." The poll itself was co-sponsored by QSP Reader's Digest, which conducts fundraising magazine sales in schools (Hurst, 2004).

Figure 4.1 shows the general growth in references to school commercialism in popular, business, and education publications from 1990 through June 2004.

The commercial messages that find their way into schools reflect a wide range of content, marketing junk food, soft drinks, popular culture, and even the self-interested positions of corporations on controversial public policy issues. Moreover, they deliver a broader ideological message that promotes consumption as the primary source of well-being and happiness. Equating the good life with consump-

Figure 4.1. Combined Total Citations, All Categories, All Presses, By Year

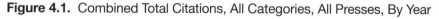

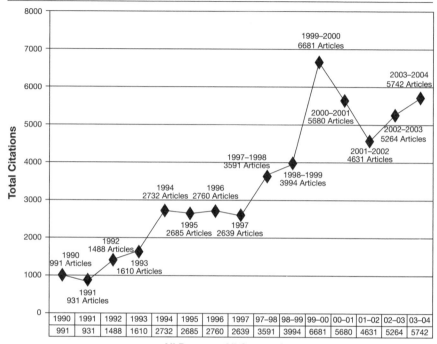

All Presses, All Categories

	1990	1991	1992	1993	1994	1995	1996	1997	97–98	98–99	99–00	00–01	01–02	02–03	03–04
	991	931	1488	1610	2732	2685	2760	2639	3591	3994	6681	5680	4631	5264	5742

tion is central to the ideology of marketing. Marketers teach that one should be perpetually dissatisfied and that dissatisfaction can best be alleviated by consuming something. In essence, marketing seeks to replace humane values with mercantile ones. By equating "more" with "good," the culture of consumption teaches that more televisions, more toys, more clothes—more of everything an American can buy—result in more happiness.

The ethical heart of the problem posed by marketing in schools is seen vividly by contrasting the thoughts of Edward Bernays, the father of the American public relations industry, and John Dewey. Bernays (1928) saw democratic civic life as a marketplace every bit as much as economic life and, in that context, considered propaganda "a perfectly legitimate form of human activity" (p. 11) essential to keeping the wheels of politics and commerce turning while preserving social stability. Conversely, Dewey viewed individuals as active members of real communities who would, through "educative experiences," advance in knowledge, self-control, and freedom, in the process progressively improving the democratic community. But where Dewey sought the integrative experiences in the service of the individual and the community, advertising seeks to destroy continuity and fragment experience while encouraging us to give into our irrational impulses for the purpose of manipulating our behavior.[3]

CERU'S FINDINGS: FOR-PROFIT
SCHOOL MANAGEMENT INDUSTRY GROWING RAPIDLY

The second line of investigation I pursue at CERU is tracking the for-profit K–12 school management industry. In the annual CERU reports on schoolhouse commercializing trends, there has been considerable variation over the years in the number of media references to privatization in all of its forms, including voucher programs and for-profit management of charter and district schools. Nevertheless, in 1990 there were 47 references, while by 2003–2004 the number of references had increased to 1,100 (Molnar, 2004; see also Molnar 1996, 1998, 1999, 2002, 2003; Molnar & Morales, 2000; Molnar & Reaves, 2001).

This is not surprising. Over the last two decades, public policies have sought to advance a market-driven approach to public education, operating under the theory that competition among schools will produce better educational outcomes. More and more for-profit corporations, for the most part operating under the umbrella of state charter school laws, have sprung up over the past decade. Wall Street has dubbed the for-profit firms managing or operating K–12 schools education management organizations (EMOs). The term EMO is intended to reflect similarities between such companies and health maintenance organizations (HMOs) (Toch, 1996).

The annual CERU report, *Profiles of For-Profit Education Management Organizations*, lists and provides selected demographic information about these companies and the schools under their management (Molnar et al., 2005). For the purposes of the *Profiles*, a company is considered an EMO if it is operated for profit, manages a school that receives public funds, and has open enrollment.[4]

Although the annual *Profiles* report labels education management companies as "profitable" and "not profitable," in the case of privately held companies the designation is based on the companies' self reports. Unlike publicly traded companies,, privately held companies are not required by law to make earnings statements public. Also, it is likely that a substantial number of EMOs operating a small number of schools are not included in the *Profiles*. At this point there is no way to effectively track such small providers systematically.

Voucher programs in which private schools would compete for public tax dollars were the original model for for-profit, market-driven education. The unpopularity of vouchers with the public has, however, limited voucher programs to a handful of locations. The Milwaukee voucher program was launched in 1989. It is limited to low-income residents of the Milwaukee Public School District. Cleveland has had a similar program since 1995. In 1999, the state of Florida established a program that makes students eligible for vouchers if they attend a school labeled failing by the state, and it now offers a separate voucher program for disabled students. Most recently, in 2004 Congress established a voucher program in the District of Columbia. For the most part, however, voucher advocates have suffered repeated defeats on ballot initiatives, including lopsided votes in

California and Michigan in 2000 (Booth & Sanchez, 2000). In state legislatures, meanwhile, voucher proposals have also failed widely; in 2004 alone, voucher bills were defeated in 26 states, according to a lobbying group opposed to vouchers (People for the American Way, n.d.). A 2003 Colorado voucher law was struck down by the state supreme court in 2004.

Instead of voucher programs, public charter schools, operating outside of the body of regulations governing public district schools, have turned out to be the dominant model for market-based school reform. In contrast to unpopular voucher proposals, charter schools have enjoyed strong bipartisan support, further contributing to their growth. The growth of charter schools helped to encourage the growth of companies to manage them and, less frequently, directly sponsor them. Additionally, some school districts began in the 1990s to contract with private companies to manage district schools.

The result was the creation of the EMO industry. The most familiar EMO is probably Edison Schools Inc. Edison was founded with the intent of creating a chain of private, tuition-charging schools. Although the company has denied it, observers have widely assumed that its original business plan was premised on the assumption that federal policy would encourage the adoption of voucher systems nationwide—a development that would have effectively created a taxpayer-subsidized market for the company's schools. Giving that assumption further credence, as vouchers failed to gain traction, the company shifted its game plan. Instead of an operator of private schools, it became a manager of public district and charter schools. Edison is a marker for the EMO industry as a whole.

The passage of No Child Left Behind (NCLB) has fostered further changes in the for-profit education industry. Edison has joined a number of firms in providing the kind of supplemental education services funded under the law. Historically, these services were provided in niche markets by companies that offered, for example, tutoring, test preparation, and remedial instruction. NCLB funds these services and provides funding or incentives for school districts to contract with private vendors for such additional services as teacher training, summer school, and curriculum development. Moreover, the NCLB provision that makes conversion to charter school status a remedy for "failing" schools is also likely to bolster the demand for school-management firms.

The importance of these provisions to the industry is evident in Edison's own data. In 2004–2005, for example, Edison Schools reported that it had contracts to serve 250,000 students. The Edison student numbers for the first time included students whose schools use Edison programs and products as well as those enrolled in Edison-managed public schools and charter schools (Edison Schools, 2004). Of the quarter-million students Edison reported serving in 2004–2005, only 66,482 were actually enrolled in Edison-managed schools. This represents a decrease of 3,959 students from the 2003–2004 school year (Molnar et al., 2005).

So-called virtual schools represent another source of growth in the EMO industry. These schools, sometimes also known as "online charter" or "virtual charter" schools, offer an Internet-based curriculum outside of the conventional brick-and-mortar setting of traditional public and charter schools. They frequently cater to children who were previously home-schooled. Where legislation has enabled such schools, state education dollars pay for children who enroll in them. Virtual schools appear poised to generate substantially larger profits than conventional charter schools, because they still receive the same amount of per-student funding as their traditional public school counterparts, despite not having to support a physical structure financially (Stephens, 2004). The 2004–2005 *Profiles* (Molnar et al., 2005) identifies six companies that manage virtual schools.

By 2004, more students were enrolled in schools managed by EMOs than at any time since the Education Policy Studies Laboratory (EPSL) began tracking the industry in 1998–1999 (see Table 4.1). The 2004–2005 *Profiles* identifies 59 firms managing 535 schools enrolling 239,766 students in 24 states and the District of Columbia. This is four-and-a-half times the number of firms reported in the first-year edition of the *Profiles*, 1998–1999, and is up from 51 in the 2003–2004 report.

Charter schools account for a large and growing majority of EMO contracts: 86.3% of the privately managed schools covered in the 2004–2005 *Profiles* are charter schools. At the same time, the 59 EMOs profiled in 2004–2005 account for 31%, or 175,350, of all students (565,648) enrolled in charter schools and 41.3% (114,591) of all charter primary school students (277,240).

In 2004–2005, the *Profiles* report for the first time compared the average enrollment of managed schools with the average enrollment of all public schools in the United States. The 2004–2005 *Profiles* defines "large EMOs" as EMOs that manage 10 or more schools and "small EMOs" as EMOs managing nine or fewer schools. Among the charter schools managed by large EMOs, 65.5% have

Table 4.1. Number of Companies, Schools, and States Profiled by Year

School Year	Number of Companies Profiled	Number of Schools Managed by Profiled Companies	Number of States in Which Profiled Companies Operate
1998–99	13	135	15
1999–2000	20	230	21
2000–01	21	285	22
2001–02	36	368	25*
2002–03	54	406	26*
2003–04	51	463	29*
2004–05	59	535	26*

* This number includes the District of Columbia.

enrollments above the average U.S. charter school enrollment. The majority of students attending charter schools run by 12 of the 14 large EMOs are in schools with enrollments that exceed the national average for comparable charter schools. Students attending charter primary schools managed by 10 of the 14 large EMOs are likely to be enrolled in schools that are larger than the average U.S. charter primary school. (The comparisons exclude virtual charters.)

These enrollment figures contrast markedly with overall charter enrollment trends, as well as with one of the ostensible benefits of charter schools. A report by RPP International (2000) found that the median size of charter schools (137 students) was much smaller than that of district schools (475 students). Although research has generally found that smaller class size and smaller school size have academic benefits (Finn, 2002; Howley, 2002), schools managed by large EMOs tend to have larger-than-average enrollments. This makes business, if not education, sense. Since public funding for schools is based on enrollment, with more students resulting in more money, it is not unreasonable to conclude that the larger enrollments of primary schools managed by large EMOs are the result of a strategic business decision. Simply put, EMOs can increase profits by increasing school size and by focusing on managing primary schools, where the cost of providing education is relatively cheaper than at the middle or high school levels.

CERU: RECENT DEVELOPMENTS

In November 2004, CERU received a grant from the Robert Wood Johnson Foundation to conduct a national survey examining specific commercial activity in a representative national sample of elementary, middle, and high schools. The foundation funds original research aimed at improving health and health care. Its priorities include addressing specific improvements in targeted health and health care challenges over a defined time period and promoting community-based projects that improve health and health care outcomes for society's most vulnerable people. CERU conducted a national telephone survey of a stratified random sample of 721 schools from a list of 76,609 schools provided by the Common Core of Data (CCD).[5]

This survey provides the clearest picture to date of the types and extent of advertising to which children are currently exposed at school. More complete results may be found in the final report of the survey, but some highlights are worth noting here. The survey divided commercial activities into two general categories: (1) commercial activity that generally requires the consent of school officials (sponsored programs, exclusive agreements, incentive programs, space advertising, and naming rights) and (2) commercial activity that generally does *not* necessarily require official consent (supplementary materials, fundraising, and many forms of electronic marketing). Such activities often occur at the classroom level, and school officials may not be aware they are taking place.

A consistent pattern emerges in commercial activities that require the involvement of school officials. When schools report engaging in advertising with a corporation that sells foods of minimal nutritional value or foods high in fat and sugar content, overwhelmingly their *only* activity is with such a corporation. The report also has documented officials' estimates of activities that did not require their consent—for instance, the use in individual classrooms of commercial materials—but those estimates may be low. Finally, while the income schools receive from advertising is often cited as the reason for engaging in contracts with corporations, the survey found that most schools receive little or no monetary compensation as a result of commercial activities.

The impact of marketing on children's food preferences is made clear by the 2005 Institute of Medicine report *Food Marketing to Children and Youth: Threat or Opportunity?* (McGinnis, Gootman, & Kraak, 2006). Given the individual and social consequences, it is hard to imagine any morally defensible justification for marketing junk food to children in general and in schools in particular.

CERU: THE IMPACT

The work of CERU has drawn the attention of the media, public officials, and engaged citizens. The EPSL contacts database—consisting of media, organizations, and individuals in policy groups or in government—contains the names and contact information of more than 6,000 individuals. Between July 1, 2004, and June 30, 2005, 407 people contacted the lab, primarily to request interviews or information and assistance of some sort. Its website logged 3.9 million hits, more than 1 million page views, and 570,750 visits from 333,075 unique visitors. Academics associated with EPSL were cited 553 times in 209 popular publications, ranging from online news services, television broadcasts, and magazines to newspapers, academic journals, and federal documents. Publications making use of EPSL findings included the *Dallas Morning News*, the *Dayton Daily News*, the Arizona *East Valley Tribune*, and *Education Week*. Government organizations, research units, and state education leaders requested EPSL's participation in surveys and advice on its areas of expertise. The Government Accountability Office, for example, requested my participation in a survey about programs designed to prevent or reduce childhood obesity, as did researchers conducting the California Health Interview Survey.

CERU illustrates how, with an ongoing research context and solid academic and financial support, a public intellectual can engage important and relevant policy topics. It is important to note, however, that the Commercialism in Education Research Unit and the Education Policy Studies Lab are not traditional academic units, such as departments. Nor are they organized around the individual research projects of a researcher or group of researchers. This has several significant implications for understanding the possibilities for encouraging more academics to function as public intellectuals. Traditional departments are organized primarily to support teaching, with research driven by the interests and energy of individual faculty members. Academic departments lack the resources to create and maintain a contacts database, draft press releases, generate mass e-mailings, or respond to hundreds of press requests for interviews; nor are they interested in undertaking those tasks. Thus, any public role played by faculty members is on their own time and, at times, at their own peril. External funders (with the exception of right-wing foundations) are not interested in building and maintaining infrastructure. They are primarily interested in providing short-term funds to academics who are willing to pursue lines of investigation that are a priority to them. When the money disappears, so does the infrastructure that supported the project. The result of these factors is an academic interest in public intellectuals without the institutional arrangements to support them.

In this regard CERU/EPSL does not provide a model. CERU, for example, is supported by a funder with a long-term commitment to the issue of school commercialism that wants CERU to be in the public eye and is comfortable with the idea that its funding supports organizational infrastructure. There are, at the moment, very few progressive funders willing to provide funds on this basis. Even if there were many funders willing to provide the necessary funding, however, they would have a hard time finding many academics with either the skill or the interest in doing the nitty-gritty, little-valued (at least at this point) work necessary to create and maintain the kind of academic organization required to transform the term *public intellectual* from an academic abstraction into a practical reality.

NOTES

1. For a detailed description of these categories, see Molnar (2004).
2. See, for example, Sherry (2004).
3. These ideas are elaborated upon in Chapter 4 of Molnar (2005).
4. For details on the methodology of the *Profiles* reports, see Molnar et al. (2005).
5. For complete details of the survey and its findings, see Molnar, Garcia, Boninger, Merrill, & Griffin (forthcoming).

REFERENCES

A conversation with Giant Cement Holding Inc.'s Terry L. Kinder. (2003, July 1). Cement Americas. Retrieved November 28, 2005, from http://cementamericas.com/mag/cement_conversation_giant_cement/

Archer, J. (2004, February 4). Private charter managers team up. *Education Week,* pp. 1, 15.

Berdik, C. (2004, May 30). Your all-mall mater. *Boston Globe*, p. D2.

Bernays, E. L. (1928). *Propaganda*, New York: Liveright.

Booth, W., & Sanchez, R. (2000, November 9). Drug reform initiatives receive support of voters; gun control also popular; school vouchers not embraced. *Washington Post*, p. A48.

Council for Corporate and School Partnerships. (2002, September 25). Council led by former U.S. education secretaries provides guidelines for model school business relationships. Press release distributed by PR Newswire for the Council for Corporate and School Partnerships.

Edison Schools Inc. (2004, September 20). Edison Schools to serve more than 250,000 students in 2004–2005. Retrieved November 29, 2004, from www.edisonschools.com/news/news.cfm?ID=174

Finn, J. (2002). Class-size reduction in grades K–3. In A. Molnar (Ed.), *School reform proposals: The research evidence* Tempe: Education Policy Studies Laboratory, Arizona State University. Retrieved July 22, 2005, from http://www.asu.edu/educ/epsl/EPRU/documents/EPRU%202002-101/Chapter%2002-Finn-Final.htm

Gaunt, J. (2004, January 15). "Your ad here" has new meaning in Dist. 300. *Chicago Daily Herald*, p. 3.

Howley, C. (2002). Small schools. In A. Molnar (Ed.), *School reform proposals: The research evidence.* Tempe: Education Policy Studies Laboratory, Arizona State University. Retrieved July 22, 2005, from http://www.asu.edu/educ/epsl/EPRU/documents/EPRU%202002-101/Chapter%2003-Howley-Final.htm

Hurst, M. D. (2004, January 21). Parent poll: Schools using fund raising for basics. *Education Week, 23*(19), 3.

Kaufman, D. (2003, November 24). Channel One outlasts its critics; in-school commercials remain a sore point for opposition. *Television Week*, p. 18.

Mabe, L. (2003, August 31). Pepsi high. *St. Petersburg Times*, p. 1D.

McGinnis, J. M., Gootman, J. A., & Kraak, V. I. (2006). *Food marketing to children and youth: Threat or opportunity?* Washington, DC: The National Academies Press.

Miguel, E. (2003, November 24). Cash talks. *Forbes*, p. 48.

Mohl, B. (2004, April 4). Commercial break: A company profits from taking kids on field trips to retail outlets, but what are they learning? *Boston Globe*, Business section, p. 1.

Molnar, A. (1996). *Giving kids the business: The commercialization of America's schools.* Boulder, CO: Westview.

Molnar, A. (1998). *Sponsored schools and commercialized classrooms: Tracking schoolhouse commercializing trends.* Milwaukee: Center for the Analysis of Commercialism in Education, University of Wisconsin–Milwaukee.

Molnar, A. (1999). *Cashing in on kids: Second annual report on trends in schoolhouse commercialism.* Milwaukee: Center for the Analysis of Commercialism in Education, University of Wisconsin–Milwaukee.

Molnar, A. (2002). *What's in a name? The corporate branding of America's schools. The fifth annual report on trends in schoolhouse commercialism.* Tempe: Education Policy Studies Laboratory, Arizona State University.

Molnar, A. (2003). *No child left unsold: The sixth annual report on schoolhouse commercialism trends, year 2002–2003.* Tempe: Education Policy Studies Laboratory, Arizona State University.

Molnar, A. (2004). *Virtually everywhere: Marketing to children in America's schools: The seventh annual report on trends in schoolhouse commercialism, year 2003–2004.* Tempe: Education Policy Studies Laboratory, Arizona State University.

Molnar, A. (2005). *School commercialism.* New York: Routledge.

Molnar, A., Garcia, D., Boninger, F., Merrill, B., & Griffin, E. N. (forthcoming). *School-community partnerships for healthy nutrition practices.* Tempe, AZ: ASU Educational Policy Studies Laboratory.

Molnar, A., Garcia, D., Sullivan, C., McEvoy, B., & Joanou, J. (2005). *Profiles of for-profit education management organizations, 2004–2005.* Tempe: Education Policy Studies Laboratory, Commercialism in Education Research Unit, Arizona State University.

Molnar, A., & Morales, J. (2000). *Commercialism@School.com. Third annual report on trends in schoolhouse commercialism.* Milwaukee: Center for the Analysis of Commercialism in Education, University of Wisconsin–Milwaukee.

Molnar, A., Morales, J., & Vander Wyst, A. (1999). *Profiles of for-profit education management companies, 1998–1999.* Center for Education Research, Analysis and Innovation, University of Wisconsin–Milwaukee.

Molnar, A., Morales, J., & Vander Wyst, A. (2000). *Profiles of for-profit education management companies, 1999–2000.* Center for Education Research, Analysis and Innovation, University of Wisconsin–Milwaukee.

Molnar, A., Morales, J., & Vander Wyst, A. (2001). *Profiles of for-profit education management companies, 2000–2001.* Center for Education Research, Analysis and Innovation. Retrieved December 12, 2004, from http://www.asu.edu/educ/epsl/EPRU/epru_2001_ Research_Writing.htm

Molnar, A., & Reaves, J. A. (2001). *Buy me! Buy me! Fourth annual report on trends in schoolhouse commercialism.* Tempe: Education Policy Studies Laboratory, Arizona State University.

Molnar, A., Wilson, G., & Allen, D. (2003). *Profiles of for-profit education management companies, 2002–2003.* Tempe: Education Policy Studies Laboratory, Education Policy Research Unit. Retrieved December 12, 2004, from http://www.asu.edu/educ/epsl/ CERU/Documents/EPSL-0301-102-CERU.pdf

Molnar, A., Wilson, G., & Allen, D. (2004). *Profiles of for-profit education management companies, 2003–2004.* Retrieved December 12, 2004, from http://www.asu.edu/educ/ epsl/EPRU/epru_2004_ Research_Writing.htm

Molnar, A., Wilson, G., Restori, M, & Hutchison, J. (2002, January) *Profiles of for-profit education management companies, 2001–2002.* Tempe: Education Policy Studies Laboratory, Education Policy Research Unit, Arizona State University.

Patterson, J. (2003, August 8). Dist. 300 ponders football scoreboard donation. *Chicago Daily Herald*, p. 4.

People for the American Way. (n.d.). Vouchers hit dead end. Retrieved November 29, 2004, from http://www.pfaw.org/pfaw/general/default.aspx?oid=16044

Pitts, E. L. (2003, July 21). Stores open doors to field trips. *Chattanooga Times Free Press*, p. B1.

Reading, writing and shopping. (2004, April 26). *Buffalo News*, p. A7.

RPP International. (2000). *The state of charter schools: 2000.* Washington, DC: Office of Educational Research and Improvement, U.S. Department of Education. Retrieved April 11, 2005, from http://www.ed.gov/pubs/charter4thyear/index.html

Sherry, A. (2004, May 23). Schools unequal in search for funds. *Denver Post*, p. A1.

Stephens, S. (2004, July). Ohio virtually booming with cyber schools. *Cleveland Plain Dealer.* Retrieved July 20, 2004, from http://www.cleveland.com/news/ plaindealer/ index.ssf?/base/news/1088328740108431.xml

Toch, T. (1996, January 8). Do firms run schools well? *U.S. News & World Report*, p. 46.

CHAPTER 5

Trudge Toward Freedom: Educational Research in the Public Interest

WILLIAM AYERS

I N THIS CHAPTER I CHAMPION the idea that educational researchers can gain sustenance and perspective by drawing on the humanities—poetry, film, theater, and imaginative literature—in their search for knowledge and under-standing. In our research, our teaching, and all our scholarly enterprises, our central goals include enlightenment and emancipation, human knowledge and human freedom. I outline an approach to educational inquiry that appeals to an expansive view of humanity focused on such questions as: what interests does our research serve? What forms of inquiry might encourage people to be more creative and active problem solvers? How?

• • •

Gwendolyn Brooks, who won the Pulitzer Prize for poetry in 1954, and served as poet laureate of Illinois from 1985 until her death in 2000, never left her bustling and bracing neighborhood and, perhaps more important, never left the commitments and concerns that animated her intelligence and her heart: the lives of the children and families—indeed, the lives of all the ordinary people of Chicago's South Side. At a massive celebration of her life, one of her former students read this poem to her memory:

GWENDOLYN BROOKS
(1917–2000)

Sometimes I see in my mind's eye a four- or five-
year-old boy, coatless and wandering
a windblown and vacant lot or street in Chicago
on the windblown South Side. He disappears
but stays with me, staring and pronouncing

me guilty of an indifference more callous
than neglect, condescension as self-pity.

Then I see him again, at ten or fifteen, on the corner,
say, 47th and Martin Luther King, or in a group
of men surrounding a burning barrel off Lawndale,
everything surrounding vacant or for sale.
Sometimes I trace him on the train to Joliet
or Menard, such towns quickly becoming native
ground to these boys who seem to be nobody's
sons, these boys who are so hard to love, so hard
to see, except as case studies.

Poverty, pain, shame, one and a half million
dreams deemed fit only for the most internal
of exiles. That four-year-old wandering
the wind tunnels of Robert Taylor, of Cabrini
Green, wind chill of an as yet unplumbed degree—
a young boy she did not have to know to love.

—Anthony Walton

There's a dissent in this poem that mirrors the life and work of Gwendolyn` Brooks—a refusal of received wisdom, a challenge to the policing proclivities of the social sciences, and an invitation to a possible way forward, a way out.

Sketching a familiar landscape, cycling back through the clichés attached so glibly to the city and city kids—coatless and wandering, the windblown streets and the vacant lots—Walton highlights the disciplining bent of so much of what we call social science research—"so hard/to see, except as case studies." He points to us, questioning our innocence and reproaching our willed ignorance, as he contextualizes and undermines the orthodoxy that had slipped so easily into place a moment ago: "an indifference more callous/than neglect," he writes, "condescension as self-pity."

And then that sudden, surprising last line: "a young boy she did not have to know to love." Indeed, here is the common faith of educators, not necessarily a distinct forward path, but a direction certainly.

In a concise and provocative way, this poem illuminates the themes and challenges I want to develop further. It invites us—in the spirit of Gwendolyn Brooks—to open our eyes to our shared humanity, to challenge orthodoxy, (especially our own dogma and received thinking), and to engage our world more freely and more fully, with both imagination and hope.

• • •

I begin deliberately with a poem in an effort to remind us of the centrality of the humanities and of humanism as principle, guide, and source in our scholarly and intellectual pursuits—our lives as students, our efforts as teachers, our projects as researchers. Jane Hirshfield (2003) writes that, "Great poetry is not a donkey carrying obedient sentiment in pretty forms, it is a bird of prey tearing open whatever needs to be opened." And Langston Hughes invents an entire vocabulary to underline the potential power of poetry to illuminate, to educate, to nourish the human core:

> Poetry possesses the power of worriation. Poetry can both delight and disturb. It can interest folks. It can upset folks. Poetry can convey both pleasure and pain. And poetry can make people think. If poetry makes people think, it might make them think constructive thoughts, even thoughts about how to change themselves, their town and their state for the better. Some poems, like many of the great verses in the Bible, can make people think about changing all mankind, even the whole world. Poems, like prayers, possess power. (quoted in Alexander, 2004, p. 23).

I turn to the humanities in the spirit of Hughes and of his many descendents, including Gwendolyn Brooks, who imagines a disruptive role for the arts in asking whether man loves art. Her answer: "Man visits art but cringes. Art hurts. Art urges voyages." I turn to the arts precisely because they urge voyages, voyages we must undertake with a sense of hope and urgency at this precise moment, voyages that might contribute to opening the desicated discourse on educational research and school improvement so dominant just now.

Humanism is built on the idea that human life is indeterminate, expansive, and interconnected, that there exists a special human capacity for knowledge of who and what we are in the world. Humanism embraces all the things we make through our own labor, including history as an ongoing human construction, and all other forms of expression as well: research and language and every manner of goods and works and products. Indeed, every humanist is always a kind of researcher, drawn—in the spirit of cooperation, sharing, and being-in-common—to explore and expand every bit of it. Because humanism invites the input and engagement of all, there is no obvious conflict between the practice of humanism and the pursuit of democracy—humanism, like democracy, unleashes an energy toward enlightenment and freedom.

This exploration requires a leaning outward, a willingness to look at the peopled world, at the sufferings, the accomplishments, the perspectives and the concerns of others, at their twisty, dynamic movement through time, and an awareness—sometimes joyous, but just as often painful—of all that one finds. It requires, as well, a leaning inward toward self-knowledge, a sense of being alive and conscious in a going world.

In each direction the humanist researcher acknowledges that every person is entangled and propelled, and sometimes made mute, by a social surround, that each also has a wild and vast inner life. We inhabit an infinite and dynamic world, a world in motion, and we are ourselves unfinished, unruly sparks of meaning-making energy; history, as always, charges relentlessly forward; the world is always and forever in-process. But going inward without consciously connecting to a larger world leads to self-referencing and worse, narcissism as truth; traveling outward without noting your own embodied heart and mind can lead to ethical astigmatism, to seeing other three-dimensional human beings as case studies or data, their lived situations reduced to the "field."

C. Wright Mills (1959), sociologist and passionately engaged intellectual, reminds students and young scholars that "the most admirable thinkers within the scholarly community . . . do not split their work from their lives. They . . . take both too seriously to allow such dissociation, and they want to use each for the enrichment of the other" (p. 195). Mills sees this dissociation as endemic and epidemic, seductive and utterly corrosive. For Mills, consistent and disciplined attention to both work and life is necessary for the best scholarly efforts.

"The starting point of critical elaboration is the consciousness of what one really is," Antonio Gramsci (1971) wrote in his *Prison Notebooks*, "and is 'knowing oneself' as a product of the historic process to date, which has deposited in you an infinity of traces, without leaving an inventory" (p. 73). Gramsci's sense of the infinite and the ineffable tied up inexorably with the concrete and the real urges us to cultivate the ability to simultaneously trust and be skeptical of personal experience, to enhance our scholarly production with personal insight. Mills asks us to understand people as social and historical actors in all their wild variety, to keep our eyes open to the largest image of humanity and to a powerful image of history as something being made and remade by actual people. Personal problems have an often hidden but nonetheless insistent social and shared aspect; social problems and issues naturally have particular and individual iterations. Life is made in the balance and in the tension of both, and scholarship must somehow work, as well, within this apparent contradiction.

For W. J. T. Mitchell (2005) the demanding standard humanism sets is to strive for "complexity without mystification, dialectics without the disabling equivocation of ambivalence . . . recognition of the baffling limits of human knowledge without obscurantism or quietism; and a recognition of the situatedness and contingency of every utterance without a surrender to relativism and without a sacrifice of abiding principles" (p. 101). Difficult enough, but Mitchell adds that humanism sets itself in opposition to "the tendency to obfuscation and mystification; the cult of expertise, whether in academic jargon or the prattlings of policy wonks; the counter cult of false transparency in the oversimplified sound bites of the punditocracy; the simplistic binarisms . . . ; and the reductionism of mass media 'information'" (p. 101). All of this, Mitchell argues, requires "an agile, improvisational sense of balance coupled with a dogged and tireless preparation for the next moment of struggle" (p. 101).

Of course, being conscious can never mean being *fully* conscious—we are all more or less conscious, contingently aware, and at the same time entirely incomplete. As researchers and humanists, we must struggle to approach others as the active knowledge-creators and meaning-makers that they are, as agents and experts on their own lives; we approach ourselves as works-in-progress, too, both incomplete and provisional.

The humanist ambition is for every human being to reach a fuller measure of his or her own humanity. Any research grounded in humanism is necessarily a lively activity, a raucous and participatory pursuit—open to every background and class and condition in its perpetual asking of new questions, its continual discoveries, its ceaseless and essential reformulations and revisions and unique revelations.

But while acknowledging humanization as goal and purpose, we note that dehumanization can be both policy and practice; we enter, then, the contested space of school and society, of scholarship and intellectual life.

●   ●   ●

The literary critic Edward Said (1994) explores this contested space in much of his work, but perhaps most pointedly in *Representations of the Intellectual*, in which he offers, in effect, a brief for the conduct of intellectual life. The book is crisp, concise, small in size—the perfect companion to cram into your backpack between your toothbrush and your bottle of water, and as necessary a part of daily survival as either of those.

The intellectual, he argues, must strive to become "an individual endowed with a faculty for representing, embodying, articulating a message, a view, an attitude, philosophy or opinion to, as well as for, a public" (p. 11). For Said, "this role has an edge to it," for the intellectual must recognize the necessity of opening spaces "to raise embarrassing questions, to confront orthodoxy and dogma (rather than to produce them), to be someone who cannot easily be co-opted by governments or corporations, and whose *raison d'être* is to represent all those people and issues that are routinely forgotten or swept under the rug" (p. 12).

All intellectuals, of course, "represent something to their audiences, and in so doing represent themselves to themselves" (p. xv), and Said is speaking in favor of a particular stance, a distinct approach to intellectual life. Whether you're a straight-up academic or a freelance writer, a down-and-out bohemian essayist or an itinerant speech-maker, an educational researcher or a teacher or a consultant to the state, you represent yourself based on an idea you have of yourself and your function: Do you think you're providing a balanced, disinterested view, or are you delivering objective advice for pay? Are you an expert offering high-level program evaluation, or are you teaching your students some essential truth? Perhaps you imagine you're advocating an eccentric if important idea. What do you want to represent? To whom? For what purpose? Toward what end, and in the interest of what social order?

Said notes that "the world is more crowded than it ever has been with professionals, experts, consultants, in a word with *intellectuals*" (p. xv), and that this creates as a central task the requirement to search out and fight for relative independence from all manner of social and institutional pressures, to authentically choose oneself against a hard wall of facts: "At bottom," Said argues, "the intellectual . . . is neither a pacifier nor a consensus-builder, but someone whose whole being is staked on a critical . . . sense of being unwilling to accept easy formulas, or ready-made clichés, or the smooth, ever-so-accommodating confirmations of what the powerful or conventional have to say, and what they do," (p. 23)—a description befitting Anthony Walton's poem. This unwillingness cannot be simply a passive shrug of the shoulders or a cynical sigh. For Said, as for Gwen Brooks, the unwillingness to accede involves publicly staking out a space of refusal.

Said exhorts intellectuals to work on the basis of a particular principle he takes to be universal: "that all human beings are entitled to expect decent standards of behavior concerning freedom and justice from worldly powers or nations, and that deliberate or inadvertent violations of these standards need to be testified and fought against courageously" (pp. 11–12).

This is the fulcrum for us, the central and primary plot point, the root out of which limbs and branches might grow requiring all manner of other, unforeseen choices. I should point out immediately that this essential first choice in no way lays out a neat road forward—choose the way of opposition and you do not inherit a set of ready-made slogans or a nifty, easy-fit party line. There are no rules—and for some this might prove difficult, perhaps even fatal—or any gods whatsoever who can be called upon to ease specific, personal responsibility. Each of us is out there on our own, with our own minds and our own hearts, our own ability to empathize, to touch and to feel, to recognize humanity in its many unexpected postures, to construct our own standards of truth about human suffering that must be upheld despite everything. "Real intellectuals," Said writes, "are never more themselves than when, moved by metaphysical passion and disinterested principles of justice and truth, they denounce corruption, defend the weak, defy imperfect or oppressive authority" (p. 6). Said is uninterested in allying with the victors and the rulers whose very stability he sees as a kind of "state of emergency" for the less fortunate; he chooses instead to account for "the experience of subordination itself, as well as the memory of forgotten voices and persons" (p. 35).

This does not mean that intellectuals are required to be, in Said's term, "humorless complainers" or whiny Cassandras—a character who, he points out, was not only unpleasant but unheard. It does mean that intellectuals work at "scouring alternative sources, exhuming buried documents, reviving forgotten (or abandoned) histories and peoples" (p. xviii). This, for Said, can be "a lonely condition, yes, but it is always a better one than a gregarious tolerance for the way things are" (p. xviii).

Said returns again and again to the notion of the authentic intellectual as a person who chooses to create an identity in part as exile—restless, in-motion, unsettled and unsettling, a person who does not feel entirely at home in his or her home—and in part as amateur—exuberant, passionate, committed, and full of delight. The intellectual lives willfully as an engaged outsider, a gleeful disrupter of the status quo, an advocate, a critic of orthodoxy and dogma, stereotype and received wisdom of every kind, all the reductive categories that limit human thought and communication. Said's intellectual works hard to maintain a kind of doubleness—something akin to DuBois's double consciousness in which African Americans were compelled, he argued, to see society and the world as both Americans *and* simultaneously as Black people, this duality being a synthesis and therefore greater than either perspective by itself. Said urges us to see our individual and collective situations in this way, as both insiders and outsiders, participants in the fullness of social life but simultaneously removed from and slightly askance to it. We must cultivate a state of steady alertness if we are to speak the unwelcome truth—as we understand it—to power.

"It is a spirit in opposition, rather than in accommodation," Said writes, "that grips me because the romance, the interest, the challenge of intellectual life is to be found in dissent against the status quo at a time when the struggle on behalf of underrepresented and disadvantaged groups seems so unfairly weighted against them." (p. xv) This points toward a research ideal we might strive toward, a path to pursue, and it illuminates as well a series of pitfalls along that path, problems that, if not exactly solved, must somehow be met and engaged. The ideal is knowledge, enlightenment, and truth on the one hand, and on the other, human freedom, emancipation, liberation. That this core of humanism is unachievable in some ultimate or final form can be discouraging to those whose mood is heavy, but it can also set a standard within the existential boundaries of our lived lives and provide, then, both focus and energy for our efforts.

In the world of teaching and learning, of schooling and education, Said's concept of the intellectual's role resonates with particular force. We live in a time when the assault on disadvantaged communities is particularly harsh and at the same time gallingly obfuscated. Access to adequate resources and decent facilities, to relevant curriculum, to opportunities to reflect on and to think critically about the world—all are unevenly distributed along predictable lines of class and color. Further, a movement to dismantle public schools under the rubric of "standards and accountability" is in place and gaining force. This is the moment within which we have to choose who to be as scholars and intellectuals, as teachers and researchers, as citizens. This is the time to figure out how, in Howard Zinn's provocative phrase, "to earn our keep in this world." (Zinn, 1997, p. 499)

I'm advancing the idea that educational researchers need to draw sustenance and perspective from the humanities in order to better see the world as it is. Whatever we find that is out-of-balance must be challenged, the devastating taken-for-granted dissected, exposed, illuminated. Whatever else we bring to our research, our teaching, and our scholarly enterprises, the core of all our work must be human knowledge and human freedom, both enlightenment and emancipation. Humanism needs to be present, and its presence acknowledged.

● ● ●

Human beings, and particularly intellectuals and researchers, are driven by a long, continuous "I don't know." It's a tiny phrase that soars on huge and propulsive wings, for it awakens the imagination. It is, after all, not the known that pushes and pull us along, although we must be serious about preparation, work, discipline, and labor. Doing research can be hard work, and a researcher can feel (if she is like others who've gone down this path) as if she's crashed into a wall—overwhelmed, uncertain, deeply confused and dislocated in turn. But if she stays with it, if she dives into the wreckage, she will likely find moments of relief, exhilaration, self-discovery, and even of joy.

There is a long tradition of socially conscious research whose avowed purpose is to combat silence, to defeat erasure and invisibility. "Socially conscious" may not be quite right—after all Ronald Reagan, Mussolini, and Pol Pot were all aware. It's certainly a mistake to imagine that anyone has a monopoly on social consciousness. Perhaps "socially responsible" gets closer, or "socially just"—but I want to point to larger goals and particular perspectives without being constrained by any formal system whatsoever, and I work hard to dwell beyond the well-lit prison of a single, shiny idea. What I'm after is research for social justice, research to resist harm and redress grievances, research with the explicit goal of promoting a more balanced, fair, and equitable social order. Several questions can serve as guideposts for this kind of inquiry:

- What are the issues that marginalized or disadvantaged people speak of with excitement, anger, fear, or hope?
- How can I enter a dialogue in which I will learn from a specific community itself about problems and obstacles they face?
- What endogenous experiences do people already have that can point the way toward solutions?
- What is missing from the "official story" that will make the problems of the oppressed more understandable?
- What current or proposed policies serve the privileged and the powerful, and how are they made to appear inevitable?
- How can the public space for discussion, problem posing, and problem solving be expanded?

There is no single procedure, no computer program that will allow this work to take care of itself; there is no set of techniques that is orderly, efficient, and pretested that can provide complete distance from a phenomenon under study or from the process of inquiry itself. Researchers draw on judgment, experience, instinct, common sense, courage, reflection, further study. There is always more to know, always something in reserve. We're never exactly comfortable, but neither are we numb or sleepwalking. We don't get harmony, but we do get a kind of arching forward—always reaching, pursuing, longing, opening, rethinking.

Researchers must peer into the unknown and cultivate habits of vigilance and awareness, a radical openness, as we continually remind ourselves that in an infinite and expanding universe our ignorance is vast, our finiteness itself all the challenge we should need to propel ourselves forward. Knowing this, we nourish an imagination that's defiant and limitless, and like the color blue or love or friendship, impossible to define without a maiming reductiveness. The goal is discovery and surprise, and in the end it is our gusto, our immersion, our urgency, enthusiasm, and raw nerve that will take us hurling toward the next horizon. We remind ourselves that the greatest work awaits us and that we are never higher than when we're not exactly certain where we're going.

●   ●   ●

Howard Zinn (1997), the eminent historian and activist scholar who has written about these issues for decades, bemoans the honor, status, prestige, and pay academics garner "for producing the largest number of inconsequential studies in the history of civilization" (p. 499). Zinn insists that we take note of and remember what motivated us to become teachers, scholars, scientists in the first place: We wanted to save lives, expand happiness, enable others to live more fully and freely. All of this is somehow rendered suspect in the insistent call for neutrality, objectivity, disinterested and discipline-based inquiry. His indictment: "Like politicians we have thrived on public innocence, with this difference: the politicians are paid for caring, when they really don't; we are paid for not caring, when we really do" (pp. 499–500). Like Said and Mills, he is urgent to resurrect the intellectual as engaged and caring, to close the "gap between the products of scholarly activity and the needs of a troubled world" (p. 500), to challenge the tenets of professional mythology, and to resist a situation where *we* publish while others perish.

Toward this end Zinn points out several commonplaces that undermine clear thought and judgment in all the intellectual precincts, from research project to academy to school to journal. These include the injunctions to: carry on only "disinterested scholarship"; "be objective"; "stick to your discipline"; remember that "scientific" means "neutral"; and believe that there is no room in the world of ideas for something as suspect as emotions.

Zinn's refutation of these commandments begins with a defense of knowledge as a form of power, a particular kind of power that can be employed against the naked power of brute force. Knowledge has the power to undermine and, perhaps, to overthrow force. But to do so, knowledge must be freely sought, explicitly linked to moral purposes, and tied to conduct. It must stand for something.

Universities are, of course, multimillion dollar enterprises governed by boards of trustees who oversee their operations. These boards are often the equivalent of millionaire clubs, overwhelmingly peopled by the owners of the means of production and information, the captains of the military-industrial complex. Such people are not neutral, and the disinterested university is a myth. The only question in this twisty, distorted, and always contested context is what and whose interests will be served and by whom.

Within this disputed space objectivity is not a self-evident good. "If to be objective is to be scrupulously careful about reporting accurately what one sees," Zinn writes, "then of course, this is laudable" (p. 504). If, for example, "objectivity" were to mean getting all the evidence one can and making judgments in light of that, well, of course. But, Zinn points out, while a metalsmith would be a fool to tinker or deceive in regard to accurate and reliable measurements, if "the metalsmith has determined in advance that he prefers a plowshare [to a sword]" (p. 504), that determination in no way asks for distorted measurements. Just so a scholar: that she prefers peace to war, national sovereignty to occupation, and women's equality to patriarchy requires no distortion.

Calls for "balance" in teaching and scholarship, which draw force from a perceived tie to "objectivity," are similarly peculiar and precarious. If the purpose of education is to seek the truth through evidence and argument, "balance" could only sensibly mean: "Find and present all the evidence you can." If by "balance" people mean the equal presentation of contradictory perspectives, the classroom and the scholarly journal become little more than sites of incessant bickering. But the classroom task, the obligation of the scholarly journal, is not quibbling; rather, it is to achieve judgment based on the widest and deepest available evidence. This means open debate, continuous inquiry, dialogue, *and* taking a stand. In reality, calls for "balance" are often in the service of a particular ideology. If an historian speaks about Palestinian rights at Columbia University today, for example, the call goes up for "balance." If an Israeli diplomat defends Israeli policies at the same place, there is no comparable hue and cry.

As with "objectivity" and "balance," so it goes with educational "research," an enterprise as we know it today constructed and catapulted after World War II on a wave of federal money. In education a sentence that begins, "The research says . . . " is too often meant to silence debate. It evokes Science, which is assumed to be larger than life: the expected response is awe and genuflection. It functions as a kind of bludgeon wielded on several sides of the school wars. It's contrapositive— "There is no research that shows . . ."—plays a similar role of quashing discussion. So, for example, a principal in Chicago, resisting the idea of bringing in a literature unit based on rap poetry, told me recently that there is no research that links studying rap with improved test scores. This may be true, but when I pointed out that Shakespeare's *Romeo and Juliet* was required reading, and asked what research links the study of Shakespeare to higher scores, he said I was being ridiculous.

But if not on objectivity, balance, and research, on what base does a claim for attention rest? Here things get sticky. For many academics that claim is primarily one of status, pedigree, affiliation, or the mantle of science. I'm reminded of the comment of my then-5-year-old son, Malik, at the awarding of my doctorate: "You're a doctor, Poppy, right?" he asked brightly. "But not the kind who can help anybody, right?" Right. And I thought then of the wisdom of the Wizard of Oz, handing over a diploma—a Th.D., Doctor of Thinkology—to the elated and suddenly notably less hapless Scarecrow: "There are plenty of professors who haven't any more brains than you have," says the Wizard. "The one thing they have that you don't is a diploma."

The alternative to status claims is to claim authority on the basis of content, on the power of evidence and argument, the representation of ideas to and for a public. Mills argues that academics create for themselves a vicious circle: in order to claim status, they too often adopt an obscure, impenetrable style; yet that grandly opaque style too often contributes to isolation and peripheral status. For Mills (1959), intellectuals must break the cycle and fight toward clarity of both substance and style: "To overcome the academic *prose*," he writes, "you have first to overcome the academic *pose*" (p. 219). He urges intellectuals to clarify as honestly as they can the claims they offer, the actual difficulty of their subjects, and the audience they hope to reach.

Mills (1963) describes the responsibility of the intellectual in the modern world:

> The independent artist and intellectual are among the few remaining personalities equipped to resist and to fight the stereotyping and consequent death of genuinely living things. Fresh perception now involves the capacity to continually unmask and to smash the stereotypes of vision and intellect with which modern communications swamp us. These worlds of mass-art and mass-thought are increasingly geared to the demands of politics. That is why it is in politics that intellectual solidarity and effort must be centered. If the thinker does not relate himself to the value of truth in political struggle, he cannot responsibly cope with the whole of live experience. (p. 299)

Be a skeptic, a narcissist. Trust your experience, and doubt your experience. This is maturity.

If there is an urgency to the researcher's or scholar's message—a real belief that the content matters—the prose tends toward directness. Like Mills, I urge my graduate students to imagine themselves in an auditorium filled with educators—teachers, administrators, a smattering of academics. They are to address the assembly on an issue of immediate importance, something they themselves think and care about. They intend to be informed by, but not enslaved to, their inquiry, their research, their data. This clears away much of the performative underbrush. Cut the bullshit: Speak!

●   ●   ●

"Science is a great and worthy mistress," W. E. B. DuBois (1975/2001) wrote, "but there is one greater and that is Humanity which science serves" (p. 42). It's important to underline the point: Research cannot be neutral. It occurs in contexts, in an historic flow, a cultural surround, a social and economic condition. It serves humanity—or some other mistress. Like education, it is designed either to perpetuate the status quo or to take the side of the disadvantage and underrepresented, to stand for humanization or to accede to dehumanization.

What interests, tendencies, or classes does our research precisely serve? What will invite people to become more aware, more critical, creative, active and productive, more free? While researchers might not know definitively *a priori* how to answer these questions, there are three commitments that might help each of us to make sounder judgments, to construct a more hopeful and workable standard by which we can examine our efforts.

In what follows I turn to the artistry of the actor and teacher Anna Deavere Smith (1993) because, like that of Gwendolyn Brooks, it has much to teach us regarding each commitment: about seeing other human beings more fully and more fairly; about challenging orthodoxy; about linking what we know to what we do.

OPENING OUR EYES/SEEING THE PERSON

Every human being, no matter who, is a gooey biological wonder, pulsing with the breath and beat of life itself, eating, sleeping, pissing and shitting, prodded by sexual urges, evolved and evolving, shaped by genetics, twisted and gnarled and hammered by the unique experiences of living. Every human being also has a unique and complex set of circumstances that makes his or her life understandable and sensible, bearable or unbearable. This recognition asks us to reject any action that treats anyone as an object, any gesture that *thingifies* human beings. It demands that we embrace the humanity of every student and every research collaborator, that we take their side. Further, it might inspire in us a sense of reverence or humility, and more than a little awe—humility because we are face to face with our own limits, our own smallness; awe because we are simultaneously in touch with the infinite.

Anna Deavere Smith (1993) captures something of this humility and awe in a riveting series of theater pieces that she calls *On the Road: A Search for American Character*, in which she interviews people—often in situations of conflict and stress—and later performs their characters, using their own words. In her one-woman show she might be a Baptist preacher, a drug dealer, a Muslim minister, a Hassidic mother, and a rebbe in quick succession. Whatever image or stereotype or categorical thinking one brings to any of these characters is exploded in Smith's portrayals—each is more than we ever thought, deeper, fuller, more surprising than we imagined. Each has dimensions we didn't know existed. The experience is both humbling and exhilarating.

Smith transforms herself on stage with astonishing speed and effect, and her major vehicle is words, how they're chosen and constructed, how they work with us and on us to shape an identity. Smith says she tries to create a space where the person she's talking with experiences his "own authorship," her own "natural 'literature.'" She claims that everyone in time "will say something that is like poetry." (Smith, 1993, p. xxxi). Her interest, remember, is the American character, and "the process of getting to that poetic moment is where 'character' lives" (p. xxxi).

Smith's work is rooted in empathy—it depends on seeing and listening to people's stories, their poetry, their own meanings, the specific words they choose to present to the world. This is an essential lesson for teachers and researchers, for this kind of seeing and listening goes beyond the surface and the superficial, requiring both effort and consciousness. The intent is honest representation, the approach is genuine and generous regard, and the work itself is arduous. "To develop a voice," she says, "one must develop an ear" (p. xxviii). She wonders: If a female actor has an inhibition about acting like a man, or a Black actor portraying a White person, does this point to an inhibition about seeing a man or hearing a White person? "Does the inability to empathize start with an inhibition," she asks, "or a reluctance to see? Do racism and prejudice instruct those inhibitions?" (p. xxviii). As teachers and researchers, what do we see when we look at our students, our field sites? What instructs our imaginations or our inhibitions?

A distinct inhibition on our ability to hear or see others fully or fairly is the reduction of humanity into categories, a practice that characterizes society in all areas, a practice so widespread that we hardly notice. We live within our own inflamed identities with such fierceness that we tend to obliterate complexity, nuance, and truth. "I'm a feminist," "I'm a philosopher," "I'm a teacher," "I'm an editor." Even if true, the words say too much, take up too much space and cast too large a shadow. Edward Said insists that no Muslim is just a Muslim, no Christian just a Christian, no Jew just a Jew. We are each an entire universe, sailing through space. We are always more.

And yet we find our visions limited, our inhibitions schooled. I remember seeing a cartoon around Mother's Day in which a bewildered-looking young man is trying to pick out a card from a display that is conveniently categorized: Biological, Adoptive, Single, Earth, Nursing, Unfit, Unwed, and on and on. The cartoon is silly, of course, and a little sad—it portrays how we actually think about mothers, how we are informed and also limited. Our inhibitions instruct our language.

Take one particular label from that fictional card display: Single. We've all heard the term *single mother* used over and over in a wide range of contexts, and we've likely said it ourselves. It has a slightly negative ring—there's something condemnatory about it, a mildly pathological undertone, a rebuke. But what substantively does the term tell us? What work—revelatory, concealing—does the term actually do? How does it instruct us or reveal us?

A woman I know interviewed people within a few square blocks of a poor neighborhood on Chicago's South Side. She reported no less than 28 distinct ways—and didn't claim that she had covered the entire territory—in which people described themselves as single mothers: living with grandparents, living with boyfriend, living with aunt, living with best friend and her child, living with same-sex partner, sister and sister's husband living next door and helping out, mother living around the corner, child's father paying rent, and on and on. A few felt abandoned by men, a few others liberated from them; some were doing well, others not so well; a few had adopted children or were their legal guardians, and one said, "I chose to be a mother without a life-partner—I'm single by choice." The variety is dazzling, the scope and range and specific meaning-making seemingly endless. Women were happy and sad, optimistic and despairing, energetic and engaged moms as well as alienated and reluctant ones.

This complex reality is, of course, swept away with the lazy label "single mother": the rough edges are all sanded off, the differences homogenized and stuffed into a simple gray bag. It is difficult to see this when the blinders are being applied—in this case, hidden in the policing language of social science. We utter the term over and over—single mother, single mother—as if it points to one specific condition, something objective, immutable. Our eyelids are feeling heavy, and before long we're completely in the hands of the carnival hypnotist.

In the worlds of schools, education, research on teaching we have become accustomed to the toxic habit of labeling, focusing relentlessly on presumed deficits, failures, and shortcomings. B.D., L.D., A.D.D., T.A.G., D.A.P. Whatever this alphabet soup of signifiers points to, one seemingly unintended consequence is the reduction of our capacity to see the three-dimensional, contradictory, complex, dynamic, in-motion, on-a-voyage human beings before us. The labels aggregate when we ought to individualize, pathologize when we might search more vigorously the side of possibility. At the very least we might insist that these kinds of representations be written in disappearing ink. And further we must somehow, in the face of all this, remind ourselves of the largest, most hopeful image of human beings and challenge ourselves as teachers, scholars, and researchers to live within that expanded and generous territory.

A commitment to seeing the person requires a radical reversal: Teachers and researchers, whatever else they do, must become student of their students, fully human subjects who become a source of knowledge and information and energy, actors, speakers, creators, constructors, thinkers, doers—a teacher as well as a learner. Together students and teachers, researchers and subjects explore, inquire, investigate, search, ask questions, criticize, make connections, draw tentative conclusions, pose problems, act, seek the truth, name this and that phenomenon, circle back, plunge forward, reconsider, gather steam, pause, reflect, reimagine, wonder, build, assert themselves, listen carefully, and speak. It doesn't end.

CHALLENGING ORTHODOXY

There's a delightful bit of satire aimed at deflating the pomposity and dogma of the critical theorists, a piece that circulates regularly in the academy. In one version credulous graduate students are presented with three lists of words, stacked up in column A, column B, and column C fashion. The task is simply to pick a word—any word—from each column and then arrange them, A + B + C. Column A contains words like: critically, culturally, politically, historically, institutionally, intellectually (add your own words here!). Column B: transformative, emancipatory, grounded, structured, mediated, contextualized, informed, powerless, and so on. And Column C: discourse, pedagogy, epistemology, authority, ideology, praxis, reality. Try it: "critically emancipatory pedagogy"; "historically grounded discourse" . . . Shazam! It works! Like the Scarecrow, you're smarter already.

I remember visiting a perfectly lovely Montessori school in Chicago years ago. On the tour for prospective parents the director kept up a steady refrain— "Maria Montessori believed . . ." or "Maria Montessori thought that . . ."—with every classroom interaction we observed. It sounded like Muzak, it felt like an initiation—my eyes were feeling heavy. Later, in informal conversation over coffee, someone mentioned the humanist psychologists Carl Jung and Carl Rogers, and I noted that Jung had once said that he was glad to be Jung and not a Jungian, because he could still change his mind. The director didn't miss a beat: "Maria Montessori said the same thing." When your dogma is full-up and full-blown, it broaches no interruption. Dr. Johnson is said to have muttered something like, "The grimmest dictatorship is the dictatorship of the prevailing orthodoxy."

Dogma is a tricky thing—easy to see in an opponent's position, much harder to apprehend when it's your own. The mindless orthodoxy of others is glaring in its foolishness, while your own has the comforting odor of common sense. Educational researchers who hope to contribute to a more humane and decent school experience and social order find themselves in the position where challenging orthodoxy is an essential, indispensable stance. As scholars we must be aware of the stakes, and aware as well that there is no simple technique or linear path that will take us to where we need to go and then allow us to live out settled scholarly lives, untroubled and finished.

The pitfalls are many: the cult of the certified expert (Said [1994] points out that "expertise . . . has rather little to do with knowledge" [p. 79]), the seduction of specialization; the drift toward power with its authoritative posture and its inevitable political agendas. Knowing that pitfalls are many and deep might help us develop a vision to traverse and resist.

LINKING CONSCIOUSNESS TO CONDUCT

Stanley Kunitz (1997), former poet laureate of the United States, wrote that "poets are not easily domesticated . . . and they can be outrageous; but they are also idealists and visionaries whose presence is needed . . . to clear the air of corruption and hypocrisy, to mock oppression, and to challenge [spiritual] apathy" (p. 11). To clear the air of corruption and hypocrisy, to mock oppression, to challenge apathy and urge us to act on what the known demands—poets, yes, by all means, and also teachers and citizens, students and activists, scholars, intellectuals, researchers.

Idealism in this sense is a synonym neither for naïveté nor for the superstitious and willful abandonment of reality—the poet/teacher/student/scholar is always leaning forward, on a quest for knowledge, for emancipation, for enlightenment, ultimately for the truth. If our destiny is to fall short—if enlightenment is always partial and truth, in any ultimate senses, always elusive—that in no way diminishes the importance of our attempt. We search for truth as an ethical imperative, a moral stance, and a guide to action; we long for freedom as the essential human task; we act because we have no other choice.

• • •

What are the challenges to humanity today? What does the hope for democracy demand now? Edward Said points out that "our country is first of all an extremely diverse immigrant society, with fantastic resources and accomplishments, but it also contains a redoubtable set of internal inequities and external interventions that cannot be ignored." (Said, 1994, p. 99) We are faced with the enduring stain of racism and the ever more elusive and intractable barriers to racial justice, the rapidly widening gulf between rich and poor, and the enthronement of greed. We are faced as well with aggressive economic and military adventures abroad, the macho posturing of men bonding in groups and enacting a kind of theatrical but no less real militarism, the violence of conquest and occupation from the Middle East and Central Asia to South America.

Encountering these facts thrusts us into the realm of human agency and choice, the battlefield of social action and change, where we come face to face with some stubborn questions: Can we, perhaps, stop the suffering? Can we alleviate at least some of the pain? Can we repair any of the loss? There are deeper considerations: Can society be changed at all? Is it remotely possible—not inevitable, certainly, perhaps not even likely—for people to come together freely, to imagine a more just and peaceful social order, to join hands and organize for something better, and to win? Can we do anything?

If a fairer, more sane and just social order is both desirable and possible, if some of us can join one another to imagine and build a participatory movement for justice, a public space for the enactment of democratic dreams, our field opens slightly. There would still be much to be done, for nothing would be entirely settled. We would still need to find ways to stir ourselves and our students from passivity, cynicism, and despair, to reach beyond the superficial barriers that wall us off from one another, to resist the flattening social evils like institutionalized racism, to shake off the anesthetizing impact of the authoritative, official voices that dominate so much of our space, to release our imaginations and act on behalf of what the known demands, linking our conduct firmly to our consciousness. We would need to reconceptualize ourselves as "stunt-intellectuals," the ones who are called upon when the other intellectuals refuse to jump off the bridge. We would be moving, then, without guarantees, but with purpose and with some small spark of hope.

• • •

In 1967 at the age of 50, with the rat-tat-tat of revolution in the air and an exuberant sense of change sweeping throughout the whole world, Gwendolyn Brooks—
with several books of poetry, a novel, and a Pulitzer Prize under her belt—wrote
of the grand rebirth of consciousness during the early days of the Black arts movement:

> I who have "gone the gamut" from an almost angry rejection of my dark skin . . . to
> a surprised queenhood in the new black sun—am qualified to enter at least the kinder-
> garten of new consciousness now. New consciousness and trudge-toward-progress.
> I have hopes for myself. (quoted in Alexander, 2004, p. 44)

"New consciousness and trudge-toward-progress"—we're reminded that it is
only the urgency of youth that can set the pace and the tone of what is to come, of
what is to be done, and still, in the grace and fullness of age we might learn to follow along, to enter at least the kindergarten of the new. Because I have hopes for
my students and my young colleagues, because I have ambitions for my children
and my grand-daughter, I also have hopes for myself.

REFERENCES

Alexander, E. (2004). *The Black interior*. St. Paul, MN: Graywolf.

DuBois, W. E. B. (2001). *The education of Black people: Ten critiques, 1906–1960*. New
York: Monthly Review Press. (Original work published 1975)

Gramsci, A. (1971). *The prison notebooks: Selections* (Q. Hoare & G. Nowell-Smith,
Trans.). New York: International Publishers.

Hirshfield, J. (2003, March/April). Telescope, well bucket, furnace: Poetry beyond the
classroom. *Writer's Chronicle, 35*(5), 14–21.

Kunitz, S. (1997). *Passing through: The later poems new and selected*. New York: Norton.

Mills, C. W. (1959). *The sociological imagination*. New York: Oxford University Press.

Mills, C. W. (1963). *Power, politics, & people: The collected essays of C. Wright Mills* (I.
L. Horowitz, Ed.).New York: Ballantine.

Mitchell, W. J. T. (2005). Secular divination: Edward Said's humanism. In H. Bhabha &
W. J. T. Mitchell (Eds.), *Edward Said: Continuing the conversation* (pp. 99–108). Chicago: University of Chicago Press.

Said, E. W. (1994). *Representations of the intellectual*. New York: Pantheon.

Smith, A. D. (1993). *Fires in the mirror*. New York: Anchor/Doubleday.

Zinn, H. (1997). *The Zinn reader: Writings on disobedience and democracy*. New York:
Seven Stories.

CHAPTER 6

"This *Is* America" 2005: The Political Economy of Education Reform Against the Public Interest

PAULINE LIPMAN

A S THE CATASTROPHE OF HURRICANE KATRINA and its aftermath unfolded on televisions across the world, there was a public expression of shock. As poor, mostly African American residents of New Orleans were left stranded day after day without food, water, sanitation, or rescue, even newscasters broke out of their scripts to express outrage, demanding "Where's the help?" A tearful parish president outside of New Orleans begged for help from the federal government on CNN. And African Americans abandoned to the New Orleans Coliseum even as newscasters reported their plight on TV and radio, echoed what hip-hop artist Kanye West dared to say on national TV,[1] that the government had abandoned storm victims in the Gulf because many of them were poor and Black. Repeatedly, TV news anchors and ordinary people asked, "How could this happen in the United States, the richest country in the world?"

Rather than a shocking aberration, this callous disregard for human life and public safety exposed what in fact was reality in the United States in 2005 for all too many people. As one Gulf storm victim proclaimed on national news, "This *is* America." I will argue that we cannot understand education policy and its implications outside this context. The aftermath of Hurricane Katrina and the devastation of New Orleans was a concentrated expression of the U.S. political economy and racial politics. New Orleans and the Gulf region are an icon for what is happening across the country. Katrina revealed that roughly one-third of the population of New Orleans lives below the poverty line and 80% of these are African American.[2] More than half of the Black households in the city did not have a car—and thus had little means of escape from the hurricane since there was little in the way of public provision for evacuation. Meanwhile, the Bush administration had cut the U.S. Army Corps of Engineers' New Orleans District budget for shoring up levees by 44% as part of the agenda to cut funding for government services (Parenti, 2005). The rebuilding phase also exemplifies urban development in the United States today. It was ushered in with suspension of the Davis Bacon Act, requiring contractors to pay prevailing wages for the cleanup. The federal government awarded billions of dollars in no-bid contracts and eliminated fuel pollution standards while contractors imported low-wage Mexican laborers even as thousands of New Orleans workers remained without jobs. And the city was put under military control, including by for-hire military contractors such as Blackwell, which is employed in Iraq. As federal relief efforts threatened to be funneled to rebuilding casinos, hotels, and the wealthy sections of the city, the mayor appointed an official commission to oversee rebuilding that was headed by venture capitalist and real estate mogul Joseph C. Canizaro, called by a fellow New Orleans business leader the "local Donald Trump" (Rivlin, 2005). Canizaro hailed the hurricane disaster as an "opportunity" to rebuild the city on new terms, none of which referred to the hundreds of thousands displaced African Americans and thousands of Hondurans who lived in the poorest wards of the city.

Katrina submerged New Orleans, but it surfaced what too many people in the United States already knew through direct experience about the punishing effects of the major transformations in the global and national economy and shifts in social policy over the past 30 years. Post-Katrina New Orleans epitomizes an economic and political landscape in which social wealth has been redistributed upward, impoverishment has expanded, the public sphere has been drastically cut, and resources have been transferred from social needs to the military. While these policies have affected people across the board, Katrina laid bare their extreme racialization. Civil rights leader Jesse Jackson, enroute to New Orleans for relief efforts, commented to the press, "In this same city of New Orleans where slave ships landed, where the legacy of 246 years of slavery and 100 years of Jim Crow discrimination, that legacy is unbroken today" (Democracy Now, 2005). Indeed, across the United States, the burden of these policies falls disproportionately on African Americans and other people of color.

This volume addresses education research in the public interest, that is "those decisions and actions that further democracy, democratic practices, equity, and social justice" (prospectus for this book). From this perspective, the full weight and implications of current education reforms can only be understood by attending to their meaning in the present political-economic context. Arguably, one's educational experience is more important than ever in determining what kinds of job one will have, whether one will have access to college, and whether schooling will prepare one to participate actively and critically in the political life of society. The goal of this chapter is to explore connections between current education reforms and the political economy and, specifically, implications for economic and social justice and democracy.

ACCOUNTABILITY, STANDARDS, AND CHOICE

Since the 1980s, education reform has moved away from a focus on equity to a focus on standards, accountability, and market mechanisms to improve schools. The policies enacted in the 1970s—from affirmative action, to bilingual education, to Title IX (equity for girls and women)—were a response to the African American civil rights movement and social movements of other oppressed groups in the 1960s and 1970s. To be sure, these policies fell far short of producing educational equity and social inclusion. In some cases they were a weak rendition or distortion of the liberatory goals of those who fought against institutionalized racial segregation and for the right to be taught in their own languages and to have equal access to the full range of school resources. Some of the policies of that era (Title I, bilingual education) were cast as compensatory. Framed by liberal policymakers in Washington and in state governments, these policies often did not begin with the knowledge and history and active participation of the people who were the target of change. As Joyce King (2005) notes in the preface to *Black Education*, these reforms, like others before and since, began with a colonial model of "we know what is best for you" (p. xxii). In addition, they failed to fundamentally redistribute resources or equalize funding or make up for past discrimination. Still, the general direction of reforms in this era was framed by the demand for equity and redistributive justice, group access and collective advancement.

Beginning in the 1980s, the discourse and direction of educational reform has shifted to quality, competition, and individual choice as the putative path to educational improvement for all (see Petrovich & Wells, 2005). Janice Petrovich (2005) summarizes the shift:

> Earlier strategies [1960s and 1970s] favored distributive justice, but since the early 1980s, strategies have favored economic growth. Equity-minded policies of the 1960s and 1970s argued for a stronger government role, for laws protecting civil rights, for publicly funded efforts to repair and compensate for historical forms of discrimination. The "excellence" oriented policies of today argue for lower taxes and less government regulation, for more choices and competition to improve quality, for rewards to those who succeed and clear consequences for those who don't. In the public discourse, the balance has shifted from concerns for group access to individual merit; from equity to quality; from entitlement to choice. (p. 7)

The shift to accountability and standards came to the forefront in the 1990s in Texas state policy (McNeil, 2000) and in Chicago (Lipman, 2004), and was instantiated in Clinton's Goals 2000. But George W. Bush's 2002 No Child Left Behind (NCLB) Act made these policies the law of the land. NCLB also opened up public education to the market by facilitating takeovers of "failing" public schools by private education management organizations (EMOs) and private provision of supplemental education services. At the same time, a system of centralized regulation of schools through high-stakes accountability and standards gives federal and state governments greater power to shape what is taught, how it is assessed, and which schools and teachers will be disciplined or rewarded. This combination of a weak state in relation to the education market and a strong state in regulation of testing, standards, and accountability has been discussed at length by a number of scholars (see Apple, 2001). There is also increased militarization of urban public schools serving low-income students of color. In addition to the proliferation of high-tech surveillance, policing, and zero-tolerance policies, little-discussed provisions of NCLB authorize closer cooperation among police, the juvenile justice system, the U.S. military, and schools. Further, NCLB has shifted policy to emphasize the learning of English with little support for the development of academic or bilingual competency of students who come to school speaking a language other than English (Gandara, Moran, & Garcia, 2004).

What are the consequences of this constellation of education policies in the context of a dramatically changing national and global economy? In particular, what are the implications for equity, democracy, and social justice?

THE POLITICAL ECONOMIC CONTEXT: FROM REDISTRIBUTION TO MARKETS

These education policies are part of a neoliberal global economic and social agenda to maximize profits by promoting the primacy of the market, reducing the cost of labor, and privatizing all spheres of economic and social life.[3] This agenda favors efficiency, or "cost effectiveness," and individual responsibility over equity and negates public responsibility to redress historical inequalities (e.g., through affirmative action, minority set-asides in government contracts, and community reinvestment). Privatization of public services effectively replaces the public interest with private interest, a shift most famously captured in British Prime Minister Margaret Thatcher's declaration that there is no English society, only individual English families (Saltman, 2000).

In the United States in the 1980s and 1990s, neoliberal policies produced massive deindustrialization and outsourcing of jobs to low-wage countries or low-wage, non-union workers in the United States. Full-time stable unionized jobs with social benefits were replaced with part-time and low-wage work, particularly in service industries, or no work at all (Moody, 1997; Ranny, 2004). Moreover, every sphere of economic, social, cultural, and biological life is now a potential commodity, from Social Security, to education, to the human genome. Over the past 20 years, we have experienced the dismantling of social programs that favor redistribution of resources and their replacement by legislation that favors individual responsibility and private providers of social services.

The result is growing social inequality and a degraded quality of life for working-class, low-income, and even middle-income people. Pressures on families have increased as social supports have been eliminated, real wages have been reduced, and urban areas in particular have lost jobs and investment in infrastructure (Anyon, 2005). While a small percentage have amassed enormous wealth and a strata of professional knowledge workers at the headquarters of globalization have benefited, the majority of U.S. workers are working longer hours for less pay and fewer social benefits (Sassen, 1998). According to Anyon (2005), during the economic boom of 1999, 41.3% of those working in the United States earned poverty-zone wages (p.19). Immigrant workers displaced by the global effects of neoliberalism are increasingly filling low-wage service and manufacturing jobs, while many African Americans can find no jobs at all in the new economy. As cities are gentrified for high-salaried professionals, working-class people and low-income people, particularly people of color, are being pushed out of central areas into already impoverished urban neighborhoods and inner-ring suburbs (Venkatesh, Celimli, Miller, Murphy, & Turner, 2004), as well as being criminalized and controlled through stepped-up policing and incarceration—as evidenced by the fact that almost 1 million African Americans are incarcerated (Brown, 2003; Parenti, 1999). The magnitude of the economic and social crisis visited on African American communities in particular is captured by Arundhati Roy's (2003) observation that Bangladeshi men have a better chance of making it to the age of 40 than African American men in Harlem. We are also living in an increasingly militarized society with a proliferation of surveillance, military spending for the 2005 fiscal year at $420.7 billion ("Highlights," 2004), and preemptive war as foreign policy. The everyday life experiences behind these statistics became, for a brief moment, prime-time spectacle in the wake of Hurricane Katrina. They gave a glimpse of the social landscape on which current educational policy plays out.

LABOR STRATIFICATION, GROWING INEQUALITY, AND EDUCATION POLICY

The labor market of the 21st century is high segmented and economically polarized. Sanjek (1998) sums up this trend: "The new jobs that appeared during the Reagan years came mainly in two varieties: high-skill, high-pay and low-skill, low-pay. A vast recomposition of the U.S. labor market was under way" (p. 124). Chicago provides a clear example. From 1967 to 1990, Chicago manufacturing jobs declined from 546,500 (nearly 41% of all local jobs) to 216,190 (18% of total jobs) while nonmanufacturing jobs went from 797,867 (59%) in 1967 to 983,580 (82%) in 1990 (Betancur & Gills, 2000, p. 27). Dislocated manufacturing workers were left with lower-wage service and non-union manufacturing work (including day labor, part-time, and sweatshop work). In 1998, 76% of the jobs with the most growth in Illinois paid less than a livable wage, and 51% of these jobs paid below half a livable wage (National Priorities Project, 1998). While some workers are recycled through these new labor positions, others are pushed into the informal economy or the ranks of the unemployed. At the opposite end of the employment scale, there is growth in high-paid jobs in the knowledge economy and business and professional services. U.S. Department of Labor data (1986–1999) on the 50 largest U.S. cities confirm a barbell labor structure with growth in high- and low-paid jobs and a decline in the share of mid-skilled, middle-income administrative and skilled production work (precision production, craft, and repair work) for which one needs a high school diploma (Skinner, 2004). This barbell economy is particularly evident in states with large numbers of low-wage foreign-born workers (Frey, cited in Skinner, 2004). The result of simultaneous upgrading, downgrading, and exclusion of labor is a highly segmented work force[4] and a social structure that is economically polarized on the basis of class, race, national origin, and gender.

As mid-skilled workers have been displaced into low-skilled, low-paid jobs, good jobs for high school graduates have declined. A student who enters the labor market after high school graduation today cannot expect the same opportunity in the labor force as his or her parents (Skinner, 2004). Anyon (2005) notes that a typical working-class job of the future is retail sales at WalMart, the largest private employer in the world with over a million workers, with average pay of $20,030 in 2000. In a stratified economy increasingly focused on information processing and the production of knowledge, education "is becoming an increasingly important criterion for determining who joins which group" (Flecha, 1999, p. 66).

What are the implications of high-stakes education accountability in this context? Emerging evidence suggests that despite the claim that no child should be left behind, in practice, despite some improvements in test scores, high-stakes testing is intensifying curriculum differentiation between high-scoring and low-scoring schools. While low-scoring schools (which generally serve low-income students and students of color) are driven to focus more on preparation for high-stakes tests that emphasize basic skills and closed-ended tasks, high-performing schools (which generally serve more affluent and Whiter student bodies) are able to maintain a more well-rounded, open-ended, and richer curriculum (see Lipman, 2004; McNeil, 2000, Valenzuela, 2005). Early evidence also suggests that putting schools on probation may drive out highly skilled and committed teachers (Lipman, 2004; Mintrop, 2004) and, in one cross-site study, did not provoke teachers to incorporate more pedagogies centered on higher-order thinking and problem solving even when mandated assessments called for it (Mintrop, 2004). An unequal curriculum in elementary school due to the regime of high-stakes testing leads to differential access to high school opportunities, such as selective magnet and college-prep programs, and differential preparation for college. In short, the overemphasis on testing and the use of standardized tests to make high-stakes decisions about students, such as grade retention, exacerbates already existing unequal opportunities to learn based on race, class, and tracking (Valencia & Villarreal, 2005). Clark, Madaus, and Shore (2005) summarize this process:

> From the time children enter kindergarten, testing is strongly implicated in their life chances. . . . For those on the wrong side of these decisions, they result in an accumulation of disparities in access to educational opportunities and resources, including promotion to the next grade, graduation from high school, and admission to college. This additive process is especially relevant in the case of non-Asian minority students because their scores on standardized tests are generally lower than those of other students. (p.104)

In other words, to the extent that high-stakes accountability policies prompt low-scoring schools to engage in education as test preparation—rather than as intellectually challenging work, expanded access to advanced courses, and the capacity for critical and analytical thought—they further institutionalize unequal opportunities to learn. This has greater consequences than ever before for one's life chances. For example, national data indicate that Black students in particular need more opportunities to learn complex mathematics, and this disparity takes on greater significance today because of the centrality of math and science in the new economy (Tate, 2004). The relationship between educational attainment and income appears to be stronger than ever (Petrovich, 2005). As Dennis Carlson (1996) argues:

> The "basic skills" restructuring of urban schools around standardized testing and a skill-based curriculum has been a response to the changing character of work in post-industrial America, and it has participated in the construction of a new post-industrial working class...of clerical, data processing, janitorial, and service industry jobs." (pp. 282–283)

Equally important is the effect on developing an informed, thoughtful, and critical citizenry. In the face of growing economic inequality, war, environmental crises, and racial marginalization, education for democratic public participation is more important than ever. Youth need the intellectual tools and sociopolitical perspective to examine social issues, critique media, link social problems to their historical and political contexts, and articulate more just social arrangements. A diet of test-driven teaching, especially for low-income students of color, clearly limits the opportunity to develop these tools in school. For example, William Tate (2004) argues that mathematical and science literacy is crucial to understanding contemporary political issues, and Black students' lack of access to complex mathematics instruction is a limiting factor in their understanding of these issues. Civil rights leader Bob Moses has called mathematical literacy the civil rights issue of today: "In today's world, economic access and full citizenship depend crucially on math and science literacy" (quoted in Tate, 2004, p.148).

The Market and Education Policy

A key feature of neoliberal economic policy is opening up new areas of social life, including health care and education, to the market. Charter schools, the creation of choice within public education, and privatization of education services, such as after-school tutoring, are examples of this. What are their implications in the current economic context?

The charter school issue is complex. There are those who advocate for charter schools because of their pro-market and pro-privatization orientations. On the other hand, progressive educators and communities of color have used the greater flexibility and autonomy of charter schools to develop culturally centered and social justice–oriented curricula and schools administered by their communities. Examples are Afro-centric schools, semi-autonomous Native American schools, and social justice charter schools (Rofes & Stulberg, 2004; Wells, Scott, Lopez, & Holme, 2005). Charter schools offer choice in curriculum and school focus and can open up the possibilities for more democratically developed and administered public schools that respond to the needs, interests, and values of communities of color in a context in which high-stakes testing and accountability are narrowing these possibilities in regular public schools.

However, in the larger neoliberal context, charter school reform may end up overall reinforcing inequality and reducing democratic participation. The charter school reform market philosophy is grounded in the notion that private entities can administer public institutions more efficiently when forced to compete with other private entities. Thus, in Illinois, as with most state charter school laws, charter schools receive less per-pupil public funding than regular public schools, plus most of them must use a portion of that funding to cover facility costs. Amy Stuart Wells and colleagues (2005) point out that limited public resources force many charter schools to contract out school administration to EMOs and create funding partnerships with business groups or corporations. Also, because the climate in which they must survive is one of high-stakes standardized tests and competition for limited resources, certain types of charter schools have a greater possibility of success than others. Charter schools that adhere to the underlying market philosophy, trim budgets to reduce operating expenses (lower teacher wages and more narrowly focused student services, for instance), and contract out services to EMOs, while pursuing educational programs that focus on student success on high-stakes standardized tests, are more likely to succeed in the charter school reform environment. Meanwhile, those that use charter school reform to develop and administer schools around notions of community participation, democracy and nontraditional and nondominant forms of valued knowledge must fight a fierce counterstream of overarching neoliberal policy. For example, in Chicago, the fastest-growing charter school force is the Chicago Charter School Foundation, which develops and oversees market-modeled charter schools operated by EMOs, which generally use curricula based on traditional knowledge, such as the CORE Knowledge Curriculum (see Core Knowledge, 2005). This is not a curriculum that will necessarily give students access to the forms of knowledge and dispositions valued in the knowledge economy or give them tools for critical participation in democratic public life.

Charter schools transfer public funds to private organizations. They are a form of public–private partnership that opens up public education as a source of direct capital accumulation. This process works by "shaving off" aspects of the education system to private providers (Robertson & Dale, 2003) and making their employees non-union. Roger Dale (1989/90) points out that "Before education can be brought into the marketplace and made subject to consumer choice; a range of possible alternatives has to be created" (p. 9). Privately operated charters eliminate public participation in their governance. Unlike public schools, which must take all students who live within their attendance areas, even charters that admit students by lottery are open to selection mechanisms, both formal and informal, that can enforce exclusion by race, ethnicity, class, immigrant status, and so on. These include attracting students most likely to fit the school's ethos, parents who have the knowledge of school options, and those with the means to afford transportation. In a high-stakes testing environment, there is greater likelihood that attractive charter schools will find ways to exclude low-scoring students and/or students more expensive to educate. These include students who require special education services, need bilingual education, or have special needs.

Charter schools are part of a larger discourse of school choice that includes selective magnet schools and public schools that mirror elite private schools for a few students alongside greater standardization and centralized regulation for the majority of schools. For example, in New York City, high-scoring schools serving more affluent and Whiter communities have been given greater flexibility in curriculum and instruction while low-scoring schools are subject to greater regulation. In Chicago, new elite magnet high schools and new Montessori elementary schools have been created at the same time that the majority of the schools are driven by accountability mandates. The result is an increasingly dual education system that parallels and reinforces a dual labor force and expands the private sphere at the expense of the public.

Magnet schools are a kind of weighted-choice system within public education that privileges the fortunate few and reinforces individual over public interest. They mean that the families privileged to attend them have less incentive to support improvement in neighborhood schools for the majority (Petrovich, 2005). As many public schools in urban areas become driven by high-stakes testing, these schools will become more attractive to those who can gain admission. Introducing choice in one part of the system "facilitate(s) a shift from collectivism to individualism, from a view that a common school is desirable to one that encourages parents/consumers to shop around and maximize *their* children's opportunities of enjoying an 'uncommon' education"—a shift from universalism to selectivity, from egalitarianism to hierarchy (Dale, 1989/90, pp. 12–13). Thus, schools are no longer part of the public interest but are commodities available to the most savvy and attractive consumer. In short, choice and charter schools both result from neoliberal economics and also reinforce its inequalities and its erosion of public institutions.

Militarization and Education Policy

In an economy in which good jobs for high school graduates are increasingly limited, and in a political context that favors U.S. world dominance and preemptive war and regime change through U.S. military force (Project for a New American Century, 1997), the future of a generation of young African Americans and Latinos is more likely to be in low-wage jobs, the U.S. military, or the prison system than in the offices powering the new informational and service economy (Parenti, 1999). Current education policies contribute to these unequal life chances not only through differentiated curricula but also through a lock-down school culture. "In these schools, replete with metal detectors, armed guards, and periodic searches, poor youth, especially African American and other youth of color, are being subjected to increased levels of physical and psychological surveillance, confinement, and regimentation" (Brown, 2003, p. 127) that mirror the most tightly disciplined low-wage jobs.

If these schools represent the "low-wage track," the criminalization of school offenses through zero-tolerance school discipline policies has established a "school house to jail house" track (Advancement Project, 2005). With zero tolerance, the number of student suspensions and expulsions has increased exponentially and disproportionately for African American and Latino youth, with negative consequences for grades, pass rates, and graduation rates. Policies that push youth out of school leave them with few options in the current economy. It is even more troubling that zero-tolerance discipline policies couple traditional school punishments with referrals to police and juvenile justice authorities. What was once a school suspension now turns into a potential juvenile criminal record and the first step into the penal system. In a context in which many African American and other youth of color are a surplus labor force, the swelling prison industrial system has become an integral part of the new economy (Parenti, 1999). The role of school policy in a school-to-prison pipeline is cause for deep concern.

Under the rationale of drug and violence prevention—real concerns of many students and parents—NCLB has made zero tolerance national policy, instigating more policing of youth rather than addressing underlying causes of violence in schools (Advancement Project, 2005). NCLB makes it easier for school districts and law enforcement "to share information regarding disciplinary actions and misconduct by students"; establishes Project Sentry to "identify, prosecute, punish, and supervise juveniles who violate state and firearms laws"; establishes the School Security Technology and Resource Center in partnership with the Sandia National Laboratory and the National Law Enforcement and Corrections Technology Center to employ new surveillance and policing technology in schools; and "shields" teachers, principals, and school board members from federal liability arising from classroom discipline practices. These measures, which primarily affect schools serving low-income students of color, are an institutionalized escalation of the surveillance of youth and the criminalization of African American and Latino youth in particular. The control of youth of color through surveillance and criminaliation coupled with highly regimented schools is necessary for an economy that includes both a large low-wage sector and exclusion of labor. Christian Parenti (1999) argues that those excluded are "rendered economically useful as raw material for a growing corrections complex" (p. 137).

NCLB also requires schools to provide the military with the student records of all high school juniors (unless students request that their records be withheld) and to give military recruiters the same access to schools and student information as colleges have. This is turning some high schools into military recruitment centers at a time when joining the military may mean being on the battlefield. There is also a proliferation of military programs in high schools, and in several cities there are new public military high schools. These schools are a partnership between the military and public school systems. Chicago is a national leader in this trend. As of fall 2005, Chicago had four high schools run jointly by the Chicago public schools and branches of the armed services and two more reported to be in the planning stages. All students in these schools are required to be Junior Reserve Officer Training Cadets (JROTC) and to take as part of their core subjects JROTC Leadership Education and Training classes. Chicago also has military middle schools. All the CPS military schools are located in communities of color.

The military school option, or "military prep track," is grounded in sedimented educational and economic inequalities. In the first place, the need for more education funding, especially in underfunded urban school districts, makes school systems vulnerable to offers of additional funds from the military. For example, the U.S. Navy gave the Chicago public schools $1 million to upgrade Senn High School as a naval academy. Second, in today's economy, joining the military may be one of the few viable options for working-class and low-income youth. The growth of military-prep high schools capitalizes on these strata of the future labor force, for whom prospects of college or a stable well-paying job are increasingly scarce as college tuition costs increase and the labor market is stratified. In low-income communities, military high schools may also be one of the few options for a safe school environment, for development of leadership skills (albeit in the military model), and for the promise of college funding for those who go on to join the military. These schools acculturate youth to the military system of rules and authority and serve as a means of screening and recruitment for military service (Lipman, 2003) at a time when the military's recruitment is down despite spending $8 billion in advertising alone. High school and middle school military programs have become a key element of the recruitment strategy by reaching students at a young age.

POLITICAL-ECONOMIC RECONSTRUCTION
OF CITIES AND METROPOLITAN REGIONS

The restructuring of the world economy is transforming cities and the metropolitan regions surrounding them. From Baltimore to Chicago to New York, corporate-center development is the chief economic strategy. This strategy is creating dual cities: spatially, economically, socially, and racially. At one end are downtown corporate, financial, tourist, and leisure zones and upscale gentrified neighborhoods carved out of abandoned manufacturing space and displaced working-class neighborhoods (Smith, 1996). At the other are socially isolated, deeply impoverished communities of color and rapidly expanding low-income immigrant neighborhoods (Sassen, 1998). These cities exemplify the barbell economy of high-paid professionals (primarily White) and low-paid service workers (primarily people of color, immigrants, and women). This restructuring of cities is facilitated by public–private partnerships, use of public funds for private development, and policies that facilitate development through displacement of working-class people and especially people of color (Brenner & Theodore, 2002).[5] This strategy shifts social wealth, land, and resources to the private sphere in the name of growth and public progress. "Rather than being in the public interest, such strategies merely serve the particularistic interests of corporate elites and their public sector allies in urban governing coalitions" (Imbroscio, 2004, p. 25).

The inequality produced by this fundamental political-economic reconstruction of many major urban centers in the United States. encourages and is reinforced by the dualization of education in these cities. Chicago has built new selective magnet high schools and international baccalaureate programs in high schools to attract middle-class professionals to the city's economy. These schools, with afternoon colloquia, rigorous seminar-style classes, state of the art equipment, and spacious hallways in new or revamped buildings rival the most expensive private schools in the city. They are in many ways, for the city's corporate/political elite, a necessary alternative to their polar opposite—the majority of public schools, which are driven by a basics, test-driven, regimented curriculum. Basic high schools that serve the future low-wage workforce and even high schools with more varied curricula that serve working-class students are thoroughly unviable as a public school option for the upper end of Chicago's dual labor force. The new college-prep magnet high schools and new Montessori elementary schools are located in gentrified, gentrifying, and affluent areas.

Metro regions as well as cities are becoming more economically, racially, ethnically, and culturally heterogeneous and economically differentiated.[6] "The new anchors of regional development—airports and their peripheral development, new universities and associated science parks, recreational theme parks, whole-sale marketing areas, and even new office and financial centers—are often located on the urbanizing fringe" (Simmonds & Hack, 2000, p. xx). Concentrations of high- and low-paid service and manufacturing, leisure, and transportation indus-tries are locating in edge cities and metro-region towns. While some suburban areas remain bastions of White affluence, others have become racially, ethnically, and economically diverse ports of entry for immigrant workers and dislocated urban African Americans. Still others are "inner-city suburbs," economically im-poverished relocation points for African Americans driven out of the city by gen-trification and the destruction of public housing. Thus, the economic dualization of metro regions is also spatial.

Metro regions are becoming more economically, racially, ethnically, and cul-turally diverse as immigrants and low-income people of color are pushed out of central cities by gentrificaiton and new immigrant workers are moving directly to edge cities and towns on the periphery of urban areas (Soja, 1999). For ex-ample, the combined effects of immigration and urban gentrification have turned some Southwest Chicago ring suburbs into virtual extensions of Chicago Mexi-can neighborhoods. According to 2000 census data, "racial and ethnic minorities" made up 27% of U.S. suburban populations, up from 19% in 1990, and "minori-ties" were responsible for the bulk of suburban population gains in the 102 major metro areas (Frey, 2001). In some towns and suburbs in metro regions, the loca-tion of low-wage manufacture and service jobs in suburban areas as well as the increased cost of housing in gentrifying cities are producing concentrations of low-wage immigrants and African Americans alongside new middle- and upper-middle-class housing developments.

As a result, many of the traditionally defined "urban school" issues—inad-equate school funding, racial and cultural diversity, deep economic disparities—are becoming metro-region issues. Some school districts in edge cities and small towns on the city periphery look more like urban school districts than the homo-geneous small towns of just a decade ago. Looking at it from the standpoint of a democratic and inclusive society, this increasing racial and cultural diversity offers a new opportunity for these areas to broaden their curriculum and draw on the cosmopolitan, urban, and transnational experiences of new student popula-tions. This is the democratic potential offered by racial and cultural diversity to enrich the education of all students and prepare them more fully to participate in a diverse democratic society.

However, NCLB may exacerbate racial, ethnic, and class tensions and social polarization in these communities. Under NCLB, achievement data must be dis-aggregated by race/ethnicity and English-language proficiency—a provision that would mark a step forward if used to address educational inequity. But in the pres-ent high-stakes accountability environment, the failure of racial/ethnic subgroups or language-minority students to meet test score benchmarks can lead to blaming immigrant and African American students and their families for a school's failure to meet NCLB targets. In fact, my data suggest this is already happening not only in urban schools (Lipman, 2004) but also in suburban schools (Lipman, 2005). In one Chicago metro-region town, affluent White residents of a new housing development initiated a referendum to withdraw from a district that was about 50.8% White, 34.5% Hispanic (Latino), 7.6% African American, and 6.8% Asian American and create their own school district (Lipman, 2005). Supporters of the referendum claimed the lower test scores of low-income students (read: students of color) were bringing down their schools. In another community, developers of a new, expensive housing development petitioned the school district to create a charter school that would have no bilingual education programs.

The increased presence of immigrant and African American students complicates normative White, Eurocentric notions of the curriculum, whose identities schools should valorize, and what language(s) and cultures should be central or even recognized. Teachers are confronted with new pedagogical questions and possibilities for a more democratic and inclusive educational practice. For example, in my research in Chicago metro-region communities, I found schools that, in the mid-1990s, developed dual-language (Spanish–English) programs that supported bilingualism/biculturalism for both English- and Spanish-speaking children. Such programs can challenge the way language works as a form of power to marginalize students who do not speak standard English. However, despite growing immigration and linguistic diversity in U.S. schools, NCLB requirements that prioritize English acquisition and require students to quickly transition to English undermine these possibilities. *Bilingual* is nearly eliminated from federal education policy language, and expenditures for English-language learners are on the decline (Gandara et al., 2004). Under accountability and standards reforms, schools are pressured to transition students to English, with a negative impact on the quality of learning, and even committed bilingual education teachers are driven to reproduce a subtractive English-first curriculum (Alamillo, Palmer, Viramonte, & Garcia, 2005; see also Lipman, 2004). At a time when classrooms and communities across the United States, not just in urban areas, are more racially, ethnically, linguistically, and culturally diverse, these policies set practical limits and symbolic parameters not only on the educational success of bilingual students but on who "belongs" in these communities.

CONCLUSION

Research on high-stakes accountability, standardization, privatization, and militarization of schools suggests that these policies exacerbate education inequalities and contribute to broader economic and social inequality. They also turn attention away from actual inequalities by proposing that all that is need to close the achievement gap and improve school safety is more standardized testing and punitive measures against schools, teachers, and students (Wells, Holmes, Revilla, & Atanda, 2004). At the very moment when inequality is increasing and education holds ever greater importance for one's life chances, there is a decrease in investment in public education as a public good. Instead, there are more sanctions for failure built on a history of inequality.

In many respects NCLB's call to "leave no child behind" resonates with the failure of earlier equity-oriented policies to actually produce equity. Racially desegregated schools too often resegregated students to within-school inequitable educational opportunities and outcomes. The failure to fully fund and adequately staff bilingual education programs contributed to the low achievement of second-language learners and left bilingual education open to attack by anti-bilingual conservatives. The crisis in urban schools serving working-class students and students of color due to starving them of resources and imposing a curriculum of miseducation and militarized schooling is answered by a system of accountability to a uniform set of standards without addressing these fundamental and deeply rooted inequalities and colonial knowledge systems (see King, 2005). In fact, NCLB accountability and English-acquisition provisions work against curricula and pedagogies that challenge colonial knowledge and have proven successful in specific communities. A generation of research and practice supports education that is grounded in the knowledge, experiences, languages, and cultures that children bring to school and that challenges racism and supports the development of sociopolitical consciousness (Ladson-Billings, 1994; Lee, 2005). NCLB institutionalizes the reversal of these practice and this knowledge bases where they have taken hold in schools and teacher education programs. The inevitable failure of many schools as a result of NCLB clears the way for arguments against public education and for privatization. As Wells and colleagues (2004) have shown in relation to the implementation of *Brown v. Board of Education*, the political-economic context can be decisive. Current policies driving education in the United States negate the context of public education when that context is one of increasing cultural and racial diversity coupled with economic inequality, racial marginalization, and militarization.

School reform alone cannot affect education without addressing inequalitiy in the economy and society. This is the urgent, larger agenda calling for engagement by educators, communities, youth, enlightened policymakers, and the public at large (Anyon, 2005; Noguera, 2003; Wells et al., 2004). But schools can play a more immediate role in preparing students to engage in the construction of this agenda. The neoliberal model of education is a human capital model—preparing workers (differentially) for the new economy. This is education in the private interest. Education in the public interest calls for students to be prepared with the tools of engaged and critical public participation in a diverse, heterogeneous democracy that is under siege.

The current regime of oppressive testing, militarized schools, and cultural white-washing is beginning to produce seeds of this countermovement. One example is the soical justice–oriented schools that are forming in various cities in reaction to current policies and grounded in the historical memory of educational and social struggles for justice. In Chicago, for example, since the fall of 2005, there are seven social justice–oriented high schools or high school academies, most brand new. The UCLA IDEA center summer seminar in critical social research for Los Angeles high school students of color provides a national model of preparing youth to study social theory and develop the research skills to be effective actors in their schools and communities beyond high school. Across the United States a powerful anti-military-recruitment campaign is involving youth in discussion and action related to war and military recruitment of low-income students of color. There are traditions of education in the public interest to draw on. To cite one of them, as Joyce King (2005) notes, " . . . privileging community well-being and the welfare of humanity, is at the conceptual and methodological center of transformative research and action in Black education" (p. 34).

NOTES

1. Before his microphone was abruptly cut, West faced the camera and declared, "George Bush doesn't care about Black people" (de Morales, 2005).
2. *The New York Times* reported that 35% of the city's Black residents—almost 110,000 people—were living in poverty, according to the 2000 census.
3. Neoliberalism is characterized by unregulated global flows of capital—transnational speculative investment, multinational agreements to liberalize trade such as the North American Free Trade Agreement, and structural adjustment policies directed against nations of the global South by the IMF and World Bank requiring countries to cut social spending and reduce wages in exchange for loans. It also strives to cheapen labor by lowering wages, breaking unions, reducing workers' benefits, exporting jobs to countires that can offer the cheapest labor, and degrading health and safety standards (see Moody, 1997; Ranny, 2004).
4. In information-processing sectors and some high-tech manufacturing, there is a simultaneous upskilling and downgrading of labor. For example, while some clerical work requires greater information-processing skills, it is often part time and temporary. The same is true for robotized and high-tech manufacturing, which requires many fewer workers than in the industrial era but workers with the education to program computers, troubleshoot, and solve problems in digitalized production processes. Despite increased demand for skills, many of these jobs lack the benefits and security of previously unionized industrial jobs.
5. In Chicago, for example, the demolition of 19,000 units of public housing has cleared the way for development of vast tracts of the city for condominiums and upscale housing and retail complexes.
6. Some (e.g., New York, Los Angeles, Chicago) are global cities—command posts in the global economy and centers of finance and global business services. Others are reinventing themselves as niche cities in the global economy (e.g., Miami and Houston) while remaining largely Rust Belt cities, hulks of their former industrialized past, with smaller emergent service sectors in which White workers have been refashioned as service

labor and many formerly industrial African American workers have little opportunity in the formal economy.

REFERENCES

Advancement Project. (2005). *Education on lockdown: The schoolhouse to jailhouse track.* Retrieved June 6, 2005, from www.advancementproject.org/reports/FINALE-OLrep.pdf

Alamillo, L., Palmer, D., Viramontes, C., & Garcia, E. E. (2005). California's English-only policies: An analysis of initial effects. In A. Valenzuela (Ed.). *Leaving children behind: How "Texas-style" accountability fails Latino youth* (pp. 201–224). Albany: State University of New York Press.

Anyon, J. (2005). *Radical possibilities: Public policy, urban eduation, and a new social movement.* New York: Routledge.

Apple, M. (2001). *Educating the "right" way: Markets, standards, God, and inequality.* New York: RoutledgeFalmer.

Betancur, J. J., & Gills, D. C. (2000). The restructuring of urban relations. In J. J. Betancur & D. C. Gills (Eds.), *The collaborative city: Opportunities and struggles for Blacks and Latinos in U.S. cities* (pp. 17–40). New York: Garland.

Brenner, N., & Theodore, N. (2002) Cities and the geographies of "actually existing neoliberalism," *Antipode, 34*(3), 349–379.

Brown, E. (2003). Freedom for some, disciplining for "others." In K. J. Saltman & D. A. Gabbard (Eds.), *Education as Enforcement: The militarization and corporatization of schools* (pp. 127–151). New York: Routledge.

Carlson, D. (1996). Education as a political issue: What's missing in the public conversation about education? In J. L. Kincheloe & S. R. Steinberg (Eds.), *Thirteen questions: Reframing education's conversation* (2nd ed.; pp. 281–291). New York: Peter Lang.

Clark, M., Madaus, G., & Shore, A. R. (2005). Testing and diversity in college admissions. In J. Petrovich & A. S. Wells (Eds.), *Bringing equity back: Research for a new era in American educational policy* (pp.103–135). New York: Teachers College Press.

Core Knowledge. (2005). Charlottesville, VA: The Core Knowledge Foundation. Retrieved August 10, 2005, from http://www.coreknowledge.org/CK/index.htm

Dale, R. (1989/90). The Thatcherite project in education: The case of the City Technology Colleges. *Critical Social Policy, 9*, 4–19.

de Morales, L. (2005, September 3). Kanye West's torrent of criticism, live on NBC. *Washington Post*, p. C01. Available online at http://www.washingtonpost.com/wp-dyn/content/article/2005/09/03/AR2005090300165.html

Democracy Now. (2005). Retrieved September 10, 2005, from http://www.democracynow.org/article.pl?sid=05/09/07/1415225&mode=thread&tid=25

Flecha, R. (1999). New educational inequalities. In M. Castells, R. Flecha, P. Freire, H. A. Giroux, D. Macedo, & P. Willis (Eds.), *Critical education in the new information age* (pp. 65-82). Lanham, MD: Rowman & Littlefield.

Frey, W. H. (2001) *Melting pot suburbs: A census 2000 study of suburban diversity.* Washington DC: Brookings Institute, Center on Urban & Metropolitan Policy.

Gandara, P., Moran, R., & Garcia, E. (2004). Legacy of *Brown: Lau* and language policy in the United States. *Review of Research in Educaiton, 28*, 27–46.

Highlights of the FY'05 budget request. (2004). Retrieved October 20, 2005, from http://64.177.207.201/static/budget/annual/fy05/

Imbroscio, D. L. (2004). The imperative of economics in urban political analysis: A reply to Clarence N. Stone. *Journal of Urban Affairs, 26*(1), 21–26.

King, J. E. (Ed.). (2005). *Black education: A transformative research and action agenda for the new century.* Mahwah, NJ: American Educational Research Association/Erlbaum.

Ladson-Billings, G. (1994). *Dreamkeepers: Successful teachers of African American students.* San Francisco: Jossey-Bass.

Lee, C. D. (2005). The state of knowledge about the education of African Americans. In J. E. King (Ed.), *Black education: A transformative research and action agenda for the new century* (pp. 45–71). Mahwah, NJ: American Educational Research Association/Erlbaum.

Lipman, P. (2003). Chicago school policy: Regulating Black and Latino youth in the global city. *Race, Ethnicity and Education, 6*(4), 331–355.

Lipman, P. (2004). *High stakes education: Inequality, globalization, and urban school reform.* New York: Routledge.

Lipman, P. (2005) Metropolitan regions—New geographies of inequality in education: The Chicago metroregion case. *Globalization, Societies, and Education, 3*(2), 141–163.

McNeil, L. (2000). *Contradictions of school reform: Educational costs of standardized testing.* New York: Routledge.

Mintrop, H. (2004). *Schools on probation: How accountability works (and doesn't work).* New York: Teachers College Press.

Moody, K. (1997). *Workers in a lean world.* London: Verso.

National Priorities Project. (1998). *Working hard, earning less: The story of job growth in Illinois* (Grassroots Factbook, Vol. I, Series 2). Northampton, MA: Author.

Noguera, P. (2003). *City schools and the American dream: Reclaiming the promise of public education.* New York: Teachers College Press.

Parenti, C. (1999). *Lockdown America: Police and prisons in the age of crisis.* London: Verso.

Parenti, M. (2005). How the free market killed New Orleans. Retrieved September 6, 2005, from http://www.zmag.org/sustainers/content/2005-09/03parenti.cfm

Petrovich, J. (2005). The shifting terrain of educational policy: Why we must bring equity back. In J. Petrovich & A. S. Wells (Eds.), *Bringing equity back: Research for a new era in American educational policy* (pp. 3–15). New York: Teachers College Press.

Petrovich, J., & Wells, A. S. (Eds.). (2005). *Bringing equity back: Research for a new era in American educational policy.* New York: Teachers College Press.

Project for the New American Century. (1997). Statement of principles. Retrieved July 28, 2005, from http://www.newamericancentury.org/statementofprinciples.htm

Ranny, D. (2004). *Global decisions, local collisions: Urban life in the new world order.* Philadelphia: Temple University Press.

Rivlin, G. (2005, September 29). A mogul who would rebuild New Orleans. *New York Times*, pp. C1, C4.

Robertson, S., & Dale, R. (2003, June). Changing geographies of power in education: The politics of rescaling and its contradictions. Paper presented at the joint BERA/BAICE conference on Globalization, Culture, and Education.

Rofes, E. E., & Stulberg, L. M. (Eds.). (2004). *The emancipatory promise of charter schools.* Albany: State University of New York Press.

Roy, A. (2003). Instant-mix imperial democracy: Buy one, get one free (A lecture spon-

116   Policy and Politics

sored by the Center for Economic and Social Rights). Retrieved August 8, 2003, from http://zmag.org/content/print_article.cfm?itemID=3637&sect

Saltman, K. J. (2000). *Collateral damage: Corporatizing public schools—A threat to democracy.* Lanham, MD: Rowman & Littlefield.

Sanjek, R. (1998). *The future of us all: Race and neighborhood politics in New York City.* Ithaca, NY: Cornell University Press.

Sassen, S. (1998). *Globalization and its discontents.* New York: The New Press.

Simmonds, R., & Hack, G. (2000). Introduction. In R. Simmonds & G. Hack (Eds.), *Global city regions: Their emerging forms* (pp. 3–7). London: Spon Press.

Skinner, C. (2004). The changing occupational structure of large metropolitan areas: Implications for the high school educated. *Journal of Urban Affairs, 26*(1), 67–88.

Smith, N. (1996). *The new urban frontier: Gentrification and the revanchist city.* New York: Routledge.

Soja, E. W. (1999). In different spaces: The cultural turn in urban and regional political economy. *European Planning Studies, 7*(1), 65–75.

Tate, W. F. IV (2004). *Brown,* political economy, and the scientific education of African Americans. *Review of Research in Education, 28,* 147–184.

Valencia, R. R., & Villarreal, B. J. (2005). Texas' second wave of high-stakes testing: Antisocial promotion legistlation, grade retention, and adverse impact on minorities. In A. Valenzuela (Ed.), *Leaving children behind: How "Texas-style" accountability fails Latino youth* (pp. 113–152). Albany: State University of New York Press.

Valenzuela, A. (Ed.). (2005). *Leaving children behind: How "Texas-style" accountability fails Latino youth.* Albany: State University of New York Press.

Venkatesh, S. A., Celimli, I., Miller, D., Murphy, A., & Turner, B. (2004, February). *Chicago Public Housing transformation: A research report.* New York: Center for Urban Research and Policy, Columbia University.

Wells, A. S., Holmes, J. J., Revilla, A. T., & Atanda, A. K. (2004). How society failed school desegragation policy: Looking past the schools to understand them. *Review of Research in Education, 28,* 47–99.

Wells, A. S., Scott, J. T., Lopez, A., & Holme, J. J. (2005). Charter school reform and the shifting meaning of educational equity: Greater voice and greater inequality? In J. Petrovich & A. S. Wells (Eds.), (2005). *Bringing equity back: Research for a new era in American educational policy* (pp. 219–243). New York: Teachers College Press.

PART II

The Making of the Public Subject

Hopes of Progress and Fears of the Dangerous: Research, Cultural Theses, and Planning Different Human Kinds

THOMAS S. POPKEWITZ

NATIONAL DISCUSSIONS ABOUT SCIENCE and policy in the media have given attention to the selective governmental omission of scientific data from reports that range from environmental impact statements to the "hiding" of statistical data about police profiling.[1] This censorship of science is important in its implications to debates about what constitutes public interests. Other forms of censorship of science have received little or no attention. The censorship in No Child Left Behind, the title for national legislation to improve the quality of schools for the poor and people of color, is an exemplar. That censorship lies in the federal mandate that the methods for studying the effects of school reform be *evidence-based and scientifically based inquiry*. At first glance, the phrase is seductive. Who could be against evidence or science to understand school reforms? But the clarion call for science is not that simple.[2] Since the knowledge of science emerges through its methods (theory and methods are intertwined in the production of knowledge), the practices to establish what counts as "data" carries a strong threat to the public spaces in which the issues and interests in a democracy are clarified.[3]

This chapter examines the censorship of science by asking about the system of reason in which the debates about *evidence-based and scientifically based inquiry* and the public interest occur. My concern is with the grid of institutions, ideas, and technologies that give intelligibility to the prescriptions and critiques of school reforms. That system of reason inscribes science as planning to change the condition of society through changing children. The system of reason about planning change had crossed ideological lines in the social and education sciences by the early decades of the 20th century (Popkewitz, 2005). It is so commonplace today that it often seems that the pedagogical task of research is only about who has the right cultural thesis about how people should live so that science can plan accordingly through theories of learning and development. But this is *not how it works*, to play with the current trope. The planning of people, I argue, is the effect of power rather than a strategy to illuminate power or even to clarify what works. The sciences and policies to plan people produce comparative principles of recognition and difference that qualify and disqualify individuals for participation.

This chapter focuses on the "reason" of planning in the education sciences and its relation to what gets worked on in schooling as the public interest. The first section examines sciences that related to educational reforms at the turn of the 20th century. Different strands of American progressive education were interventions designed to change urban conditions, community interactions, and modes of living. Dewey's pragmatism, Thorndike's behaviorism, and the Chicago School of community sociology, discussed here, overlapped in a trans-Atlantic social Protestant reform movement to address "The Social Question." The Social Question was perceived as how to change the moral disorder produced by the conditions and modes of living of the urban poor, immigrants, and racial groups. The reform sciences embodied twin cultural theses in planning. There were cultural theses embodied in the hope of the sciences to find the right standards for producing the enlightened cosmopolitan citizen of the nation. The hope of the future embodied fears about urban dangers and its dangerous people. The comparative system of reason in the urban sciences recognized the need to include populations previously excluded that simultaneously gave focus to difference. The comparative distinctions and divisions made it impossible for the urban child ever to be "average." The second section focuses on the twin cultural theses of hope and fear in contemporary reforms of school curriculum standards and urban education. The hope of today's future is the cosmopolitan Learning Society and the lifelong learner. The recognition of hope for an inclusive society is evoked with the phrase *all children* that is a continual reiteration in the reforms—"all children will learn." The word *all*, I argue, embodied the unspoken cultural thesis about a mode of living signified as the lifelong learner. The dangers to and the dangerous for the future of society is *the child left behind*, the child who does not have the qualities of "all" children. The characteristics and capabilities of the child left behind and the urban child overlap to produce a particular human kind targeted for the administration in education research, policy, and curriculum standards.

My focus on the systems of reason goes against the grain. While it is fashionable to differentiate theory and practice, this division mystifies and eludes more than it clarifies. The educational sciences are material practices.[4] The principles generated in categories and classifications of educational research enter into school pedagogy, community programs, media, and literature to form the objects of planning who children are and should be. Second, historicizing "educational thought" is a strategy of change that does not inscribe the planning of the people as the principle of action. The diagnosis of the systems of pedagogical reason is to make fragile the causality of present arrangements and thus to open up possibilities other than those of the present. Without examining the systems of recognition and difference inscribed in the planning of research, the particular patterns of power and resistance can overlap and maintain the very rules and standards that undermine inclusive public interests.

The discussion about *the reason* of scientific planning accepts the challenge of those who brought together this volume; that is, to think about how education research can address the pressing educational and social problems of inequity that confront us. The historical argument about planning as the goal of the social and pedagogical sciences is not against planning and science as contributing to the public interest. Just the opposite. Planning is important for seeking rectifications of pressing social problems that range from controlling disease to enabling the state to fulfill is moral obligations to further civil rights and to provide social safety nets. My concern with planning is the dangers of science in *making people* in a democratic society, which I return to in the conclusion. Examining progressive and contemporary education research makes it possible to consider the changing intellectual tools of the education sciences of planning and their comparative systems of recognition and difference. The comparative "reasoning" shapes and fashions not only what is constituted as the objects of research. The systems of recognition and difference in research enter into what is constituted as public interests.[5]

SCHOOLING AS CHANGING SOCIETY BY CHANGING PEOPLE

There is an almost religious belief that the purpose of science is to plan society. That planning is not natural to science, nor is the idea of planning planned.

Planning is embedded in the modern state, which took responsibility for the planning of society through the planning of the citizen whose participation (agency) was necessary for governing. The governing through planning had a particular quality in modern republicanism and its democratic notions. Democracy transformed politics from an activity dependent on a conception of public (as opposed to private) life into a matter of social life and the life of society (Cruikshank, 1999). The founding figures of the American and the French Republics recognized this transformation. Democratic participation was "something that had to be solicited, encouraged, guided, and directed" (Cruickshank, 1999, p. 97). The maintenance of the nation was dependent on making the citizen a self-governing agent in public affairs.

The purpose of modern schooling is to *remake society through remaking the child as the future citizen.* One might say that the problem of social (re)construction of society through schooling was placed at the foot of the child. Jefferson spoke of the need for education to create the citizen who embodied the cosmopolitan principles of the nation. The different progressive pedagogical ideas of John Dewey,

G. Stanley Hall, Edward L. Thorndike, and George Counts in the 20th century provided different visions of planning the child and society; they did not differ in the vision that science can plan the future. The planning embodied cultural theses for planning the modes of life of the future citizen whose actions were to guarantee the values of the Republic. For Dewey, "the future of our civilization" was dependent on a particular style of thinking, "seeing," feeling, and acting through the habits of science. The nation was narrated as embodying the potential of being the most advanced civilization. If this future was to occur, it depended "upon the widening spread and deepening hold of the scientific habit of mind, the problem of problems in our education is therefore to discover how to mature and make effective this scientific habit" (quoted in Reuben, 1996, p. 63). The mode of living that guaranteed civilization in Dewey's pragmatism did not distinguish between universalized Christian values, the general development of ethics in secular society, and the practices of democracy (see, e.g., Popkewitz, 2005).

Thorndike's sciences of education went in a different direction from Dewey but did not reject the notion of planning of the child as a means to plan for a progressive society. Science, for Thorndike, was a method to observe and classify the innate qualities of humans in order to increase the efficiency and stability of the social order. The science of education would eliminate, according to Thorndike, disagreement about the facts of child development.

The making of public interests through planning the child appears in the politically radical thesis of George Counts that education is a central institution in the social reconstruction of society. His famous speech to the Progressive Education Society, "Dare the Schools Build a New Social Order," challenged teachers "to assume unprecedented social responsibilities" as "we live in a difficult and dangerous time" (Counts, 1932/1980, p. 106). The school pedagogy was to inscribe a cosmopolitan reason whose principles provide "an intelligent and determined effort" of schools to "develop the capacities and redeem the souls of common men and women." Teachers "owe it to the young" to give them a better "legacy of spiritual values . . . [so] . . . our children be enabled to find their place in the world, be lifted out of the present morass of moral indifference, be liberated from the senseless struggle for material success, and be challenged to high endeavor and achievement" (Counts, 1932/1980, p. 107).

To bring these different positions together in relation to the history of social and education sciences would follow as: One may want to debate positivism's tenuous life in the sciences, but Comte's phrase about the need to organize/plan society to enable *progress and order* embodied a more general way of thinking about science as serving public interests. The different sciences of childhood and the family, for example, were technologies to stabilize the uncertainties embodied in democracy, and to guide and give direction to change and the public interest through the administration of individuality. Education sciences were to make visible the interior of the child's mind and calculate the principles of thought that enabled the self-governing individual. One pillar of "reason" that gives plausibility to today's No Child Left Behind reforms is the notion of science as a planning technology of society through the planning of the child. The standards of learning and teaching are, as I will later discuss, principles that order, classify, and differentiate who the child is and should be.

THE FEARS AND HOPES ABOUT
WHO IS AND WHO IS NOT CHANGEABLE

The cultural theses in planning for the modern child in progressivism and in today's child left behind is one of a more inclusive society. This planning brings into focus another pillar in the reasoning of planning. In the past and today, the narratives of hope for an inclusive society embody fears. The fears are about the dangers to and the dangerous of society. The dangers and dangerous at the turn of the 20th century were linked to a range of causes, including industrialization and urbanization, that centered attention on the city. The fears, however, were not only about changing urban conditions. The intellectual tools of the social and pedagogical sciences embodied a continuum of values that compared and divided the qualities of those who do not and cannot participate in the progress of society. Whether we like it or not, the twins of hope and fear are embodied in the sciences of planning schooling and its "child."

The inscriptions of fears are inscribed as an abjection, the dual processes of recognition and the production of cultural spaces of difference (Kowalczyk & Popkewitz, in press). A *comparative mode of thought differentiated the poor and racialized groups from the social "body."* Particular populations were targeted as a special problem in the gesture toward the interests of the whole, signified as the hope of democracy. The distinctions and comparison were expressed as The Social Question, a phrase of trans-Atlantic Protestant social and political reformers at the turn of the 20th century. The perceived moral disorder of the city was linked with questions of urbanization, race, and social class (Rodgers, 1998). The new social and educational sciences were a search to reconstruct a moral order within the city and reverse what was perceived as the alcoholism, prostitution, delinquency, "loss" of culture and family ties, and lack of the basic foundations of inner moral restraint.

The urbane Protestant reformers of the city studied the poor as what Jane Addams, a leader of the Settlement House Movement working with urban immigrants and African Americans, called "types and groups." Research was to identify the conditions that produced urban moral decay and work with government for effective reforms to eliminate the evils of the city and purify its citizens of moral transgressions. Surveys, ethnographies, and interviews—tools of the new disciplines of sociology and psychology—mapped the conditions of the city and daily life of the immigrants from southern and eastern Europe, the poor, and "Negroes" (see, e.g., Lasch-Quinn, 1993).

The Planning of the Moral Life of the Urban Family

The urban family was central to social planning. The family was the earliest and most immediate place to apply the paradigm of self-abridgement of culture that linked individuality to collective belonging and "the home" of the nation. The domestic sciences at the turn of the 20th century, for example, ordered and classified modes of living for the urban family. Scientific approaches were to be brought into child rearing, nutritional practices, and the physical care and cleanliness of the home to prevent disease. The rationalizing of the home merged medicine with social science and moral questions to order the life of the family as modern and scientific. The settlement house movements were not only about immigrant families and their cultures. Narratives of African Americans were about the moral degeneration of the family, framed as the consequence of the harsh system of slavery that "obliterated morality, family integrity, social organization and even culture and civilization itself" (Lasch-Quinn, 1993, p.11). The changes in the *habitus* of the urban home also entered into modes of communication and organization of the "cosmopolitan" family of the middle classes to change gendered relations. What middle-class family today does not makes shopping lists and seek to rationally order "healthy" cultural patterns for child rearing? Dewey and Thorndike (and let's not forget Freud) live together in today's home.

Theories of the child, family, community, and teacher education embodied inscriptions to govern the agentive individuals who managed their lives, carried out responsibilities that are not only for self-development and growth but also for standardized public virtues that enable the conferring of that agency. The invention of a range of technologies enabled the family to inscribe the norms of public duty while not destroying its private authority. Rose (1999) refers to these as technologies of *responsibilization.*

> The government of freedom, here, may be analyzed in terms of the deployment of technologies of *responsibilization.* The home was to be transformed into a purified, cleansed, moralized, domestic space. It was to undertake the moral training of its children. It was to domesticate and familiarize the dangerous passions of adults, tearing them away from public vice, the gin palace and the gambling hall, imposing a duty of responsibility to each other, to home, and to children, and a wish to better their own condition. The family, from then on, has a key role in strategies for the government of freedom. It links public objectives for good health and good order of the social body with the desire of individuals for personal health and well-being. A "private" ethic of good health and morality can thus be articulated on to a "public" ethic of social order and public hygiene, yet without destroying the autonomy of the family—indeed by promising to enhance it. (p. 74)

The cultural theses of the family and the child were connected to (and, for some, disconnected from) narratives of collective belonging and "home." That "home" was the nation defined as the American Exceptionalism, perceiving the nation and the citizen as a unique human experiment for moving civilization to-ward the highest ideals of human values and progress. American Exceptionalism embodied the nation as the Chosen people that formed a unique human experi-ment in bringing liberty and freedom. The notion of the "Providential Nation," as Glaude (2000) argues, embodied a racial destiny and difference under a rhetoric of consensus.

American Exceptionalism is embodied in the different trajectories that form progressive movements and the different curriculum projects about the new school (see Kliebard, 1986). The cultural values of a Chosen People circulated in the approaches to the sciences of planning the child. As with the political and so-cial reforms, Exceptionalism in progressive education was an almost evangelical and redemptive faith that education could improve and possibly perfect society through projects of modernizing and creating the modern self (see, e.g., Reese, 2002).

The Exceptionalism of the nation embodied comparison that situated its citi-zens as representing the most advanced civilization and recognized and differenti-ated those who were not located in the space of the Chosen People. A continuum of values positioned others at a less advanced stage of development. The latter groups were recognized in the hope of rescue and inclusion yet differentiated as disqualified from participation. Inscribed in the education science was a recogni-tion of those whose difference prevented progress and the pursuit of happiness, the latter expressed as an aim of schooling by Edward L. Thorndike that juxta-posed the hope of schooling with fears about those whose behaviors posed danger to the future society. One can read much of the 20th-century education sciences as being about changing people whose qualities and characteristics lie outside the norms and values that able the pursuit of happiness. The hope of inclusion in the sciences, however, functioned as a comparative system to inscribe and normalize notions of deviance.

To reorder urban life and the urban individual, the social and educational sci-ences assumed that modern progress destabilized existing hierarchies through reformist agendas (Eisenstadt, 2000; Wittrock, 2000). This destabilizing of tradi-tions looked to the future as an elimination of the immorality carried from the past. The national Exceptionalism would overcome the evils of modernization inherited from the Old World, which inhibited progress. The sciences of urban life and education would tackle the conditions of the city through reconfiguring the values and norms through which families and their children planned their daily life. The urban design of streets and transportation systems and the design of the inner characteristics of individuality were related in a field of practices that merged public interests projected into the Exceptionalism of the nation with the self-governing patterns of the urban child and family.

Planning of the child was a "civilizing" practice. School pedagogy was to re-move old cultural traditions from the patterns of daily life and replace them with other cultural theses.[6] Pedagogical practices were inscription or intellectual tools that linked individuality to collective narratives of national belonging. Dewey's pragmatism was a project to design the child by eliminating past traditions in order to construct a modern self, an individual whose modes of reflection and participation were directed toward actions for the future. Pragmatism was to inscribe a cosmopolitan mode of living positing that "the evil of the wrong kind of development is even greater [as] . . . the power of thought . . . frees us from servile subjection to instinct, appetite, and routines" (Dewey, 1910, p. 23). Hope and fear were also embodied in Thorndike's behaviorism. The scientific basis of teaching was "to produce and to prevent changes in human beings; to preserve and increase the desirable qualities of body, intellect and character and to get rid of the undesirable." This scientific knowledge was to give "the teacher the working of human nature so they can control it through their teaching" (Thorndike, 1906/1962, p. 60).

The removing of past traditions to "civilize," however, is not removing traditions but a process of memorializing and forgetting that reinvents traditions. The veneration of the new and the revising/replacing of the old traveled across social and cultural spheres—from architecture to the schooling of children. "The modern projects itself as the new, the actual, the contemporary. While remembering former modernities, we evoke their pastness to authenticate the newness of 'what's new' and yet filter the contemporary through a gauze of the particles of the past" (Jaguaribe, 2001, p. 333).

School subjects memorialized collective narratives through the hopes of progress and the fears of the dangerous. Music education by the turn of the 20th century, for example, was to mold the population into cosmopolitan, democratic citizen (the hope) and eliminate juvenile delinquency and other evils of society (the fears) through providing for productive use of leisure and self-cultivation (Gustafson, 2005). Listening habits were classified as age-appropriate behavior that inscribed a scale of value from an immature or primitive human development to a fully endowed capacity that corresponded to race and nationality. Singing embodied the child who expressed a home life of industriousness and patriotism set against racial images and narratives of Blacks and immigrants. Music was related to the health of the child, with jazz described in the 1920s as causing disease in young girls and in society as a whole. A growing body of psychoacoustics literature gauged the effects of musical sound and systematized means of observing music's internal "motor" nature in external behaviors such as dance movements, inattentiveness, musical taste, excitation, and foot-tapping. Carl Seashore, a psychology professor, claimed that a full 10% of the children tested for "hereditary" musical talent were unfit for musical appreciation. The child who did not learn the music was "distracted," a determinate category bound to moral and social distinctions about the child as a drifter, a name-caller, a gang-joiner, a juvenile offender, a joke-maker, a potential religious fanatic, having acute emotional stress and an intense interest in sex.

The Urban Community and the Urban Child of Chicago Sociology

The notion of community emerging in the new social sciences and settlement house movements sought to counter the urban moral disorders and threats to American exceptionalism. Much of the work of the Chicago Settlement House Movement, the University of Chicago community sociology, the social psychology of George Herbert Mead, and John Dewey's pragmatism were design projects for planning society through planning the family and the child. The planning joined the hope of a new urban society through rescue and the fears of the urban communities by the cosmopolitan.

Theorizing about community, social settlement house programs, and school curricula embodied a comparative method that differentiated qualities of morality/immorality in modes of living. The patterns of interactions and networks of individuals were domains of a moral community thought "lost" in urbanization and industrialization. The notions of community in American sociology were linked to German social theories about the fall and resurrection of the city as a center of culture, belonging, and home. Community in German theories (*Gemeinschaft*) was the imagined pastoral congregation where a community of believers came closest to nature and God prior to modernity. This pastoral model was destroyed in the abstract relations of society *(Gesellschaft)* as modernity produced alienation. The planning of smaller patterns of communication and interaction through notions of community reinscribed past images in the new urban conditions and people. The sociologist George Herbert Cooley (1909), for example, espoused communication systems reestablishing the family on universal Christian principles that stressed a moral imperative to life and self-sacrifice for the good of the group. Cooley thought that proper socialization in the family and the neighborhood would enable the child to shed the greed, lust, and pride of power that were innate to the infant—and thus mold the child as fit for civilized society.

The school had a particular place in this governing. The pedagogical sciences were devices to intervene in the development of childhood and ultimately to influence what society would be. Dewey's notions of "intelligent action," Cooley's interactions, and Thorndike's behaviorism overlapped to fabricate human kinds for the school to work on. The school as a place of learning and of community was to remake the family through images of Protestant moral values and rational, scientific processes of ordering experience and action.

The early incorporation of teacher education into the university can be read as a project that was to fabricate the cosmopolitanism of the urban teacher. Professionalization projects brought teachers into university courses at the turn of the 20th century. Teacher education embodied fears of the urban teachers' Old World traditions in which values and beliefs were tied to ethnicity and radical socialist ideas brought from Europe. University education was to reshape and fashion allegiances as an American cosmopolitanism (Murphy, 1990). The cosmopolitanism of the professionalization of the teacher was seen as a "civilizing" practice that redesigns lines of authority in school administration, weeds out those of "less" desirable ethnic and social origins, and instills a sense of loyalty to the school principal, superintendent, and educational professorate (Murphy, 1990). Thorndike likened schooling to the building of a house's foundation. Teacher education was to make the teacher into the builder who knows "how to erect a frame, how to lay a floor and the like with reference to what is to be built; the teacher should often study how to utilize inborn tendencies, how to form habits, how to develop interests and the like with reference to what changes in intellect and character are to be made" (Thorndike & Woodworth, 1901/1962, p. 57).

The two are inseparable historically as context and discourses overlap.

The comparative differentiating and distinguishing of cultural theses is historically at the "heart" of a science associated with the "consciousness" of modernity. The subject of the planning of society through the planning of individuality inscribes comparison as a consciousness of programs in the public interest. The categories of behavior, community, and problem solving were ordering devices that shaped the objects of observation and scrutiny. Those objects of recognition and difference embodied the hope and fear as comparative humankinds. The categories of the social and psychological sciences circulated as the problems to be worked on to plan the school in the name of a common good. Programs, books, self-help literature, and magazines were produced to enable the design of schools as communities—to develop children's learning and to enable the family to provide a healthy environment for children's growth. While today's public and professional debates about *evidence-based and scientifically based inquiry* are made in the name of the public interests, the comparative system of classifying, recognizing, and dividing still remain to undermine the inclusive aims at the outset.

CONTEMPORARY CURRICULUM STANDARDS, NO CHILD LEFT BEHIND, AND URBAN EDUCATION: DIVIDING DIFFERENT HUMAN KINDS

Like progressive education, major reform research programs about curriculum standards reforms,[7] No Child Left Behind, and urban education inscribe comparative systems of reasoning in the planning of society through the planning of the child. The hope of inclusion embodies a mode of life that I call the unfinished cosmopolitan, called in research the *lifelong learner*. To rescue the child left behind is to rescue that child whose characteristics, I argue below, are those of the "urban" child. The policies and reform research embody a continuum of values through the juxtaposition of the phrase that instruction should be equal in "all children learning" with the child left behind. The word *all* functions to inscribe unspoken standards about a particular child (the lifelong learner) that differentiates and distinguishes the qualities of the child left behind. In the following section, I will pursue how the "reason" of policy and research produces that child as a particular human kind that does not "fit" the standards that are to serve as inclusive.

Standards as Cultural Theses About The Unfinished Cosmopolitan

Curriculum standards, discussions of what works, and *evidence-based and scientifically based inquiry* are not merely about whether or not to apply standards. The distinctions and categories about the child and school subjects in curriculum reforms and research are inscriptions of cultural theses about who the child is and should be. To consider this politics of standards in the reform curriculum, it is helpful to consider standards as inventions to develop the capacity of the state to have direct knowledge and access to what was previously opaque. There is just so far that one can compare and administer goods and people when measurement means talking about *a hand, a foot, a cartload, basketful, handful,* or *within earshot*. Reliable means of enumerating and locating its population; gauging wealth; and mapping land, resources and settlements were produced in order to intervene and regulate the realm. Educational standards are analogous to creating a uniform system of taxes and the development of uniform measurements.

The centralizing of measurement to provide standards, oddly enough, was important to Enlightenment notions of the equitable republic. The installing of the metric system was to create an equal citizen. The Encyclopedists writing immediately prior to French Revolution, for example, saw the metric system as an intellectually important instrument to make France "revenue-rich, militarily potent, and *easily administered"* (Scott, 1998, p.32). If the citizen did not have equal rights in relation to measurements, then it was assumed that the citizen might also have unequal rights in law. Inconsistency among measurements, institutions, inheritance laws, taxation, and market regulations was seen as the greatest obstacle to making a single people. The measurement standards were at once a means of administrative centralization, commercial reform, and cultural formation.

Current debates about school standards fit into this notion of *easily administered* citizens. Standards of curriculum are brought into the public arena as ensuring that schools serve diverse social interests by being equal for *all* children (*all* children learn) and with *no child left behind*. The phrases are seductive because they generalize public commitments to address and redress the conditions produced by poverty, discrimination, and school failures. Ignored in the focus on outcomes are the distinctions and differentiations mobilized to order the problems of educational research and through which public interests are given concrete form. Standards to measure and compare human kinds, as in the past, embody comparative systems of recognition and difference that I discussed earlier as a double narrative of hope and fear.

The comparative quality is embodied in the juxtaposition of expressions that all children are to learn and that *no child is left behind*. The two phrases stand in relation to each other as a continuum of values that normalize the qualities and characteristics of the child. The phrase *all children* is a gesture toward an equal system. The *all* embodies unspoken cultural theses about a universalized child for whom the school plans to secure a future of progress and individual happiness. I say unspoken because the *all* appears in the standards literature and standards reform research as if everyone "knows" who that child is. There is an anthropological "Other" child encountered in the reform literatures and sciences of pedagogy. That child is comparatively spoken about as the child left behind, targeted for intervention for not being the universalized child. The "all children" and the child left behind are two distinct human kinds in the planning of schooling.

The cultural thesis of *all* children embodies a human kind that I have spoken about elsewhere as *the unfinished cosmopolitan* (Popkewitz, 2004). Across European Union and U.S. policy, curriculum planning and research involves the social reconstruction of society through making the child as a cosmopolitan lifelong learner. The lifelong learner lives in the future—"The Information Society" and "The Learning Society" (Lawn, 2003; Popkewitz, Olsson, & Petersson, in press). Hargreaves (2003), for example, rejects the materialism and marketization of contemporary neoliberal reform in favor of school reforms to prepare for the future of a knowledge society that "is really a learning society . . . [that] process(es) information and knowledge in ways that maximize learning, stimulate ingenuity and invention and develop the capacity to initiate and cope with change" (p. xviii). The child inhabits the Learning Society with "a cosmopolitan identity which shows tolerance of race and gender differences, genuine curiosity toward and willingness to learn from other cultures, and responsibility toward excluded groups within and beyond one's society" (Hargreaves, 2003, p. xix). The lifelong learner's agency is distinguished as an individual's voice that gives self-actualization, freedom, and empowerment that brings the ethical and moral reconstruction.

What are the qualities of life in the recognition of "all children"? Across the standards literature in school subjects is the *unfinished cosmopolitan* who problem-solves and works collaboratively in communities (see, e.g., Popkewitz & Gustafson, 2002). The problem solving is a thesis about an autonomous and responsible mode of living that involves continuous decision making or problem solving. The problem-solver is a particular kind of human whose rules and standards for participation are calculated and given an order in research that, for example, speaks about notions of tentativeness and attentiveness, or processes that entail "risk taking," and "guess and check" (Popkewitz, 2004).

Whereas schools in the past sought to replace the home as the primary site of socialization, today's reforms bring the parent into the school as one of the many lifelong learners of the Learning Society (Popkewitz, 2003).[8] The unfinished cosmopolitan seems to cross national boundaries as an imagined community of a "Knowledge" or "Learning Society" in the continual pursuit of knowledge and innovation. Descriptions of the lifelong learners are of an entrepreneurial individual that appears to give value to economic values and neoliberal notions of market.

But the entrepreneurial individual circulates in the reforms as a cultural register about a mode of living, not as one of economics. The mode of living embodies a belonging and "home" in multiple communities where choice is directed to problem-solving and continuous innovation. Learning psychologies and communication and interactional theories form connections of practices that lie inside of the imagined communities and outside of history.

As in Progressive reforms, the pedagogical notions of community connect the scope and aspirations of public powers with the personal and subjective capacities of individuals. At one level are narratives about problem solving and community as linking *all* individuals to social or economic progress and the revitalization of democracy. The stories of the problem solving child, for example, are about the mode of life of an individual faced with constant changes in society. In a statement resonating across American school subject reforms, the National Council of Teachers of Mathematics' (2000) model for curriculum standards reform argues that the student needs to be prepared for the future where change is "a ubiquitous feature of contemporary life, so learning with understanding is essential to enable students to use what they learn to solve the new kinds of problems they will inevitably face in the future" (pp. 20–21).

The classroom community is thought of as a "participation structure" concerned with creating fluid identities. Research projects focus on communication patterns that mediate the "interactions between intervention and setting" (Design-Based Research Collective, 2003, p. 5). The "community of learners" mediates identity through the specific communication systems of the classroom. Children are to live as autonomous learners continuously involved in self-improvement and ready for uncertainties through working actively in communities of learning (see, e.g., National Council for Teachers of Mathematics, 2000).

Whatever the merits of problem solving and community, the notions are never merely descriptive of some natural reasoning of the child, something natural to the child that the research merely recoups, or without systems of values that relate individuality to collective belonging. "Problem solving" and community are distinctions that demarcate, preserve, and make administrable what are perceived as the salient features of a child's inner characteristics and capabilities.

The notion of problem solving and community embody a particular type of planning of *the self*. The project of life is to design one's biography such that there is movement from one social sphere to another, as if life were a planning workshop that had a value in and of itself. Action is a continual flow of problem solving to design not only what will be done but also the future of who that person will be. The agency of the individual is directed to problem solving to chase desire. This desire lies in the infinite choices that one can make in the pursuit of continuous innovation. The only thing that is not a choice is the choice of choosing. The "ubiquitous" uncertainty of the future that mathematics education tames has less to do with learning the disciplinary norms of mathematics than with the inscription of a particular cultural thesis about life as planning one's future of continuous innovation and choice through a self-improvement process of problem solving (Popkewitz, 2004).

Earlier 20th-century classrooms as a place of socialization where the child internalized preestablished collective universal norms of identity are today a re-designed space of living. The location of responsibility is no longer traversed through the range of social practices directed toward a single public sphere—the social. Responsibility is located in diverse, autonomous, and plural communities that constitute the common good. It is a mode of life that shapes individual empowerment as bound to perpetually constructing one's own practice in "communities" of learning. The empowerment of freedom is talked about as if there are no enclosures. Yet there was the expression of a fatalism in a series of interviews of teachers, administrators, and government official that make resistance less possible (see Lindblad & Popkewitz, 2004). That fatalism is spoken about as an inevitable element in globalism, whose ubiquitous features make it impossible for the individual, to quote a French high school textbook, "to escape the flux of change" (Soysal, Bertiloot, & Mannitz, 2005, pp. 24–25). The above studies create an irony as the notions of community and problem solving in curriculum reforms embody talk about empowerment that overlaps with the feelings of fatalism. The autonomous self that innovates in the communities of learning elude the internments and enclosures of historicity that shape and fashion agency, freedom, and participation.

Further, there is a paradox of reducing spheres of agency through the boundaries inscribed in the participatory structures of problem solving and community in school standards reforms and research. This is evident in studies of school textbooks. Science education textbooks across different nations, for example, have changes over a period of time to give students greater opportunities for participation. That flexibility and participation in learning occurs with more and more of the world represented by the iconic images of the expertise of science (McEneaney, 2003). Thus, while there is greater participation of the student, that participation occurs in narrow arenas of choice as the expertise of science is consecrated as the authoritative knowledge for daily life.

Standards as Human Kinds:
Cultural Theses About the Urban Child Left Behind

The cultural thesis embodied in *all* children *makes possible the differentiation of particular segments of the population as a special problem. The "all" is a rhetorical strategy that unites all parts of the social whole*, The Learning Society. The child left behind is recognized as needing to be included in the Learning Society, yet different. Professional curriculum standards policies and research, for example, recognize members of population groups of the children left behind as different from "all children," occupying a double space.[9] The child left behind exists in a social space of social disintegration (the loss of "civilization") and of moral degeneration that coexists with the hope of rescue and redemption through the proper planning. The contemporary *child left behind* is as urban as was the child of the Social Question of progressive reform movements. School planning to change the conditions of urban life retains comparative practices to change people. And the sciences and state policies in today's reforms are to correct the school conditions to work toward an equitable and just society. The child left behind in reforms, however, is not merely a continuation of the past. Today's pedagogical hope is to produce the unfinished cosmopolitan child who acts with republican ideals and a democratic mode of living.[10] The hope of inclusion coexists with fears of the dangers and dangerous, signified as the child left behind.

The child left behind and the urban child have an overlapping territory of membership. The qualities of the urban child were expressed comparatively in an ethnographic study of urban and rural schools (Popkewitz, 1998). The categories of recognition and difference for the urban and rural child were psychologically and sociologically the same. For the practical purposes of planning, the children of the urban and rural schools were "urban."

What were these categories of recognition and difference? Psychological, social, and pedagogical categories overlap as distinctions of the child acted on in pedagogical interventions. Psychological dangers of low self-esteem and a poor self-concept give expression to the inner qualities of the urban verses the nonurban child. The comparative norms of the latter silently traverse the reform and research texts as unspoken distinctions about the dispositions and sensitivities lacking in the child left behind.

The urban teachers, for example, talked about urban children as having "street-wise" intelligence. The word signified a way of thinking and acting that was different from an unspoken mode of acting with "intelligence." The deployment of street-wise intelligence is a strategy to recognize and give equal value to the mode of living of the urban child (Popkewitz, 1998). The distinction of street-wise intelligence operates practically to give pedagogical direction to how teachers can work toward the public interest that *all children learn*. The street-wise intelligence embodied a distinction of teachers' hope and faith that the innate potential of the child can be drawn out by school reforms to rectify the qualities of the child that prevent success. Street-wise intelligence is also a comparative distinction between the urban child, who learns by doing, and the learning of others, who manipulate abstract ideas.

The psychological qualities of the urbanness of the child left behind do not stand alone but are reassembled with social categories about, for example, dysfunctional families, single-parent households, juvenile delinquency, and homes without books to read. A determinate category of the urban child is formed as the child "who live[s] in poverty, students who are not native speakers of English, students with disabilities, females, and many nonwhite students [who] have traditionally been far more likely than their counterparts in other demographic groups to be victims of low expectations" (National Council of Teachers of Mathematics, 2000, p. 13). The assembly of psychological and social characteristics of the "urban" child has little to do with geographical place. It is a cultural thesis. Children who live in the high-rise apartments and brownstones of American cities are not classified in the space of urban education. The children of the brownstone appear as "urbane" and cosmopolitan, not "urban." And the *urban* child is not only of the city but is also assigned to particular children in suburban and rural schools who occupy that cultural space (Popkewitz, 1998).

The distinctions are not only of the classroom. They circulate in policy statements about school standards as well as international reporting about the conditions of education. Whereas statistical reporting in the 1960s focused on distinctions of social stratification, finer and finer distinctions about the socially excluded in educational reporting have developed that follow along those the teachers deployed (Lindblad & Popkewitz, 2002). *Who said that research does not get into the classroom?*

"Urban" is a particular assembly of cultural categories that positions the poor and racialized population for recognition and differentiation. The distinctions and differentiations that make for the "Other" in schooling can be related to the work of sociologist Pierre Bourdieu. Bourdieu's (1979/1984) study has enabled us to think of the production of differences through differential systems of recognition and distinctions that divide and organize people's participation. For example, Bourdieu examined the systems of recognition and distinctions among French primary teachers, secondary teachers, professionals, and engineers in how they "appreciated" art, organized their homes with furniture and art, as well as made choices about food, movies, and education. These patterns of distinctions and appreciations were different from, for example, those of office workers and small-shop salespeople. Bourdieu (1989/1996) also explored how the school system consecrates a social nobility through performing a series of cognitive and evaluative operations that realize social divisions. To use Bourdieu's study, distinctions between the child who problem-solves and the urban children who learn by doing embody an unequal playing field built on different characteristics and capabilities of the individual. *The child left behind is one whose difference is never "of the average."*

THE HOPED-FOR AND THE DANGEROUS: CONCLUDING THOUGHTS ON SCIENCE AS A COMMITMENT TO PUBLIC INTERESTS

This chapter began with a notion of censorship that focused on systems of reason in which research and policy practices are framed. My interest in censorship, however, focused on the productive qualities in of the system of reasoning in generating principles of reflection, action, and differentiation. Embedded in the planning of the human sciences are cultural theses about modes of living whose effects are to divide. This politics of knowledge brings me to the initial call for this volume.

How does the argument tackle the relation of the public interest and research?

First, the systems of reason in school reform research are historical practices that have a double effect. The efforts of reforms and social science to change the condition of people change people. That changing of people embodies comparative distinctions and a continuum of values. This was evident in the early progressive reform research to respond to the Social Question of the urban child and family and its mutations that circulate in No Child Left Behind. The reform gestures about "all children" are intended to unite and unify the whole in general values that express public interests. The concrete strategies to search for a unified society, however, bring to the fore comparative distinctions that embody the twins of hope of the cosmopolitan and fear of different human kinds who embody dangerous modes of life. Research and policy overlap in their double systems of recognition of and differentiation about the dangers and dangerous to an imagined unified whole.

Second is the question of whether science as the planning of people is in the public interest. In general, it is clear that planning in a democratic society is an important part of the state's moral and economic obligations to its citizens. There would be no national civil rights agenda or control of disease without it. My question, however, is more specific. Does science as an expertise of planning people work in the public interest? While it seems natural and "right" that science can provide efficient and effective paths to a more democratic and just society, this stance has little historical justification and in fact can be politically dangerous, if not always bad. Democracy is not efficient; but where planning is appropriate to promote collective interests, it should reside in democratic processes, not in the prophesies and prophets of science. The objects of planning and intervention in the educational sciences are not naturally there for researchers to "use" but effects of power that continually need to be problematized. After a hundred years of such planning, perhaps it is time to rethink planning as part of what makes science relevant to change and its commitments to democracy and the public interest.

Third, research needs to consider how particular patterns of power and resistance can act mutually, if unwittingly, to reinforce principles that differentiate and divide through its systems of reason—what I spoke about throughout this chapter as the grid of institutions, ideas, and technologies of research that give intelligibility to the prescriptions and critiques of school reforms. This caution directs attention to the expertise of research as not merely an epiphenomenon that directs attention to how ideas and reason are used to further interests and "forces" in society. Knowledge is a constitutive and productive element in the making of worlds. The argument of this chapter is that the problem of public interest in science is to make visible the objects of representation and distinctions. Critical race, postcolonial, and feminist scholarship have continually directed attention "to learn to what extent the effort to think one's own history can free thought from what it silently thinks, and so enable it to think differently" (Foucault,1978, p. 9).

To consider research as embedded in assemblies of ideas, institutions, and technologies that help to bring social relations into being does not eliminate the commitments to act. Rather it is to address the politics of schooling that takes planning as a given project of change. Contemporary critiques of reform policy tend to focus on who benefits or is handicapped as a consequence of reforms. Class, gender, and racial implications of the standards reform movement are examples. Such critiques are necessary to bring attention to groups omitted or prevented from public conversations and the allocation of values in a democracy. This focus on the subjects of participation, while necessary, is not sufficient without taking into account the systems of reason through which the objects of recognition and difference in planning people are constructed as the subjects of policy and research.

Making fragile the causality of history in the making of "the self" is a theory of change. It avoids the inscription of subject as the object of planning by focusing on the inscription tools through which the objects of scrutiny and planning are produced. The folk wisdom of the university today is that researchers need to "talk" to policymakers, teachers, and communities. I am not against such talk but question the politics of the very distinctions of that talk, which divides "ideas," "texts," and discourse from the "real" world of teachers' practice and experience. This thinking about knowledge as distinct from practice functions as what Gaston Bachelard called epistemological obstacles that hide and obscure how practices are produced as effects of power. "Practice" is not an unmediated reality. Practice is something felt, seen, thought about, and acted on through a historical assembly of ideas, institutions, and events. Joan Scott (1992), a feminist historian, has argued that the politics of change need to "*attend to the historical processes that, through discourse, position subjects and produce [our] experience* (pp. 25–26). The distinction between nominalist (discourse, text) and realist (contexts) needs to be unthought in the practices of social and education sciences and the public interests. The bifurcated world distances, divide, erases, and hides how expert knowledge works dialectically in forming of social relations. Marx, among others, understood that words are not merely words or epiphenomena but productive, material elements in the daily construction of who "we" are and who is disqualified from being that "we." The realists of education are the least realist.

NOTES

1. As I wrote different drafts, people were generous with their time to respond in a way that continually pushed my thinking about what was said and not said. Anthony Brown, Kefferlyn Brown, Carl Grant, Tuula Gordon, Ruth Gustafson, Jamie Kowalczyk, Julie Mc-

Cloud, Amy Sloane, and the Wednesday Group seminar were among the people gracious in their time. I realize that with all this help there should be no faults in what follows. That is not the case and makes obvious that the limitations of the arguments are clearly mine.

2. I am using science in its general sense of asking questions and seeking disciplined and systematic methods to answers to these questions, not in the narrow utilitarian, positivist, or empiricism senses of science. Regarding the question of the politics of science embodied in current national reforms, see, for example, St. Pierre (2004).

3. Democracy and participation are *topoi*, terms that everyone seems to know and that need no author. While not rejecting the terms as dispositions in formulating public interests, my strategy is to examine the concrete practices through which the objects of public interest are constructed for intervention and administration.

4. I use materiality not to "see" the social and educational sciences as causal actors but to give attention to a particular expertise in the production of the objects of reflection and participation formed through assemblies of ideas, institutions, and technologies.

5. I use the word *constituted* and later will use the word *concretely* advisedly. The words are used to direct attention to the systems of recognition and difference through which research makes the child visible and administrable. My argument is that the practices of schooling and research generate principles through which notions of the public good are given a specificity in the pedagogical administration of the child. This is not to say they produce what is taken abstractly as public good or they serve as a causal agent. While current debates continually invoke notions of equity, justice, democracy, and empowerment, for example, what is at issue is not the commitment to these terms but the particular systems of reason that orders, differentiates, and divides the practices of reflection and participation. Having said this, it is odd to me that most education research leaves the productive qualities of school knowledge unscrutinized by assuming that the systems of reason are merely a reflection or epiphenomenon of some superstructure or ideology.

6. There was debate about what this shedding of the past in remaking the present. Some reformers sought an Americanization process that homogenized different populations through Old World traditions. Others, like Dewey, saw value in using certain elements of what immigrants, for example, brought as cultural dispositions as adding and enriching American values. The hyphenation of this American identity (e.g., Italian-American, Polish-American) is an exemplar of the latter, although the linguistic positioning privileges what follows the hyphen. At the same time, notions of difference circulated through, for example, eugenics that inscribed racialized and gendered distinctions about who could and could not be Americanized.

7. I find that the general contemporary argument for or against standards makes sense if one thinks of schooling in the centralized/decentralized states of the United States. State educational ministries around the world establish standards as a prerequisite of the state's obligations to scrutinize social interests and the public interest. But the differences in state traditions does not remove the question of what constitutes standards.

8. The literature about the rationalization of the home still exists, only now spoken about in a different register than the domestic sciences. The home is *pedagogicalized*; that is, the standards and rules of schooling move into the home more directly through such research about parents reading to their child and making the home a surrogate classroom. This is discussed in Popkewitz (2003), and cross-nationally in Popkewitz, Olsson, and Petersson (in press).

9. I draw on two particular studies of the "urban" child in making this observation; see, for example, Popkewitz (1998) and Lindblad and Popkewitz (2004).

10. The hope of the reform of schooling is to push thinking outside comparative distinctions about the dangers in multicultural education and culturally relevant pedagogy (see., e.g., Grant & Sleeter, 2003; Ladson-Billings, 2001).

REFERENCES

Bourdieu, P. (1984). *Distinction: A social critique of the judgment of taste* (R. Nice, Trans.). Cambridge, MA: Harvard University Press. (Original work published 1979)

Bourdieu, P. (1996). *The state nobility: Elite schools in the field of power* (L. C. Clough, Trans.). Stanford, CA: Stanford University Press. (Original work published 1989)

Cooley, C. (1909). *Social organization; A study of the larger mind.* New York: Charles Scribner's Sons.

Counts, G. S. (1980). Dare the school build a new social order? In L. Dennis & W. Eaton (Eds.), *William George S. Counts: Educator for a new age* (pp. 98–107). Carbondale, IL: Southern Illinois University Press. (Original work published 1932)

Cruikshank, B. (1999). *The will to empower: Democratic citizens and other subjects.* Ithaca, NY: Cornell University Press.

Design-Based Research Collective. (2003). Designed-based research: An emerging paradigm for educational inquiry. *Educational Researcher, 32*(2), 5–8.

Dewey, D. (1910). *How we think.* Boston: D.C. Heath.

Eisenstadt, S. N. (2000). Multiple modernities. *Daedalus, 129*(1), 1–29.

Foucault M. (1978). *History of sexuality: The use of pleasure* (R. Hurley, Trans.). New York: Pantheon Books. (Original work published 1976)

Glaude, E., Jr. (2000). *Exodus! Religion, race, and nation in early nineteenth-century Black America.* Chicago: University of Chicago Press.

Grant, C., & Sleeter, C. (2003). *Making choices for multicultural education: Five approaches to race, class and gender* (4th ed.). New York: Wiley.

Gustafson, R. (2005). *Merry throngs and street gangs: The fabrication of Whiteness and the worthy citizen in early vocal instruction and music appreciation, 1830–1930.* Unpublished doctoral dissertation, University of Wisconsin–Madison.

Hargreaves, A. (2003). *Teaching in the knowledge society: Education in the age of insecurity.* Maindenhead, UK: Open University Press.

Jaguaribe, B. (2001). Modernist ruins: National narratives and architectural forms. In D. P. Gaonkar (Ed.), *Alternative modernities* (pp. 327–349). Durham, NC: Duke University Press.

Kliebard, H. (1986). *Struggle for the American curriculum.* London: Routledge & Kegan Paul.

Kowalczyk, J., & Popkewitz, T. (in press). Multiculturalism, recognition and abjection: (Re)-mapping Italian identity *Policy Futures in Education.*

Ladson-Billings, G. (2001). *Crossing over to Canaan: The journey of new teachers in diverse classrooms.* San Francisco: Jossey-Bass.

Lasch-Quinn, E. (1993). *Black neighbors. Race and the limits of reform in the American settlement house movement, 1890–1945.* Chapel Hill: The University of North Carolina Press.

Lawn, M. (2003). The "usefulness" of learning: The struggle over governance, meaning, and the European education space. *Discourse, 24*(3), 325–336.

Lindblad, S., & Popkewitz, T. (Eds.). (2002). *Statistical information and systems of reason on education and social inclusion and exclusion in international and national contexts. A report from the EGSIE project* (Uppsala Reports on Education, No. 38). Uppsala University, Sweden: Department of Education.

Lindblad. S., & Popkewitz, T. (2004). Educational restructuring: Governance in the narratives of progress and denials. In S. Lindblad & T. Popkewitz (Eds.), *Controversies in educational restructuring: International perspectives on contexts, consequences and implications* (pp. 69–96). Greenwich, CT: Information Age Publishing.

McEneaney, E. (2003). Elements of a contemporary primary school science. In G. S. Drori, J. W. Meyer, F. O. Ramirez, & E. Schofer (Eds.), *Science in the modern world polity: Institutionalization and globalization* (pp. 136–154). Stanford, CA: Stanford University Press.

Murphy, M. (1990). *Blackboard unions: The AFT & the NEA 1900–1980.* Ithaca, NY: Cornell University Press.

National Council for Teachers of Mathematics. (2000). *Principles and standards for school mathematics.* Reston, VA: Author.

Popkewitz, T. (1998). *Struggling for the soul: The politics of education and the construction of the teacher.* New York: Teachers College Press.

Popkewitz, T. (2003). Governing the child and pedagogicalization of the parent: A history of the present. In M. Bloch, K. Holmlund, I. Moqvist, & T. Popkewitz (Eds.), *Governing children, families and education. Restructuring the welfare state* (pp. 35–62). New York: PalgraveMacmillan Press.

Popkewitz, T. (2004). The alchemy of the mathematics curriculum: Inscriptions and the fabrication of the child. *American Educational Research Journal, 41*(4), 3–34.

Popkewitz, T. (Ed.). (2005). Inventing the modern self and John Dewey: Modernities and the traveling of pragmatism in education. New York: PalgraveMacmillan Press.

Popkewitz, T., & Gustafson, R. (2002). The alchemy of pedagogy and social inclusion/exclusion *Philosophy of Music Education Review, 10*(2), 80–91.

Popkewitz, T., Olsson, U., & Petersson, K. (in press). The learning society, the unfinished cosmopolitan, and governing education, public health and crime prevention at the beginning of the twenty-first century. *Educational Philosophy and Theory.*

Reese, W. (2002). *Power and the promise of school reform: Grassroots movements during the Progressive era.* New York: Teachers College Press.

Reuben, J. (1996). *The making of the modern university: Intellectual transformations and the marginalization of morality.* Chicago: University of Chicago Press.

Rodgers, D. (1998). *Atlantic crossings. Social politics in a progressive age.* Cambridge, MA: The Belknap Press of Harvard University.

Rose, N. (1999). *Powers of freedom: Reframing political thought.* Cambridge, UK: Cambridge University Press.

Scott, J. (1991). The evidence of experience. *Critical Inquiry, 17,* 773–797.

Scott, J. (1992). The evidence of experience. In J. Butler & J. Scott (Eds.), *Feminists theorize the political* (pp. 22–40). New York: Routledge.

Scott, J. (1998). *Seeing like a state: How certain schemes to improve the human condition have failed.* New Haven, CT: Yale University Press.

Soysal, Y., Bertiloot, T., & Mannitz, S. (2005). Projections of identity in French and German history and civics textbooks. In H. Schissler & Y. Soysal (Eds.), *The nation, Europe, and the world. Textbooks and curricula in transition* (pp. 13–34). New York: Berghahn Books.

St. Pierre, E. (2004). Refusing alternatives: A science of contestation. *Qualitative Inquiry, 10*(1), 130–139.

Thorndike, E. L. (1962). Principles of teaching. In G. M. Joncich (Ed.), *Psychology and the science of education. Selected writings of Edward L. Thorndike* (pp. 55–69). New York: Bureau of Publications, Teachers College, Columbia University. (Original work published 1906)

Thorndike, E. L., & Woodworth, R. S. (1962). Education as science. In G. M. Joncich (Ed.), *Psychology and the science of education. Selected writings of Edward L. Thorndike* (pp. 48–69). New York: Bureau of Publications, Teachers College, Columbia University (Original work published 1901)

Wittrock, B. (2000). Modernity: One, none, or many? European origins and modernity as a global condition. *Daedalus, 29*(1), 31–60.

Democracy, Diversity, and Social Justice: Educating Citizens for the Public Interest in a Global Age[1]

JAMES A. BANKS

A THOUGHTFUL CITIZENRY that believes in democratic ideals and is willing and able to participate in the civic life of the nation is essential for the creation and survival of a democratic society. Reflective and active democratic citizens make decisions and take action in the *public interest*, which Ladson-Billings and Tate (2005) define as actions and decisions that "further democracy, democratic practices, and social justice." To educate citizens so that they will make decisions and take actions in the public interest, the schools must promote political, economic, and cultural democracy. Historically, schools in nation-states throughout the world have eschewed cultural democracy and emphasized cultural assimilation and the eradication of the cultures and languages of students from diverse racial, ethnic, language, and religious groups (Banks, 2004a).

CHALLENGES TO THE ASSIMILATIONIST NOTION OF CITIZENSHIP

An assimilationist conception of citizenship education existed in most of the Western democratic nation-states prior to the rise of the ethnic revitalization movements of the 1960s and 1970s. A major goal of citizenship education in these nations was to create nation-states in which all groups shared one dominant mainstream culture. It was assumed that ethnic and immigrant groups had to forsake their original cultures in order to fully participate in the nation-state (Patterson, 1977).

The ethnic revitalization movements of the 1960s and 1970s strongly challenged the assimilationist conception of citizenship education. These movements, triggered by the civil rights movement in the United States, echoed throughout the world. French and Indians in Canada, West Indians and Asians in Britain, Indonesians and Surinamese in the Netherlands, and Aborigines in Australia joined the series of ethnic movements, expressed their feelings of marginalization, and worked to make the institutions within their nation-states responsive to their economic, political, and cultural needs.

Indigenous peoples and ethnic groups within the various Western nations—such as American Indians in the United States, Aborigines in Australia, Maori in New Zealand, African Caribbeans in the United Kingdom, and Moluccans in the Netherlands—want their histories and cultures to be reflected in their national cultures and in the school, college, and university curricula (Eldering & Kloprogge, 1989; Gillborn, 1990; Smith, 1999). Multicultural education was developed, in part, to respond to the concerns of ethnic, racial, and cultural groups that feel marginalized within their nation-states (Banks & Banks, 2004).

The right of ethnic and cultural minorities to maintain important aspects of their cultures and languages has been supported by philosophers and educators since the first decades of the 1900s. Drachsler (1920) and Kallen (1924)—of immigrant backgrounds themselves—argued that the Southern, Central, and East European immigrants who were entering the United States in large numbers had a right to retain parts of their cultures and languages while enjoying full citizenship rights. Cultural democracy, argued Drachsler, is an essential component of a political democracy.

Woodson (1933/1977) made a case for cultural democracy when he argued that a curriculum for African American students should reflect their history and culture and harshly criticized the absence of Black history in the curriculum. He stated that schools, colleges, and universities were "mis-educating" Black students because they were not teaching them about African cultures and civilizations. Ramírez and Castañeda (1974) maintained that cultural democracy requires that teaching methods used in the schools reflect the learning characteristics of Mexican American students as well as help them become bicognitive in their learning styles and characteristics.

Canadian political theorist Kymlicka (1995) and U.S. anthropologist Rosaldo (1997), make arguments today that echo those made by Drachsler (1920), Kallen (1924), and Woodson (1933/1977) in the first decades of the 1900s. Both Kymlicka and Rosaldo contend that immigrant and ethnic groups should be able to participate fully in the national civic culture while maintaining aspects of their cultures and that the dominant culture of the nation-state should reflect their experiences and cultures. Kymlicka calls this concept "multicultural citizenship"; Rosaldo refers to it as "cultural citizenship."

In order for all citizens in U.S. society to experience political, economic, and cultural democracy—and to make decisions and take actions in the public interest—teachers need to have the knowledge, skills, and attitudes to create democratic classrooms and schools and to implement a *culturally relevant* (Ladson-Billings,

1994) or *responsive* curriculum (Gay, 2000). Research indicates that when teachers use knowledge about the social and cultural context of their students when planning and implementing instruction, the academic achievement of students can increase (Au, 1980; Lee, 1995; Philips, 1972; Piestrup, 1973).

To support the goals of a political and cultural democracy and enhance the academic achievement of all students, teachers can gain insights from the research on culturally responsive teaching. This research provides information about the social contexts and purposes of education, the influence of culture on learning and schooling, and culturally responsive curricula, pedagogy, and assessment (Gay, 2000; Ladson-Billings, 1994).

Increasing Diversity in the World

There is increasing diversity as well as increasing recognition of diversity in nation-states throughout the world. After World War II large numbers of people emigrated from former colonies in Asia, Africa, and the West Indies to the United Kingdom to improve their economic status. Since the late 1960s, thousands of people from diverse language, cultural, racial, and religious groups have immigrated to nations such as Germany, France, and the Netherlands. Australia and Canada have also experienced increased diversity caused by immigrant groups seeking better economic opportunities.

Nations that traditionally have been thought to be homogeneous, such as Japan and Sweden, now acknowledge their diversity. Although the population of the United States has been diverse since the founding period, its ethnic composition has changed dramatically since 1965, when the Immigration Reform Act was passed. In the late 19th and early 20th centuries, most immigrants to the United States came from Europe. Today, most come from Asia and Latin America. A significant number also come from the West Indies and Africa. The United States is now experiencing its largest influx of immigrants since the late 19th and early 20th centuries (Suárez-Orozco, Suárez-Orozco, & Quin, 2005). The U.S. Census projects that ethnic groups of color—or ethnic minorities—will increase from 28% of the nation's population today to 50% in 2050 (U.S. Census Bureau, 2000).

Racial, cultural, ethnic, language, and religious diversity is also increasing in schools throughout the Western world, including the United States (Banks, 2004a). Forty percent of the students enrolled in U.S. schools in 2002 were students of color. This percentage is increasing, primarily because of the increase of Mexican American students. In some of the nation's largest cities, such as Chicago, Los Angeles, Washington, DC, New York, and San Francisco, half or more of the public school students are students of color. In 2004, 58.9% of the students in the Seattle school district were ethnic minorities. In 2002, students of color made up 65.2% of the student population in the public schools of California, the nation's most populous state (California State Department of Education, 2000).

Language and religious diversity is also increasing in the nation's student population. About 20% of the U.S. school-age population speaks a language other than English at home (U. S. Census Bureau, 2000). Immigrant students are the fastest-growing population in U.S. public schools. The percentage of African Americans who are foreign born is increasing. The census estimates that 8% (2.2 million) of the African American population is foreign born ("Snapshot," 2005).

There is a wide racial and cultural gap between teachers and students. While 40% of the nation's students are ethnic minorities, most of the nation's teachers are White and speak only English. White teachers make up about 86% of the nation's teachers (Cochran-Smith, Davis, & Fries, 2005). The percentage of White teachers in the nation's schools will not change in the foreseeable future. The vast majority (80%–93%) of the students enrolled in college and university programs that prepare teachers are White.

Diversity: Opportunities and Challenges

The significant changes in the racial, ethnic, and language groups that make up the nation's population create a demographic imperative for educators to respond to diversity. Diversity offers both opportunities and challenges to our nation, to schools, and to teachers. Diversity enriches our nation, communities, schools, and classrooms. Individuals from many different groups have made and continue to make significant contributions to American society. Diversity also provides our society with many different and enriched ways to identify, describe, and solve social, economic, and political problems.

Diversity also provides schools, colleges, and universities with an opportunity to educate students in an environment that reflects the reality of the nation and the world and to teach students from diverse groups how to get along and how to make decisions and take actions in the public interest. A diverse school environment enables students from many different groups to engage in discussions to solve complex problems related to living in a multicultural nation and world.

Diversity also poses serious challenges to our nation, to schools, and to teachers. Research indicates that students come to school with many stereotypes, misconceptions, and negative attitudes toward outside groups (Stephan & Stephan, 2004; Stephan & Vogt, 2004). Here is an example from a study by Van Ausdale and Feagin (2001):

> Carla, a three-year old child, is preparing . . . for resting time.
> She picks up her cot and starts to move it to the other side of the classroom. A teacher asks what she is doing. "I need to move this,"explains Carla. "Why?" asks the teacher. "Because I can't sleep next to a nigger," Carla says, pointing to Nicole, a four-year-old Black child on a cot nearby. "Niggers are stinky. I can't sit next to one." Stunned, the teacher, who is white, tells Carla to move her cot back and not to use "hurting words." (p. 1)

Without curriculum intervention by teachers, the racial attitudes and behaviors of students become more negative and harder to change as they grow older. Consequently, an important aim of multicultural education is to provide students with experiences and materials that will help them develop positive attitudes and behaviors toward individuals from different groups (Stephan & Stephan, 2004; Stephan & Vogt, 2004).

The wide gap between the academic achievement of students of color such as African Americans and Mexican Americans and Whites and groups of Asian Americans such as Chinese and Japanese Americans is another important challenge in diverse schools and to a multicultural society. I will discuss research related to closing the academic achievement gap between Whites and most groups of color later in this chapter.

Education and Diversity

During the last three decades my research has focused on ways to reform schools so that they will increase the academic achievement of diverse groups and help all students develop democratic racial attitudes and a commitment to democracy and social justice. Education in a democratic society should help students acquire the knowledge, attitudes, and skills needed to become productive workers within society as well as develop the commitment, attitudes, and skills to work to make our nation and the world just places in which to live and work. We should educate students to be effective citizens of their cultural communities, the nation, and the world.

Goals of Multicultural Education

An important goal of multicultural education is to improve race relations and to help all students acquire the knowledge, attitudes, and skills needed to participate in cross-cultural interactions and in personal, social, and civic action that will help make our nation and world more democratic and just. The goal of multicultural education is to teach students to know, to care, and to act to promote democracy in the public interest.

Multicultural education is consequently as important for middle- and high-income White suburban students as it is for students of color who live in the inner city. This story about a wealthy child near Hollywood from *The Shortchanged Children of Suburbia* (Hechinger, 1967) indicates why multicultural education is needed by all of the nation's students:

> The story is told about a little girl in a school near Hollywood who was asked to write a composition about a poor family. The essay began: "This family was very poor. The mommy was poor. The Daddy was poor. The brothers and sisters were poor. The maid was poor. The nurse was poor. The butler was poor. The cook was poor. And the chauffeur was poor . . ." (p. 5)

Multicultural education fosters the public good and the overarching democratic goals of the United States. It also helps students to acquire the knowledge, attitudes, and skills they need to make decisions and to take action in the public interest. Multicultural education is trying to *Americanize* America and to help it actualize the ideals stated in its founding documents: the Declaration of Independence, the Constitution, and the Bill of Rights. That is the essence of the multicultural education project, which has brought the nation closer to the democratic values stated in its founding documents.

School-based reforms are needed to help students learn how to live together in civic, moral, and just communities that respect and value the rights and cultural characteristics of all students. Such efforts are made more difficult because a large percentage of students attend single-race schools and because segregation often exists within racially and ethnically mixed schools that use tracking and special programs to meet the special needs of various student groups (Oakes, 2005). According to Sowell and Oakley (2002):

> The average White child attends a school that is over 78% White. The average Black child attends a school that is over 57% Black. The average Hispanic child attends a school that is over 57% Hispanic. The average Asian child attends a school that is over 19% Asian."

The Dimensions of Multicultural Education

What have we learned in the last three decades about ways in which schools can be reformed in order to increase the academic achievement of students from diverse groups, improve race and ethnic relations, and educate students so that they will make decisions and take actions that promote democracy and the public interest?

I have categorized the major research and scholarship that has been done over the last 30 years into five dimensions, which I call the *dimensions of multicultural education*. I discuss this research comprehensively in the *Handbook of Research on Multicultural Education* (Banks, 2004b). In this chapter, I will briefly describe each of these dimensions and some of the significant insights that have been gained from research, scholarship, and wisdom of practice in the last three decades. The five dimensions are (1) content integration, (2) the knowledge construction process, (3) an equity pedagogy, (4) prejudice reduction; and (5) an empowering school culture and social structure.

Content Integration. Content integration describes the extent to which teachers use examples and content from a variety of cultures and groups to illustrate key concepts, principles, generalizations, and theories in their subject area or discipline. Research indicates that when teachers include examples of content from different racial and ethnic groups, students develop more positive racial attitudes toward these groups and their stereotypes of other groups are challenged (for reviews of this research see Banks, 2001; Stephan & Stephan, 2004). Research also indicates that students become more engaged and active learners when teachers incorporate information about their cultures, histories, and experiences into the curriculum (Gay, 2000; Ladson-Billings, 1994).

The Knowledge Construction Process. The knowledge construction process describes the extent to which teachers help students understand, investigate, and determine how the cultural assumptions, frames of references, perspectives, and biases in a discipline influence the ways in which knowledge is constructed within it. Scholarship in ethnic studies and women's studies indicates that knowledge in the popular culture, in the media, and in textbooks reflects the biographies, perspectives, and cultural experiences of the scientists, social scientists, and historians who created that knowledge.

The knowledge in the school curriculum and in textbooks has a powerful influence on how students view and experience the world. I will give an example from the textbooks that I used in school in the 1950s.[2] I was an elementary school student in the Arkansas delta in the 1950s. One of my most powerful memories is the image of the happy and loyal slaves in my social studies textbooks. I also remember that there were three other Blacks in my textbooks: Booker T. Washington, the educator; George Washington Carver, the scientist; and Marian Anderson, the classical singer. I had several persistent questions throughout my school days: Why were the slaves pictured as happy? Were there other Blacks in history beside the two Washingtons and Anderson? Who created this image of slaves? Why?

The image of the happy slaves was inconsistent with everything I knew about the African American descendants of enslaved people in my segregated community. We had to drink water from fountains labeled "colored," and we could not use the city's public library. But we were not *happy* about either of these legal requirements. In fact, we resisted these laws in powerful but subtle ways each day. As children, we savored the taste of "White water" when the authorities were preoccupied with more serious infractions against the racial caste system. The civil rights movement that emerged in the 1960s, which consisted of marches and protests, contradicted the notion that African Americans in the South were happy with their condition.

Throughout my schooling, these questions remained cogent as I tried to reconcile the representations of African Americans in textbooks with the people I knew in my family and community. I wanted to know why these images were highly divergent. My epistemological quest to find out why the slaves were represented as happy became a lifelong journey that continues, and the closer I think I am to the answer, the more difficult and complex both my question and the answers become. The question—*Why were the slaves represented as happy?*—has taken different forms in various periods of my life, such as "Why did a book like *The Bell Curve* (Herrnstein & Murray, 1994)—which argues that Blacks are genetically inferior to Whites—remain on *The New York Times* best-seller list for 15 weeks and sell a million copies within the first 18 months of its publication?"

I now believe, along with other scholars—such as Harding (1991), Code (1991), Collins (2000), and Jacobson (1998)—that the biographical journeys of researchers greatly influence their values, their research questions, and the knowledge they construct. The knowledge they construct mirrors their life experiences and their values.

I discovered through historical research that the paradigm of the happy slaves was constructed by Ulrich B. Phillips (1918/1966) and described in his 1918 book, *American Negro Slavery*. Phillips, a descendant of slave owners, emphasized the benign treatment of the slaves and their happiness. The Phillips slavery paradigm was institutionalized in the popular culture and in schools, colleges, and universities. Mainstream historians did not seriously challenge it until the late 1950s, the 1960s, and the 1970s, when it was critiqued by historians such as Elkins (1959), Stampp (1969), and Blassingame (1972). However, the Phillip slavery paradigm was challenged from the academic margins by African American scholars such as Carter G. Woodson and W. E. B. DuBois when *American Negro Slavery* was first published in 1918.

An Equity Pedagogy. An equity pedagogy exists when teachers modify their teaching in ways that will facilitate the academic achievement of students from diverse groups. Culturally relevant or culturally responsive teaching—a form of equity pedagogy—is used to help close the achievement gap (Gay, 2000; Ladson-Billings, 1994).

Many explanations have been given for the achievement gap between White students and students of color such as African Americans, Mexican Americans, and Native Americans. Multicultural education theorists and researchers believe that the difference between the home cultures of minority students and the school culture is a major reason for the low academic achievement of minority students. During the last three decades researchers have been investigating ways in which teachers can make use of elements from the cultures of students to increase their academic achievement.

Researchers have described ways in which the languages, dialects, and home cultures of low-income students and students of color can be used to motivate them to learn. Many studies describe the differences between the school culture and the home cultures of students from diverse groups. Researchers have described the ways in which verbal interactions differ in the school and in the homes of Navajo students (Philips, 1983) and how language use differs among White middle-class teachers, the White working class, and the Black working class (Heath, 1983).

Some researchers have described how teachers can use the home language of low-income African American students, called Black English, as a vehicle to help them master Standard English (Delpit & Dowdy, 2002). In 1996, a contentious national debate over Black English occurred when the Oakland public school district proposed using Black English as a vehicle to teach African American students Standard English. This recommendation is quite consistent with research by linguists. Research indicates that an effective way to teach students a second language is to build on their home language or dialect rather than try to eradicate it (August & Hakuta, 1997; Piestrup, 1973).

Some studies provide evidence to support the idea that when teachers use culturally responsive teaching, the academic achievement of minority students increases. Au and Kawakami (1985) found that if teachers used participation structures in lessons that were similar to the Hawaiian speech event "talk story," the reading achievement of Native Hawaiian students increased significantly. They write:

> The chief characteristic of talk story is *joint performance*, or the cooperative production of responses of two or more speakers. For example, if the subject is going surfing, one of the boys begins by recounting the events of a particular day. But he will immediately invite one of the other boys to join him in describing the events to the group. The two boys will alternate as speakers, each telling a part of the story, with other children present occasionally chiming in. (p. 409; emphasis in original)

Talk story is very different from recitations in most classrooms, in which the teacher usually calls on an *individual* child to tell a story.

Lee (1993) found that the achievement of African American students increases when they are taught literary interpretations with lessons that use the African American verbal practice of signifying. Signifying is "a genre within African American speech that involves ritual insult—as in playing the dozens. Signifying always involves . . . [a] high use of figurative language" (C. Lee, personal communication, February 5, 2005). Horowitz and colleagues summarize an important finding by Heath:

> Shirley Brice Heath (1983) discovered that African American children in a Southern community did not answer obvious, factual questions to which they assumed the teacher knew the answer. This kind of questioning, such as—"What color is this dish?" "How many fingers do I have?—common in many middle-class homes, was not part of their experience where questions were used only when the asker [really] did not know the answer. The result was that they did not answer such obvious questions, and teachers assumed they were less able learners. (Horowitz et al., 2005, p. 115).

Prejudice Reduction. Theory and research in this dimension focus on the characteristics of students' racial attitudes and how teaching methods and materials can change them. Research indicates that the use of multicultural textbooks, other teaching materials, and cooperative teaching strategies that enable students from different racial and ethnic groups to interact positively in equal-status situations help students develop democratic racial attitudes (Banks, 2001; Stephan & Vogt, 2004). These kinds of materials and teaching strategies can also result in students choosing more friends from outside racial, ethnic, and cultural groups.

Since the 1940s, a number of curriculum intervention studies have been conducted to determine the effects of teaching units and lessons, multicultural textbooks and materials, role playing, and other kinds of simulated experiences on the racial attitudes and perceptions of students. These studies indicate that curriculum materials and interventions can help students develop positive racial attitudes and perceptions.

These studies provide guidelines that can help teachers improve intergroup relations in their classrooms and schools. Trager and Yarrow conducted one of the earliest curriculum studies in 1952. Titled *They Learn What They Live*, it examined the effects of a democratic multicultural curriculum on the racial attitudes of children in the first and second grades. The curriculum had a positive effect on the attitudes of both the students and teachers. *This study indicates that in order for students to learn democracy, they must experience a democratic school and curriculum.*

Research indicates that when schools create *superordinate* groups—groups with which members of all the groups in a situation identify—relations are improved (Banks et al., 2001). When membership in superordinate groups is salient, other group differences become less important. Creating superordinate groups stimulates liking and cohesion, which can mitigate preexisting animosities. An example of a superordinate group is a basketball team that includes Black, White, and Mexican American students who are working together to beat an opponent. In this situation, race and ethnicity become less important than beating the opponent.

In school settings there are many superordinate group memberships that can be created or made salient. For example, it is possible to create superordinate groups through *extracurricular activities*. There are also many existing superordinate group memberships that can be made more salient, such as the classroom, the band, the school, the community, the state, and the nation.

An Empowering School Culture. An empowering school culture is used to describe the process of restructuring the culture and organization of the school so that students from diverse racial, ethnic, language, and social-class groups will experience educational equality and cultural empowerment. Research and theory indicate that creating a successful school for low-income students and students of color requires restructuring the culture and organization of the school.

Research indicates that the culture of some schools fosters academic achievement and that the culture of other schools does not (Brookover, Beady, Flood, Schweitzer, & Wisenbaker, 1979). Schools of the same social-class composition have significantly different effects on student achievement. Some schools in low-income communities—as well as in high-income communities—have cultures that foster high academic achievement. Researchers call these schools "effective" or "improving" schools. Other schools in both low- and high-income communities have cultures that do not foster high academic achievement.

Levine and Lezotte (2001) have identified the important characteristics of effective or improving schools. They include:

- a safe and orderly environment,
- a shared faculty commitment to improve achievement,
- an orientation focused on identifying and solving problems,
- high faculty cohesion and collaboration,
- high faculty input in decision-making, and
- school wide emphasis on recognizing positive performance. (pp. 525–526)

Education for National and Global Citizenship

Because we live in a global society that is highly interconnected, an effective education for the 21st century prepares students for thoughtful citizenship in their communities, the nation, and the world. Worldwide immigration and globalization raises new questions about how to prepare students for thoughtful and active citizenship. Multicultural societies are faced with the problem of constructing nation-states that reflect and incorporate the diversity of their citizens and yet have an overarching set of shared values, ideals, and goals to which all of its citizens are committed. Diversity and unity must be balanced in multicultural nation-states.

Only when a nation-state is unified around a set of democratic values such as justice and equality can it protect the rights of cultural, ethnic, and language groups and enable them to experience cultural democracy and freedom. In a democratic society, ethnic and immigrant groups should have the right to maintain important elements of their ethnic cultures and languages as well as participate in the national civic culture.

Nationalists and assimilationists throughout the world worry that if they allow students to maintain identifications with their cultural communities, they will not acquire sufficiently strong attachments to their nation-states. They have a "zero-sum conception of identity" (Kymlicka, 2004, p. xiv). The theoretical and empirical work of multicultural scholars indicates that *identity is multiple, changing, overlapping, and contextual, rather than fixed and static*—and that thoughtful and clarified cultural identifications will enable people to be better citizens of the nation-state. Writes Ladson-Billings (2004):

> The dynamic of the modern (or postmodern) nation-state makes identities as either an individual or a member of a group untenable. Rather than seeing the choice as either/or, the citizen of the nation-state operates in the realism of both/and. She is both an individual who is entitled to citizen rights that permit one to legally challenge infringement of those rights while simultaneously acting as a member of a group. . . . People move back and forth across many identities, and the way society responds to these identities either binds people to or alienates them from the civic culture. (p. 112)

Balancing Unity and Diversity

Balancing unity and diversity is a continuing challenge for multicultural nation-states. Unity without diversity results in hegemony and oppression; diversity without unity leads to Balkanization and the fracturing of the nation-state. A major problem facing nation-states throughout the world is how to recognize and legitimize difference and yet construct an overarching national identity that incorporates the voices, experiences, and hopes of the diverse groups that compose it. Many ethnic, language, and religious groups have weak identifications with their nation-state because of their marginalized status and because they do not see their hopes, dreams, visions, and possibilities reflected in the nation-state or in the schools, colleges, and universities (Ladson-Billings, 2004).

The diversity brought to Europe by immigrants from its former colonies has increased racial, ethnic, and religious tension and conflict. The establishment of a policy by the French government—which bans the wearing of religious symbols in public schools such as the headscarf worn by Muslim girls—is a desperate attempt by a nation with a strong assimilationist history and ideology to deal with religious expression in the public sphere. As worldwide immigration increases diversity on every continent, nation-states are searching for ways to balance unity and diversity (Banks et al., 2005). The four Muslim young men who are suspected of being responsible for the bombings of the London underground on July 7, 2005, had immigrant parents but were British citizens who grew up in Leeds. However, they apparently were not structurally integrated into British mainstream society and had a weak identification with the nation-state and other British citizens.

The Western world is perplexed, exhausted, and fear ridden as it attempts to envision and implement viable and creative strategies to respond effectively to the intransigent conflicts in the Middle East and Islamic suicide bombers (Barber, 2003). These events have resulted in bombings that have created a reign of terror throughout the world—including the attacks on the Pentagon and the World Trade Center on September 11, 2001; the bombings of four commuter trains in Madrid, Spain, on March 11, 2004; the bombings in the London transportation system on July 7, 2005; and the bombing of a Red Sea resort at Sharm el-Sheikh in Egypt on July 23, 2005.

The Development of Cultural, National, and Global Identifications

Assimilationist notions of citizenship are ineffective today because of the deepening diversity throughout the world and the quests by marginalized groups for cultural recognition and rights. *Multicultural citizenship* is essential for today's global age (Kymlicka, 1995). It recognizes and legitimizes the right and need of citizens to maintain commitments both to their cultural communities and to the national civic culture.

Nussbaum (2002) states that we should help students develop cosmopolitanism. Cosmopolitans view themselves as citizens of the world who will make decisions and take actions in the *global public interest*. Nussbaum states that their "allegiance is to the worldwide community of human beings" (p. 4). Cosmopolitans identify with peoples from diverse cultures throughout the world. Nussbaum contrasts cosmopolitan universalism and internationalism with parochial ethnocentrism and inward-looking patriotism. Cosmopolitans "are ready to broaden the definition of public, extend their loyalty beyond ethnic and national boundaries, and engage with difference far and near" (W. C. Parker, personal communication, July 18, 2005). Cosmopolitans view the public interest globally and are concerned with threats to the world community such as global warming, the HIV/AIDS epidemic, and sustainable development.

Students should develop a delicate balance of cultural, national, and global identifications (Banks, 2004a). Cultural, national, and global experiences and identifications are interactive and interrelated in a dynamic way. Each needs to be developed in the schools. Students should develop cultural, national, and global identifications that are critical and thoughtful. They should not be nonreflective and unexamined.

Nationalism and national attachments in most nations are strong and tenacious. Globalization and nationalism are coexisting and sometimes conflicting trends in the world today (Banks et al., 2005). An important aim of citizenship education in the public interest is to help students develop global identifications and commitments. The ways in which people are moving back and forth across national borders today challenge the notion of educating citizens to function in one nation-state. Many people have more than one national identity and live in multiple places. Students also need to develop a deep understanding of the need to take action as citizens of the global community to help solve the world's difficult global problems and to make decisions and take actions that will enhance democracy and promote the public interest in their cultural communities, their nation, and the world.

DEMOCRACY, DIVERSITY, AND THE PUBLIC INTEREST

The increasing diversity throughout the world today and the increasing recognition of diversity—as well as the intractable problems that the world faces—require a reexamination of the ends and means of citizenship education if is to serve the public interest (Parker, 2003). Assimilationist conceptions of citizenship education that eradicate the cultures and languages of diverse groups will be ineffective in a transformed "flat" world (Friedman, 2005). In the flat world described by Friedman, scientific and technological workers educated in Asian nations such as India and China are competing successfully with—and sometimes outperforming—scientific and technological workers educated at universities in the United

States. The United States can no longer take its scientific and technological superiority for granted. It is being challenged by nations such as India and China.
Effective citizenship education in a diverse and flat world will help students to
attain new knowledge, paradigms, and perspectives on the United States and the
world. The concepts, paradigms, and projects that facilitated the rise and triumph
of the West between the 16th and the 20th centuries are ineffective in the changed
world of the 21st century. Citizenship education in the United States—as well as
in other Western nations—must be reinvented so that it will enable students to see
their fates as intimately tied to that of people throughout the world and to understand why a "threat to justice anywhere is a threat to justice everywhere" (King,
1963/1994, pp. 2–3).

NOTES

1. This chapter is adapted from James A. Banks (2005).
2. This section of this chapter is adapted from James A. Banks (1998).

REFERENCES

Au, K. (1980). Participation structures in a reading lesson with Hawaiian children: Analysis of a culturally appropriate teaching event. *Anthropology and Education Quarterly,
11*(2), 91–115.
Au, K. H., & Kawakami, A. J. (1985). Research currents: Talk story and learning to read.
Language Arts, 62(4), 406–411.
August, D., & Hakuta, K. (Eds.). (1997). *Improving schooling for language-minority children: A research agenda.* Washington, DC: National Academy Press.
Banks, J. A. (1998). The lives and values of researchers: Implications for educating citizens
in a multicultural society. *Educational Researcher, 24*(7), 4–17.
Banks, J. A. (2001). Multicultural education: Its effects on students' racial and gender role
attitudes. In J. A. Banks & C. A. M. Banks (Eds.), *Handbook of research on multicul-
tural education* (1st ed.; pp. 617–627). San Francisco: Jossey-Bass.
Banks, J. A. (Ed.). (2004a). *Diversity and citizenship education: Global perspectives.* San
Francisco: Jossey-Bass.
Banks, J. A. (2004b). Multicultural education: Historical development, dimensions, and
practice. In J. A. Banks & C. A. M. Banks (Eds.), *Handbook of research on multicul-
tural education* (2nd ed.; pp. 3–29). San Francisco: Jossey-Bass.
Banks, J. A. (2005, March 3rd). *Democracy, diversity, and social justice: Education in a
global age.* Annual faculty lecture, University of Washington, Seattle.
Banks, J. A., & Banks, C. A. M. (Eds.). (2004). *Handbook of research on multicultural
education* (2nd ed.). San Francisco: Jossey-Bass.
Banks, J. A., Banks, C. A. M., Cortés, C. E., Hahn, C. L., Merryfield, M., Moodley, K. A.,
Murphy-Shigematsu, S., Osler, A., Park, C., & Parker, W. C. (2005). *Democracy and
diversity: Principles and concepts for educating citizens in a global age.* Seattle, WA:
Center for Multicultural Education, University of Washington.

Banks, J. A., Cookson, P., Gay, G., Hawley, W. D., Irvine, J. J., Nieto, S., Schofield, J., & Stephan, W. (2001). *Diversity within unity: Essential principles for teaching and learning in a multicultural society*. Seattle: Center for Multicultural Education, University of Washington.

Barber, B. R. (2003). *Fear's empire: War, terrorism, and democracy*. New York: Norton.

Blassingame, J. W. (1972). *The slave community: Plantation life in the antebellum South*. New York: Oxford University Press.

Brookover, W., Beady, C., Flood, P., Schweitzer, J., & Wisenbaker, J. (1979). *School social systems and student achievement: Schools can make a difference*. New York: Praeger.

California State Department of Education. (2000). Retrieved July 14, 2004, from http://data1.cde.ca.gov/dataquest

Cochran-Smith, M., Davis, D., & Fries, K. (2005). Multicultural teacher education: Research, policy, and practice. In J. A. Banks & C. A. M. Banks (Eds.), *Handbook of research on multicultural education* (2nd ed.; pp. 931–975). San Francisco: Jossey-Bass.

Code, L. (1991). *What can she know? Feminist theory and the construction of knowledge*. Ithaca, NY: Cornell University Press.

Collins, P. H. (2000). *Black feminist thought: Knowledge, consciousness, and the politics of empowerment* (2nd ed.). New York: Routledge.

Delpit, L., & Dowdy, J. K. (Eds.). (2002). *The skin that we speak: Thoughts on language and culture in the classroom*. New York: The New Press.

Drachsler, J. (1920). *Democracy and assimilation*. New York: Macmillan.

Eldering, L., & Kloprogge, J. (1989). *Different cultures, same school: Ethnic minority children in Europe*. Amsterdam: Swets & Seitlinger.

Elkins, S. M. (1959). *Slavery: A problem in American institutional and intellectual life*. New York: Grosset & Dunlap.

Friedman, T. L. (2005). *The world is flat: A brief history of the twenty-first century*. New York: Farrar, Straus & Giroux.

Gay, G. (2000). *Culturally responsive teaching: Theory, research, and practice*. New York: Teachers College Press.

Gillborn, D. (1990). *Race, ethnicity, and education*. London: Unwin Hyman.

Harding, S. (1991). *Whose science? Whose knowledge? Thinking from women's lives*. Ithaca, NY: Cornell University Press.

Heath, S. B. (1983). *Ways with words: Language, life, and work in communities and classrooms*. New York: Cambridge University Press.

Hechinger, F. M. (1967). Foreword. In A. Miel with E. Kiester Jr. *The shortchanged children of suburbia*. New York: Institute of Human Relations Press, The American Jewish Committee.

Herrnstein, R. J., & Murray, C. (1994). *The bell curve: Intelligence and class structure in American life*. New York: The Free Press.

Horowitz, F. D., Darling-Hammond, L., & Bransford, J., with Comer, J., Rosebrock, K., Austin, K., & Rust, F. (2005). Educating teachers for developmentally appropriate practice. In L. Darling-Hammond & J. Bransford (Eds.), *Preparing teachers for a changing world: What teachers should learn and be able to do* (pp. 88–125). San Francisco: Jossey-Bass.

Jacobson, M. F. (1998). *Whiteness of a different color: European immigrants and the alchemy of race*. Cambridge, MA: Harvard University Press.

Kallen, H. M. (1924). *Culture and democracy in the United States*. New York: Boni & Liveright.

King, M. L., Jr. (1994). *Letter from a Birmingham jail.* New York: HarperCollins. (Original work published 1963)

Kymlicka, W. (1995). *Multicultural citizenship: A liberal theory of minority rights.* New York: Oxford University Press.

Kymlicka, W. (2004). Foreword. In J. A. Banks (Ed.), *Diversity and citizenship education: Global perspectives* (pp. xiii–xviii). San Francisco: Jossey-Bass.

Ladson-Billings, G. (1994). *The dreamkeepers: Successful teachers of African American children.* San Francisco: Jossey-Bass.

Ladson-Billings, G. (2004). Culture versus citizenship: The challenge of racialized citizenship in the United States. In J. A. Banks (Ed.), *Diversity and citizenship education: Global perspectives* (pp. 99–126). San Francisco: Jossey-Bass.

Ladson-Billings, G., & Tate, W. F. (2005). Prospectus for this book submitted to Teachers College Press.

Lee, C. D. (1993). *Signifying as a scaffold for literary interpretation: The pedagogical implications of an African American discourse genre.* Urbana, IL: National Council of Teachers of English.

Lee, D. C. (1995). A culturally based cognitive apprenticeship: Teaching African American high school students skills in literary interpretation. *Reading Research Quarterly, 30*(4), 608–630.

Levine, D. U., & Lezotte, L. W. (2001). Effective schools research. In J. A. Banks & C. A. M. Banks (Eds.), *Handbook of research on multicultural education* (pp. 525–547). San Francisco: Jossey-Bass.

Nussbaum, M. (2002). Patriotism and cosmopolitanism. In J. Cohen (Ed.), *For love of country* (pp. 2–17). Boston: Beacon.

Oakes, J. (2005). *Keeping track: How schools structure inequality* (2nd ed.). New Haven, CT: Yale University Press.

Parker, W. C. (2003). *Teaching democracy: Unity and diversity in public life.* New York: Teachers College Press.

Patterson, O. (1977). *Ethnic chauvinism: The reactionary impulse.* New York: Stein & Day.

Philips, S. U. (1972). Participant structures and communicative competence: Warm Springs children in community and classroom. In C. B. Cazden, V. P. John, & D. Hymes (Eds.), *Functions of language in the classroom* (pp. 370–394). New York: Teachers College Press.

Philips, S. U. (1983). *The invisible culture: Communication in classroom and community on the Warm Springs Indian Reservation.* Prospect Heights, IL: Waveland Press.

Phillips, U. B. (1966). *American Negro slavery.* Baton Rouge: Louisiana State University Press. (Original work published 1918)

Piestrup, A. M. (1973, July). *Black dialect interference and accommodation of reading instruction in first grade.* Monographs of the Language-Behavior Research Laboratory, No. 4. Berkeley: University of California.

Ramírez, M., III, & Castañeda, A. (1974). *Cultural democracy, bicognitive development, and education.* New York: Academic Press.

Rosaldo, R. (1997). Cultural citizenship, inequality, and multiculturalism. In W. V. Florres & R. Benmayor (Eds.), *Latino cultural citizenship: Claiming identity, space, and rights* (pp. 27–28). Boston: Beacon.

Smith, L. T. (1999). *Decolonizing methodologies: Research and indigenous peoples.* New York: Zed Books.

Snapshot of the African American/Black Market. Retrieved February 9, 2005, from www. magazine.org/marketprofile

Sowell, J., & Oakley, D. (2002). *Choosing segregation: Racial imbalance in American public schools, 1990–2000.* Albany, NY: Lewis Munford Center. Retrieved February 28, 2005, from http://mumfordl.dyndns.org/cen2000/SchoolPop/SPReport/SPDownload.pdf

Stampp, K. M. (1969). *The peculiar institution: Slavery in the ante-bellum south.* New York: Knopf.

Stephan, W. G., & Stephan, C. W. (2004). Intergroup relations in multicultural education programs. In J. A. Banks & C. A. M. Banks (Eds.), *Handbook of research on multicultural education* (2nd ed.; pp. 782–798). San Francisco: Jossey-Bass.

Stephan, W. G., & Vogt, W. P. (Eds.). (2004). *Education programs for improving intergroup relations.* New York: Teachers College Press.

Suárez-Orozco, M. M., Suárez-Orozco, C., & Quin, D. B. (Eds.). (2005). *The new immigration: An interdisciplinary reader.* New York: Routledge.

Trager, H. G., & Yarrow, M. R. (1952). *They learn what they live: Prejudice in young children.* New York: Harper & Brothers.

U.S. Census Bureau. (2000). *Statistical abstract of the United States* (120th ed.). Washington, DC: U. S. Government Printing Office.

Van Ausdale, D., & Feagin, J. R. (2001). *The first r: How children learn racism.* Lanham, MD: Rowman & Littlefield.

Woodson, C. G. (1977). *The mis-education of the Negro.* New York: AMS Press. (Original work published 1933)

CHAPTER 9

Multiculturalism, Race, and the Public Interest: Hanging on to Great-Great-Granddaddy's Legacy

CARL A. GRANT

IN THE EARLY 19TH CENTURY, Alexis de Tocqueville (1848/2001) re-marked that "the prejudice rejecting the Negro seems to increase in proportion to their emancipation, and inequality cuts deep into mores as it is effaced from laws" (p. 316). Almost 100 years later, in 1944, Gunnar Mydral observed that there is a "vicious circle" of cumulative causation. He contended that this "vicious circle" included self-sustaining processes in which the failure of African Americans to make progress justified for Whites the prejudicial attitudes that, when reflected in social and political action, ensured that African Americans would not advance. More than 60 years later, racial equity has not come to pass for African Americans, who have been the primary target of racism and a racist discourse; and racial equity and multiculturalism at the institutional and individual level of society continues to be resisted. Many Americans have difficulty accepting and affirming that both the *ideal* and *everyday practice* of democracy are for both the Whites and non-Whites in the population. It is as if the tenets of democracy (e.g., equality, social justice), as expressed in documents such as the Declaration of Independence and the U.S. Constitution, are for only some citizens. Why is this so, 50 fifty years after *Brown v. Board of Education* and 40 years after the Civil Rights Act of 1965?

This chapter offers several reasons why this is so. The first reason is that a dual structure has historically existed and continues to exist, which causes and facilitates different treatment of America's White and non-White people. The second reason is that Americans for the most part live in a *plural society,* which can be defined as racially/ethnically segregated communities within cities and states (Ringer, 1983; U.S. Census Bureau, 2005); the plural society does not actively facilitate communication and cooperation across racial and ethnic groups, and therefore it resists multiculturalism. This notion of the plural society is quite different from the *pluralistic society,* which is meant to convey a sense of multiple voices and perspectives drawn into one culture and community. The third reason is the marginalization of multiculturalism and race in society and multicultural education in school as they are situated within a struggle between the democratic ideals of the country and the United States Constitution and the affirmation of these ideals.

My argument is not new. Mydral (1944), Ringer (1983), and others have made somewhat similar arguments. What, then, is my contribution to this conversation on race and multicultuaralism? It is to remind the reader not to forget the strength and evil of racism or its chameleon-like nature. Acts of racism at the institutional and personal level change in keeping with changes in society. This change allows the flow of power and privilege to remain at the mercy and to serve the pleasures of the dominant group. Another reason for placing racism at the center of my argument is that this chapter is being written during the time of the No Child Left Behind Act (NCLB) and Hurricane Katrina, when actions by the government surrounding both seek to obscure race and inequality.

NCLB, with its focus on principal/teacher/student accountability policies predicated on the use of *scientific* research in the classroom backed up by randomized trial design and instructional practices approved by the What Works Clearinghouse, stipulates ways in which educators (e.g., teachers and principals) should act (or not act) that obscure race and inequality. NCLB does not take into account the existence of a dual and racist structure in society and racial divisions, constructed out of racism and a racialized discourse, that affect African American and other children in the United States. NCLB naively assumes that all children are potential recipients of both U.S. democratic ideals and the practice of those ideals. In other words, the reasoning behind NCLB is that equality (when it is considered) is a technical issue, not a structural one. Thomas Popkewitz (personal communication, October 1, 2005) argues that NCLB is about "finding the right technologies/research of what works and [it] penalizes those not working hard enough" (teachers do not try hard enough; the poor decided not to work, or not to get in their non-existent cars to leave New Orleans). The problem and the solution, according to government officials, lie not in structural reforms (repairing levees or dealing with inequity and race) but instead with the individual and local initiatives in disaster aid and schooling. (See, for example, Thomas 2005; Solomon, 2005).

Whereas NCLB has a more subtle and nuanced racism and racialized discourse, responses to and events surrounding Hurricane Katrina display a blatant form of racism and racialized discourse, highlighting the gross mistreatment of scores of African Americans. I am reminded of the 1960s, when it was snarling dogs and streams of water from fire hoses that inflicted pain on African Americans. In the wake of Katrina, African Americans suffered because they did not receive the basics of life: food, shelter, and water. Some were left to die a horrible and unnecessary death, often alone. Watching television, it was immediately obvious to me and many other African Americans that race was a key factor in the government response to the people stranded in New Orleans, most of whom were Black (Thomas, 2005). The media were slow to see the race card floating and wading in the water and standing on the rooftops. What television and newspapers first reported was that Blacks were looting and robbing. However, cries of racism arose when race could not be ignored or mentally pushed away as the television pictures showed the horrible conditions that African Americans were facing.

The un-muting of racism has not, however, brought forth a discussion and/or public conversation (I am speaking as much about talk around the watercooler and in the halls of government as I am about public hearings) that is consistent in size and scope with that which was unveiled to the American public in New Orleans. There is a silence and/or superficial discussions. Discussion of racism for the most part has been connected to governmental officials who neglected to perform their job. Political leaders postured about how and when they should respond and the media provided superficial reporting. Finally, with Hurricane Rita taking center stage—at the time of this writing—do you want to bet that we won't have this conversation? And not having conservations on race and racism will work in opposition to the public interest of *All* Americans.

WHAT IS "*THE PUBLIC INTEREST*" AND WHAT PUBLIC ARE WE TALKING ABOUT?

In the invitation to contribute to this book, the editors helpfully provided a meaning of "the public interest," stating "We . . . argue that public interest is not merely the aggregation of many individual private interests. Rather, the public interest involves those decisions and actions that further democracy" (prospectus, Ladson-Billings & Tate, personal communication, 2005). They, like Water Lippman, see the public interest as divorced from private interest and also supported by a social justice/benevolent discourse. Walter Lippman stated, "The public interest may be presumed to be what men would choose if they saw clearly, thought rationally, acted disinterestedly and benevolently" (quoted in Bell & Kristol, 1965, p. 5). Such has not been the case for NCLB and Hurricane Katrina; men (government officials) have not seen clearly, thought rationally, nor acted benevolently in a timely and efficient manner. Instead, especially in the case of Hurricane Katrina, there was a neglect and negligence of the highest order.

Debates regarding the public interest have been with us, and have influenced the direction of society, for centuries (e.g., Jean-Jacques Rousseau's *The Social Contract*, 1762/1999). Some (e.g., Hess, 2003) argue that the conceptualization of the public interest, meaning a common good that transcends the wants or needs of individuals, was discussed as the "general will" by Rousseau. The "general will," according to Rousseau, is a concern with the public interest rather than with private interests. In addition, Rousseau reminds us that if the will of the majority is acting in support of the selfish interests of a particular social class or group, then the will of the majority may unfairly deny the legal rights of an opposing minority. The dominant group in America and its group members' selfish concern with their own group's interests have supported the dual structure and plural society and created a dilemma for many Americans, including educators.

METHOD: "HOMEWORK" BEFORE PROCEEDING

As part of my preparation for writing this chapter, I looked at how other professions discuss the idea of "the public interest." I discovered Rosemary Stevens's (1971/1996) highly acclaimed book *American Medicine and the Public Interest.* What I took from this book, which chronicles the growth, development, and acceptance of medical specialization, is the importance of history and the analysis of that history, as well as the importance of critically reading about what is currently taking place in one's field (and the rest of society).

I also read Irving Louis Horowitz and Jonathan B. Imber's (2002) article "Scientific Endeavor, Professional Aims and Public Interests." What I took from the article was a statement directed toward social science, which I appropriated for myself to share with other educators:

> There is no other agency in our culture, whose role is to ask long range and if need be, abruptly irreverent questions of our democratic institutions, and to follow these questions with research and the systematic charting of the way ahead. The responsibility is to keep everlastingly challenging the present with the question: *What is it that we human beings want and what things would have to be done, in what ways and in what sequence, in order to change the present so as to achieve it?"* (p. 11; emphasis added)

History, analysis, responsibility, and continuing to challenge are key ingredients for this assignment.

RACIST DUALITY: A RESISTANCE TO MULTICULTURALISM—
A LONG AND DEEP HISTORY

Resistance to multiculturalism did not start with European Americans' decision to keep African Americans in their place, as, for example, with the *Dred Scott* case in 1857, when the U.S. Supreme Court denied citizenship rights to Blacks and decreed that enslaved people do not become free when taken into free territory, nor with the *Plessy v. Ferguson* decision in 1896 to uphold the doctrine of "separate but equal." Nor did resistance to multiculturalism start with the action of Black people against racist acts when, for example, in 1954, Rosa Parks refused to give her bus seat to a white man; when Ruby Bridges and others integrated schools in the South in the 1960s (Bridges, 1999); or when Blacks started to integrate the schools in Boston, Chicago, and San Francisco (Metcalf, 1983).

Resistance to multiculturalism started during colonial times. Ringer (1983) argues that there is a racist "duality" deeply rooted in America's past, and this duality is built into its structural and historical origins. He contends that the dual treatment of Blacks and Whites is derived from the twofold processes of colonization and colonialization that were generated by the White Europeans' conquest and settlement of the New World. The English colonies were molded in British racial, religious, and national image, and this colonist heritage was expressed in the Declaration of Independence and the Constitution. It was through this heritage that the sovereignty of the people was reaffirmed in both the political state and the national community. In each, Ringer (1983) states, "'We the People' were to share rights and immunities and were to be defined as citizens. Within the Domain of the People, universalistic, egalitarian, achievement-oriented, and democratic norms and values were to be the ideals . . . Membership in this People's Domain, though, was confined, in the colonist society, to whites" (p. 8).

The place of Blacks, who were the central target for racist acts and racialized discourses that supported the enslavement of Black people and the brutal mistreatment of other non-Whites in the developing United States, was at the lowest level of society. English colonists subjected both Indians and Blacks to brutality and fraud. Indians, for example, were conquered and removed from their land; treaties were broken, and they were treated as savages or "noble" savages (Berkhofer, 1978; Costo & Henry, 1970; Pearce, 1988). In 1661, the Virginia legislature was the first to legalize slavery. Blacks were brought into the colonies as slaves and treated as dehumanized property (Bullock, 1967; Logan & Cohen, 1967). Years later, the *return* of Blacks to some African countries (e.g., Liberia) was considered by some White Northerners who were opposed to slavery, but also believed that emancipated African Americans had no place in White society (Ringer, 1983).

The dual structure, particularly as it related to slavery and African Americans, emerged unscathed during the writing of the Declaration of Independence, the Constitution, and other promulgations of American democratic ideals. As a result, Blacks, Indians, and other minorities were not only excluded from the newly created People's Domain of the Constitution, but they also continued to be exploited for their labor (African Americans), to be deprived of their land (American Indians), and in general to be treated as conquered subjects or property (Ringer, 1983).

Of course, the dual structure has not remained unchallenged. Social challenges have brought about some positive changes. Slavery was abolished in 1865, and Indians have not been removed from their lands for decades. Jim Crow laws have been struck down, and the "separate but equal" doctrine was overturned in 1954. Racial inequities on the whole are not nearly as blatant and overt as they once were. In fact, racial tolerance and respect is an accepted way of life. In addition, resistance to multiculturalism has weakened over the past several decades. Teachers ask for it, and parents and administrators do not object to the teachers' requests (Grant & Sleeter, 1996). Nevertheless, the legacy of the dual structure remains; multiculturalism—except in weakened forms, such as "human relations" ("Let's all just get along") or "food, fairs, and festivals"—is resisted; and acts of racism and a racialized discourse continue to operate against the public interest.

Racism, although changed in form and application, is viable and resilient at the institutional and personal level; it continues to prevent Blacks and other minorities from achieving full equality and from enjoying the benefits that come with living in a multicultural society. Three examples illustrate the resilient and chameleon-like quality of racism.

Example 1: Racist acts such as red-lining and white flight, which were somewhat common practices in the housing market 50 years ago, are not often practiced today. I can recall in 1951 that my family was searching for a different house in Chicago. We were "moving on up." We were purposely not shown property in some areas (red-lining). The action of the real estate agent was not blatant racism, but more subtle: "I don't think you would like to live in that community; the schools are not very good, etc, etc." He was usually referring to White neighborhoods. After some time—we were persistent—we purchased a house. For the next 2 days, a police car was stationed outside of our house. Within 3 to 4 days, the entire neighborhood underwent a total change from all White to all Black. Today, the old form of red-lining is gone; it is rare that a police car has to be stationed outside of an African American home to protect the family from racist acts, and it's also rare that a person of color will see an entire neighborhood undergo a total racial change in the matter of a few days. Nevertheless, today racist acts still are used to control African Americans' shopping for a home. On September 14, 2005, *Washington Post* staff writer Sandra Fleishman (2005) reported the results of a federal study that shows that many minorities are more than two or three times as likely as Whites to receive high-priced mortgages. Fleishman states that "about 32 percent of blacks and 20 percent of Hispanics took out high-cost conventional loans in 2004 to buy a home, compared with 9 percent of non-Hispanic whites, according to the Fed." In addition, "About 35 percent of blacks and 19 percent of Hispanics got high-cost refinance loans, compared with just under 13 percent of non-Hispanic whites, the analysis says" (p. D1). Quoting John Taylor, president of the National Community Reinvestment Coalition, Fleishman states "I think the fairest statement you can make is that if you're a minority, you're twice as likely as a white to get a higher-cost loan" (p. D1).

Example 2: In 1954, the Supreme Court delivered a major blow to the dual structure that regulated the way Blacks and Whites lived. The Supreme Court in *Brown* v. *Board of Education* declared that "separate but equal" educational facilities are "inherently unequal" and that segregation is therefore unconstitutional. With the *Brown* decision, segregated washrooms, movie theaters, lunch counters, and restaurants disappeared. And in time, segregation in other areas of society, such as sports, began to come to an end. For example, in the 1950s, Black athletes increasingly became football players at colleges that had historically enrolled only White students. This integration merely inspired a different form of segregation. Black athletes were instructed to be invisible except on Saturday during the football game. Walter (2005) states that Black athletics "were instructed by their coaches to do two main things: remain passive in the face of racial insults, and above all do not date white women" (p. 5). Along with this segregation, it was argued that African Americans were not smart enough to play quarterback at the college or professional level. It is only within the past few years that we have come to see African Americans playing quarterbacks and more than two or three Black head football coaches at major colleges. In addition, seeing Blacks as mangers or as executives at the college or professional level still is an event waiting to happen. Walter (2005) states the following:

> It is true that Black athletes face enormous obstacles in obtaining positions in the coaching, managing, and executive ranks of professional sports as well as in college and university ranks. These obstacles are not reduced by the number of Black athletes who graduate with marginal skills, who do not graduate at all, or who play successfully in the professional leagues. In short, there is little correlation between the excellence or athletics abilities and the mobility many whites have between the playing field and the coach's clipboard. (p. 7)

Example 3: In education, segregated schools, which were declared not in keeping with the principles of democracy in 1954, are with us today. In *The Shame of the Nation: The Restoration of Apartheid Schooling in America,* Jonathan Kozol (2005) informs the American public that the dual structures are still in place and describes their effects on children:

> What saddens me the most during these times is simply that these children have no knowledge of the other world in which I've lived most of my life and that the children in that other world have not the slightest notion as to who these children are and will not likely ever know them later on, not at least on anything like equal terms, unless a couple of these kids get into college. Even if they meet each other then, it may not be the same, because the sweetness of too many of these inner-city children will have been corroded by that time. Some of it may be replaced by hardness, some by caution, some by calculation rooted in unspoken fear. I have believed for 40 years and still today that, we would be an infinitely better nation if they knew each other now. (p. 11)

THE "PLURAL SOCIETY"
AS A RESISTANCE TO MULTICULTURALISM

Many racial groups make up the population of the United States, and multiracial populations have inhabited the United States before colonial times. However, for the most part the racial groups—African Americans, American Indians, Asian Americans and Latinos—live in their groups, mostly apart from other racial groups. J. S. Furnivall (1956) calls this arrangement, with different racial groups living in different sections of the city/area side by side, but separately within the same political unit, a *plural society*. Since colonial times, the plural society in the United States has been dominated by White Americans who have enacted a number of government policies (e.g., *Dred Scott*, 1857; *Plessy vs. Ferguson*, 1896; Exclusion Act of 1882; Immigration Act of 1924) to legitimate and/or support the plural structure. In addition to judicial and legislative polices, presidential initiatives—such as President Jackson advocating the policy that removed the Cherokee west of the Mississippi; President Wilson extending Jim Crow segregation into the federal service, and President Roosevelt signing the executive order that authorized the placement of Japanese Americans into interment camps during World War II—have all maintained the plural society (Ringer, 1983).

It was in the 1960s, Ringer (1983) argues, that the United States for the first time in its history extended the promise of full membership in the People's Domain under the legal-normative umbrella of the American creed to persons of all races. In the 1960s and 1970s, legislative and judicial actions (e.g., Civil Rights Act, 1964, and Voting Rights Act, 1965; Elementary and Secondary Education Act, 1965; *Brown v. Board of Education*, 1954; Bilingual Education Act, 1968; *Diana v. State Board of Education*, 1970; *Lau v. Nichols*, 1974; Fair Employment Practice Commission [FEPC]) were put into effect by Congress, the judiciary, and several presidents to dismantle (even make illegal in some cases, e.g., school segregation) legislation and presidential initiatives that supported the plural society.

However, Ringer (1983) states, "The strongly embedded petrified effects of the now illegal plural structures were not dislodged by these actions; instead they continued to rut the paths of most nonwhites and to limit their chances and opportunities in the People's Domain" (p. 12). In the plural society, in part because of how it is structured, cross-racial socialization and integration are still low among non-White group members. For example, over the years there has been an increase in residential integration across racial lines. However, data from the 2000 Census (U.S. Census Bureau, 2005) show that, in spite of some decline between 1980 and 2000, residential segregation is still high for African Americans. Asians and Pacific Islanders, as well as Latinos, have tended to experience increases in residential segregation. In addition, there are inhospitable feelings among non-White members groups. A Harris poll in the early 1990s reported the following:

- 46 percent of Hispanics and 42 percent of African Americans agreed that Asians are "unscrupulous, crafty and devious in business"—in contrast to 27 percent of Whites;
- 68 percent of Asians and 49 percent of African Americans agreed that Hispanics tend to "have bigger families than they are able to support"— in contrast to 50 percent of the whites;
- 33 percent of Hispanics and 22 percent of Asians believed that African Americans, "Even if given a chance, aren't capable of getting ahead"—in contrast to 12 percent of the whites;
- 48 percent of Hispanics, 39 percent of African Americans, and 30 percent of Asians believe that Muslims belong "to a religion that condones support of terrorism"—in contrast to the 41 percent of non-Muslim whites. (Permuttler, 2002, pp. 64, 65)

Further, because of how the economic marketplace is structured, non-White groups have been kept out of the economic mainstream and therefore kept from having an opportunity to work together with Whites. Ringer (1983) states:

> Having forcibly "created" the colonial plural society, the white European stood at its pinnacle of power and privilege. He superimposed his own political, economic, and social institutions on whatever traditional base there was and retained in his own hands the ultimate instrument of coercion and power. He introduced and installed administrative procedures and structures that enhanced his control. He created elite role models which were patterned in his own image and style and he introduced schemes of status evaluation with himself at the top. In effect, much of his energy was devoted to securing and maintaining his political, economic, and social dominance in the colony (p. 30).

Today, non-White groups' access to the marketplace is still hindered, in part because they are sometimes pitted against one another. Perlmutter (2002) argues that new manifestations of intergroup prejudice have emerged because of actual or imagined preferential treatment of some non-White groups (e.g., model minority vs. at-risk, culturally disadvantaged). Perlmutter (2002) contends that in some cases racial groups compete with one another for government benefits. In other cases, groups may battle over which racial group is the bigger victim.

In schools, very little multicultural education focuses on the plural society. Much of multiculturalism education in K–12 schools is about racial harmony, cultural awareness, and tolerance between White and non-White groups, instead of about cultural awareness, acceptance, and affirmation among the different non-White groups. In addition, much of multicultural education in schools of education centers on instructing White teacher candidates about how to teach (e.g., with classroom management methods, learning styles, instructional techniques) students of color. In other words, instruction is about how to help Whites better deal with the racial groups that were enslaved or subjugated during the early days in the nation's history. Very little attention is given to teaching non-White groups about other minorities, intraminority group prejudice, and /or intergroup tensions among native-born and immigrant groups. Further, very little instruction in multicultural education is about how to accept and affirm the culture and history of non-White groups and to celebrate their contribution to American society (Grant & Sleeter, 1996).

FAULT LINE BETWEEN BELIEFS AND PRACTICE: AVOIDING THE DILEMMA

> We seek . . . not just equality as a right and a theory, but equality as a
> fact and a result.
> —President Lyndon B. Johnson, Howard University

Up to this point, my argument has focused mostly on structural and institutional dimensions of race, multiculturalism, and the public interest. Now I wish to move the discussion more directly to my daily grind as a teacher educator. Here, I discuss pedagogy as the politics of schooling that relates to and overlaps with the structural and institutional. That is, as Popkewitz (personal communication, October 1, 2005) argues, "Race and racism embodied in the conditions which produce education, also are embodied in the images, narratives and beliefs of students as they organize reflections and actions in teaching and teacher education."

When sharing the above history with my students, I sometimes get something like the following: "That is old news. You are giving us irrelevant history. Thanks to the Internet, History Channel, and our high school teachers, we have learned about the horrors of enslavement, the Japanese in interment camps, and the abuse and mistreatment of the American Indians. What you are describing is from my great-great-granddaddy's time. We are sorry it happened, but our generation is not responsible, nor should we be connected to our great-great-grandfathers' mistakes. We believe in democratic principles such as equality, equity, and social justice."

I agree with my students' (all whom are White, except one or two) claims that they believe in the democratic principles espoused in the Constitution and the Declaration of Independence. However, it is not their beliefs as much as their actions that serve as the resistance to multiculturalism. There is a fault line, which was created in part by the dual structure and plural society, between their beliefs in democratic ideals and their practice of these ideals. Some of them are fully aware that the fault line exists, but others' are not. As noted above, many think that the civil rights movement took care of their great-great-granddaddy's racist acts because their K–12 history books and other instructional material have not been forthright (Sleeter & Grant, 1991); in addition, they have not been compelled to examine their actions to see if they are racist or to question whether they are privileged because of their skin color.

Conflict between students' beliefs in democratic ideals and their practice of these ideals causes teacher candidates and others to respond in different ways Many use common strategies for dealing with their conflict: avoidance, accommodation, aggression, compromise, and collaboration (Cloke & Goldsmith, 2000).

Those who avoid the discussion often contend that the dual treatment of Blacks and Whites for the most part came to an end in the 1960s with the humanitarian cries for freedom and justice by Blacks and others; with civil rights legislation; and with favorable court decisions for Blacks, women, individuals with disabilities, and other marginalized groups. They argue that legal-normative foundations were dismantled and Blacks and other minorities gained access and legal equality (e.g, *Brown v. Board of Education* and voting rights legislation). Sheryll Cashin (2004), in *The Failures of Integration: How Race and Class Are Undermining the American Dream,* addresses this misconception when she observes that 50 years after *Brown v. Board,* people argue that the United States should be an integrated society and that people of all races are inherently equal and entitled to the full privileges of citizenship. Contrarily, Cashin (2004) states, "Here is the reality: While we accept these values in the abstract, we are mostly pretending that they are true. At the dawn of the twenty-first century, the ideals of integration and equality of opportunity still elude us, and we are not being honest or forthcoming about it" (p. x).

Others show accommodation toward multiculturalism by readily accepting, for example, the ethnic studies course that they are required to take. However, over the next one or two semesters, they tend to argue that they are receiving too much multicultural education. Teacher candidates contend that less attention should be directed toward multicultural issues and more attention should be directed toward more traditional topics in teacher preparation, such as classroom management and discipline. In short, teacher candidates argue that their interests, and therefore the public interest, are not being served when they have class assignments that require them to apply a critical race analysis to the K–12 curriculum and their schooling. Some in this group claim that although there could be a race, culture, and income gap between them and a good number of the students they will teach, it is not in their immediate professional and personal interests to have a teacher preparation curriculum that rigorously addresses multiculturalism. They say that some multiculturalism is good, but not too much.

Still others deal with multiculturalism by generating a host of responses such as aggression/anger, guilt, shame, and despair. Beverly Tatum (1992) makes this point when she argues that students do not wish to engage in race-related discussion and content because it generates guilt, shame, and/or anger and despair—and that they may lead to resistance toward multiculturalism. Tatum (1992) states the following:

As many educational institutions struggle to become more multicultural in their students, faculty, and staff, they also begin to examine issues of cultural representation within their curriculum. This examination has evoked a growing number of courses that give specific consideration to the effect of variables such as race, class, and gender on human experience—an important trend that is reflected and supported by the increasing availability of resource manuals for the modification of course content. . . . Unfortunately, less attention has been given to the issues of process that inevitably emerge in the classroom when attention is focused on race, class, and/or gender. It is very difficult to talk about these concepts in a meaningful way without also talking and learning about racism, classism, and sexism. The introduction of these issues of oppression often generates powerful emotional response in students that range from guilt and shame to anger and despair. If not addressed, these emotional responses can result in student resistance to oppression-related content areas. Such resistance can ultimately interfere with the cognitive understanding and mastery of the material. This resistance and potential interference is particularly common when specifically addressing issues of race and racism. (pp. 1–2)

Still others are silent (in public places) about their dilemma between democratic beliefs and practices. It seems as if they have worked out a compromise within themselves as to when and where they may discuss issues of race and racism. Julie Landsman (2001), in *A White Teacher Talks About Race,* provides an observation about the silence in public around the discussion of racial duality:

In college and high school today, most white teachers are hesitant to bring up what stares at us with brown or blue eyes, what is so obvious when we see a coffee-colored, freckled, or dark blue-black hand resting on a white page. We believe we are "colorblind," a notion from the '50s, and from the Reagan years when it was considered wrong to recognize our differences. We white people hide from the fact of skin color difference. We often fail to speak directly at work about students who are different from ourselves. We do speak about it, though. After work, at dinner tables, we use euphemisms, code words: "welfare problem," "poverty problem," "crime problem," assuming these mean something other than what they are—a back-handed way of talking about what we believe is a 'race problem.'" (p. xi)

Similarly, many education researchers and scholars who advocate democratic principles marginalize or avoid multiculturalism in their work. During the past academic year, I was invited to review and evaluate two education handbooks. In each volume, the attention to multiculturalism was minimal. By "minimal," I mean there may be some reference to multiculturalism without attention to it or to the problems and issues living in a multicultural society brings with it. At best, there were one or two of the chapters in each handbook where race and/or multiculturalism were addressed. For example, in the handbook that focuses on research methods, one of the chapter authors, Kelly (in press), argues that there is a need to include oppressed groups' voices when conducting research in order to prevent "ideological distortions" (p. 10). Another chapter author, Banks (in press), argues that mainstream academic knowledge not only maintains the status quo but also perpetuates institutionalized racism; therefore, a multicultural analysis that takes into account the concept of power and privilege needs to be included. Such perspectives were not included in the work of most of the other chapters. Most of the chapter authors, whom I know, espouse their belief in the democratic principles of equity, equality, and social justice. Nevertheless, their work for the most part is muted regarding race and/or racism. The upshot of this is that graduate students who use these materials are implicitly told to ignore the fault line between democratic ideals and practices. Such attention to multiculturalism and race is a form of resistance and is not in the public interest.

Still others argue that multiculturalism is not a good form of practice for actualizing the democratic ideals and that multiculturalism is not in the public interest. Mike Walters (2004), after taking a look at multiculturalism on college campuses, claimed that "multiculturalism does more damage than it does good" (p. 1). Walters states that, "The movement toward multiculturalism and diversity are flawed in conception and evil in practice. If an individual wishes to learn about people from different backgrounds, it is only fair that he begins by setting aside preconceived notions based on race, culture, sexual orientation and identity. From that blank slate, one can best begin learning about the individual's view, beliefs and experience" (p. 1). It is safe to conclude that Walters does not believe that multiculturalism on the college campus is in the best interest of the students or the public.

CONCLUSION

How do we come to understand the chasm between democratic ideals and practice so that we may have conversations and act to eliminate the dual structures and bring about a more integrated society, rather than a close plural society? Myrdal (1944), in *The American Dilemma,* offered an observation to help Americans to recognize the fault line between democratic ideal and practice and to deal with the problems and issues of race and racism. His idea is useful today. Myrdal argues that the problem of White Americans with Black Americans can be analyzed and understood only if it is located in the norms and values that describe and define the basic ideals of America as a nation and as a people. These ideals, as we note above, are written into the founding and early documents of the nation. In these documents—the Declaration of Independence, the Preamble of the Constitution, the Bill of Rights—are America's ideals: freedom, dignity, equality for all people, justice, and a fair opportunity. Thus, I hear Myrdal saying we must begin the conversation at the point where we admit that we have failed to align our practices with our democratic ideals; accept that we have a dual society and a racist discourse; and have done little as a nation to foster intergroup integration and harmony. Our acceptance of racism and the racialized discourse that supports racism will then permit us to focus the debate away from such ideas as "it's not race, it's class" or "let's not talk about race, but get the people some shelter and water." It is about race—and racism that is very resilient and has a long history—and it is there that conversation must begin. We are connected to our great-great-granddaddies, hopefully in more proud and positive than shameful and negative ways. If we forget this or remain silent, the dual structure will remain in place, the plural society will breed stronger intergroup hostility, the fault line between democratic ideals and practice will become larger, and the nation's public interest will not be served.

REFERENCES

Banks, J. (in press). Researching, race, culture and difference: Epistemological challenges and possibilities. In J. Green & P. B. E. Gregory (Eds.), *Complementary methods for research in education* (3rd Ed.).

Bell, D., & Kristol, I. (1965). What is the public interest? *The Public Interest, 1*, 1–4.

Berkhofer, R. F. (1978). *The White man's Indian*. New York: Vintage.

Bridges, R. (1999). *Through my eyes*. New York: Scholastic.

Bullock, H. A. (1967). *A history of Negro education in the South: From 1619 to the present*. New York: Praeger.

Cashin, S. (2004). *The failures of integration: How race and class are undermining the American dream*. New York: Public Affairs.

Cloke, K., & Goldsmith, J. (2000). *Resolving conflicts at work: A complete guide for everyone on the job*. San Francisco: Jossey-Bass.

Costo, R., & Henry, J. (1970). *Textbooks and the American Indian*. San Francisco: Indian Historian Press.

Fleishman, S. (2005, September 14). Minorities often pay more for mortgages: lenders required to give Fed data on subprime loans. *Washington Post*, p. D1.

Furnivall, J. S. (1956). *Colonial policy and practice*. New York: New York University Press.

Grant, C. A., & Sleeter, C. E. (1996). *After the school bell rings*. London: Falmer.

Hess, F. M. (2003, September). Public schools and the public interest. *The School Administrator*, pp. 28–31.

Horowitiz, I. L., & Imber, J. B. (2002, November/December). Scientific endeavor, professional aims and public interests. *Society, 40*(1), 8–11.

Kelly, G. (in press). Epistemology and educational research. In J. Green & P. B. E. Gregory, (Eds.), *Complementary methods for research in education* (3rd ed.).

Kozol, J. (2005). *The shame of the nation: The restoration of apartheid schooling in America*. New York: Crown.

Landsman, J. (2001). *A White teacher talks about race*. Lanham, MD: Scarecrow Press.

Logan, R. W., & Cohen, I. S. (1967). *The American Negro: Old world background and new world experience*. Boston: Houghton Mifflin.

Metcalf, G. (1983). *From Little Rock to Boston: The history of school desegregation*. Westport, CT: Greenwood.

Myrdal, G. (1944). *An American dilemma*. New York: Harper & Brothers.

Pearce, R. H. (1988). *Savagism and civilization: A study of the Indian and the American mind.* Berkeley: University of California Press.

Perlmutter, P. (2002, March/April). Minority group prejudice. *Society, 39*(3), 59–65.

Ringer, B. B. (1983). *"We the People" and others: Duality and America's treatment of its racial minorities.* New York: Tavistock.

Rousseau, J. J. (1999). *The social contract* (new ed.). London: Oxford University Press. (Original work published 1762)

Sleeter, C. E., & Grant, C. A. (1991). Race, class, gender, and disability in current textbooks. In M. Apple & L. Christian-Smith (Eds.), *The politics of the textbook* (pp. 78–110). Routledge & Chapman Hall.

Solomon, M. (2005). The problems with No Child Left Behind. Retrieved October 2, 2005, from http://www.educationnews.org/problems-with-no-child-left-behind.htm

Stevens, R. (1996). *American medicine and the public interest.* New Haven, CT: Yale University Press. (Original work published 1971)

Tatum, B. D. (1992). Talking about race, learning about racism: The application of racial identity development theory in the classroom. *Harvard Educational Review, 62*(1), 1–24.

Tocqueville, A. de (2001). *Democracy in America.* New York: Signet. (Original work published 1848)

Thomas, E. (2005, September 19) How Bush blew it. *Newsweek,* pp 30–38.

U.S. Census Bureau. (2005). Housing patterns. Available at http://www.census.gov/hhes/www/housing/housing_patterns/housing_patterns.html

Walter, J. (2005) The changing status of the Black athlete in the 20th century United States. Retrieved October 22, 2005, from www.americansc.org.u/Online/walters.html

Walters, M. (2004). Multiculturalsim does more damage than it does good. *The Battalion.* Retrieved December 15, 2005, from http://www.thebatt.com/media/paper657/news/2004/10/22/Opinion/Multiculturalism.Does.More.Damage.Than.It.Does.Good-777351.shtml

Public Interest and the Interests of White People Are Not the Same: Assessment, Education Policy, and Racism

David Gillborn

As I write, I try to remember when the word racism ceased to be the term which best expressed for me exploitation of black people and other people of color in this society and when I began to understand that the most useful term was white supremacy.
                                                              —bell hooks (1989, p 112)

What has become clear to me is my parents have a disdain towards "whiteworld." They came here to earn money. They came for no other reason. They don't trust white people, they don't engage with them more than they have to and certainly school was a white institution.
              —Dennis, a Black Londoner whose parents migrated to England
                        in the early 1950s (quoted in McKenley, 2004, p. 61)

INTRODUCTION

MOST WHITE PEOPLE WOULD PROBABLY be surprised by the idea of "White world"; they see only the "world", its *White-ness* is invisible to them because the racialized nature of politics, policing, education, and every other sphere of public life is so deeply ingrained that it has become normalized—unremarked and taken-for granted. This is an exercise of power that goes beyond notions of "White *privilege"*—a phrase that has become increasingly common as writers come to an awareness of the multitude of ways in which people who are identified as "white" enjoy countless, often unrecognized, advantages in their daily lives:

I have come to see white privilege as an invisible package of unearned assets that I can count on cashing in each day, but about which I was "meant" to remain oblivious. White privilege is like an invisible weightless knapsack of special provisions, assurances, tools, maps, guides, codebooks, passports, visas, clothes, compass, emergency gear, and blank checks. (McIntosh, 1988, p. 291)

Peggy McIntosh famously listed 50 privileges that accrue from being identified as White, ranging from the ability to shop without the threat of being followed to the possibility of living free from harassment and the option to act however you choose without being seen as emblematic of an entire racial group. This important work has proved useful to many critical educators trying to raise the consciousness of their students, but, as Zeus Leonardo (2002, 2004) has argued, there has been a tendency for talk of "privilege" to mask the structures and actions of domination that make possible, and sustain, the routine assumptions that work in the interests of White people and against the interests of people of color:

The theme of privilege obscures the subject of domination, or the agent of actions, because the situation is described as happening almost without the knowledge of whites. It conjures up images of domination happening behind the backs of whites, rather than on the backs of people of color. The study of white privilege begins to take on an image of domination without agents. (Leonardo, 2004, p. 138)

In addition, work on Whiteness does not always retain a sense of power and, as Michael Apple has argued, can lapse into possessive individualism whereby it can "become one more excuse to recenter dominant voices" by subverting a critical analysis and making an argument along the lines of "but enough about you, let me tell you about me" (Apple, 1998, p. xi). Such uncritical forays into Whiteness studies threaten to recolonize the field of multicultural education (McLaren, 1995; Sheets, 2000) and to mask the structural power of White identifications so that Whites are perversely portrayed as race victims (Apple, 2004; Howard, 2004), and serve to ensure that higher education remains an institution predominantly operated *by* White people *for* White people (Dlamini, 2002; Foster, 2005).

It is in this sense that many critics, especially those working within critical race theory (CRT), talk of White *supremacy* (see Delgado & Stefancic, 2001; Ladson-Billings & Tate, 1995). In these analyses, White supremacy is not only, nor indeed primarily, associated with relatively small and extreme political movements that openly mobilize on the basis of race hatred (important and dangerous though such groups are): rather, supremacy is seen to relate to the operation of forces that saturate the everyday, mundane actions and policies that shape the world in the interests of White people (see Bush, 2004; Delgado & Stefancic, 1997):

[By] "white supremacy" I do not mean to allude only to the self-conscious racism of white supremacist hate groups. I refer instead to a political, economic, and cultural system in which whites overwhelmingly control power and material resources, conscious and unconscious ideas of white superiority and entitlement are widespread, and relations of white dominance and non-white subordination are daily reenacted across a broad array of institutions and social settings. (Ansley, 1997, p. 592)

Critical race theory is sometimes attacked for placing race at the center of the analysis, seemingly to the detriment of gendered and class-based analyses. In fact, a good deal of CRT takes very seriously the intersections of raced, classed, and gendered inequities (see, for example, Parker, Deyhler, & Villenas, 1999; Wing, 1997). However, at its core, CRT demands that race and racism never be relegated to the sidelines nor imagined to be a complexifying element in a situation that is *really* about class or *really* about gender. In this chapter I adopt a CRT perspective to examine the operation of racism in the English education system—a context where both the scale of race inequity and the processes that sustain it may be surprisingly familiar to critics working in the United States. I focus on the processes by which school students are assessed, ranked, and educated differently according to official judgments about "merit" and "ability." These processes are officially presented as color-blind, value-neutral matters of professional judgment and assessment, but they act to powerfully protect White interests and marginalize the interests of people of color, especially those who identify as Black.[1]

ASSESSMENT AND EDUCATIONAL INEQUITY: WHO COUNTS?

It is striking that whenever critical scholars propose a case where racism is implicated, there is a tendency for others (usually, but not exclusively, White people) to argue that some other factor is *really* to blame. For every Black student who fails an exam or is expelled from school (forms of symbolic violence that Black students endure in disproportionate numbers [Gillborn & Mirza, 2000]), there is always another *possible* explanation. One of the clearest cases of this within the academy can be seen in the methodological questions raised about antiracist research, where (it has been argued) the failure to *prove* the existence of racism to the satisfaction of the people in question is sufficient reason to refrain from making such a damaging criticism (see Hammersley, 1995; Foster, 1993; Foster, Gomm, & Hammersley, 1996; for a reply, see Gillborn, 1998). Indeed, even in signature cases like the murder of Stephen Lawrence (a case that ultimately led to the reform of British race equality legislation) there are always additional *possible* explanations. For example, as Stephen lay dying on the pavement (having been stabbed by a gang of White youths), a 14-year-old onlooker was astonished that none of the police officers present took action in response to his injuries. The official report notes:

> She was amazed that no-one was attending to the body on the floor or trying to stem the flow of blood. She saw that there was a lot of blood and her knowledge of First Aid told her that something ought to have been done. (Macpherson, 1999, p. 57, emphasis in original)

The attending police officers claimed not to have seen that there was a significant amount of blood and to have thought it best to leave Stephen in the position in which he had collapsed. This claim, essentially one of negligence rather than racism, was *accepted* by the inquiry team. So, rather than spending more time on definitions (of racism, supremacy, etc.), it may be useful to begin by imagining a more simple set of propositions and see where that leads us. This use of an alternative narrative approach is common in critical race theory, where storytelling is frequently used to help cast familiar issues in a fresh light and view things through a new lens (see Bell, 1990, 1992; Delgado, 1995; Ladson-Billings, 1998; Ladson-Billings & Tate, 1995; Tate 1997; Williams, 1987). This is *not* to run from the disciplines of scientific rigor and conventional forms of academic disputation—readers who see no place for storytelling in science may skip forward to the end of the vignette at no great loss. My analysis rests on the use of publicly available statistics and draws on a range of empirical studies (both quantitative and qualitative). My story is not an alternative to critique—it is a complement to it, a means of shedding new light on a set of issues whose remarkably damaging consequences might otherwise be lost amid the mundane and routine processes that not only conceal race inequity but actually produce it.

THE "WRONG" RESULT: A STORY ABOUT ASSESSMENT

This story is about a deeply racist society. In this imaginary society racism saturates all public agencies. This is not a generally nice place where the occasional nasty individual spoils things. No, this is a society were racism leaves its imprint on virtually every aspect of life, from birth to death (and everything in between).

Now, of course, in a society so deeply patterned by racism, not everything is plain sailing. People don't simply accept their subjugation no matter how long it has been practiced. There are continual points of conflict and resistance, but most of the time these are kept in check and barely register on the "mainstream" consciousness. Consequently, the dominant group is able to sustain its preferred fiction; that the despised people only have themselves to blame for their misfortune. This is possible because—in this imaginary place—racism is present throughout every major part of society. Racism patterns its political system and its public services, including the police and the schools.

Until, that is, one day, something goes wrong.

One day it is discovered that, despite all the odds, the despised group is excelling in school.

Totally contrary to the dominant group's view of how things *should* be, it emerges that the despised group is really good at something. And to make matters worse, this is not something that can be dismissed as frivolous or entertaining—like being good dancers, musicians, or athletes.

It emerges that the despised group is excelling in a school test.

They are not yet outperforming the entire educational system, but it becomes clear that on one particular kind of test, they are not just holding their own—they are the very highest achievers.

The dominant group is stunned: How can this be?

Now, of course, in this imaginary racist society such a thing cannot be permitted.

But what is to be done?

An obvious solution is to simply bar the despised group from taking the test. You can't pass what you're not allowed to enter.

Good answer. And, under certain circumstances, that strategy would work. Indeed, we have an example very close to home . . .

ASSESSING MERIT OR CLOSING DOWN POSSIBILITIES? AN ENGLISH EXAMPLE

The main examination at the end of compulsory schooling in England is the GCSE (General Certificate of Secondary Education). Students' results are graded from A*, A, B, and C through to G: grades C and above are known as "higher pass grades" and at least five of these are necessary for entry to most courses in higher education or in professional education. The GCSE was introduced in 1988 and, since then, most subjects have adopted an approach known as "tiering" (see Figure 10.1). In most subjects, teachers allocate pupils to one of two separate exam tiers (in mathematics, there are currently three tiers). There is no dual entry, and the tier places a higher and lower limit on the grades available. Those in the foundation tier cannot do better than a C in most subjects—meaning that study at an advanced level may be out of the question (because the necessary grades A* to B *cannot* be awarded in that tier). In mathematics, the foundation tier currently denies even a C, which is usually taken as the minimum requirement for entry to higher education and the professions.

In a study of tiering in two London secondary schools, Deborah Youdell and I discovered that two-thirds of Black students were entered for maths in the lowest tier (Gillborn & Youdell, 2000): No matter how many questions they answered correctly, therefore, two out of three Black children could not possibly achieve the required pass grade in maths because the examination simply did not permit it.[2] Of course, these lower-ranked groups are not overtly determined on the basis of race—they are usually presented as a reflection of the pupils' capabilities, that is, their "*ability.*" But, as Bernard Coard (1971) pointed out more than 30 years ago, we should be extremely cautious whenever we are told that certain pupils (disproportionately Black pupils) are less able, less well developed, or whatever is the preferred phrase of the moment to describe those pupils who have been deemed to be outside the chosen ranks of those destined to succeed. We need this caution because, despite the façade of value-neutral standardized testing and teachers' "professional" judgment, in school the word *ability* is very often another word

Figure 10.1. Tiering and the Grades Available in GCSE Examinations (England)

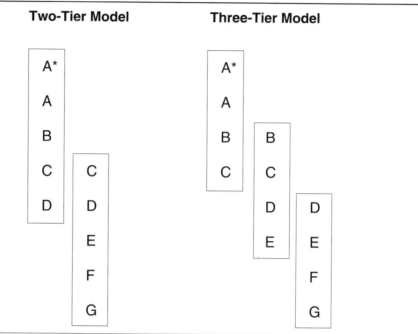

for what teachers *think/assume* children can do. Let me illustrate with a simple example. During our research, we spoke with a department head about pupils' reactions when they were told their teachers' predictions for their future exam performance:

> I found that quite strange that the kids had their estimated grades because they then came back at you and gave you earache, you know, would challenge you in the corridor and so you were under threat. You know, "why have you only given me that grade," you know? Because kids, you know, have different perceptions of themselves, they have no understanding, you know, and some of them live in cloud cuckoo land. I mean we've got, we had a whole period where we had Afro-Caribbean kids running around with gold rimmed glasses on with plain glass in them because they thought it made them look more intelligent, you know, they really had highly inflated opinions of themselves as far as academic achievement, and this is fact. I mean there were a whole group of kids that put on glasses and wandered round the corridors with gold rimmed glasses on because they really felt that they were sort of A/B

This quotation is especially illuminating because the teacher *could* have interpreted the situation in a way that shattered common stereotypes. For example, in many quarters a preferred explanation for the lower average Black attainment levels (especially among boys) is that they are somehow afraid to be seen to work hard, that they think academic effort is uncool. This is paraded in the media as the predominant cause for Black academic failure, neatly shifting the blame from the system itself (e.g. Matthews, 2004; Sewell, 2005) and the erasing of the history of the Black community's commitment to education and the evidence in front of our eyes. For example, in England, Black young people are more likely to remain in full-time education than their White counterparts (Gillborn & Gipps, 1996). Similarly, the teacher quoted above is blind to the evidence in front of him. He describes Black pupils who are confident in their abilities and he even speculates that they change their appearance so as to "look more intelligent." And yet this same teacher does not recognize the hunger and commitment before him; he sees only the stereotype—Black young people that embody unrealistic expectations and engender a sense of fear: "challenge you in the corridor" . . . "you were under threat" . . . "they really had highly inflated opinions of themselves."

Of course, schools assess pupils all the time, both informally (as above) and formally, including the use of so called "cognitive abilities tests"—essentially IQ tests by a less discredited name. And yet, amid all this testing, one simple fact is vitally important: There is no measure of educational potential; every test is a measure of *learned* competencies. Even within the ranks of the psychometric testers themselves—people who write and administer IQ tests for a living—there is now widespread agreement that there is no single thing called "ability" or intelligence and that relative scores are not fixed:

> Human abilities are forms of developing expertise . . . tests of abilities are no different from conventional tests of achievement, teacher-made tests administered in school, or assessments of job performance. Although tests of abilities are used as predictors of these other kinds of performance, the temporal priority of their administration should not be confused with some kind of psychological priority. . . . There is no qualitative distinction among the various kinds of measures. (Sternberg, 1998, p. 11)

Or to put it more simply:

> The fact that Billy and Jimmy have different IQs tells us something about differences in what they now do. It does not tell us anything fixed about what ultimately they will be able to do. (Sternberg, 1998, p. 18)

These quotes are from someone working *within* the psychometric field. The author, Robert J. Sternberg, is the IBM Professor of Psychology and Education at Yale, a major figure in contemporary "intelligence" testing, and a leading theoretician in the field of human abilities and giftedness. Sternberg has devoted considerable energy to his thesis that "abilities" are "forms of developing expertise," including several publications and the establishment of a dedicated center at Yale (see Sternberg, 1998, 1999, 2001). However, Sternberg's central argument is not as revolutionary as some might think. The Cleary Committee, appointed in the 1970s by the American Psychological Association, stated:

> A distinction is drawn traditionally between intelligence and achievement tests. A naive statement of the difference is that the intelligence test measures *capacity to learn* and the achievement test measures *what has been learned*. But items in *all* psychological and educational tests measure *acquired* behavior. (quoted in Kamin, 1981, p. 94, emphasis added)

Contrary to popular belief, therefore, there is no test of capacity to learn: *Every* test so far conceived measures only what you have learned so far. Despite all the "scientific" façade that surrounds the industry of standardized testing, therefore, we must remember that tests—all tests—measure only whether a person can perform well on that particular test at that particular time. They do not reveal differences in innate potential any more than a teacher's off-the-cuff assessment of students represents a reliable and valid measure of merit. In view of these factors, it is perhaps not surprising that White students are between two and five times more likely than their Black counterparts to be identified as "gifted and talented" in English schools.[3] In fact, the recent history of the "gifted and talented" provision is an interesting illustration of the place of race equity in education policy more generally.

In March 2002 the British government founded a national Academy for Gifted & Talented Youth at an annual cost of £20 million. The model for the academy is the Center for Talented Youth at Johns Hopkins University, founded by Professor Julian C. Stanley. In 1994, at the height of the controversy about the book *The Bell Curve* (Herrnstein & Murray, 1994), Stanley was co-signatory to a statement about IQ testing in the *Wall Street Journal* ("Mainstream Science," 1994) which asserted the fairness of IQ tests, stated that intelligence is determined by genetics more than environment, and reported an average difference between Whites and "American Blacks" of around 25 points—this would be equivalent to the average White person being more intelligent than over 80% of Black people. At the time I gave a major public lecture on race equity in London and warned that the "gifted and talented" programs would likely become yet another area where Black students were denied equity (Gillborn, 2002). The Department for Education issued a rebuttal stating that "the gifted and talented scheme will identify children by looking at ability, rather than attainment, to capitalise on the talents of the individual child, regardless of ethnic background" ("Racism Warning," 2002).[4] In a news story covering the establishment of the British Academy, the minister responsible was confident that the English scheme would not replicate the problems of its U.S. counterpart:

> The Centre for Talented Youth has been established for 21 years but it is only since 1999 that attempts have been made to reach under-represented groups. . . . Mr Timms

[the British Schools Minister] said the Centre for Talented Youth's success in including low income and minority students was modest. The Excellence in Cities gifted and talented programme meant the new English academy would be better placed to reach those pupils'. (Henry, 2002, p. 13)

Subsequently, no safeguards were put in place to ensure that minority students were dealt with fairly and, 3 years later, the underrepresentation of Black students was confirmed, but no action taken to address the situation (DfES, 2005, p. 36).

And so, if we return to the story of a mythical crude racist society, we can see that denying entry to the test might provide a solution. GCSE tiers are not widely understood (by students or parents, let alone the general public). Indeed, the case of GCSE tiering offers a neat example of how the dominant group could respond without even having to compromise its preferred narrative—that the despised group fails because of its own deficiencies rather than because of racism. The dominant group would simply report that the despised group were not good enough to take the test. But in the imaginary racist society of my story, the problem is even bigger than that.

In my story, the despised group is excelling at a test that *every* pupil must take. You see, in the place I'm asking you to imagine, the state has decreed that all children must be tested throughout their school careers. They are each stamped with a unique code number, and a log of their successes—and failures—follows them throughout the system.

And so everyone must take the test. But if the dominant group cannot restrict entry to the test, it seems that only one course of action remains: Change the test.

The test must be redesigned so that the despised group no longer succeeds.

Simple.

But, of course, such a crass and obviously racist set of events could never occur in the *real* world. There would be an outcry. Wouldn't there?

ONCE UPON A TIME, WHEN BLACK CHILDREN DID BEST

In 2000 I co-authored a national report with Heidi Safia Mirza, Professor of Race Equality at the University of Middlesex. The report was an independent review of evidence sponsored and published by the official schools inspectorate, the Office for Standards in Education (OFSTED). The work was widely reported in the media (including coverage on national TV, radio, and newspapers), and certain findings received particular attention. First, in conflict with the dominant stereotypes, we found that there was a great deal of variation in attainment by minority groups in different parts of the country. In 2000 there was no legal obligation to monitor education results by ethnic origin, but an increasing number of local education authorities (LEAs) were starting to gather this data, especially where the statistics were needed in order to bid for additional resources from the Department for Education & Skills (DfES). It was precisely this impulse that had led more than 100 local authorities to provide data that, after a somewhat protracted series of negotiations, we were able to access and analyse.[5] Contrary to expectations, we discovered that for each of the principal minority ethnic groups, there was at least one LEA where that group was the most likely to achieve five or more higher-grade GCSE passes (Gillborn & Mirza, 2000). This surprised many, including the DfES, which had previously not realized the scale of variation within (as well as between) different groups.

A second finding that startled many observers arose from the same data set. Most of the 118 LEAs on which we had data reported ethnic breakdowns from the age of 11 onward (the end of 'Key Stage 2' in the national curriculum). However, six LEAs also monitored pupils' achievements at age 5, in the so-called baseline assessments carried out when children entered compulsory schooling. The data on all six LEAs indicated that Black attainments fell relative to the LEA average as the children moved through school. The data on one LEA was especially striking. In the largest LEA in our sample (also one of the biggest authorities in the country), we found that Black children were the *highest*-achieving of all groups in the baseline assessments (see Figure 10.2).

Figure 10.2. Black Performance Relative to the LEA Average at Selected Ages, 1999

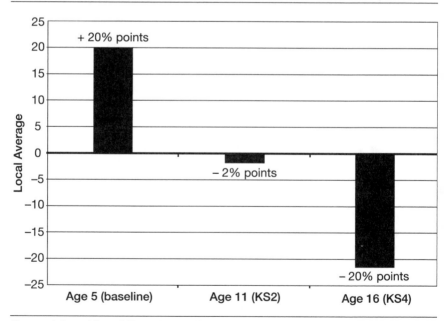

Source: Adapted from Gillborn & Mirza (2000), Figure 5.

Figure 10.3. Black Performance Relative to the National Average at Age 11 and Age 16, Ten LEAs, 1998

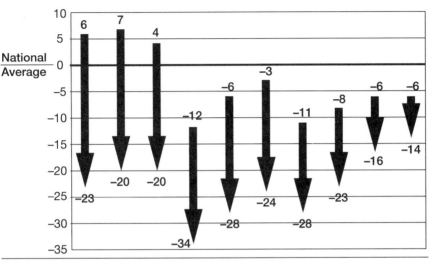

Source: Adapted from Richardson & Wood (1999), Table 4.

At age 5, Black children were significantly more likely to reach the required levels: 20 percentage points above the local average. At age 11, however, Black children in the same LEA were performing *below* the local average. And at age 16, the end of compulsory schooling, the inequity was so bad that Black children were the *lowest*-performing of all the principal groups—21 percentage points below the average (Gillborn & Mirza, 2000).

In the report, we noted that previous work had already begun to document the relative decline in Black attainment at later stages in the education system. A year earlier research for the pressure group Race on the Agenda (Richardson & Wood, 1999) had shown a similar pattern between the ages of 11 and 16. Their study included data on 10 LEAs in and around London, showing that between the end of primary school and the end of secondary school, on average, African Caribbean pupils dropped 20 percentage points relative to the national average (see Figure 10.3). Prior to the OFSTED report, therefore, data were already suggesting that Black/White inequalities might be worsening as children move through the system. What marked out the OFSTED report for particular attention, however, was the prominence of the report's sponsor and the range of our data. Unlike previous analyses, the data in Figure 10.2 started at age 5, much earlier than any other available data. In addition, by showing Black children as the *highest* achievers in the baseline assessments, the data fundamentally challenged the assumption that Black children entered the school system poorly prepared (a common argument at the time). This was an important finding that quickly passed into the wider arena of debate on race and achievement: This view of Black children's attainments is now very widely cited. For example, the OFSTED report is often used as a major source on race and education in textbooks.[6] The finding on 5-year-olds has passed into received wisdom and is widely quoted, for example, by newspapers as part of the context for wider debates, and it is frequently cited by politicians:

> According to government figures, black pupils start primary school with some of the highest scores in baseline assessments of initial ability. But after two years they begin to slip behind other pupils.
>
> *The Guardian*, March 8, 2005, p. 7

> When African and Afro-Caribbean children start school at five they do as well in tests as white and Asian children. By the age of 11 their achievement levels begin to drop off. By 16 there has been a collapse.
>
> Diane Abbott, MP, March 2005

It is remarkable that in such a short time (less than 5 years) this once-startling fact became an accepted part of the educational landscape. Unfortunately, there is something even more remarkable, because in that same 5-year period the system of assessment on entry to school changed, and so did the patterns of attainment: Black children are no longer the highest-achieving group; in fact, they are now among the *lowest* performers.

NEW ASSESSMENT, NEW OUTCOMES: A FAMILIAR STORY?

The term *foundation stage* has been officially applied to the period between a child's third birthday and the end of his or her reception year in primary school. Simultaneously, the Foundation Stage Profile has replaced the baseline assessments that used to take place when children entered primary school.[7] There are several important points to note about the Foundation Stage Profile. First, it is entirely based on teachers' judgments: The Qualifications & Curriculum Authority (QCA, 2003) describes it this way:

> Throughout the foundation stage, as part of the learning and teaching process, practitioners need to assess each child's development. . . . These assessments are made on the basis of the practitioner's accumulating observations and knowledge of the whole child. By the end of the final year of the foundation stage, the Foundation Stage Profile will provide a way of summing up that knowledge. (p. 1)

A second key point about the Foundation Stage Profile is that it is relatively complex in terms of its coverage. Overall there are six "areas of learning": personal, social, and emotional development; communication, language, and literacy; mathematical development; knowledge and understanding of the world; physical development; and creative development. These six areas include 13 different scales, which are assessed individually in relation to specific "Early Learning Goals."

A final significant point in relation to the Foundation Stage Profile is that the system was introduced only relatively recently and is still surrounded in some uncertainty. Indeed, there are important questions about the reliability of the results. When reporting on the first set of data, for example, the Department for Education & Skills (2004) stated:

> *The results should be treated with caution as this is the first year that such data have been collected.* The data result from a new statutory assessment for which teachers have received **limited** and **variable** training and the moderation of results within and between local education authorities (LEAs) has been **patchy**." (p. 1, emphasis in original)

In fact, the DfES was so worried about the quality of the assessments that when the results were first published (in June 2004), the document was entitled "experimental statistics" and the National Statistics logo was deliberately not used (DfES, 2004, p. 1). This first analysis of data from the Foundation Stage Profile made no reference to ethnicity at all. About 6 months later, however, the DfES made use of the same material in an overview of data on ethnicity and education. This time there was a partial breakdown of results in relation to the principal minority ethnic groups (DfES, 2005). This is highly significant because it was the first time that any data from the Foundation Stage Profile had been published with an ethnic component.

The DfES presentation included a brief explanation about the Foundation Stage and a note of caution about the level of teacher training involved and the moderation of results. The document then presented a breakdown of results in relation to one of the 13 scales (Figure 10.4) and a summary of key findings. The discussion begins with the following statement: "Patterns of achievement for minority ethnic groups in Early Learning Goals would appear to broadly mirror attainment gaps at older ages" (DfES, 2005, p. 8). Interestingly, there was no reference to how this finding sat alongside previous work in the field, such as the earlier baseline test results. Nevertheless, the document noted that this pattern was common across all of the 13 scales that make up the Foundation Stage Profile: "Pakistani and Bangladeshi children . . . perform less well, followed by Black African and Black Caribbean children (with all groups scoring less well than the average on all 13 of the scales)" (DfES, 2005, p. 8). There was no further data on race inequity and the Foundation Stage Profiles. The DfES document made no further mention of the foundation stage, and there was no comment at all about previous assessments of minority children's learning on entry to compulsory schooling.

The reader was left with a sense of continuity, not change. But these findings run contrary to the now widely held belief that Black children do relatively

Figure 10.4. Foundation Stage Profile 2003: Pupils Meeting or Exceeding the Expected Level, *Language for Communication & Thinking* by Ethnic Origin

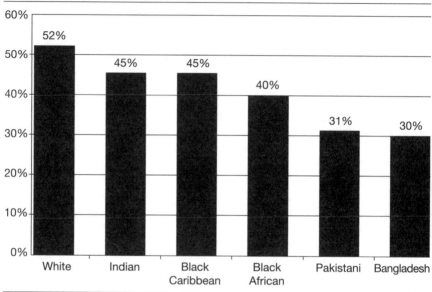

Source: DfES (2003), Figure 3.

well on entry to compulsory school. As I have already noted, this belief is widely stated and restated—it appears in textbooks, in the media, and even in political discourse. And yet the Department for Education & Skills published the first ever ethnic analysis of results from the new assessments and the pattern was reversed without comment. It is difficult to overestimate the significance of these events: the received wisdom has been turned on its head; Black children have moved from being "*over*achievers" to "*under*achievers"; and the system that has produced these outcomes is acknowledged to be based on training and moderation that was "patchy." And yet the results stand. The new pattern of attainment for 5-year-olds is reported without further comment, and one of the key issues that had raised questions about Black children's treatment in schools has been erased, almost overnight.

    And what about attainments in the local authority that Mirza and I had highlighted? The DfES data are based on national returns and, as already noted, results can differ substantially from one LEA to another. With the cooperation of that LEA, we can judge how far the national picture is reflected at a local level: The result is far from encouraging.

    Table 10.1 shows attainment in all six areas of learning in the Foundation Stage Profile broken down by ethnicity and gender. The table relates to the same

Table 10.1. Foundation Stage Assessments by Ethnic Group and Gender 2004 (Proportion of pupils achieving the majority of the early learning goals in each area of learning) (percentage points comparison with white pupils)

Ethnic Group	Personal, Social and Emotional Development			Communication, Language & Literacy			Mathematical Development			Knowledge and Understanding of the World			Physical Development			Creative Development		
	B	G	All	B	G	All	B	G	All	B	G	All	B	G	All	B	G	All
White	NA	NA	NA	NA	NA	NA	NA	NA	NA	NA	NA	NA	NA	NA	NA	NA	NA	NA
Mixed Race; White/African Caribbean	-7%	-1%	-4%	-4%	-4%	-3%	-5%	-3%	-3%	-5%	+1%	-2%	+3%	+1%	+2%	+3%	+4%	+4%
Mixed Race; White/Asian	-9%	-5%	-8%	-1%	-8%	-5%	-5%	-11%	-8%	-11%	-2%	-8%	-6%	-7%	-6%	-9%	-1%	-7%
Mixed Race Other	-10%	-7%	-8%	-7%	-10%	-8%	-10%	-9%	-9%	-11%	-9%	-10%	-4%	-3%	-3%	-11%	-7%	-10%
Indian	-7%	-7%	-7%	-5%	-9%	-7%	-8%	-12%	-10%	-15%	-13%	-14%	-5%	-8%	-6%	-12%	-9%	-11%
Pakistani	-16%	-14%	-15%	-20%	-24%	-22%	-23%	-22%	-22%	-24%	-24%	-24%	-9%	-8%	-8%	-20%	-15%	-18%
Bangladeshi	-15%	-19%	-17%	-26%	-29%	-27%	-26%	-29%	-27%	-28%	-28%	-28%	-10%	-7%	-8%	-22%	-17%	-20%
Asian; Other	-7%	-8%	-7%	-6%	-11%	-8%	-12%	-10%	-10%	-12%	-12%	-12%	+1%	=	+1%	-6%	-14%	-10%
Black Caribbean	-13%	-7%	-10%	-14%	-11%	-12%	-9%	-7%	-7%	-8%	-10%	-9%	-2%	-4%	-2%	-5%	-5%	-5%
Black African	-16%	+2%	-6%	-23%	-11%	-15%	-17%	-7%	-11%	-28%	-12%	-20%	-1%	=	=	-18%	+3%	-6%
Chinese	-9%	-5%	-6%	-2%	+2%	+1%	-5%	-4%	-4%	-16%	=	-8%	-1%	=	=	+10%	-4%	+3%
All Groups	-7%	-6%	-6%	-8%	-10%	-9%	-9%	-9%	-9%	-10%	-9%	-10%	-4%	-3%	-3%	-8%	-6%	-7%

LEA featured in the OFSTED report of 2000 (Figure 10.2). In order to retain the anonymity of the local authority, I have removed the original data and inserted a figure (positive or negative) to show how each cell's value relates to the respective White performance.[8] For example, -7% in the upper left-hand cell denotes that 7% fewer "Mixed Race White/African Caribbean" boys were judged to have met or exceeded the target when compared with White boys.

In total there are 180 different cells relating to minority attainment in the table: 159 of the cells (almost 90%) show minority children being ranked lower than their White counterparts. There are just 15 cells where minority children are ranked higher than Whites, and most of these are within the areas of "physical development" and "creative development"—domains where traditional stereotypes would more easily accept such performance.

This change in patterns of attainment is hugely important. It is these scores that schools will use to judge the progress of the students in later assessments. Potentially, the lower attainments of Black students in subsequent stages of the education system will no longer be viewed as a relative drop in performance; they may simply be viewed as performing in line with their lower starting points.

HOW DID WE GET HERE?
IT'S NOT A CONSPIRACY—ITS WORSE THAN THAT

Clearly these developments raise a series of important questions. Unfortunately, baseline assessments were not around for very long and there was no single national system—indeed, more than 90 different schemes were accredited. Consequently, it is difficult retrospectively to identify reliable information on the various approaches that were used. In contrast, the new Foundation Stage Profile is a national scheme, it is compulsory, and it is entirely teacher assessed. This latter point (the reliance on teacher assessment) may offer a clue to part of the mechanism behind the changes. Work on assessment has long argued that teachers' views of group characteristics (such as class, gender, and ethnicity) can affect their scores (e.g., see Gipps, 1994; Kornhaber, 2004). I have already discussed how these processes can operate at a classroom level, and it is widely documented that Black students tend to be overrepresented in low-ranked teaching groups when teachers' judgments are used to inform selection within schools (in systems such as tracking, setting, banding, and tiering); for relevant data and discussions, see Connolly (1998), Gillborn (2004a, b), Oakes (1990), Oakes Joseph, & Muir (2004), and QCA (2000). In addition, in their review of key debates about assessment, Sanders and Horn (1995) quote the following:

> In England in the late 1980s, when the assessments that make up the General Certificate of Secondary Education were changed to put more emphasis on performance tasks (which are assessed by classroom teachers) and less on written answers, the gaps between the average scores of various ethnic groups increased rather than narrowed. (Maeroff, 1991, p. 281, quoted in Sanders & Horn, 1995)

In addition, the change in the *timing* of the Foundation Stage Profile may be implicated in the new pattern of results. The new assessment is completed by teachers at the end of the children's "reception" year, whereas most "baseline assessments" in the previous system were completed within the first few weeks of children entering school. Some antiracist practitioners have suggested to me that the relative deterioration in Black students scores (noted previously in Figures 10.2 and 10.3) may take effect during this first year.[9]

How these changes in outcome have come about, therefore, is an important question, but even more important is the fact that the changes occurred without apparent disquiet or possibly even without being recognized. Boldly stated, the facts are simple: In recent years Black students' attainments at the start of school appear to have radically decreased relative to their White peers; this has coincided with the reform of assessment procedures at that stage; and yet the pattern is reported officially without query and without further comment. This looks suspiciously like the imaginary racist society in my earlier story.

However, there is a key difference. Unlike the society in that story, there is no suggestion here that the changes in England have been manufactured deliberately in any way. This is not to deny their impact and severity: The changes that have happened are clearly *racist in their outcome* insofar as Black students have been markedly disadvantaged. But there is no evidence of conscious intent: There is no conspiracy. It is more frightening than that. Rather than being generated by a deliberate strategy (one that is readily open to exposure and reversal), these changes appear to have resulted from the *normal* workings of the education system—a system that places race equity at the very margins of debate and takes no action when a new assessment system produces results that leave all minority groups in the wake of the White majority. Mainstream education policies are enacted with little or no regard to how they will impact on minority ethnic students (Gillborn, 2005). This is demonstrably the case in relation to GCSE tiering, in relation to selection and tracking within schools, and in relation to the assessment system more generally (see Ladson-Billings, 2004). *It is difficult to imagine a contrary situation where no action would be taken were a new assessment system to result in White children being outperformed by their peers in every minority group.*

CONCLUSION

The logics of empire are still with us, bound to the fabric of our daily being-in-the-world; woven into our posture toward others; connected to the muscles of our eyes; dipped in the chemical relations that excite and calm us; structured into the language of our perceptions. We cannot will our racist logics away. We need to work hard to eradicate them. We need to struggle with a formidable resolve in order to overcome that which we are afraid to confirm exists let alone confront in the battleground of our souls. (McLaren, 1998, p. 63)

Writing about Whiteness is increasingly fashionable, but serious, critical engagement with the structures of racial domination remains a mostly minority pastime—in every sense of the phrase. As Peter McLaren notes, understanding the processes through which White racial hegemony is structured and maintained is more than a rational exercise of the mind. These issues touch on deeply ingrained, often visceral aspects of our "daily being-in-the-world."

In this chapter I have adopted a position informed by my ongoing attempt to apply critical race theory to an analysis of educational inequity in England (see also Gillborn, 2004c). I have tried to follow William Tate's (1999) advice and view CRT scholarship as "an enactment of hybridity" (p. 260). Consequently I have combined different narrative forms and critical sociological policy studies in an attempt to explore how White supremacy operates through the mundane realities of the day-to-day exercise of assessment practices in education.

I have described how the system of tiering operates to deny a disproportionate number of Black students the possibility of gaining higher-grade passes in the high-stakes tests that mark the end of compulsory schooling in England. Despite the rhetoric of "higher standards for all," the simple fact is that many Black students are locked into an examination that makes the best grades literally impossible to attain. I have also described how a new system of assessment for 5-year-olds appears to have erased, virtually overnight, the only part of the system where Black children were relatively successful.

In this chapter, therefore, I have used the case of assessment and testing in England to raise fundamental questions about the possibility of socially just outcomes in an education system dominated by the perspectives of White policymakers and practitioners. The evidence suggests that assessment does more than merely *record* inequity; it is implicated in the processes that *produce* and *sustain* inequity. This challenges the assumption, common to liberal democratic societies in general, that race inequity is a temporary aberration and that race is a marginal issue in society at large and in the education system in particular. A critical perspective on race and education highlights that—whatever the rhetoric—race inequity has been a constant and central feature of the education system. In this chapter I have tried to show how even the most dramatic of setbacks can happen without apparent malice, and even without comment. Until we address the presence of racism as a fundamental and defining characteristic of the education system, the present situation is unlikely to change in any meaningful sense regardless of superficial rhetorical commitments to inclusion, civil rights, and social justice.

ACKNOWLEDGMENTS

This chapter has benefited from the scholarship and support of numerous colleagues. Some of the ideas formed parts of presentations at the Three Deans seminar (London,

August–September 2005) and the British Educational Research Association (Glamorgan, September 2005). In particular, the following have offered detailed feedback and/or guidance on the text: Stephen J. Ball, Gregg Beratan, Jannette Elwood, Dorn Gillborn, Gloria Ladson-Billings, Grace Livingston, Gordon Stobart, Sally Thomas, Carol Vincent, and Deborah Youdell.

NOTES

1. By "Black" I mean children who identify their ethnic heritage as broadly "Black Caribbean" or "Black African." In some educational research a composite Black group is used (also sometimes known as "African Caribbean"). In other sources separate groups are counted. These complications are inevitable given the fluid nature of "race" categories and the variety of approaches used in contemporary research.

2. In the spring of 2005 the Qualifications & Curriculum Authority (QCA) announced plans to remove the three-tier model in mathematics from 2006 onward. The restrictions and inequities built into the two-tier model, however, will remain unaltered.

3. Among the reforms meant to "raise standards" in urban schools, the British government has introduced the so-called "gifted and talented strand" whereby schools may identify between 5% and 10% of their pupils for additional lessons and specially targeted resources: 10% of White pupils enjoy this additional resource compared with 4% of "Black Caribbean" pupils and 2% of those identifying as of "Black African" ethnic heritage (DfES, 2005, p. 36).

4. The idea that there is a difference between "ability" and "attainment," of course, neatly demonstrates that the Department for Education share the belief in the fallacy that it is possible to identify inner *potential* rather current *performance*.

5. One hundred eighteen LEAs granted permission to use their data on the understanding that they would not be identified by name in the report.

6. Gillborn and Mirza (2000) is a prominent source in many introductory texts, including Browne (2002), where it is one of three principal sources used to introduce the section on race and educational attainment; see also Haralambos and Holborn (2004) and Holborn and Langley (2004).

7. The introduction of the Foundation Stage Profile completed a system whereby every child is now subject to national system of assessment at the ages of 5, 7, 11, 14, and 16. Each child's results are individually recorded by the Department for Education & Skills.

8. This percentage point difference is calculated by subtracting the White performance from the respective minority ethnic performance. Hypothetically, for example, if 40% of White students reached the target but only 30% of "Black Caribbean" students, then the value for the latter would be -10%.

9. Antiracist colleagues working in early education have suggested to me that Black students are often viewed as relatively advanced when they first enter school: unlike many White students, frequently they can write their names and read simple sentences (a sign of the high value placed on education in minority households). However, it is possible that even during the very first year of schooling, such positive evaluations are overridden by teachers who come to see them stereotypically as a source of trouble while, on the other hand, their White peers have longer to catch up and show what they are capable of.

REFERENCES

Abbott, D. (2005, March 8). Black boys continue to fail but segregation is not the solution. *Daily Express*, p. 12.

Ansley, F. L. (1997). White supremacy (and what we should do about it). In R. Delgado & J. Stefancic (Eds.), *Critical White studies: Looking behind the mirror* (pp. 592–595). Philadelphia: Temple University Press.

Apple, M. W. (1998). Foreword. In J. L. Kincheloe, S. R. Steinberg, N. M. Rodriguez, & R. E. Chennault (Eds.), *White reign: Deploying Whiteness in america* (pp. ix–xiii). New York: St. Martin's Press.

Apple, M. W. (2004). Making White right: Race and the politics of educational reform. In M. Fine, L. Weis, L. Powell Pruitt, & A. Burns (Eds.), *Off White: Readings on power, privilege, and resistance* (2nd. ed.; pp. 74–85). New York: Routledge.

Bell, D. (1990). After we're gone: Prudent speculations on America in a post-racial epoch, *St. Louis University Law Journal*, reprinted in R. Delagado, & J. Stefancic (Eds.), (2000). *Critical race theory: The cutting edge* (pp. 2–8). Philadelphia: Temple University Press.

Bell, D. (1992). *Faces at the bottom of the well: The permanence of racism.* New York: Basic Books.

Browne, K. (2002). *Introducing sociology for AS level.* Cambridge, UK: Polity.

Bush, M. E. L. (2004). Race, ethnicity and whiteness. *Sage race relations abstracts, 29*(3–4), 5–48.

Coard, B. (1971). *How the West Indian child is made educationally subnormal in the British school system.* London: New Beacon Books.

Connolly, P. (1998). *Racism, gender identities and young children: Social relations in a multi-ethnic, inner-city primary school.* London: Routledge.

Delgado, R. (1995). *The Rodrigo chronicles: Conversations about America and race.* New York: New York University Press.

Delgado, R., & Stefancic, J. (1997). Introduction. In R. Delgado & J. Stefancic (Eds.), *Critical White studies: Looking behind the mirror* (pp. xvii–xviii). Philadelphia: Temple University Press.

Delgado, R., & Stefancic, J. (2001). *Critical race theory: An introduction.* New York: New York University Press.

Department for Education & Skills (DfES). (2004). *Experimental statistics first release.* (SFR 25/2004). London: Author.

Department for Education & Skills (DfES). (2005). *Ethnicity and education: The evidence on minority ethnic pupils.* London: Author.

Dlamini, S. N. (2002). From the other side of the desk: Notes on teaching about race when racialised, *Race Ethnicity & Education, 5*(1), 51–66.

Foster, K. M. (2005). Diet of disparagement: The racial experiences of Black students in a predominantly White university, *International Journal of Qualitative Studies in Education, 18*(4), 489–505.

Foster, P. (1993). "Methodological purism" or "a defence against hype"? Critical readership in research in "race" and education, *New Community, 19*(3), 547–552.

Foster, P., Gomm, R., & Hammersley, M. (1996). *Constructing educational inequality: An assessment of research on school processes.* London: Falmer.

Gillborn, D. (1998). Racism and the politics of qualitative research. In P. Connolly & B. Troyna (Eds.), *Researching racism in education* (pp. 34–54). Buckingham, UK: Open

University Press.

Gillborn, D. (2002). *Education and institutional racism: A professorial lecture.* London: Institute of Education, University of London.

Gillborn, D. (2004a). Racism, policy and contemporary schooling: Current inequities and future possibilities. *Sage Race Relations Abstracts, 29*(2), 5–33.

Gillborn, D. (2004b). Ability, selection and institutional racism in schools. In M. Olssen (Ed.), *Culture and learning: Access and opportunity in the classroom* (pp. 279–297). Greenwich, CT: Information Age Publishing.

Gillborn, D. (2004c, September). *Critical race theory: What is it and what use is it to British antiracism?* Paper presented at the annual meeting of the British Educational Research Association (BERA), Manchester, UK.

Gillborn, D. (2005). Education policy as an act of White supremacy: Whiteness, critical race theory and education reform, *Journal of Education Policy, 20*(4), 485–505.

Gillborn, D., & Gipps, C. (1996). *Recent research on the achievements of ethnic minority pupils* (Report for the Office for Standards in Education). London: Her Majesty's Stationery Office.

Gillborn, D., & Mirza, H.S. (2000). *Educational inequality: Mapping race, class and gender—A synthesis of research evidence* (Report #HMI 232). London: Office for Standards in Education.

Gillborn, D., & Youdell, D. (2000). *Rationing education: Policy, practice, reform and equity.* Buckingham, UK: Open University Press.

Gipps, C. V. (1994). *Beyond testing: Towards a theory of educational assessment.* London: RoutledgeFalmer.

Hammersley, M. (1995). *The politics of social research.* London: Sage.

Haralambos, M., & Holborn, M. (2004). *Sociology: themes and perspectives.* London: HarperCollins.

Henry, J. (2002, March). America's most gifted, *Times Educational Supplement*, p. 13.

Herrnstein, R. J., & Murray, C. (1994). *The bell curve: Intelligence and class structure in American life.* New York, The Free Press.

Holborn, M., & Langley, P. (2004). *AS and A-level student handbook.* London: HarperCollins.

hooks, b. (1989). *Talking back: Thinking feminist, thinking Black.* Boston: South End Press.

Howard, P. S. S. (2004). White privilege: For or against? A discussion of ostensibly antiracist discourses in critical Whiteness studies. *Race, Gender & Class, 11*(4), 63–79.

Kamin, L. J. (1981). *Intelligence: The battle for the mind: H. J. Eysenck versus L .J. Kamin.* London: Pan Books.

Kornhaber, M. L. (2004). Assessment, standards, and equity. In J. A. Banks & C. A. McGee Banks (Eds.), *Handbook of research on multicultural education* (pp. 91–109). San Francisco: Jossey-Bass.

Ladson-Billings, G. (1998). Just what is critical race theory and what's it doing in a *nice* field like education? *International Journal of Qualitative Studies in Education, 11*, 7–24.

Ladson-Billings, G. (2004). New directions in multicultural education: Complexities, boundaries, and critical race theory. In J. A. Banks & C. A. M. Banks (Eds.), *Handbook of research on multicultural education* (pp. 50–65). San Francisco: Jossey-Bass.

Ladson-Billings, G., & Tate, W. F. (1995). Toward a critical race theory of education. *Teachers College Record, 97*(1), 47–68.

Leonardo, Z. (2002). The souls of White folk: Critical pedagogy, Whiteness studies, and globalization discourse. In G. Ladson-Billings & D. Gillborn (Eds.), *The Routledge-Falmer reader in multicultural education* (pp. 117–136). London: RoutledgeFalmer.

Leonardo, Z. (2004). The color of supremacy: Beyond the discourse of "White privilege." *Educational Philosophy and Theory, 36*(2), 137–152.

Macpherson, W. (1999). *The Stephen Lawrence inquiry* (CM 4262-I). London: Her Majesty's Stationery Office.

Maeroff, G. I. (1991). Assessing alternative assessment, *Phi Delta Kappan, 73*(4), 273–281.

Mainstream science on intelligence. (1994, December 13). *Wall Street Journal*, p. A18.

Matthews, D. (2004, August 19). Academic failure, a contempt for authority, and violence—we can't blame it *all* on racism, *Daily Mail*, p. 30.

McIntosh, P. (1988). White privilege and male privilege: A personal account of coming to see correspondences through work in women's studies. In R. Delgado & J. Stefancic (Eds.), (1997), *Critical White studies: Looking behind the mirror* (pp. 291–299). Philadelphia: Temple University Press.

McKenley, J. (2004). *Second-generation perspectives on the transmission of educational values in the parenting of Black British families of Caribbean origin.* Unpublished doctoral dissertation, Institute of Education, University of London.

McLaren, P. (1995). White terror and oppositional agency: Towards a critical multiculturalism. In P. McLaren (Ed.), *Critical pedagogy and predatory culture: Oppositional politics in a postmodern era* (pp. 117–144). New York: Routledge.

McLaren, P. (1998). Whiteness is . . . the struggle for postcolonial hybridity. In J. L. Kincheloe, S. R. Steinberg, N. M. Rodriguez, & R. E. Chennault (Eds.), *White reign: Deploying Whiteness in America* (pp. 63–75). New York: St. Martin's Press.

Oakes, J. (1990). *Multiplying inequalities: The effects of race, social class, and tracking on opportunities to learn mathematics and science.* Santa Monica, CA: Rand.

Oakes, J., Joseph, R., & Muir, K. (2004). Access and achievement in mathematics and science In J. A. Banks & C. A. McGee Banks (Eds.), *Handbook of Research on Multicultural Education* (pp. 69–90). San Francisco: Jossey-Bass.

Parker, L., Deyhle, D., & Villenas, S. (Eds.). (1999). *Race is . . . race isn't: Critical race theory and qualitative studies in education.* Boulder, CO: Westview.

Qualifications & Curriculum Authority (QCA). (2000). *Pupil grouping and its relationship with gender, ethnicity and social class: A summary of the research literature.* London: Author.

Qualifications & Curriculum Authority (QCA). (2003). *Foundation stage profile: Handbook.* London: Author.

Racism warning over curriculum plans. (2002). Retrieved November 25, 2005, from http://news.bbc.co.uk/1/hi/education/1867639.stm

Richardson, R., & Wood, A. (1999). *Inclusive schools, inclusive society: Race and identity on the agenda* (Report produced for Race on the Agenda in partnership with Association of London Government and Save the Children). Stoke-on-Trent, UK: Trentham.

Sanders, W. L., & Horn, S. P. (1995). Educational assessment reassessed: The usefulness of standardized and alternative measures of student achievement as indicators for the assessment of educational outcomes. *Education Policy Analysis Archives, 3*(6). Retrieved April 4, 2004, from http://epaa.asu.edu/epaa/v3n6.html

Sewell, T. (2005, March 8). Sorry, we can't just blame racism for Black boys' failings, *Daily Mail*, p. 12.

Sheets, R. H. (2000). Advancing the field or taking center stage: The White movement in multicultural education, *Educational Researcher, 29*(9), 15–21.

Sternberg, R. J. (1998). Abilities are forms of developing expertise. *Educational Researcher, 27*(3), 11–20.

Sternberg, R. J. (1999). Intelligence as developing expertise, *Contemporary Educational Psychology, 24*, 259–375.

Sternberg, R. J. (2001). Giftedness as developing expertise: A theory of the interface between high abilities and achieved excellence. *High Ability Studies, 12*(2), 157–179.

Tate, W. F. (1997). Critical race theory and education: History, theory, and implications. In M. W. Apple (Ed.), *Review of research in education* (Vol 22; pp. 195–247). Washington DC: American Educational Research Association.

Tate, W. F. (1999). Conclusion In L. Parker, D. Deyhle, & S. Villenas (Eds.), *Race is . . . race isn't: Critical race theory and qualitative studies in education* (pp. 251–271). Boulder, CO: Westview.

Williams, P. J. (1987). Alchemical notes: Reconstructing ideals from deconstructed rights. *Harvard Civil Rights—Civil Liberties Law Review.* Reprinted in R. Delagado & J. Stefancic (Eds.), (2000). *Critical race theory: The cutting edge* (pp. 80-90). Philadelphia: Temple University Press.

Wing, A. K. (Ed.). (1997). *Critical race feminism: A reader.* New York: New York University Press.

PART III

The School and Curriculum as Sites of Education Research in the Public Interest

Curriculum and Students: Diverting the Public Interest

CATHERINE CORNBLETH

Of course we're teaching to the state standards in reading and math. We've aligned our curriculum, texts, and testing with the standards. In fact, last summer, I was a member of our school's curriculum mapping team, and I've volunteered to be an item-writer for the state tests. We want our students to do well on the state tests and our school to be recognized as a good school. That reflects well on teachers too. So, we're moving to more data-driven decision making so we can tell which students are most at-risk of not passing and what are their particular weaknesses. (elementary school teacher)

Ninety-six percent of our eleventh graders passed the Regents U.S. History and Government exam the first time around this year. We really worked to get that passing rate up, and it's paying off. Our district moved up in the *Business First* newspaper rankings this year. (high school principal)

Her SAT scores were good but probably not good enough for the kind of college we'd like her to attend. So we're sending her to a tutoring program that our friends recommended highly, and she'll take the SAT again next semester. (parent)

On both the immediate and delayed posttests, the experimental treatment group significantly outscored the control group at the .0001 level. (researcher)

W HILE HYPOTHETICAL, ALL FOUR of these "quotes" could easily be real. They certainly sound like what I've heard in my daily life as a university professor frequently engaged in school-based research or reading scholarly journals and the popular press. In none of these cases, or countless others we could muster, is there a hint of substance—of what some students are or are not learning or of what the experimental treatment entails. Even the "U.S. History and Government Regents exam" doesn't reveal which or whose history, perspectives, or analytical skills are assessed or deemed correct. We are too often too taken by numbers to ask about their meaning or implications, let alone educational (in contrast to statistical) significance or standard errors of measurement. When, for example, was the last time that you or someone you know asked about the meaning or educational significance of a student or school test score or a p-value? Or of its social or political implications?

I begin with this small screed in an effort to call attention to one of the ways in which I believe that educators and education researchers can and should further research in the broader public interest, rather than research that primarily serves self- or special interests. (These arguments about research also carry implications for education policymaking and practices in the public interest.) We can, and I would argue should, nurture wide-ranging and well-informed skepticism, questioning, and a "show me" approach that probes beyond slogans, claims, and surface appearances more generally—regardless of their source. What would be an example? How do you know that? What's the supporting evidence? Who benefits as a result of that? Concurrently, we can and should both expect and welcome similar critical review of our own work.

The intent here is not to play "gotcha" but to test (and refine and strengthen) our findings and interpretations as well as reveal and consider their wider ramifications, socially and politically as well as pedagogically. This is a key part of how I understand public interest research. Public interest research, following the ASIPI (Association for Science in the Public Interest, www.public-science.org/), is distinguished by public involvement, public availability of results, and beneficiaries. My particular concern lies with those fractions of the public who lack the resources, financial and other, to access better or the best education and future for their children, however they define that future. They constitute, I suspect, the nondominant 75–80% of the U.S. population (see Correspondents of the *New York Times*, 2005).

In making a case for research in the public interest, I focus on curriculum and students, two interrelated areas with which I have a long-standing personal and academic acquaintance. Three illustrations are offered in support of my call for informed skepticism and questioning: the discussions cum debates about scientifically based research; the establishment of higher standards as a basis for the selection, organization, and treatment of curriculum knowledge; and some of the consequences of No Child Left Behind (NCLB) and similar state-level, testing-accountability legislation in practice. In each case, I wonder about the extent to which educators, researchers, policymakers, and members of the general public recognize that attention is being diverted, intentionally or inadvertently, from underlying issues and the broader public interest in a democracy such as the United States might become.

SCIENTIFICALLY BASED RESEARCH

Arguments about preferred or "better" forms of research in education date back at least a century. I grew up professionally in the 1975–1985 period during which critical perspectives and ethnographic field study methods were gaining acceptance, sometimes only grudgingly. Mistakenly, I thought that our profession had moved beyond seeking after a 19th-century version of "hard science." The current fray is supposedly about "scientifically based research" (SBR) and dates to language in the 1999 Reading Excellence Act, later incorporated with some modifications into NCLB as the Reading First initiative (see Eisenhart & Towne, 2003).

The 1999 Reading Excellence Act marked the first appearance in federal education law of definitions of education research. The purpose was to specify the kinds of research that service providers could use as a rationale for decisions regarding program expenditures. NCLB defined SBR more narrowly as hypothesis-testing within experimental or quasi-experimental designs, preferably with random assignment. Later federal legislation (e.g., ESRA, the Educational Sciences Reform Act of 2002) defined the kinds of education research that would be funded somewhat more broadly and more attuned to research in school settings. Over the course of 3 years, definitions were modified to admit a greater range of research.

Meanwhile, at the behest of the Office of Educational Research and Improvement (OERI; specifically, the National Educational Research Policy and Priorities Board), the National Research Council established a committee in late 2000 "to investigate what constitutes scientific research in education" (Eisenhart & Towne, 2003, p. 32). That committee's report, *Scientific Research in Education* (National Research Council, 2002) "argued that scientifically based research is defined by a set of principles . . . , not by research methods (quantitative or qualitative), and that the principles guiding scientific research in education are in many ways the same regardless of method" (p. 33).

The Education Sciences Reform Act (in 2002), among other things, replaced OERI with the Institute of Educational Studies (IES) and offered another definitional framework for scientifically based research in education that can receive federal funding—one that can be seen to be influenced by *Scientific Research in Education*, congressional testimony, and feedback from the field. While one could argue whether any definition should be written into federal law, this one is relatively broad and does not reduce research to methods or procedures. It could, however, be more or less narrowly interpreted.[1]

Whether in support of or opposition to scientifically based, or simply, scientific research in education, too many discussants confuse (or simply lump) definitions, purposes (e.g., program selection, research funding), and sources (e.g., NCLB, SBR, ESRA). A more serious problem, from my vantage point, is joining in any debate that reduces education research to methodological squabbles, "my research versus your research." Such recurring squabbles in academic circles not only waste time, energy, and other resources (though one may score short-lived "points"), but more importantly, they deflect attention from the purposes–perspectives–paradigms of educational research and from substantive aspects of education such as curriculum and students. Arguing within a framework set by others, such as about the procedures of scientifically based or scientific research in education, most often serves to maintain the status quo, which in turn serves the dominant interests that framed the debate if for no other reason than it accepts without question that SBR (whatever it is) is good. Instead, *Scientific Research in Education*, for example, did not argue methods or procedures; it conceptualized education research in a relatively broad and accessible postpositivist manner (Eisenhart, 2005).

If experimental or quasi-experimental research examined not only "what works" or "what works best" but also *for whom* and *for what* and *in what settings*, it would have much more potential to serve the public interest. Which students perform well or better with which methods in what settings for what kinds of outcomes? It is unlikely that the same methods work equally well for all students (I thought we learned that by the late 1970s) or, for instance, for learning both historical chronology and comprehension (I thought we learned that by the 1980s), or in groups/classes of 7, 17, 27, and 37 (I thought we learned that by the 1990s). What might happen if more education researchers recalled or called for scientific or scientifically based research on education to respond to questions such as these? What I'm suggesting here is a reshaping of this and other education research debates to address substantive issues and questions of who benefits from one or another framing and position. Private interests, special interests, or a broader public interest or set of public interests? It could be a matter of strategic redefinition of "scientific research" and other slogans or forced choices.[2]

The most harmful threat to the public interest stemming from the current push for scientific research in education and the scientific research procedures debate, as I see it, lies in the diversion of attention and other resources from issues and research questions that simply do not fit the referred procedures and the "what works (best)" question. How, for example, does school culture shape students' understandings of themselves, individually and collectively? In what ways do racism and sexism appear to limit or enhance some students' opportunities to learn in school? With such knowledge, interventions could be devised, tried, and evaluated to alleviate documented ill effects and not only support equity and social justice but also likely increase the achievement of students previously disadvantaged by school culture and practices. But if we do not even ask these kinds of questions and receive at least encouragement if not tangible support for pursuing them, the social-pedagogical status quo is maintained and too many students "fall through the (expanding) cracks." In Walker's language (2005), the current debate privileges some research and researchers while silencing other research voices.

HIGHER STANDARDS FOR
CURRICULUM KNOWLEDGE AND STUDENT LEARNING

In the previous instance, about scientifically based research, attention is diverted from substantive questions—such as the distribution of educational opportunities and benefits—to treatment A vs B horse race studies and tugs of war about research procedures. Neither challenges existing educational systems. In this instance, about curriculum standards and student learning, attention is diverted from substantive questions—such as "What vision or version of science or America is transmitted to future generations?"—to claims of rigor and pursuit of higher test scores. Never mind what students might be learning.

I focus on history and social science as a specific case, particularly on questions of incorporating the diversity that has characterized the United States since its beginnings, because this is an area that I know well and the evidence is both ample and vivid. Beyond the diversion of attention from selection, organization, and treatment of curriculum knowledge, in some cases the rhetorical emphasis on "higher standards" actively seeks to constrain or standardize curriculum knowledge. Standardization is a response to the increasing diversity of the U.S. population and various groups' efforts to be recognized and included—both of which can be seen as threatening established interests.

By curriculum knowledge, I refer to that knowledge (broadly defined to include what some people distinguish as beliefs, attitudes, values, and skills) that is selected to be taught in schools, including opportunities for students to critique and construct as well as to receive existing knowledge. What is selected, how it is organized and treated or taught, and to which groups of students it is distributed matter mightily in terms of educational opportunities and benefits, both individual and collective, both pedagogical and political. The ongoing discourse of higher standards, assessment, and accountability, however, preempts consideration of both curriculum knowledge and student learning at the same time that it tends toward standardization and cultural containment. Whether these are purposeful or unintended consequences is a question for another time.

Within the limits of this chapter, I draw primarily on two sources—my own earlier essay, "National Standards and Curriculum as Cultural Containment?" (Cornbleth, 2001) and Sleeter and Stillman's (2005) "Standardizing Knowledge in a Multicultural Society." Efforts toward what I call cultural containment have a long history in the United States, well documented by historians such as Joyce Appleby in her OAH (Organization of American Historians) presidential address, "Recovering America's Historic Diversity: Beyond Exceptionalism" (1992), and education scholars such as Michael Olneck (1989, 1990, 1993). In a masterful analysis, "Moral Majorities and School Curriculum: Historical Perspectives on the Legalization of Virtue," Tyack and James (1985) show how now-dominant groups, having ensconced their experiences and perspectives in school curricula, now guard against the efforts of "others" for inclusion of their histories, cultures, experiences, and perspectives.

It is well established that public schooling in the United States has served and continues to serve purposes of Americanization and assimilation—of building a national citizenry—in large part by controlling curriculum knowledge through curriculum policymaking and by shaping the conditions of curriculum practice. Perhaps because of the disparate beginnings and relatively brief history of the United States, national leaders have sought a common national identity if not a common culture. Particularly in the past century, the notion of common culture has gained mass appeal, seemingly as a defense against changing circumstances and/or diversification associated with industrialization, urbanization, immigration, technological innovation, and globalization as well as external enemies of the moment. The movement toward national curriculum standards and student assessments can be seen as part of a recurring search for certainty and stability through common practice if not consensus.

Alongside the renewed nation-building and nationalizing efforts in the United States is a countermovement toward racial/ethnic/cultural (but not necessarily political or economic) diversity. As the latter gains momentum, it spurs the former, especially among those who have benefited from established arrangements of power and privilege. Efforts to renew the nation-building purposes of public schooling also have been given impetus by globalization. As economies and popular cultures, for example, become increasingly globalized, nation-states may be in danger of losing their separate identities and raisons d'être. Yet, the nation remains a potent source of identity and loyalty for many citizens. The nation, like the local community or region in an earlier age, is a symbolic anchor in a rapidly changing and often hostile world. Disputes about the vision of the nation to be passed on to future generations via school curricula can be seen as competing efforts to reset that symbolic anchor.

Over the past 20 years, both national standard-setting activities and case studies of state-level curriculum policymaking in California and New York illustrate that increasing racial/ethnic/cultural diversity in the United States is being met once again with efforts to contain that diversity by curricular as well as other means. As the student body becomes less European-based, social studies curriculum guidelines seem to be becoming more so, despite the appearance of multicultural inclusion. Many of those involved in state curriculum policymaking and national standard-setting activity seem oblivious to multicultural identities, either ignorant of the social demographics or wishing them away.

The 1987 social studies curriculum guidelines and 1990 state-approved school textbooks in California, for example, have been described aptly as "put[ting] everyone in the covered wagon" (Joyce E. King, quoted in Waugh & Hatfield, 1992, p. A18). In other words, non-Europeans have been invited into the story of America on terms set by others. "The price of the ticket," to borrow from James Baldwin (1985), has been high. More specifically:

> California's version of American history was based on an immigrant perspective that in effect subjugated Native Americans, African Americans, and former Mexican citizens in the Southwest to the status of ride-alongs, rather than primary participants and shapers of America's dynamic hybrid culture. (Cornbleth & Waugh, 1995/1999, p. 12)

And the immigrant prototype has been European, most often 17th-, 18th-, or early 19th-century Western and Northern European, largely ignoring Asian and more recent Central and South American immigrant experience.

There is no equivalent to the Euro-immigrant narrative of California's story of America in the New York social studies or national history standards documents. New York simply returns to a traditional view of U.S. political history with a few mentions of "individuals and groups who represent different ethnic, national, and religious groups" (NYSED, 1996, p. 5), usually unspecified except for "Native American Indians."

The voluntary national history standards were developed by UCLA's National Center for History in the Schools, then co-directed by U.S. historian Gary Nash and elementary social studies educator Charlotte Crabtree, with funding from the NEH (National Endowment for the Humanities) when it was headed by Lynne Cheney and the Education Department when Diane Ravitch was assistant secretary. A few years later, in 1994, Cheney led the conservative critics of the resulting standards. Nash and his group bowed to the conservative opposition and revised the standards; they did not, however, give in entirely or give up and run. For example, the revised edition omits (from Era 2, Colonization and Settlement, 1585-1763) the previously included reference to the interaction of various groups, the "early arrival of Europeans and Africans in the Americas, and how these people interacted with Native Americans" (NCHS, 1994, p. 35). In the revised 1996 "basic" edition, the standards do not specifically mention Native Americans until Era 4, Expansion and Reform, 1801–1861. Generally, the experiences of other-than-European groups are grafted onto a conventional, chronological U.S. political chronicle.

In the social studies curriculum policies adopted in New York and California over the past two decades, and in the 1996 revised national U.S. history standards, claims of national unity overwhelm acknowledgment of diversity, and the Western cultural heritage is emphasized. The view that the nation was built by, and derives its strength from, diverse individuals and groups is minimized, as if diversity and unity were mutually exclusive. Despite repeated reference to "the nation's commonalities," "common community," "shared community," "national unity," "common culture," and "ways people are unified by many values, practices, and traditions," few specifics are provided beyond the rarely disputed democratic political ideals on which the nation was founded. Nor do these policy documents explain how supposed commonality translates into unity.

Multicultural knowledge and national identities are muted in at least two ways in these curriculum policies. While the documents can be seen as allowing for or encompassing multiple perspectives and group experiences, specific examples are very conventional and rarely explicitly multicultural. The language such as New York's "significant reform movements" illustrates a major way in which racial/ethnic/cultural diversity can be diluted and diminished. Defenders of the language can and do point to it as enabling consideration of diversity (e.g., the civil rights movement, immigration reform since 1965). Skeptics point out that "significant reform movements" can be investigated without ever mentioning racial/ethnic/cultural diversity—by, for example, investigating the environmental movement. Second, without specification, educators who might be amenable to teaching about multicultural America but lack the requisite knowledge receive no guidance. By default if not explicitly, these curriculum policies also suggest that individual identities are monocultural (e.g., Black, White, Asian, or Native American Indian), and each cultural group is treated as homogeneous.

Curriculum policymaking, including syllabus revision (New York) or creation of a framework (California) and standards, is always a matter of knowledge control—of trying to control the knowledge to be made available to students in classrooms across the district, state, or nation. Controlling curriculum knowledge means selecting some knowledge to be included and other knowledge to be kept out. One way to keep knowledge out is to ignore it. Omission is especially effective with newer knowledge that probably is not familiar to experienced teachers or other adults who completed their formal education some time ago. Another way to keep knowledge out is to include so much other knowledge that there is little or no room for anything else. Both of these tactics have been employed in New York to discourage meaningful attention to racial/ethnic/cultural diversity in social studies curriculum practice.

Sleeter and Stillman's (2005) content analyses of the 2001 History–Social Science Framework and Standards for California Public Schools as well as three reading–language arts–English language development standards and curriculum documents from 1997 and 1999 led them to conclude that "raising standards has become synonymous with standardizing curriculum" (p. 27) insofar as teachers are encouraged to teach to the test. Further, the standards movement can be seen as an attempt to reassert if not fully restore power relations of an earlier period, prior to the civil rights and related educational inclusion and equity movements.

In California, subject-area content standards guide the adoption of textbooks in grades 1–8 and, since the 1999 Public School Accountability Act, achievement testing (and the rewarding of high-performing schools and the sanctioning of low-performing ones). Subsequently, state policy has recommended aligning postsecondary curriculum and teacher preparation to the state standards (Sleeter & Stillman, 2005). The 1987 History–Social Science Framework and Standards document, originally contentious (see, e.g., Cornbleth & Waugh, 1995/1999), was "readopted three times with only minor updates" (Sleeter & Stillman, 2005, p. 33), most recently in 2001, suggesting public and professional apathy, resignation, or other priorities if not consensus.

As in 1987, primacy is given to history as "a story well told," language originally attributed to Diane Ravitch, one of the co-authors of the 1987 document. The dominant U.S. history storyline emerging from Sleeter and Stillman's (2005, p. 37) analysis "revolves around European and European Americans, particularly men" although there is at least rhetorical recognition of the United States as an immigrant society that has always been multicultural. For example, the Framework and Standards emphasize that U.S. "institutions were founded on the Judeo-Christian heritage, the ideals of the Enlightenment, and English traditions of self-government" (California Department of Education, 2001, p. 64; cited in Sleeter & Stillman, 2005, p. 37). These claims are true enough, but only a partial, selective account that does not serve the public interest. "The conquests of northern Mexico and indigenous peoples are marginalized and sanitized" (Sleeter & Stillman, 2005, p. 38) in part by presenting them largely through map study and timelines, not as an integral part of "a story well told." Similarly, "the historic struggle to extend to all Americans the constitutional guarantees of equality and freedom" (p. 21) falls woefully short.

Organized around the perspectives and experiences of historically dominant groups that privilege a European American immigrant story, the 2001 California History–Social Science Framework and Standards establishes the "knowledge of white English speakers as dominant" (Sleeter & Stillman, 2005, p. 39) as normative, ignoring or excluding most Californians and many Americans nationwide. "Implicitly, in an attempt to reduce the significance of the growing demographic diversity of California' students, the content standards set up a we/they perspective in which 'we' are of European, Judeo-Christian heritage and English-speaking, and 'they' are not" (p. 43). The intent, purposeful or unexamined, to control knowledge and contain cultures is quite clear.

Sleeter and Stillman (2005, p. 42) acknowledge that teachers have some "latitude for deciding how to teach history and social science," more so than in reading. However, the state curriculum guide "is so packed and backed up by state-adopted texts [through eighth grade] that it is an effort to not follow the standards" (p. 42). Based on their document analysis, Sleeter and Stillman (2005) conclude:

> Although the content standards in both disciplines rest within a specific ideology, they are presented as if there were no serious ideological debates to consider. Both present a detailed curriculum outline, and both give enough verbal recognition to cultural, racial, and linguistic diversity that teachers without a deep understanding of diverse intellectual funds of knowledge, diverse ideological perspectives, and effective pedagogy for diverse students might see the standards as fully inclusive. (p. 43)

In sum, both state and national curriculum policymakers have been downplaying the racial/ethnic/cultural diversity that has characterized the United States since its beginnings. How long or how well these containment efforts will hold remains to be seen. Curriculum policy is continually made, remade, and unmade both in official chambers and school classrooms. Public interests may yet be served.[3]

STATE-LEVEL TESTING-ACCOUNTABILITY IN PRACTICE

Much has been said and written about the intent and hopes of raising student achievement and leaving no child behind in the process. Standardized testing has become the preferred way to tell how we're doing (though it doesn't necessarily help students learn), and accountability (used nearly synonymously with testing but rarely defined) resonates well for most middle- and upper-class Americans who believe that their status is the result of the well-earned, level playing field of a meritocracy.

As Airasian (1987) has shown, standardized tests symbolize the maintenance of order, standards, and traditional educational values and practices. The general public also tends to see them as scientific, objective, and fair. The irony, if not the unconscionability, of this largely unexamined state of affairs is that its instigators (e.g., politicians and policymakers, teachers and administrators) are not being held accountable (i.e., responsible) for the apparent results in terms of curriculum and students. Yet the Bush administration has been talking about extending the testing-accountability provisions of NCLB, legislation to high schools—despite this same administration's call for scientifically based research as a basis for program selections at the state and school district levels and as a requirement for federal funding.

The evidence regarding the control and narrowing of curriculum knowledge made available to students, especially students in "lower-performing" schools, is available for those who are interested (see, e.g., Airasian, 1987, 1988; Cimbricz, 2002). Less well documented and widely known are effects on students. Who is and is not benefiting from current testing-accountability practices in schools? Research in the public interest might well investigate. Here, I draw on a case study of a single Texas elementary school that, if at all representative of what is occurring nationwide, should shame policymakers, educators, researchers, and the general public into reexamining conceptions and assumption as well as policy and practices regarding achievement and accountability.

While most of the public discourse refers to NCLB, several states, including California, New York, and Texas, already had their own testing-accountability systems in place and have yet to fully experience the separate impact of NCLB implementation. The experiences of students, teachers, and administrators at one Texas elementary school with the Texas Accountability System since its inception in 1993 and the more recent Student Success Initiative (SSI) are instructive. Boober-Jennings (2005) spent the spring of 2003 in an intensive study (participant-observation, interviews, document analysis, informal interactions) of the urban Beck Elementary School (BES) in the Brickland Independent School District (both pseudonyms). BES is a relatively high-performing school with "an economically disadvantaged minority population" (p. 236), at least 75% of the total, in a metropolitan area. It has been rated as "acceptable" by the Texas Education Agency—but not yet as "recognized," which requires at least 80% of students who take the state test to pass it. Both administrators and teachers seemed to have "a considerable desire" (p. 237) to achieve a "recognized" rating. What Boober-Jennings found in response to her investigation of how the school district and school modified their policies and practices in response to the Texas Accountability System and the SSI, which mandates passing a third-grade reading test in order to be promoted to fourth grade, can be summarized as follows:

> I came to understand the constellation of practices used at BES to increase aggregate test scores as a form of "educational triage.". . . That is, teachers divided students into three groups—safe cases, suitable cases for treatment, and hopeless cases—and rationed resources to those students most likely to improve the school's scores. Through a series of practices, including focusing on "bubble kids" (those on the threshold of passing the test), targeting resources to the "accountables" (those students included in the school's accountability rating), and decreasing the size of the accountability subset . . . by referring students for special education, teachers diverted resources to students most likely to increase aggregate pass rates—the "suitable cases for treatment"—and away from those viewed as hopeless cases. Some of these practices were supported at the district level under the auspices of "data-driven decision making," while others, such as referring students for special education to remove them from the accountability subset, were not. (Boober-Jennings, 2005, pp. 232–233)

Four themes emerged in Boober-Jennings's (2005) analysis of educational triage at BES: (1) the adoption of presumably neutral or objective "date-driven decision making" that legitimated or rationalized diverting attention and other resources from low-performing students who were deemed unlikely to improve enough to pass the state test(s); (2) school personnel's use of data in a manner that created "the impression, if not the reality, of improvement" (p. 233); (3) the use of "loopholes in the accountability system" (p. 233) to exclude students (e.g., special education students) who might lower the school's aggregate test scores; and (4) understanding how and why "teachers willingly participate in educational triage" (p. 233), despite their stated commitment to helping children learn. Boober-Jennings's account is based on the school district or institutional environment's "equating of 'good teaching' with high test scores . . . [which] shapes teachers' professional identities" (p. 233) and encourages competition among them (rather than collegiality that might spawn collective resistance to test score preoccupation). School personnel seemed unaware of how their data-driven practices did not merely predict, but actively produced, differential student outcomes. In sum, "a singular focus on increasing aggregate test scores rendered school-wide discussion of the 'best interests of children' obsolete" (p. 260).

To what extent and in what ways do other statewide or nationwide testing-accountability policies and practices provide differential (dis-)incentives for attending to some students more or more effectively than to others? Who is benefiting from current practices? What are the public interests here, particularly with respect to curriculum and students?

CONCLUDING COMMENTARY

So, what might we make of these three cases taken together: scientifically based research, higher standards for curriculum knowledge and student learning, and state-level testing-accountability in practice? Among the not terribly far-fetched interpretations is that all three illustrate how public, professional education and research, as well as political policy attention, is being diverted from important questions about curriculum and students—specifically, curriculum knowledge and students learning, or "who has opportunities to learn what?"

This diversion has at least two noteworthy aspects. One already highlighted is that involvement in any of these debates, on terms already set by others, is unlikely to change very much in terms of redirecting attention to curriculum, students, or related equity issues. Second, school conditions with respect to curriculum, students, and equity remain pretty much as they have been, thus sustaining privilege and disadvantage educationally, socially, and politically. Public interests continue to be neglected in favor of special or private interests, and the difficult questions tend not to be raised or pursued. In short, such neglect maintains existing forms of social stratification, hierarchy, and power relations.

It is past time to reclaim curriculum knowledge and student learning, as well as to step back from the hot-button issues, to refuse to be drawn into others' debates on their terms, and to critically examine what we are about as education researchers and where we're headed purposefully, not by default. The effects of neglect and default are "real," whether or not they are intended. In effect, I am calling for *activist research* of various forms, activist in the sense that it raises questions challenging conventional wisdom, informs critical reform efforts, and contributes to a healthier and more equitable society and democracy—in other words, activist research in the public interest.

NOTES

1. Subsequently the National Research Council produced a 2004 report, *Advancing Scientific Research in Education*, and appointed a committee to investigate the "quality of evidence" in behavioral and social science research. Meanwhile, the recently created IES appears to be taking a narrower view of acceptable, scientific research. If ever one wondered about the socially constructed nature of science or research, there should be little doubt now.

2. While my ideas about reshaping the debate go back at least a decade, such as Cornbleth and Waugh (1995/1999), I have been reenergized by George Lakoff's recent work, such as *Don't think of an elephant!* (2004).

3. Both Sleeter and I have evidence that some "maverick" teachers refuse to be so contained; however, they are not representative of most teachers in this first decade of the 21st century.

REFERENCES

Airasian, P. W. (1987). State mandated testing and educational reform: Context and consequences. *American Journal of Education, 95*(3), 393–412.

Airasian, P. W. (1988). Symbolic validation: The case of state-mandated, high-stakes testing. *Educational Evaluation and Policy Analysis, 10*(4), 301–313.

Appleby, J. (1992). Recovering America's historic diversity: Beyond exceptionalism. *Journal of American History, 79*(2), 419–431.

Baldwin, J. (1985). *The price of the ticket: Collected nonfiction 1948–1985.* New York: St. Martin's/Marek.

Boober-Jennings, J. (2005). Below the bubble: "Educational triage" and the Texas accountability system. *American Educational Research Journal, 42*(2), 231–268.

California Department of Education (CDE). (1987, 2001). *History–social science framework and standards for California public schools.* Sacramento, CA: Author.

Cimbricz, S. (2002). State-mandated testing and teachers' beliefs and practice: A review of research. *Educational Policy Analysis Archives, 10*(2). Retrieved December 15, 2005, from http://epaa.asu.edu/epaa/v10n2.html

Cornbleth, C. (2001). National standards and curriculum as cultural containment? In C. Cornbleth (Ed.), *Curriculum politics, policy, practice: Cases in comparative context* (pp. 289–328). Albany: State University of New York Press.

Cornbleth, C., & Waugh, D. (1999). *The great speckled bird: Multicultural politics and education policymaking.* New York: St. Martin's/Mahwah, NJ: Lawrence Erlbaum. (Original work published 1995)

Correspondents of the *New York Times.* (2005). *Class matters.* New York: Times Books.

Eisenhart, M. (2005). Science plus: A response to the responses to *Scientific research in education. Teachers College Record, 107*(1), 52–58.

Eisenhart, M., & Towne, L. (2003). Contestation and change in national policy on "scientifically based education research." *Educational Researcher, 32*(7), 31–38.

Lakoff, G. (2004). *Don't think of an elephant!* White River Junction, VT: Chelsea Green.

National Center for History in the Schools (NCHS). (1994). *National standards for United States history, Grades 5–12.* Los Angeles: University of California, Los Angeles, NCHS.

National Center for History in the Schools (NCHS). (1996). *National standards for history, Basic ed.* Los Angeles: University of California, Los Angeles, NCHS.

National Research Council. (2002). *Scientific research in education.* Washington, DC: National Academies Press.

New York State Education Department (NYSED). (1996). *Learning standards for social studies* (rev. ed). Albany: Author.

Olneck, M. R. (1989). Americanization and the education of immigrants, 1900–1925: An analysis of symbolic action. *American Journal of Education, 97*, 398–423.

Olneck, M. R. (1990). The recurring dream: Symbolism and ideology in intercultural and multicultural education. *American Journal of Education, 98*, 147–174.

Olneck, M. R. (1993). Terms of inclusion: Has multiculturalism redefined equality in American education? *American Journal of Education, 101*, 234–260.

Sleeter, C., & Stillman, J. (2005). Standardizing knowledge in a multicultural society. *Curriculum Inquiry, 35*(1), 27–46.

Tyack, D. B., & James, T. (1985). Moral majorities and the school curriculum: Historical perspectives on the legalization of virtue. *Teachers College Record, 86*(4), 513–535.

Walker, V. S. (2005). After methods, then what? A researcher's response to the report of the National Research Council. *Teachers College Record, 107*(1), 30–37.

Waugh, D., & Hatfield, L. D. (1992, May 28). Rightist groups pushing school reforms. *San Francisco Examiner*, p. A18.

CHAPTER 12

Making Educational History: Qualitative Inquiry, Artistry, and the Public Interest

TOM BARONE

INTRODUCTION

MOST OF US FOR WHOM EDUCATIONAL STUDIES is our chosen field see ourselves as engaged in an ongoing quest to make the world of schooling a better place. Our efforts, simultaneously personal and professional, are fueled by hopes for an educational enterprise guided by our moral compasses, a felt need to realign its policy and practice, and therefore its outcomes, with our own sense of educational virtue.

I cannot more aptly describe the nature of my own quest than did Maxine Greene in articulating hers. Greene (1988) characterized her own lifelong struggle as one of "connect[ing] the undertaking of education . . . to the making and remaking of a public space" (p. xi).

But in recent times those with opposing interests, most from outside the field of education, have made the pursuit of that quest more problematic. Working diligently toward the downsizing of that public space, they have, from my point of view, moved to denigrate the public schools and to castigate those who live and work within them, in favor of a less expansive vision, one guided by a narrow, private, corporatist ideology. Little I have seen and heard over the last few years leads me to believe that these forces are in decline.

As academic professionals, one of the most important outlets for pursuing our quest is our scholarship. And for some educational researchers, quantitative and qualitative alike, it is there more than anywhere that frustration and even futility reign, with a sense that the realm of schooling has been largely untouched by our painstaking efforts to study that world and to reveal what we have found. Indeed, since the November 2004 elections, a few colleagues, in personal conversations, have expressed to me their doubts that progressive educational researchers, even in collaboration with like-minded academic colleagues and public school educators, can ever effect the realignment of schooling in America with their aspirations for it.

Despite the ongoing trials and recent disappointments, my quest, and hopefully yours, is not easily retired. But as we witness the educational landscapes of the public school and the academy devolving around us, I feel the need to support our longings, to revive our yearnings, for making a positive difference through our scholarly research. And to that end I quote the following words of Jean Paul Sartre (1948/1988): "The world and man reveal themselves by undertakings. And all the undertakings we might speak of reduce themselves to a single one, *making history*" (p. 104, emphasis added).

Sartre was not, of course, directly addressing the world of educational research, but from those pithy words I extrapolate the following: As educational inquirers, parts of our professional selves are indeed defined by our notions of the educationally true, good, and beautiful. We do indeed reveal these parts of our selves within and among other locations, our research projects. And it is through those undertakings that we must continue to strive to make educational history.

To that end, this chapter represents a tentative foray into a realm of possibilities. In it I explore merely one avenue for redressing the dire state of education though our work as educational scholars and researchers. It is divided into two parts. In the first I attempt to more fully articulate the nature of the obstacles that we face as educational researchers in our efforts at making educational history. In the second I suggest some features of qualitative research, especially arts-based research, that might serve us in our quest.

THE PROBLEM

In the last few years we have witnessed the greatest intervention of the federal government into the field of education in the history of the United States, a deep intrusion into the once public space of the classroom for the purpose of managing the transactions between those who live and work there. The consequences of this intervention, intended and otherwise—but largely, I believe, pernicious—are too varied and widespread to catalogue here. But among them has been the reinforcement of frame factors that have served to diminish the professional autonomy of teachers and administrators, deskilling them, as Michael Apple would say, and severely hampering them from engaging in history-making practice, which is to say, praxis.

Among the available forms of resistance to this institutional oppression of educators is a quiet subversion of these externally generated policy mandates from behind the closed classroom door. But while some degrees of professional freedom surely remain for educational practitioners, the omnipresent standardized exam, like Foucault's panopticon, renders subterfuge more problematical.

Subterfuge, moreover, does little to alert noneducators to the extent of the damage currently being inflicted on the educational process. While signs of discontent with practices such as high-stakes testing have emerged among scattered clusters of laypeople, conventional suppositions on which harmful policy mandates are based go largely unchallenged; within the general public, confusion remains widespread.

Writing in the 1920s, John Dewey (1927/1954) observed that a "public that is organized in and through those officers who act in behalf of its interests," including policymakers, is critical to the health of a democracy. He further noticed that the public of the time "is in eclipse, unsure and uncertain. . . . The public seems to be lost; it certainly is bewildered" (pp. 15–16). With other social and educational progressives, I detect nowadays a similar "eclipse of the public." The populace seems lost, distracted, largely unconcerned as one of the last bastions of hope for what Dewey called the Great Community—the public school—is betrayed by policymakers who are failing to act in the public's interests in ways that most do not fully comprehend.

Schneider and Ingram (1997) have identified the kind of politics that operates when the public is bewildered, lost, befuddled, betrayed. They call it *degenerative politics* (cited in Smith, 2004). Degenerative politics depends and feeds on an organized, usually public, display of entertainment. This theatrical display, designed to manipulate social reality toward a desired end, constitutes what Edelman (1988) calls *the political spectacle*. Of the several elements identifiable within that spectacle, I will mention three here.

The first significant element in this public pageant is that of skewed imagery, a series of distorting pictures lodged in the public consciousness. The second is a symbolic language, a set of abstract words, devoid of concrete referents, to which meanings are nevertheless assigned. Third, the words and images live in a mutually supportive relationship within an overarching storyline, similar to what the postmodernist social critic Jean-Francois Lyotard (1979) would call a master narrative.

Master narratives are meta-stories that aim to bring final meaning to cultural phenomena. These are stories that we cling to for a comfort and familiarity otherwise denied us in an increasingly jarring and bewildering world. A narrative provides a kind of coherence to the symbolic language and images, just as the words and images drive and illuminate the story, free to operate within the political spectacle, to pervade public awareness.

The words, images, and meta-story that are serving to confuse the public about educational matters are, of course, part of a more inclusive cultural narrative about issues of childhood, race, gender, social class, intellectualism, and private initiative versus public good. In teasing out the ways in which this vocabulary, imagery, and narrative pertain to education, I blend my own ideas with those of Mary Lee Smith (2004), who has transported some of Edelman's (1985, 1988) notions about the political spectacle into the educational arena.

The public has been bombarded with images of indolent and insolent school children, especially children of color; of uninterested, incompetent, mostly female teachers who are responsible for those children's purported deficiencies; and of the rare, isolated hero-teachers who, on behalf of their students, combat, without a posse of colleagues, a corrupt and stifling school bureaucracy. Finally, there are the manufactured images of the aloof, impractical, theory-obsessed teacher educator, portrayed as the ultimate apologist for the self-serving educational establishment.

Meanwhile, conversations about education these days are riddled with words and phrases such as *accountability, high standards,* and *freedom of choice.* Who, asks Smith (2004), could disagree with these words? And yet, she notes, the meaning of each term can vary within alternative contexts. For example, *accountability* suggests something quite different to accountants, to educators, and to testing experts. But those who use the term within the political spectacle "gloss over real differences in definitions and values" in favor of a privileged meaning that serves the narrow interests who seek to maintain the political spectacle.

Within the meta-story that flows from and through these words and images, children, public school teachers, administrators, and professors of education are stereotyped and scapegoated. Members of the educational establishment are portrayed as not responsible to the motivational forces of the free market. Because they have placed our nation's social, cultural, and economic well-being in jeopardy, they themselves are in constant need of surveillance, or "accountability." Most importantly, the public (a.k.a. "government") schools in which they work require a dose of private-sector competition to cure what ails them.

Because this master narrative is an artifact crafted within a degenerative politics, it is not, ultimately, a useful one. This is because it draws its breath from an air of unreality. Edelman (1985) suggests that the pictures within the political spectacle "create a moving panorama taking place in a world the public never quite touches," its members never actually experiencing it for themselves (p. 5). The images associated with words such as *accountability,* and the meta-story they support, lack concrete referents and so "float free of specific meaning. . . . No tether ties these words [and images] . . . to the world of experience and intractable concrete details" (Smith, 2004, p. 13). Nor are the meanings of the words, images, and story within the meta-narrative tied to debilitating cultural forces, details of which might reveal teachers and students as the victims rather than the perpetrators of social crimes. Instead, unwarranted meaning is arrogated to these words and images by those in a position to do so. The result is a public that is "held in a kind of thrall" (Smith, 2004, 13).

My favorite evidence of the extent of this psychological bondage continues to be the annual Phi Delta Kappa/Gallup poll of the public's attitudes toward the public schools (Rose & Gallup, 2004). Year after year, the poll has demonstrated a sizable gap between the views held about the quality of schools with which respondents are directly familiar, and their views of those with which they are not.

In the 2004 poll, 70% of parents from across the nation awarded an A or a B to the school attended by their oldest child. Asked to grade all public schools nationally, only 26% of the same parents chose an A or B.

How to account for this paradox? Between the parents' direct experiences of the nearby schoolhouse and their impressions of the distant classrooms inhabited by other people's children lies the political spectacle churning out distorted language and clichéd imagery. These words and images are rife within the products of the commodified and banalized mass media, especially the electronic visual media (Males, 1999) such as film, TV sitcoms, and newsmagazines, the commercial aims of which are, paraphrasing Abbs (2003), as far removed from actual experience as an amusement arcade is from teaching philosophy.

Those aims are indeed to bewilder and befuddle, to mystify and indoctrinate. The evidence from that Gallup poll (and elsewhere) suggests that while the flow from the popular media may be limited in its capacity to affect profoundly the meanings we derive from "actual" experiences, it remains sufficiently powerful to transform the benignly distant and unfamiliar into the fearfully strange and exotic. Unfortunately, however, it is within this anxiety manufactured within the political spectacle that much of today's educational policy is being fashioned.

The difficulties of removing the blindfolds should not be minimized. The political spectacle has allowed the seeds of misperception to be planted deep within the collective subconscious. Indeed, discussions in the media about educational matters almost inevitably betray assumptions built on the imagery within the master narrative. When even the National Federation of Teachers condescends to the language of educational standards and teacher accountability, the extent of the problem is more clearly registered.

The seeds are certainly buried below the cultural topsoil of political partisanship. While the 2004 platforms of the two major parties surely reflected, to some degree, the interests of different constituencies, the rhetoric on both sides floated above the meaning of terms such as *accountability* and *educational standards—* and even the ways in which a child may be left behind.

Of course, in a political campaign the spectacle reaches its height; indeed, dueling pageants vie for center stage. A campaign hardly represents an opportune moment for educating an electorate. Perhaps, in the wake of that campaign, with the spectacle lingering but its fever diminished, the time is right to intensify our efforts at intervening in history through our scholarship, even as we refuse to create a spectacle of our own.

WHAT TO DO?

So what are the various research approaches available to us for the kind of intervention of which I speak? The list of qualitative inquiry strategies has grown more extensive in recent decades to include the various forms of case studies, participatory action research, phenomenological research, hermeneutical research, cultural studies, critical ethnography, postmodernist approaches, poststructuralist approaches, and postcolonialist approaches, autoethnography, narrative research, life history, performative ethnography, and so on.

All have been recast, as we know, as a kind of *blacklist* of research methodologies (indeed, one that disparages all nonexperimental forms of educational research). But recast by whom? Are the proponents of a new, aggressively retrogressive research orthodoxy the same policymakers and politicians who benefit from a degenerative politics? If so, does their disdain for these research approaches reflect a concern that the methodologies might facilitate a remaking of the history that they feel they own? The presence of such a fear would support my own beliefs about the potential of these alternative research genres, and so offer hope.

In addressing the possibilities of making educational history through alternative genres of educational research, I focus primarily on the kind known as *arts-based*. I am wondering about the potential of a research approach that, boldly but not rudely, humbly and not arrogantly, intervenes in the current state of educational affairs, one that expands the reach of our scholarship because of (*not despite*) the fact that it is profoundly aesthetic, one that *both* finds its inspiration in the arts *and* leads to progressive forms of social awareness. I am thinking of an approach to research on educational phenomena that alters the world by raising questions, one that makes history by providing a catalyst for the changing of minds. And among the candidates whose minds might be changed are the members of the general public currently under the sway of the political spectacle.

This is, as we know, not the usual audience for educational researchers of any stripe. Instead, career success for members of the professoriate has largely depended on the degree to which our texts inform and persuade professional colleagues within our circumscribed discursive subcommunities. But some cultural observers have reinforced our discomfort with this narrow audience, expressing concerns about the tendency of academic writing to alienate readers unprepared to penetrate the opaque prose of disciplinary specialization. Russell Jacoby (1987), in particular, has insisted that even writings by academics with emancipatory intentions have not served to resist, but rather to contribute to, a general decline in public discourse.

In the last few decades, some educational researchers have abandoned the traditional premises, procedures, protocols, and modes of representation of the quantitative and qualitative social sciences for those of the arts. But arts-based researchers have thus far only rarely abandoned the traditional conception of the research audience. For those who have, the alternative audiences have included, among others, educational practitioners and policymakers, the informants whose experiences have been represented in the research text, those who commission evaluations of educational programs, and the researcher him- or herself.

I am—emphatically—not suggesting that arts-based researchers cease addressing any audience they desire to address. But I am imagining research projects that reach out to an audience that transcends one consisting only of colleagues and those alternative readers and viewers. Such an audience might include laypeople of all social categories, privileged and otherwise; those who might be identified as members of an intelligentsia or literati; and those who do not know the meaning of those words, residents of the many red states and the slightly fewer blue states— all of us who are, or should be, active participants in the larger civic culture, and all of us who have been, in varying degrees, captivated by the spectacle.

I am envisioning educational inquirers who undertake the reclaiming and redirecting of history by communicating directly with the general public through research that is based in the arts. But what characteristics of art and arts-based research hold promise in this regard? Two will be highlighted here. First, I am recommending research that is *socially engaged*, and second, research that is *epistemologically humble*. I begin with the notion of social or political commitment in art and arts-based research.

Socially Engaged Arts-Based Research

We have learned from various postmodernist theorists that power relationships inevitably inhabit every human activity and cultural artifact. All science is, therefore, inherently political, as is all art. But like some science, art can be emancipatory—and in more than one sense. For Nelson Goodman, art can free us from entrenched, commonsensical ways of viewing the world. By calling for and yet resisting "a usual kind of picture," writes Goodman (1968), "it may bring out neglected likenesses and differences . . . and in some measure, remake our world" (p. 33).

Goodman sees the emancipatory potential of art in its capacity to obviate and undercut facets of a prevailing worldview. Other definitions of art seem to emerge out of a more specific concern for inequities within the sociopolitical relationships in a culture. Art of this sort, more directly focused on the effects of social practices and institutions on human beings, operates out of what bell hooks (1994) calls an *outlaw culture*, one that promotes "engagements with . . . practices and . . . icons that are defined as on the edge, as pushing the limits, disturbing the conventional, acceptable politics of representation" (pp. 4–5).

Outlaw art represents a kind of assertively political project similar to what Sartre called socially engaged literature. Sartre (1948/1988) also viewed the primary aim of art as a challenge to the established interests within society, seeing the artist as "in a state of perpetual antagonism toward the conservative forces which are maintaining the balance he needs to upset" (p. 81).

Both hooks and Sartre are recommending artistic projects that move to shape and influence the public consciousness by critiquing the politically conventional and the socially orthodox. And artists throughout the ages have succeeded in doing so—from Sophocles to Bertoldt Brecht, from Victor Hugo to Richard Wright, from Pablo Picasso to Judy Chicago, from Spike Lee to Gregory Nava, from photographer Lewis W. Hine to Dorothea Lange, to name but a few is to omit untold numbers of others.

Their work reflects the spirit of more recent activist art, which, as Nina Felshin (1995) put it, has attempted to "change the conversation" by "exposing issues to a public view as a means of sparking *public* debate" (p. 37, emphasis added) and ultimately to stimulate social change. That is the sort of artistic stimulus that stands tall against the zeitgeist maintained through the political spectacle, one that offers hope that history can indeed be made through the personal quest of the artist.

I am obliged to report that I have, up to this point in the relatively short history of the genre, not been privy to a completely unblemished work of arts-based research, one sufficiently powerful, by itself, to redirect the educational conversation in the manner suggested by Felshin. But some, in their closely observed, imaginatively crafted renderings of the struggles of teachers and young people, have confirmed my beliefs about the potential of alternative research genres to upset the balance maintained within the spectacle.

Take, for example, the ethnodrama *Street Rat* (Saldana, Finley, & Finley, 2005), a piece of arts-based research that focuses on the lives of some homeless youths in New Orleans. The play was adapted by Johnny Saldana, Susan Finley, and her son Macklin from a research story composed by the Finleys (Finley & Finley, 1999) and from poetry written by Macklin (Finley, 2000). In April 2004, I attended a production of this ethnodrama directed by Saldana.

The script, based on participant-observer Macklin's experiences with his informants, moved briskly from an introduction of the two main characters, Roach and Tigger, to complications arising partly from their relationships with each other and their homeless friends, to a dramatic climax as violence nearly erupts, and finally to a touching denouement, a scene in which Tigger and Roach, obviously filling a void in each other's lives left there by others, declared in their garbage-strewn living quarters that they were, at least for the time being, home. The narrative drive of the story was punctuated by the recitation of poems of various lengths, composed by Macklin, who thereby became, himself, a character in the play.

Other touches added to the production's effective *mise-en-scène*. Absent a proscenium arch, audience members were seated in a black-draped, rectangular room, its floor shared with the actors. The minimal props, authentic costuming, and background music were all carefully designed and selected to advance the vision of the director and his collaborators.

The formal attributes of *Street Rat* were matched by its content. The telling details in the lives of Roach, Tigger, and their comrades enabled me to dwell within an otherwise largely unavailable world of homeless young people. Through an array of concrete images, particular forms of intelligence were revealed to me, the structure of moral codes laid bare. Through a cascade of specific utterances and gestures, I was granted access to their personal hopes, dreams, and motivations.

As an example of socially engaged research, this play addressed sociopolitical phenomena that remain hazy within the spectacle. Indeed, it was willing to refocus on—that is *re*-search—a part of what the postmodern theorist Nelson (1987) lists as

> the neglected . . . the forgotten, the irrational, the insignificant, the repressed, the borderline, the eccentric, the sublimated, the rejected, the nonessential, the marginal, the peripheral, the excluded, the tenuous, the silenced, the accidental, the dispersed, the disqualified, the deferred, the disjointed . . . [all that which] the modern age has never cared to understand in any particular detail, with any sort of specificity. (p. 7)

But the glimpse that this play affords us of a hidden or unfamiliar world is not an act of mere voyeurism. It is, rather, a work of what Stone (1988) calls *moral fiction*, one that aims to "establish the connections between [debilitating] social forces and individual lives" (p. 76). The socially committed play accomplishes what good outlaw art can: It "open[s] up institutions and their practices for critical inspection and evaluation" (Lincoln & Denzin, 2003, p. 377). The play's carefully embodied observations, the results of the researcher's scrutiny and artistry, challenge the arrogation of meanings within the political spectacle. It is indeed potentially emancipating in the strong sense advocated by hooks and Sartre.

Epistemologically Humble Arts-Based Research

Still, an arts-based research project geared to subvert the master narrative and confound the political spectacle must be more than socially committed. It must also be epistemologically humble.

Of course, the master narrative that serves the political spectacle, operating within a modernist epistemology that gravitates toward final knowledge, lacks all humility. Master narratives possess a totalizing character as they aim to impose order on the world from a distinct, if often hidden, ideological point of view, one that appears to be authoritative, final, exclusionary of alternative viewpoints, all-knowing.

A disposition of this sort in the social researcher represents the attitude of an epistemological bully. (Note that I have dampened down Lyotard's [1979] over-heated epithet of *epistemological terrorist*). "Arrogant bully" is, I think, an appropriate term for an epistemological stance that attempts to impose its own singular view of the world on its audience. But adopting a stance of epistemological modesty in projects of social inquiry entails more than the exchange of a social science methodology for an arts-based approach. Artists and arts-based researchers, however high-minded their emancipatory intentions, may produce works as exclusionary, monologic, and hegemonic as other sorts of projects. This happens whenever, to paraphrase Sartre, the would-be artist, eager to change minds, zealous to make history, forgets to make art.

Image, language, and story are indeed the tools and the products of artists. But socially committed research that evidences an interrogatory rather than an authoritative attitude must not resemble, on the one hand, the self-abnegation of political eunuchs, nor, on the other, the ersatz artistry of dogmatists, propagandists, ideologues, and rigid partisans. My hope is for a politically vital arts-based research, the kind that challenges the comfortable, familiar, dominant master narrative, not by proferring a new totalizing counternarrative but by luring an audience into an appreciation of an array of diverse, complex, nuanced images and partial, local portraits of human growth and possibility.

This implies that arts-based research has the power to involve members of the public in history-making dialogue, or in what I call *conspiratorial conversations*. A conspiracy suggests a communion of agents engaged in exploratory discussions about possible and desirable worlds. When an arts-based work engenders an aesthetic experience in its readers or viewers, empathy may be established, connections made, perceptions altered, emotions touched, equilibria disturbed, the status quo rendered questionable. Individual voices of audience members may be raised in common concern—either within the artistic textual engagement itself (between reader and text) and/or afterwards, among members of an audience of readers or viewers. In these conversations, ideas and ideals may be shared for the purposes of an improved reality. Plots may be hatched against inadequate present conditions in favor of more emancipatory social arrangements in the future.

How can a piece of arts-based research effectively engender conspiratorial moments? To create the possibility of conspiracy, the artist must first imagine what Wolfgang Iser (1974) calls an *implied readership*. Implied readers are those who actively participate in the composition of textual meaning" (p. xii). But this term "incorporates both the pre-structuring of the potential meaning by the text, and the reader's actualization of this potential by the reading process" (p. xii).

"Street Rat" was pre-structured by the Finleys and Saldana in a manner that pulled me, implied *viewer*, member of the public, into the world of the play, enticing me to reconstruct the illusion first imagined by the playwrights. In such a textual re-creation, wrote Dewey (1934/1958), "there is an ordering of the elements of the whole that is in form, although not in details, the same as the process of organization the creator of the work consciously experienced. . . . Without an act of recreation the object is not perceived as a work of art" (p. 307).

In this process of formal reconstruction, the viewer lives momentarily in a virtual world, bracketed off from the world of experience external to the work. Phenomenologist aestheticians would argue that the viewer thereby experiences a piece of subjective life, partakes of the vision of the artist as embodied in the prestructured work. But some works may not allow for an easy return from that vision into the world outside. Indeed, a work that is only technically accomplished can have an effect opposite to that of promoting conspiracy. While beguiling formal qualities can lure an audience into imagining another world, this hypothetical space is a realm of fantasy. Like the educational spectacle, a formal masterwork may create its own detachment as it bedazzles its viewers into acquiescence with its vision, offering a sublime illusion, never really, as Edelman would say, "touching the world."

Some works of propaganda are like this—technically marvelous, formally beautiful. But they do not emancipate. Lacking nuance, closed to disconfirming evidence, they seek only to indoctrinate, to lull into quietude. This kind of propaganda is, in fact, akin to kitsch, a debased kind of art that sentimentalizes everyday experiences.

Works of kitsch can evoke emotions that are based on nostalgia, or they may construct imaginary enemies. These elements of kitsch are found in the popular media's characterizations of teachers as either singularly heroic or collectively incompetent, their tales in which the intelligence and moral fiber of today's youth compare poorly to those of yesteryear, their images of public schools as out of control (Edelman, 1995). In kitsch, as in propaganda, a clear, controlled, unsentimental rethinking of mainstream truths and realities is sacrificed on the altar of the meta-narrative. But in their privileging of form over substance, their refusal to attend to the blemishes on the face of the prevailing master narrative, both propaganda and kitsch are disqualified as art, as research, and as catalysts for conspiracy.

Conspiracy is more likely to result from engagements in which aesthetic content grounds a work of art in the closely observed particulars of experience. The merely beautiful, or otherwise kitschy, work is thereby conditioned, planted in virtual space and time. A work that is closed in on itself is opened up to previously unimagined meanings.

The particulars that constitute the aesthetic content of *Street Rat* are what a traditional social scientist would call *data*. But here those data were carefully selected, edited, shaped, fashioned, dramatized, with an artistic end in mind. The aesthetic content of the play, in close relationship to its theatrical qualities, advanced in a credible fashion an understanding of these troubled youngsters, kids who, throughout their lives at home and in school, and later on the streets, were rarely either seen or heard. And now, along with the previously transparent forces that served to deform their lives, they were.

But just as form can become an imperial presence in the arts-based text, so can substance. Indeed, in many of the pieces of socially committed educational research to which I have been privy, aesthetic substance has hardly been the victim of an aesthetic sin. It has been the sinner. In that sort of work a regard for bombast over seductiveness can mean that formal qualities are casualties of the unrestrained political outrage of the socially committed researcher.

Now, minor imbalances of substance over form can be found in even the best socially committed arts-based research, including *Street Rat*. In that work, the sources of the street kids' alienation from their families, schools, and society in general, suggested within the more prosaic dialogue of the script, were successfully reinforced and amplified by the vivid imagery and driving rhythms of the poems interspersed throughout the text. Occasionally, however, anger overtook artistry, and stridency and shrillness prevailed. The poetry, hovering above the dramatized display of particular, contextualized injustices, seemed too obviously designed for the speedy delivery of a facile social message.

Considering the other attributes of this ethnodrama, those unfortunate lapses are easily forgiven. But in encounters with other emancipatory-minded arts-based projects, I have sometimes found myself cringing at a heavy-handedness in pursuit of noble goals. And even those who enjoy being preached to in a choir should remember that sermonizing the likeminded does not a conspiracy make. At their best, socially engaged arts-based research projects aim to entice into meaningful dialogue. Sympathetic outsiders are not merely the progressivist faithful, nor are they politically entrenched neoconservative ideologues. They are, instead, all those potential allies who have been temporarily mesmerized by the spectacle.

A successful enticement of sympathetic outsiders requires more than mere emotional discharge, which, as Dewey (1934/1958) reminds us, "is a necessary but not a sufficient condition of expression" (p. 61). Emotion that is effectively expressed through art is the result of a thoughtful composition of significant subject matter into an aesthetic form in which that emotion is embodied. Absent the artistic expression to which Dewey has alluded, there looms a reduced capacity to persuade profoundly, to move viewers affectively and cognitively into a skepticism regarding social pieties and platitudes.

Instead there is the kind of alienation that Carol Becker (1994) suggests is the product of some activist art:

> Art may be focused directly on the issues of daily life, but, because it seeks to reveal contradictions and not obfuscate them, art works which should spark a shock of recognition and effect catharsis actually appear alien and deliberately difficult. Art easily becomes the object of rage and confrontation. [And artists], frustrated by the illusion of order and well-being posited by society, . . . [may] choose rebellion as a method of retaliation. . . . [I]n so doing, they separate themselves from those with whom they may actually long to interact. (p. xiii)

This alienation may in fact be seen as the mirror image of that produced by either the beautiful-but-clueless or the kitschy. Again there are totalitarian tendencies, a lack of interest in or failure to facilitate democratic engagements with viewers who might be sympathetic outsiders. While *Street Rat* is a largely effective, socially engaged work that managed not to alienate, but to compel the attention of a limited, localized public audience, a second politically committed work has managed to secure a wider audience, although not as a full-fledged work of art. Indeed, it may offer hope regarding the degree of artistry necessary for a piece of qualitative research to promote conspiracy.

The book is *Doing School* by Denise Clark Pope (2001). Its subtitle reveals its political interests: *How We Are Creating a Generation of Stressed Out, Materialistic, and Miseducated Students.* The book explores the culture of competition in a comprehensive California high school as it traces the tensions between the felt needs of students and the materialistic brand of success expected of them. And at least at its narrative center, it avoids an authoritative stance, striking an effective balance between aesthetic form and substance. The author maintains an eye for telling detail, even as she wisely avoids the off-putting stridency of which Becker speaks. She transforms her informants into quasi-literary characters, transmuting her own concerns into the form of biographical portraits of five ethnically diverse students, fashioning for inspection the idiosyncratic life worlds of these students and the common social forces that operate to diminish them.

Still, in its student portraits, *Doing School* never really achieves the formal power of great literature. In reading the student stories, there is little danger of entrapment in sublime illusion. And in an analytical chapter entitled "The Predicament of Doing School," one finds a text more traditionally ethnographic than artistic. The text becomes more expository and didactic, less concerned with representing individual lives than with explaining, analyzing, comparing, and generalizing. Finally, in its last two pages, the format of the book shifts dramatically as appendices in the form of charts neatly condense into rows and columns general information about its central characters and the behaviors they exhibited in pursuit of success.

Doing School, unlike *Street Rat,* is, therefore, hardly activist art. In fact, its author makes no artistic claims for it at all. Instead, the book defies labels, serving, I suggest, as an example of the kind of genre blurring that, so prevalent nowadays, first emerged in social research in the 1970s, during Denzin and Lincoln's (2000) so-called "third moment" in the history of qualitative research. Still, if its quasi-literary center is seen as a core out of which the analytical content is extrapolated, then the project might indeed be identified, if not as artistic, then as arts-*based.*

The limited formal attributes of *Doing School,* like those of many qualitative research texts, certainly seem sufficient for facilitating readers' reconstruction of the text. Without feeling bullied by either textual form or content, this reader accepted the invitation to dwell vicariously in the lives of these young people. So it was that, through these portraits, I came to regard these students not as "other people's children" who populate a vague and distant campus but as specific human beings who harbor recognizable dreams in the face of debilitating circumstances.

Indeed, Denise Clark Pope (personal conversation) has suggested that, more than any other aspect of the book, the student stories account for its surprisingly positive reception among the lay public. A significantly better "seller" than most books about educational issues, *Doing School* has received much publicity, from interviews of the author on CNN, public television stations, national radio shows, and local news media to the creation of a conference at Stanford investigating the possibilities of school change. During that time, Pope addressed approximately 12,000 people who were primarily attracted, she says, to both the substantive topic and the readable style of the book. When it comes to hatching conspiracies, *Doing School* seems good enough.

Pope and, in a different way, Saldana have been able to entice members of the public into dialogues about meaning, about the nature of educational virtue, connecting that philosophical concern to features of the debilitating sociopolitical matrix in which young people live their lives. Appealing to a wide audience that apparently includes sympathetic outsiders, they seem to have generated the kind of public discussion that cuts through the miasma of the political spectacle.

They have accomplished this, I believe, by effectively calling into form the particulars of human life, thereby opening up their readers and viewers to the multiplicities of experience in the lives of young people. But, to return to Iser's (1974) notion of the implied reader, there is always the corresponding responsibility of the percipient of the work to assert him- or herself in the actualization of its potential. Conspiracy is—to repeat—a dialogue, not a monologue.

Again, when particulars are called into form by an artist, they can come to mean more than they originally meant in the so-called real world outside the work of art. But after reconstructing the meaning contained in the personal vision of the artist, vigilant percipients may assert their own influence over the work. Sensing a pull toward a closed, formal meaning may produce a healthy skepticism of the work and a desire to dismantle it. Finding their own voices as interpreters and critics, the percipients may, I mean, interrupt the illusion of the work. Becoming what Belsey (1980) would call a *revolutionary reader*, they move beyond the role of textual consumer to speak back to the work, to assign their own meanings to it. No longer is it just "reality" that means more than it originally meant. By dismantling the work, and transporting it into their own experiential landscapes, the percipients make it mean something different than it meant to the artist.

This means, of course, that the artist has lost a degree of control over the work. Sometimes the loss is complete, the artist's original vision vandalized. Indeed, Marcuse (1964/1991), Said (1993), and others remind us that, throughout history, once-radical artworks have been co-opted and tamed by conservative cultural forces for their own purposes. All texts are, of course, vulnerable to an audience free to engage in that which Stuart Hall (1980) characterizes as an *oppositional reading*, one that rejects what a *preferred* reading accepts. In this kind of reading from an oppositional ideological ground, hopes for a spectacle-confounding, conspiratorial engagement are dashed.

Because an artistic engagement depends on the *twin* responsibilities of the artist and the viewer, no matter how potent the prestructuring of the artwork, the artist's reach is limited. Or as Herbert Read (1966) wrote: "The eye is thoroughly corrupted by our knowledge of traditional modes of representation, and all the artist can do is to struggle against the schema and bring it a little nearer to the eye's experience" (p. 71).

I hope that arts-based researchers will never abandon that struggle. Nor, having produced our broadly accessible work, should we fear relinquishing control of it to the public. For this is, I believe, a profound and necessary gesture of epistemological generosity wherein a deeply committed arts-based educational researcher, abandoning the monovocal text out of faith in the social imagination, invites others to engage in a truly dialogical conversation about educational possibilities.

This invitation represents a refusal to reach toward indoctrination, and is born of an understanding that as artists and arts-based researchers we can never, strictly speaking, change minds. We must believe that people, within genuine dialogue, change their own minds. So instead we move to *artfully* coax them into collaborative interrogations of stale, tired, taken-for granted facets of the educational scene.

It is, I believe, precisely our humble stance, our speaking in tentative tones, our refusing to parade around in the uniform of a master narrator that justifies our projects of arts-based research. Wayne Booth (1961) made the point in writing about the rhetoric of fiction. "I am not," he wrote, "primarily interested in didactic fiction, fiction used for propaganda or instruction. My subject is the technique of non-didactic fiction, viewed as the art of communicating with readers" (p. 1). And we, too, refuse to advance our small, inviting, carefully observed portraits of schoolpeople from a stance of omniscience. Nor do we, in self-defeat, attempt to erase ourselves from our works, refuse to inscribe in them our educational visions, abandon our quests.

In our efforts to create history-making works of arts-based research, we continue to work toward a public expression of a personal *point of view*, even as we remain observers who, while committed, are open to the world. Convinced that a conspiracy must play itself out in its own dialogical space, may we arts-based researchers ask the trenchant questions rather than provide the easy answers, with no desire to replace a master narrative with a totalizing alternative—let alone one that is preconceived.

CHALLENGES AND POSSIBILITIES

Of course, there are considerable challenges to what may seem like a grandiose, even quixotic, vision of an arts-based educational research community that has succeeded in cutting through the educational spectacle on behalf of genuine educational reform. Engaged in research that is not only (a) arts-based or (b) emancipatory-minded, but (a) *plus* (b), we are swimming against the current of traditional methodological orthodoxy now reinforced, in a fit of political nostalgia, by federal policymakers. We are also working under the increasing weight of the corporate university, wherein those members of the professoriate who secure extramural grant monies to replace dwindling public revenues for higher education are rewarded with enhanced professional status. We are pushing against our own perceived lack of talent for crafting meaningful works of arts-based research, and against an academic culture that refuses to support the fostering of those talents in the next generation of educational researchers. We are choosing to ignore those, often otherwise enlightened, members of our own educational community who would suggest that we leave the generation of conspiracies to professional artists who are not educationists. And, perhaps most difficult, we are attempting to cut through a seemingly impenetrable, commodified popular culture that is antagonistic toward the thoughtful, challenging, nonkitschy, inexpensively produced artifacts, whether as films, novels, short stories, poems, television programs, or theatre.

How can we keep hope alive in the midst of these challenges?

In *Changing Minds*, Howard Gardner (2004) posits a spectrum of mind-altering creativity with two poles. Located at one end, capital C change is the result of the capital C creativity of capital C change agents. Gardner's examples from the arts and sciences, and fields of public policy, include historical figures such as Einstein, Picasso, de Gaulle, Freud, and the like. At the other pole are the "teachers, parents, and storekeepers who are satisfied with 'lowercase mind change,' changing the mental representations of those for whom they have [direct] responsibility" (Gardner, 2004, 132). But Gardner credits his colleague Csikszentmihaly with suggesting (in Feldman, Csikszentmihaly, & Gardner, 1994) that while "most of us cannot hope to effect big C creativity, we might at least expect to be 'middle C' creators" (Gardner, 2004, 132). Understanding that we need not necessarily match the high art of the masters in order to make history might reduce the levels of performance anxiety of some arts-based researchers.

We might also eschew the "great man" model of capital C change in order to avoid the isolation of those geniuses who single-handedly turn history on its head, in favor of mutual support afforded within a collectivity of artists. Recall, for example, the politically committed American artists of the 1930s—the novelists, playwrights, cartoonists, photographers, and painters—whose work, as Edelman (1995) points out, "made poverty vivid for Americans and made them feel its miseries, so that public welfare came to be categorized by most of the public as a justifiable aid to the needy rather than a drain on the treasury" (p. 108).

The work of these artists served to question the prevailing cultural narrative and helped make possible the policy initiatives of the New Deal. Might individual arts-based researchers, each pursuing their own personal desires for the expansion of the public space through their own chosen art form, coalesce to interrogate the entrenched master narrative of our own era? And might we be joined by qualitative researchers of other genres, even social scientists, whose work, now similarly disparaged, has included, ever since its inception, elements of artistry?

Collaborative and group efforts have also been, since the 1980s, the modus operandi of many activist artists. And for those of us without sizable grant funds, the history of activist art may offer clues for feasibly penetrating the popular culture. While sometimes prone to sensationalistic excesses, these artists have nevertheless moved their work, including applied theater, exhibitions, installations, and media events, onto public sites (Felshin, 1995). Some activist artists have focused on the creating of visual images designed for consumption by the mass media. More successful, in my estimation, have been those who have targeted specific constituencies within the public, often collaborating with members of marginalized communities. Most recently, activist artists have exploited the possibilities within the electronic media.

Finally, most encouraging is surely the knowledge that our work has, indeed, already begun. Let those apologists for the master narrative feel the need to clutch their tightly sealed version of educational history closer to their bosoms. For there are now in the once politically subdued and artistically disinclined academic research community those who would challenge their history. They include Pope, Saldana, and a growing number of other socially engaged and epistemologically humble qualitative researchers. The aim of their, of our, continuing quest is to, politely but powerfully—that is to say, *artfully*—change the conversation, to persuade those to whom history and public policy rightfully belong to resist the "usual kind of picture" in favor of one that, in touching the world of education as it is, makes one wonder about what it should and can become.

REFERENCES

Abbs, P. (2003). *Against the flow: Education, the arts, and postmodern culture*. London: RoutledgeFalmer.
Becker. C. (1994). Introduction: Presenting the problem. In C. Becker (Ed.), *The subversive imagination: Artists, society, and social responsibility* (pp. xi–xx). New York: Routledge.
Belsey, C. (1980). *Critical practice*. London: Methuen.
Booth, W. (1961). *The rhetoric of fiction*. Chicago: University of Chicago Press.
Denzin, N., & Lincoln, Y. (2000). Introduction: The discipline and practice of qualitative research. In N. Denzin, & Y. Lincoln (Eds.), *Handbook of qualitative research* (2nd ed.; pp. 1–28) Thousand Oaks, CA: Sage.
Dewey, J. (1954). *The public and its problems*. Athens, OH: Swallow Press/Ohio University Press. (Original work published 1927)
Dewey, J. (1958). *Art as experience*. New York: Capricorn Books. (Original work published 1934)
Edelman, M. (1985). *The symbolic uses of politics*. Urbana: University of Illinois Press.
Edelman, M. (1988). *Constructing the political spectacle*. Chicago: University of Chicago Press.
Edelman, M. (1995). *From art to politics: How artistic creations shape political conceptions*. Chicago: University of Chicago Press.
Feldman, D., Csikszentmihaly, M., & Gardner, H. (1994). *Changing the world*. Westport, CT: Praeger.
Felshin, N. (1995). *But is it art? The spirit of art as activism*. Seattle: Bay Press.

Finley, M. (2000). *Street rat*. Detroit: Greenroom Press, University of Detroit.

Finley, S., & Finley, M. (1999). Sp'ange: A research story. *Qualitative Inquiry, 9*(2), 254–267.

Gardner, H. (2004). *Changing minds*. Boston: Harvard Business School Press.

Goodman, N. (1968). *Languages of art*. Indianapolis and New York: Bobbs-Merrill.

Greene, M. (1988). *The dialectic of freedom*. New York: Teachers College Press.

Hall, S. (1980). Encoding/decoding. In S. Hall, D. Hobson, A. Lowe, & P. Willis (Eds.), *Culture, media, language: Working papers in cultural studies, 1972–1979* (pp. 128–138). London: Hutchinson.

hooks, b. (1994). *Outlaw culture: Resisting representations*. New York: Routledge.

Iser, W. (1974). *The implied reader*. Baltimore: Johns Hopkins University Press.

Jacoby, R. (1987). *The last intellectuals: American culture in the age of academe*. New York: Basic Books.

Lincoln, Y. S., & Denzin, N. K. (2003). The revolution in presentation. In Y. S. Lincoln & N. Denzin (Eds.), *Turning points in qualitative research* (pp. 375–378). Walnut Creek, CA: AltaMira Press.

Lyotard, J.-F. (1979). *The postmodern condition* (G. Bennington & B. Massumi, Trans.). Manchester, UK: Manchester University Press.

Males, M. (1999). *Framing youth*. Monroe, ME: Common Courage Press.

Marcuse, H. (1991). *One dimensional man*. New York: Beacon. (Original work published 1964)

Nelson, J. (1987, September). *Postmodern meaning of politics*. Paper presented at the annual meeting of the American Political Science Association, Chicago.

Pope, D. C. (2001). *Doing school: How we are creating a generation of stressed out, materialistic, and miseducated students*. New Haven, CT: Yale University Press.

Read, H. (1966). *Art and alienation*. New York: Schocken.

Rose, L. C., & Gallup, A. M. (2004). The 36th annual Phi Delta Kappa/Gallup poll of the public's attitudes toward the public schools. *Phi Delta Kappan, 86*(1), 41–58.

Said, E. (1993). *Culture and imperialism*. New York: Knopf.

Saldana, J., Finley, S., & Finley, M. (2005). Street rat. In J. Saldana (Ed.), *Ethnodrama* (pp. 142–179). Walnut Creek, CA. AltaMira Press.

Sartre, J.-P. (1988). *What is literature? and other essays*. Cambridge, MA: Harvard University Press. (Original work published 1948)

Schneider, A., & Ingram, H. (1997). *Policy design for democracy*. Lawrence: University of Kansas Press.

Smith, M. L. (2004). *Political spectacle and the fate of American schools*. New York: RoutledgeFalmer.

Stone, R. (1988). The reason for stories: Toward a moral fiction. *Harper's, 276*(1657), 71–78.

CHAPTER 13

The Art of Renewing Curriculum Research

DONALD BLUMENFELD-JONES

I N THE PROSPECTUS FOR THIS BOOK, Gloria Ladson-Billings and William Tate wrote that there is a recurring "role of education research as a vehicle for working in the public interest." They wrote that "the public interest
involves those decisions and actions that further democracy, democratic practices,
equity, and social justice. In this volume we argue that education scholars can and
must undertake work that speaks to the pressing public issues related to education." This chapter explores what it means to engage in curriculum research that
works toward furthering "democracy, democratic practices, equity, and social justice" and challenges our conceptions of what we ought to be doing. In so doing
I do not stipulate which contemporary issues we ought to address as there are so
many that such a listing would be inevitably inadequate. Rather, I challenge us to
consider a renewal of the field in the public interest through more direct research
engagement both with those people who practice curriculum creation and with
those people who make daily curriculum decisions. It has been asserted by some
that curriculum studies have for too long shunned engagement with the field of
practice and focused too much on so-called theory (see, for example, the Wraga,
1999; Pinar, 1999; Wright, 2000; and Henderson, 2001 exchange in *Educational
Researcher*). You might construe the above statement about shunning engagement as reinstating the old theory-versus-practice gap that divides our field into
nearly warring camps. However, rather than adhere to such an old confusion, I
hope to show that engagement with those who perform curriculum creation and
curriculum decision making as well as engagement with the processes they use is
not a matter of favoring practice over theory but, rather, a way of enriching both
theory and practice and understanding their synergistic character.[1] Coupling this
with a concern for doing research in the public interest strengthens the possibility
of having a stronger effect on the lives of people living in schools and out. While I
recognize that this sort of call is not new, we must (and I think do) understand that
while our scholarship has produced salient and insightful critique that is directly

pertinent to the public interest concerns forwarded by Ladson-Billings and Tate, it has not been taken up in substantive ways.

This failure is not merely a matter of our not having learned how to communicate the knowledge we have developed to the people who have the power and authority to make curriculum and curriculum decisions. Rather, many of us have not considered engagement with the field of practice to be part of our work and, therefore, have not adequately conceptualized such engagement. While there has been some work in the area of curriculum deliberation as one form of researching practice—such as Reid's (1999) and McCutcheon's (2002) work on curriculum deliberation as the basis for both creating curricula and making curriculum decisions, Walker's (1988), description of a naturalistic view of the practice of making new curricula, Smith and Apple's (1991) work on textbook creation and marketing as a species of creating curricula and curriculum decision making)—even this area has not been a robust part of curriculum studies. I hope, in this chapter, to persuade you of the salience of this call for engagement with practitioners and to propose a hermeneutic, art-making approach to thinking about what it means to do research on curriculum creation and curriculum decision making.

As a way into this discussion, it is worth examining, at closer range, what might constitute "public interest." Ladson-Billings and Tate's idea can be subsumed under the idea of "freedom." That is, democracy and attention to justice are processes leading toward increasing freedom for people. The question becomes: What is this freedom that we would secure? Almost no matter where we look in the Western philosophical literature, we find a similar view of freedom. For instance, Paul Ricoeur (1992) discusses a Kantian view of freedom in terms of the ability of a person to begin an action. He writes that Kant "distinguishes two types of beginning: one which would be the beginning of the world, the other which is a beginning in the midst of the world" (p. 105). People may not be responsible for the beginning of the world, but they are certainly responsible for acting in the world. As such, Ricoeur continues, freedom flows from the ways in which our free actions "function from [a] determined series of causes" (p. 105). That is, we are not free to choose and act in any way we please. We must attend to the circumstances (causes) that inform our choices and actions. Hanan Alexander (2001), a contemporary ethicist working from a spiritual and pragmatist tradition, writes of free choice and action as "based on understanding of the positive and negative consequences of alternatives" (p. 71). This understanding constrains our freedom to choose and act by noting that our choices and actions should be guided by considering their consequences. Herbert Marcuse (1992), the Frankfurt School critical theorist, writes that "Freedom does not contradict necessity . . . but presupposes it" (p. 7) By this he means that to be free is to recognize necessity and to learn how to live within its confines, seeing "the necessary as necessary" and "elevating it to the sphere of reason" (p. 7). These views of freedom share the idea that freedom is never purely free—as in free from all influence—but, rather, functions from within the constraints of the reality within which we live.

Martin Buber (1947/1993), who works from the existentialist tradition, connects education and freedom in a way consonant with the above ideas. He writes that education is primarily about the release of powers to act in the world. It is important to stipulate what this release is not about and what it is for. It is not about the modernist desire to transform the world for our own needs and wants (see Berman, 1988, for an exposition of modernity). Nor is it about privileging the individual's attempts to gain for him- or herself as much as possible of the world's goods, an attitude that seems to pervade present-day life. Nor is it about the mundane notion of "freedom from constraints," the notion that freedom is the opposite of being coerced or compelled to do something. Rather, as Buber (1947/1993) put it,

> At the opposite pole from compulsion there stands not freedom but communion. Compulsion is a negative reality; communion is the positive reality; freedom is a possibility, possibility regained. At the opposite pole of being compelled by destiny, nature or men there does not stand being free of destiny or nature or men but to commune and covenant with them. To do this it is true that one must first become independent; but this independence is a foot-bridge, not a dwelling-place. . . . Communion in education . . . means being opened up and drawn in. Freedom in education is the possibility of communion. (p. 107)

Communion derives from late Middle English and Latin for "that which is held in common." *Com* itself means "with" and *-ion* denotes an action or condition. Thus in "communion" we take action toward the condition we hold in common (Stein & Urdang, 1966). Buber is telling us that, although we may perceive ourselves as independent (and this is a necessary step in our development), the more fundamental condition of our lives is to be held together within the scope of destiny, nature, and human beings.[2] Our independence does not supplant the constrained character of our lives (noted by all four philosophers mentioned above), and we must come to recognize our independence without being mired in it. In the light of these connections, *freedom* means understanding how living with each other affects each person; how we can respond to destiny, nature, and each other; and what constitutes our responsibilities when we live in communion with these realities. Education, dedicated to developing these understandings within and among our learners, becomes a practice of freedom. Given that Ladson-Billings and Tate's call for the public interest is directly critical of a society of selfishness and individuation over the public good, these descriptions of freedom make sense.

What can be said of education can also be said of curriculum research. As long as we ignore the fabric of communion that produces curriculum (meaning ignoring the communality of nature, history, and people that constrains what is produced and enacted and is shared by all of us), we only partially understand what curriculum means. While, in the current curriculum studies scholarship, we attend to curriculum as an expression of what might be called "the social" in the form of political, cultural, economic, and sociological analyses of curriculum (and this sort of public interest research is necessary to understand curriculum), this is not what is meant by *communion*. *Communion* means participating with each other in recognizing and living within our constraints as outlined by Kant's, Alexander's, Marcuse's, and Buber's notions of nature, destiny, and other people. Within the practices of curriculum creation and decision making, without participation in communion we will not be located in the experience of living curriculum experience and, consequently, cannot really learn what constitutes freedom and how to affect change in curriculum in the public interest. Conversely, through participation in communion, theory pertaining to concern for democracy and social justice becomes germane and is modified by its interaction with the lived experience. Even the "theory-driven" Frankfurt School theorists (Marcuse, Adorno, and Horkheimer) recognized the interrelationship between so-called theory and so-called practice. As Henry Giroux (1997) instructs us, "Critical theory insists that theory and practice are interrelated. . . . Theory and practice represent a particular alliance, not a unity in which one dissolves into the other" (p. 45). He goes on to write that "experience . . . contains in itself no guarantees that it will generate the insights necessary to make it transparent. . . . While it is indisputable that experience may provide us with knowledge, it is also indisputable that knowledge may distort rather than illuminate the nature of social reality" (p. 45). At the same time, the Frankfurt theorists often engaged in concrete studies that delved into the nature of the lived political of their time, using a theoretical cast of mind. They demurred from the idea that theory could tell all there was to tell about the phenomenon in question. In so doing, they modeled the dialectic of theory-practice by not subsuming one to the other. This paradox provides us with the careful, skeptical platform from which to examine what engagement with communion, as the basis for research into curriculum practice, might mean.

    Prior to developing the hermeneutic of public interest research (and exploring possibilities of an art-making practice for doing so), it is necessary to speak in more detail as to what is meant by "renewal." This call connects us to our history with renewal as articulated by Joseph Schwab (1988) more than 35 years ago. His contentions around what constitutes involvement with the practice of curriculum provide some hints as to what directions we can take.

ARE WE MORIBUND?
NO, BUT WHO ARE WE IN THE LIGHT OF THE PRACTICAL?
A CALL FROM HERMENEUTICS AND ART MAKING

Schwab infamously made the statement, in 1969, that the curriculum field was "moribund" (Block, 2004; Schwab, 1988). He meant that curriculum scholars were no longer engaged with the practicality of being oriented toward solving particular educational problems, which he felt was the central character of curriculum. As long as curriculum scholars did not engage in such practical work, the field was destined for, at best, obscurity and irrelevance. To be sure, what Schwab meant by "the practical" is not the present-day narrowness of accountability that, according to all the news media, is desired by the general public. Nor did Schwab intend by the practical preparation for work-life in order to take one's proper place in the world of work, which is also, according to contemporary apologists for accountability (beginning, in contemporary times, with the Carnegie Report *A Nation at Risk*), in the interest of the public. These calls (for accountability and economic salience) connect with the public interest in part because those who make the calls have engaged in a rhetorical project for convincing the public of their importance. This is accomplished by instilling fear in the public: Without such moves, the whole educational project, and consequently economic project, will be, or even is, in a state of devolution. For example, see *The Manufactured Crisis* (Berliner & Biddle, 1996), read the Carnegie Report, note the rhetoric around No Child Left Behind, and look in any newspaper reporting how poorly American students do when compared to other developed countries. The major problem with present-day policy pertains to all of the public values that are *not* addressed by these narrow versions of the public's interests and needs. It is here that "public interest" becomes the more complex vision furnished by Ladson-Billings and Tate as they draw upon deeply held notions of the rights, responsibilities, and values that are not necessarily served well by a focus on accountability and economic viability. While concern for tracking success in education and for our children's having a secure economic future may be important values, they are not the only values worth educational focus—and an exclusive focus on them is exactly the kind of practicality Schwab critiqued.

While Schwab was not being narrow, he was declaring that curriculum studies scholars had a certain task to fulfill. This task was to be engaged with the process of education in an immediate and ever-changing way. It was to see that problems arising in educational settings must have responses attending to the specifics of the situation, rather than creating general principles of action that apply equally to all situations. This differs from the contemporary accountability environment of standards and tests that are applied equally to all situations, supposedly in order to compare different sites with each other and determine who is failing and who is succeeding (and distribute educational resources accordingly as goads and punishments as well as rewards). Schwab's view of the practical is significantly more complex, focusing on how an intellectual and theoretical cast of mind can be associated with the practical. In mixing the theoretical and the practical, he is presenting an image of how life is actually lived. Life is a messy construct, and no single theory can stand in for what it is like to live that life.

Why should we focus on studying curriculum creation and decision making? One answer is given above: Curriculum creation and decision making are prime sites for working with research in the public interest. There are at least two other answers. For one, it has become a truism in curriculum studies that top-down work does not succeed in changing the curriculum situation in schools or other venues. If we perform our research absent from the scene of creation and decision making, we continue to divide ourselves from those people who are to implement those understandings. Even when we write of what is going on in specific classrooms, either the work often remains technical (how can we teach better without considering whether or not we ought to be teaching what we teach?) or the curriculum is seen from a distance through particular theoretic lenses that may not honor the complexity of the people living in those situations. While it is important to analyze curriculum from an ideological perspective or in light of the socioeconomic-political conditions within which curriculum is made and resides, we must ask ourselves how successfully we have engaged with what it means to live lives under those conditions. In all these cases, the knowledge developed through research is valuable, but it is still delivered whole-cloth to curriculum practitioners laboring in the schools and other venues. Such knowledge usually falls on deaf ears and, if taken up at all, is transformed into what the person taking up the work deems to be educative. Dan Lortie (1977), in *School Teacher*, termed this approach to teaching and curriculum implementation "the apprenticeship of observation": People place much more stock in what they have experienced than what is delivered to them as some form of truth.[3]

Yet another reason for becoming engaged in the area of practice has to do with the inevitable fact that no matter what curriculum research we practice, not to be involved with the "material" of curriculum is, perhaps, not to be involved with curriculum. Schwab (1988) certainly seems to be making this argument as he wrote:

> There will be a renaissance of the field . . . only if the bulk of curriculum energies are diverted from the theoretic to the practical . . . to the eclectic. By "eclectic" I mean the arts by which unsystematic, uneasy, but usable focus on a body of problems is effected among diverse theories, each relevant to the problems in a different way. . . . [The practical is a] complex discipline . . .concerned with choice and action, in contrast with the theoretic which is concerned with knowledge. Its methods lead to defensible decisions, where the methods of the theoretic lead to warranted conclusions. (pp. 586–587)

While Schwab wrongly divides knowledge of theory from the practical as if there is no theory in practice[4] and wrongly divorces knowledge from action (clearly we cannot act without knowing something), he does provide two interesting ideas. His call for an "unsystematic, uneasy, but usable focus on a body of problems [that is] is effected among diverse theories" has hermeneutic overtones, and his call for the "arts of the eclectic" extends the possibility of seeing curriculum practice as a sort of art form. There has been a good deal written about using the arts in educational research (see Eisner, 1994; and Chapter 12 in this volume) and arts-based educational research is a growing field. In this chapter I want to take a slightly different tack and discuss what I see as the artistic process and how this can inform research practice as well as look at curriculum practice and why it is particularly well aligned with an interest in freedom.

The remainder of this chapter will be devoted to an exploration of hermeneutics as a way into engagement. The discussion will focus on what it means to become hermeneutically aware and why direct involvement with what might be called "the stuff" of curriculum creation and decision making is central to developing a hermeneutically adept research practice in the public interest. Lest there be a fear that such engagement means becoming co-opted by the already mentioned simplistic arguments that presently beset educational policy thinking, we must see that engagement of a hermeneutic kind deliberately moves us toward the kind of complexity that marks the best theory. In discussing hermeneutics, it will be asserted that we are already always engaged in hermeneutic activity and, so, hermeneutics is inescapable.

Hermeneutics will be linked to the aforementioned art-making cast of mind, dedicated to the kind of freedom described earlier. Art-making is a practice of freedom as the artist seeks connection (communion) with her or his object of concern (landscape, people, flowers, ideas, and more), and, through the act of communion, something new is learned about that relationship and the object itself. The artist works within the constraints of a tradition with which he or she must be in constant conversation and the constraints of the materials and the object itself. The curriculum researcher, curriculum designer, and curriculum decision maker all function from within traditions and can look at the object of their interest (the curriculum research, the curriculum itself, the curriculum decisions to be made) as aesthetic visions and forms. Enacting freedom, as has already been stated, is not an act of license but, rather, an act of acknowledging such constraints and seeing what can be accomplished anew living within those boundaries. Because the character of art-making is ad hoc (as it will, shortly, be described), curriculum research on curriculum creation and decision making can be treated as an ad hoc act, as can the acts of curriculum creation and decision making themselves (see Decker Walker's [1988] now-classic work on a naturalistic model for curriculum creation, which provides hints of this). Art-making, as with hermeneutics, requires immersion in materials in order for the art to be salient. It is not sufficient for the artist to think of a work; he or she must engage with the materials for making the work. And in the interaction between vision and realization, something is learned both about the vision and the materials that redounds upon the artist as a human being. Through the act of art-making, the artist is transformed. Similarly, hermeneutics teaches that through the act of interpretation, the interpreter is changed. If there is a relationship among hermeneutics, art-making, and curriculum research on curriculum creation and decision making, then, in the act of research, the researcher is changed in that act. Thus, hermeneutics and art have something to offer an engaged curriculum research practice.

AN EXCURSUS ON HERMENEUTICS AND ART-MAKING
FOR CURRICULUM CREATION AND DECISION-MAKING
RESEARCH IN THE PUBLIC INTEREST

In hermeneutics we study the ways in which we make sense of our experience through the process of interpretation. In the act of interpretation we can develop self-understanding (Gadamer, 1988; Ricoeur, 1974) as the core to our meaningful existences and something called phronēsis (Gallagher, 1992). Hermeneutic theory recognizes that not everyone is aware that this is occurring, and, to the degree that the individual is unaware, that the person cannot make optimal use of her or his interpretive processes. While self-understanding may be fairly obvious as to meaning, the second, phronēsis, is not so obvious and needs explanation. According to Shaun Gallagher (1992), phronēsis refers to moral knowledge that involves self-knowledge but is not completed by self-understanding. Phronēsis requires that "the person who is understanding does not know and judge as one who stands apart . . . but rather . . . thinks along with the other from the perspective of a specific bond of belonging as if he too were affected" (Gadamer, quoted in Gallagher, 1992, p. 153). The person must stand in communion with another in order to develop moral knowledge. What is the process of developing self-understanding and phronēsis? The process is cyclic in character: We experience the situation in the light of our preunderstandings of what that situation might be. We then project, using our theories and preunderstandings, where the experience might be leading. Having made some initial sense of the situation, we, then, gather new information by further experiencing the situation. This further experience is filtered through our preunderstandings of where the experience might lead. Those preunderstandings and theories are modified by the experience and, based on an amalgam of experience and projecting possible endpoints, we project still other directions the situation may pursue. We continue in this mixture of experience, theorizing, and projection until we come to the "end" of the situation. At that point we have developed knowledge about ourselves in relation to the experience through questioning the experience as it unfolds and testing it against what we already know, both of which become modified by the process of questioning. In a very real sense, we become a new self, changed by the experience of making sense. Hopefully, we also—if we are really paying attention to our communion with the experience—develop phronēsis (moral knowledge situated within self-knowledge and knowledge of others).

What are the benefits of taking a hermeneutic stance toward research in the public interest? Hermeneutics recognizes the constant uncertainty of truth-finding. (This directly connects with Schwab's advocacy of research that is "uneasy.") Uncertainty stems from two facts about the process of interpretation. The person who is coming to understand through communion recognizes the limitations of her or his initial position, termed, in hermeneutics, the "horizon." The horizon is comprised of the kinds of theories and preunderstandings that the interpreter brings to the interpretive process. We cannot, initially, know more than what we already know. That is, in fact, why we enter into experience in the first place: to expand our horizon of understanding. At the same time, the people we are attempting to understand also reside within an horizon of their own. The purpose of research is to expand the horizon of both the researcher and person or persons the researcher is attempting to understand, to, as much as possible, fuse the two horizons so that the researcher comes as close as possible to understanding others and their situation (without ever losing the understanding that there can be no pure identification with another person). In this way, what is understood honors the situation of the other whom the researcher is attempting to come to understand. This recalls Dewey's definition of democracy as "associated living"; a hermeneutic research disposition has great potential for producing understandings that can enhance the democratic life. The researcher experiences how situated everyone's experience and knowledge are. This understanding allows the researcher to not be bound to any particular conclusions that he or she might have brought into the situation before beginning the research. In fact, the researcher potentially allows for the experience to disconfirm predictions that he or she might have had about the situation and allows for what is known to be modified by what is encountered. Neither experience nor theory is privileged; rather, both are understood to interact synergistically, creating potential for new knowledge. Understanding is always on the move, ever evolving and, therefore, uneasy (to use Schwab's term) and messy. Based on this description, to do curriculum research in the public interest, we must become immersed in the "stuff" of curriculum: How can we have experience if we are not so immersed? The public is immersed daily in lives, and we cannot know those lives except when we become immersed in them.

Emergence and the unending process of meaning making, immersion, and modification of what we know link directly to the practice of art-making as a model for thinking about doing curriculum research in the public interest. Thomas Barone (2001; Chapter 12, this volume), in his work on aesthetics and research, characterizes research as interested in either the "enhancement of certainty" (scientific research) or the enhancement of "ambiguity" (associated with the arts). Life, in these two senses, is far more like art than like science. Thus, to posit the practice of art-making as a model for informing public interest research also makes sense.

Returning to Martin Buber, he provides insight into the artistic process resonant with the notions of freedom used in this chapter. He situated his ideas within a philosophy of relationship. In *I and Thou* (1923/1958) he writes about two kinds of relationships we have in our lives, both of which are necessary. In the first of these, the *I–It* relationship, all the world is an object to me that I manipulate for my own ends. This is not a relationship to be decried for it is natural and inevitable. There is, however, a second relationship, the *I–Thou* relationship. In this relationship I begin to experience another in a way that brings a new reality to me about myself as well as about the other person. Buber describes it as "feeling from the other side"—and it is more than sympathy or empathy. It is a life-transforming experience. When he writes of making art, he links the *I–Thou* relationship to the practice of art. He writes:

> This is the eternal source of art: a man is faced by a form which desires to be made through him into a work. This form is no offspring of his soul, but is an appearance which steps up to it and demands of it the effective power. The man is concerned with an act of his being. (1923/1958, p. 9)

Buber is informing us that the artist has a vision of a relation in the world that stems from an *I–Thou* relationship, which he or she confronts with his or her own relation to the world. This vision is but a possibility of something that will only become apparent in the act of making the art, and this act can only be performed in the presence of the person responding with all of her or his being. If the person takes up this challenge, then a work of art will ensue. Buber goes on:

> The act includes a sacrifice and a risk. This is the sacrifice: the endless possibility that is offered up on the altar of the form. For everything which just this moment in play ran through the perspective must be obliterated; nothing of that may penetrate the work. The exclusiveness of what is facing it demands that it be so. (1923/1958, p. 10)

Buber is saying that once the artist begins work, the form limits how the vision will be realized and this must be acknowledged. While the artist might want to put everything that comes to hand into the art, this will not make for art. Art is, of necessity, always a sacrifice, a loss:

> This is the risk: the primary word can only be spoken with the whole being. He who gives himself over to it may withhold nothing of himself. The work does not suffer me, as do the tree and the man, to turn aside and relax in the world if *It*; but it commands. (1923/1958, p. 10)

Once the artist accepts the sacrifice, he or she also accepts the demand to confront the sacrifice and the vision with all his or her being. The artist experiences such a relationship when he or she commits to making art, and the experience itself will not allow the artist to see the world as merely materials bent to his or her will. (We do not want to romanticize the artist in this. Certainly artists are ruthless and taught to be competitive and treat materials and ideas as economic forms rather than as aesthetic possibilities, but that is the sociological business of art and here we are thinking of the act itself.) There is a reward for sacrifice and risk of which Buber (1923/1958) writes:

> I can neither experience nor describe the form which meets me, but only body it forth. And yet, I behold it, splendid in the radiance of what confronts me, clearer than all the clearness of the world which is experienced . . . the relation in which I stand to it is

real, for it affects me, as I affect it. To produce is to draw forth, to invent is to find, to shape is to discover. In bodying forth I disclose. I lead the form across into the world of *It*. (p. 10)

Bodying forth art is an ineffable experience, not easily discussed or described but certainly concrete as the artist grapples with the form and the materials. In the act of bodying forth or making art, the artist is changed. Something is drawn forth and invented that carries with it a discovery about the original vision relationship unknown prior to the sacrifice and risk. This discovery can only happen through the act of the art-making.

Limitation and constraint are central to the art-making process. The artist can never have materials and forms exactly as he or she might want. For instance, in Joyce Cary's (1965) comic novel *The Horse's Mouth*, Gulley Jimson, the painter/protagonist, has just been released from jail. His paints have been stolen, and he can only pinch four small pots of sample decorator paints (two red, a blue, and a white) from the oilman. He has no brushes and so must fashion one from a stump of rope. He proceeds to work on the painting he had begun before going to jail for a month. He becomes excited by the ways in which his imagination and execution work together. It is through the tension he experiences between his vision and the materials and forms to which he is limited that he produces his art. In my own experience, I was once asked to choreograph a duet for two nondancers to music not of my choosing and for a limited television space. It wasn't only a problem-solving practice. I sought a vision and then, given the severe limitations of my materials, brought that vision to life in a way I would have never predicted. This was one of my most satisfying choreographic experiences. Art thrives on limitation.

There is also an anarchic quality to art-making that, as it turns out, is similar to the practice of science. Paul Feyerabend (1970), the philosopher of science, posited that science practice is anarchic: The scientist assembles her or his practice according to what materials are at hand and what ideas are current or being offered. Science is a combination of rule and error, "errors" being "the expression of the idiosyncrasies of an individual thinker, observer, even of individual measuring instruments, depends upon circumstances" (p. 18). Errors are the "expression of the phenomena and theories [which] . . . develop in unexpected ways" (p. 18). Feyerabend wrote that errors are a collection of stories and aimless gossip and are like art: Learning proceeds from doing and trying out. Sometimes an error leads to success (think of the discovery of penicillin). Just so, hermeneutics and art, as described above, depend on error for fruitfulness. Jackson Pollock, it is said, discovered his action painting by accident and was so fascinated by it that he pursued and developed it. He did not arrive at it through rational processes. Just so, we cannot expect the practice of curriculum research in the public interest, proceeding hermeneutically and artistically, to emerge through rational processes. As with Feyerabend, we recognize the ad hoc character of all research, including hermeneutics and art-making, and note that this is an inevitable characteristic of all research rather than an accident to be fixed. The tension that emerges from such a process is not something to be bemoaned but an accepted dimension of the artistic process. It is by experiencing the tension that new dimensions of the vision are discovered because the artist must respond to the world that is actually speaking to him or her. That is what art is, fundamentally: a response to experience. If there is no experience, there can be no response.

If we view the act of curriculum research in the public interest from this hermeneutic, art-making, anarchic vantage point, we can argue that we only learn in the presence of immersion with our materials and our vision, simultaneously. As the artist communes with her or his vision and form and responds to the vagaries of the unfolding work, so, as curriculum researchers, we become available to vision and form in the scene into which we are inquiring and respond to what we find there rather than to what we wish to find there. If we enter a curriculum scene with a notion of what we think people should be doing if they are interested in democracy and social justice, then we will never discover the multiplicity that is democracy, the multiple possibilities of which we could not be aware (because we live inside our own horizons). Both hermeneutics and artistic practice provide us with a world-openness attitude, consonant with both freedom and democracy. Perhaps of equal importance, those with whom we are doing our research feel themselves invited into the process of understanding and will be, hopefully, more open to the findings we, the researchers, can offer. In this environment, one of exploration and ambiguity, something may be learned by everyone, an end devoutly to be desired.

MOVING HERMENEUTICS AND ART-MAKING
TOWARD CURRICULUM RESEARCH IN THE PUBLIC INTEREST

Even with all that has been described, it may still fairly be asked how hermeneutics and art-making link to research in the public interest, since the above descriptions do not necessarily link to the concerns of Ladson-Billings and Tate. For one thing, it is certainly true that some artists serve a politically regressive agenda. Art does not necessarily lead to forwarding the public interest. As for hermeneutics, thinkers such as E. D. Hirsch (1988) are considered conservative hermeneutic practitioners and theorists (Gallagher, 1992). Gallagher means by this that such thinkers want to use hermeneutics to develop one true interpretation of a text, event, or experience. In Hirsch's educational prescription about what every American needs to know in order to be a good citizen, he narrows this to knowing a list with which you should be familiar. This might be considered to be antidemocratic and not prone to lead toward a socially just world. Indeed, he has been criticized as simply reinscribing the old oppressions.

Under a hermeneutic, art-making approach, we cannot be sure, in analyzing Hirsch's recommendations, that he is not about promoting democracy and social justice. He may be functioning from a very different horizon from ours that it is our task to uncover, describe, and take account of in interpreting his curriculum. He is certainly functioning in an ad hoc fashion in terms of making a list (over other possibilities) and populating it in very particular ways. What happens when we enter into that list, as an artist might enter into a phenomenon, to know more about it? By engaging Hirsch in these ways, we imaginatively engage his practice of curriculum making and, in so doing, we potentially both learn new definitions of democracy and social justice and understand how he turns in the direction that he turns while espousing democratic and socially just ends. In other words, even here, where he is addressing current educational problems in ways we might decry, we might yet learn something through our inquiry about democracy and social justice of which we could not be previously aware.

Given this confusing possibility, how do we move hermeneutics and art-making as models for doing public interest research? The move needs a cast of mind or set of dispositions about democracy and social justice, rather than being wedded to one theory of democracy and social justice through which we filter what we examine. Dispositions for democracy and social justice are preferable because they leave us more open to the possibility of disconfirmation, the life-blood of hermeneutics and art-making. Once interpretation and art-making become formulaic, the results of our research practice lack the opportunity for the kind of emergent understanding necessary to both hermeneutics and art-making. Thus, with Hirsch we must be open to what we can learn by staying available to possibilities.

How can these dispositions be used? Jurgen Habermas (1972), in *Knowledge and Human Interests*, lays out a typology of social science research that can be helpful here. He names three types of research practice: the empirical-analytic, the historical-hermeneutic, and the critical-emancipatory. The first two—tracking well with quantitative and qualitative inquiry, respectively—favor a "rule" of inquiry requiring that the inquirer have no interest in the outcomes of the inquiry. The inquirer must remain entirely disinterested. The third, the critical-emancipatory, does not make this claim but openly declares that the inquirer's interest is in increasing freedom through his or her work. Habermas argues that the first two do, actually, have interests that they don't acknowledge. The empirical-analytic fulfills the human agenda of control of a situation in order to make technological advances in it. The historical-hermeneutic fulfills the human desire for consensus and understanding. It is important to note that the critical-emancipatory mode is not actually a particular mode; rather, the critical-emancipatory inquirer is willing to use, and often does use, both empirical-analytic and/or historical-hermeneutic methods. Bowles and Gintis (1976), in *Schooling in Capitalist America*, rely almost exclusively on statistics. Gary Anderson (1989) has conceptualized a critical approach to ethnography, a form of historical-hermeneutic inquiry. Pierre Bourdieu, in *Distinction* (1987), employed multiple modes of inquiry: surveys, statistical analyses of eating habits and theater attendance, interviews, analysis of art-works, and more. Bourdieu is clearly a researcher concerned with democracy and social justice.

The critical-emancipatory is a cast of mind and a set of dispositions guiding the inquirer to employ whatever modes of inquiry seem to be capable of yielding understanding for the purposes of increasing freedom. These dispositions can drive the research project without destroying the "objectivity" of the project. We can enter into curriculum research in the public interest with a hermeneutic, art-making frame of mind actively engaged in communion as we pursue empirical-analytic or historical-hermeneutic work and add to this a consistent concern for democracy and social justice. Specific curriculum research projects dedicated to examining current curriculum issues (e.g., the place of "standards" in curriculum creation and decision making and how people take them up and why) can be informed by these coordinated approaches. Locating our work in the venues of curriculum creation and decision making allows us to participate (be in communion with) the complexity of human understanding and emergent educative agendas. Rather than participate in frozen versions of what is true (as if we could actually know what is true), we enter into the messy life of curriculum, hermeneutically and artistically, helping others to see how this looser approach to both research and decision making more mirrors how we function than contradicts it. In so doing, we foster dialogue around the important concerns of democracy and social justice in the public interest.

NOTES

1. It is important to note that the relationship between theory and practice has been explicitly acknowledged in at least two sectors of the field. For many years presentations on alternatives to standard practices of curriculum creation have been presented at the annual *Journal of Curriculum Theorizing* Conference on Curriculum and Classroom Practice, better known as the Bergamo Conference. The Curriculum and Pedagogy Conference and organization and its publication, the *Journal of Curriculum and Pedagogy,* are also involved with bringing practice and theory together. James Henderson and Richard Hawthorne's work on transformative curriculum leadership (2000) and Henderson and Kathleen Kesson's work on curriculum wisdom (2003) also fit within this area. So there is some small tradition for investigating this area of curriculum studies and for joining theory and practice. I am simply asserting that it is time to consider making this work more central to curriculum studies.

2. Buber's emphasis on relationship and connection has many contemporary counterparts in education thinking. See, for instance, Barbara Thayer-Bacon's (1998) work on relational epistemology, Nel Noddings's (1984) work on the care ethic, and Blumenfeld-Jones's (2004) work on Levinasian ethics in the classroom.

3. Several caveats are important to understand this first argument. In the above it was stated that there has been much good work done in curriculum studies since Schwab's declaration. Indeed it can easily be asserted that Schwab's declaration helped spur the development termed, by William Pinar, as "reconceptualist curriculum studies." Pinar's seminal

edited volume *Curriculum Theorizing: The Reconceptualists* (1975) brought to public attention work that became the many strands of new curriculum research: critical/theoretical work, phenomenology, *currere,* hermeneutics, curriculum history, aesthetics, and more. The critical community (for example, Jean Anyon, Michael Apple, Henry Giroux, Jennifer Gore, Peter McLaren, Thomas Popkewitz, Kathleen Weiler, and more) has made many contributions to our understanding of curriculum for democracy. All of this work has been fecund, opening the field to a more robust understanding of curriculum as an idea and arena of study. And this work was not without its practical implications about better ways of educating. It is also to be understood that there are now strong and abundant political forces at work to thwart and ignore what curriculum studies scholars have produced, and it is also true that, as a society, represented in our schools, we continue to be wedded to stock curricula consisting of academic subject matter conceptualized in an academic manner that has little meaning for social justice and democracy. But, with all this in mind, the suggestion is being made that we reconsider our relationship to schools and the connection between our work and that life, to continue alongside the evolving, unfolding possibilities that began as reconceptualization.

4. There is no human practice that is not grounded in implicit theories—see Chris Argyris's influential work in this regard on "espoused theory" versus "theory-in-use" (http://www.infed.org/thinkers/argyris.htm and http://www.actionscience.com).

REFERENCES

Alexander, H. (2001). *Reclaiming goodness: Education and the spiritual quest.* South Bend, IN: University of Notre Dame Press.

Anderson, G. L. (1989). Critical ethnography in education: Origins, current status, and new directions. *Review of Educational Research, 59*(3), 249–270.

Barone, T. (2001). *Touching eternity: The enduring outcomes of teaching.* New York: Teachers College Press.

Berliner, D., & Biddle, B. (1996). *The manufactured crisis: Myths, fraud, and the attack on America's public schools.* New York: Addison-Wesley.

Berman, M. (1988). *All that is solid melts into air: The experience of modernity.* New York: Penguin.

Block, A. (2004). *Talmud, curriculum and the practical: Joseph Schwab and the rabbis.* New York: Peter Lang.

Blumenfeld-Jones, D. S. (2004). The hope of a critical ethics: Teachers and learners. *Educational Theory, 54*(3), 263–279.

Bourdieu, P. (1987). *Distinction: A social critique of the judgment of taste* (R. Nice, Trans.). Boston: Harvard University Press.

Bowles, S., & Gintis, H. (1976). *Schooling in capitalist America.* New York: Basic Books.

Buber, M. (1958). *I and Thou* (2nd Ed; R. Gregor Smith, Trans.). New York: Charles Scribner's Sons. (Original work published 1923)

Buber, M. (1993). Education. In *Between man and man* (pp. 98–122). New York: Routledge. (Original work published 1947)

Cary, J. (1965). *The horse's mouth.* New York: Harper & Collins.

Eisner, E. (1994). *The educational imagination: On the design and evaluation of school programs.* New York: Macmillan.

Feyerabend, P. (1970). *Against method: Outline of an anarchistic theory of knowledge.* Minneapolis: University of Minnesota Press.

Gadamer, H.-G. (1988). *Truth and method.* New York: The Crossroad.

Gallagher, S. (1992). *Hermeneutics and education.* Albany: State University of New York Press.

Giroux, H. (1997). *Pedagogy and the politics of hope.* Boulder, CO: Westview.

Habermas, J. (1972). *Knowledge and human interests.* Boston, MA: Beacon.

Henderson, J. (2001). Deepening democratic curriculum work. *Educational Researcher, 30*(9), 18–21.

Henderson, J. & Hawthorne, R. (2000). *Transformative curriculum leadership.* Englewood Cliffs, NJ: Prentice-Hall.

Henderson, J., & Kesson, K. (2003). *Curriculum wisdom: Educational decisions in democratic societies.* Englewood Cliffs, NJ: Prentice-Hall.

Hirsch, E. D. (1988). *Cultural literacy: What every American needs to know.* New York: Vintage.

Lortie, D. (1977). *School teacher: A sociological study.* Chicago: University of Chicago Press.

Marcuse, H. (1992). Philosophy and critical theory. In D. Ingram & J. Simon-Ingram (Eds.), *Critical theory: The essential readings* (pp. 5–19). New York: Paragon House.

McCutcheon, G. (2002). *Developing the curriculum: Solo and group deliberation.* Troy, NY: Educator's International Press.

Noddings, N. (1984). *Caring: A feminine approach to ethics and education.* Berkeley CA: University of California Press.

Pinar, W. F. (Ed.). (1975). *Curriculum theorizing: The reconceptualists.* Berkeley, CA: McCutchan.

Pinar, W. F. (1999). Gracious submission. *Educational Researcher, 28*(1), 14–15.

Reid, W. (1999). *Curriculum as institution and practice: Essays in the deliberative tradition.* Mahwah, NJ: Erlbaum.

Ricoeur, P. (1974). *The conflict of interpretations: Essays in hermeneutics.* Evanston, IL: Northwestern University Press.

Ricoeur, P. (1992). *Oneself as another* (K. Blamey, Trans.). Chicago: University of Chicago Press.

Schwab, J. (1988). The practical: A language for curriculum. In J. Gress with D. Purpel (Eds.), *Curriculum: An introduction to the field* (2nd ed.; pp. 586–607). Berkeley, CA: McCutchan.

Smith, L. C., & Apple, M. (1991). *The politics of the textbook.* New York: Routledge.

Stein, J., & Urdang, L. (Eds.). (1966). *The Random House dictionary of the English language: the unabridged edition.* New York: Random House.

Thayer-Bacon, B. J., with Bacon, C. S. (1998). *Philosophy applied to education: Nurturing a democratic community in the classroom.* Upper Saddle River, NJ: Merrill.

Walker, D. (1988). A naturalistic model for curriculum development. In J. Gress with D. Purpel (Eds.), *Curriculum: An Introduction to the field* (2nd ed.; pp. 235–248). Berkeley, CA: McCutchan.

Wraga, W. (1999). Extracting sun-beams out of cucumbers: The retreat from practice in reconcpetualized curriculum studies. *Educational Researcher, 28*(1), 4–13.

Wright, H. K. (2000). Nailing Jell-o to the wall: Pinpointing aspects of state-of-the-art curriculum theorizing. *Educational Researcher, 29*(5), 4–13.

In the Public Interest

WILLIAM F. TATE

> Let nothing be done through selfish ambition or conceit, but in lowli-
> ness of mind let each esteem others better than himself. Let each of
> you look not only for his own interests, but also the interests of others.
> Philippians 2: 3-4 (New King James Version)

UNIVERSITIES TODAY ARE OFTEN JUDGED by the amount of rev-
enue in their endowments. It is undeniable that a significant endowment
can advance the university's mission. Endowments are part of a legacy
of university partnerships that date back hundreds of years. One of the first gifts
endowing an academic professorship was awarded to a man who would eventually be named Bishop of Rochester, England. The professorship was established
to support and advance the theological mission of Cambridge University. John
Fisher was the first academic to hold the Lady Margaret Professorship. Eventually
Fisher, a man of significant academic standing, was named chancellor of Cambridge University, a position he maintained until his death. As a bishop, chancellor, and Lady Margaret Professor, many sought his counsel and held his scholarship in high regard. Eventually he became the advisor to King Henry VIII. The
King's history with women and divorce is well documented. What is sometimes
overlooked is that John Fisher, the Lady Margaret Professor, took a public stand
against the king's effort to declare his marriage to Queen Catherine null and void.
His public position, based on principle, ethics, and moral conviction, cost the first
holder of the Lady Margaret Professorship at Cambridge University his life. The
endowed professor was beheaded. It is not the prestige of the endowed professorship that symbolizes the legacy of John Fisher. Rather, his legacy, in part, was his
willingness to publicly offer a reasoned position and to stand firm in the face of
great political opposition. He looked beyond his own self-interest and defended
the rights of an individual not positioned to leverage the same public forum. He
considered the interests of others and acted. This legacy is an important reminder
and challenge for all academics and researchers hoping to conduct research in the
public interest. The purpose of this chapter is to provide a brief discussion of my

thinking about education research and the public interest. My remarks are framed as a global response to the chapters of this book. Each of the contributors to this book has provided a set of conditions that might potentially advance the work of others who desire to contribute to the educational literature with the public interest in mind. My goal is to respond to their thinking. This response is organized into three sections.

THE AMERICAN SOCIAL SCIENCE PROJECT
AND EDUCATIONAL RESEARCH

The purpose of this section is to discuss the arguments and recommendations of this book in light of the American social science project, so a brief discussion of the American social science project is warranted. In his discussion of the history of political science, Kenneth Prewitt (2005) argued that, like science more generally, American social science has since its inception revolved around two inseparable projects: a science project (more in-depth understanding of human behavior, relationships, organizations, and so on); and a national political project (advancing humankind, protecting the nation, building the economy, strengthening democracy, etc.). He further stated that American social sciences are largely American-centric. For example, political science has focused largely on the theories and practice of American political institutions and practices—Supreme Court, Congress, federalism, and elections; on American political behavior—interest groups, voter choice; on liberal political doctrine; and most revealing, on American exceptionalism. Later in its intellectual history, political science questions with a more international scope—security and strategic alliances—often turn to how the United States participates in and is impacted by matters beyond our borders. Political science is not an outliner in this regard. Economics, as seen by policy groups and universities in the United States, has capitalism as its primary theoretical reference point, with a majority of empirical work drawing on U.S. data and examples. Sociology continues to inform our understanding of urbanization, social stratification, socialization of language minorities, and industrial dislocations—all topics that were present in the United States over 100 years ago and central to the emergence of this discipline. Psychology, centered on child development, emotion, cognition, life-span development, and social relations, has evolved within the U.S. context. According to Prewitt (2005), the discipline of anthropology represents a partial exception. However, anthropology's links to the race–science movement in the 19th century, and its connections to area studies during the latter part of the 20th century, suggest that even this field has the United States as a constant point of reference. Area studies as originally supported by foundations and the U.S. federal government was part of a cold war strategy to influence the thinking and actions of new nations subject to communist proposals. Additionally, with respect to U. S. anthropology, it is as likely to involve the study of a health issue specific to a racial group in an urban or rural community of the United States as it is to the non-U.S. other. The study of the culture of science laboratories, institutions, or government agencies in the United States is now more than acceptable in the discipline. Of course, there are exceptions across all the disciplines to this U.S.-centeredness. However, the trend is worth noting and speaks directly to an implied compact related to the support of social science research. Specifically, social science is a science project with a goal to improve human conditions in the United States. The social science project in America is not without its share of tensions and contradictions. Burawoy (2005) captures the tension in his discussion of public sociology:

> Within our discipline, public sociology is caught in a contradictory position, on one side, professional sociology's concern to develop a monopoly of abstract, specialized knowledge, evaluated by peers and, on the other side, publics that demand accessible knowledge devoted to concrete issues. . . . For their part, publics want to turn public sociologists into their own policy sociologists! On the other hand, sociologists may seek to subjugate publics, demanding moral conformity to their edicts, as when traditional public sociologists turn science into sermons or when organic public sociologists ply their trade like a vanguard party. . . . Public sociology is not only challenged from outside, by the very publics it addresses, but also from within the discipline, by professional sociology. From the beginning, professional sociology has deployed the mantle of science to distinguish itself from common sense, to distinguish its analytical theory from folk theory, and to distinguish its systematic methods of data collection from random and incoherent experiences of everyday life. It has developed bodies of knowledge, subject to peer review and all too often rendered inaccessible to wider publics. Professional sociology is intended first and foremost for fellow sociologists. (pp. 74–75)

This orientation to consider the interests of colleagues in a field is largely driven by a need to establish credibility and legitimacy in the wider academic landscape, and to distinguish the work of the field from other competing disciplines. This competition is often shaped by discussions of what science is, whose meaning is contested and significant to the struggle within a field and among disciplines. The response by participants in many disciplines and fields of study was to call for a greater use of statistical modeling (Ash, 2005; NCES, 2003; Rosenburg, 1992). This has certainly been the case in education, as government officials and applied research think-tanks have raised concerns about a plethora of educational policy recommendations, folkways, and educational management strategies, using terms like *unscientific* and *lacking an evidentiary base*. As Cornbleth details in her chapter, reading instruction, curriculum standards, student learning, state accountability mechanisms, and research methods in education have been subject to intense scrutiny, with notions of science as the mechanism of critique and correction.

The chapters in this book are part of an ongoing discourse related to the U.S. social science project and education. A more complete understanding of the recommendations and strategies outlined by this set of authors in light of the U.S. social science project follows.

POLITICAL ECONOMY AND THE PUBLIC INTEREST

Education is a social investment. Despite recent claims to the contrary by some advocacy groups, education has evolved as part of a U.S. social compact and is generally a protected right (Bell, 2004). Yet, appropriately, many of the arguments found in this book extend beyond the parameters of education and such directly related policy. This section examines political economy and public interest concerns.

Anyon's chapter calls for a change in federal and metropolitan policy formulation. She argues that macroeconomic policies (e.g., minimum wage standards) have a profound influence on poverty, and that the eradication of poverty is foundational to real change in educational opportunity structures and related outcomes. Anyon's arguments cannot be separated from political ideology driven by visions of how socioeconomic status is advanced in the U.S. context. Grubb and Lazerson (2004) argued that sociologists use three simple models to represent the transmission of socioeconomic status. The models depict the differing effects of family background and education on socioeconomic status. While sociologists use the models to capture relationships and to test theories, politicians and policymakers often align their policy recommendations with one of the three models of socioeconomic advancement. The first model of socioeconomic transmission, described by Grubb and Lazerson (2004) and termed a pre-vocational pattern, is largely associated with the 18th and 19th centuries. In this era, parents were chiefly responsible for the financial success of their children. The primary mode of economic advancement involved supporting their sons to continue a family business or trade or by locating apprenticeships and appropriate marriages. Thus, in the pre-vocational pattern, family background influenced socioeconomic status (SES)—employment and earnings—of children directly, while formal schooling was largely a non-factor in determining SES.

The pre-vocational pattern represents a model of the interrelationships among family background, education, and SES associated more closely with the antebellum period. However, the pre-vocational model began to shift as capitalism developed in the United States. As Foner (1998) stated:

> Market capitalism opened numerous jobs to skilled workers, and in many crafts, owning a shop remained well within reach. Yet the increased scale of manufacturing undermined traditional skills and diminished opportunities for journeyman to rise to the status of independent master. Increasingly, wage labor, rather than ownership of productive property, became the economic basis of family survival. After 1830, the rapid increase of immigration swelled the bottom ranks of the labor force. At mid-century, over two-thirds of the workforce in Boston and New York City consisted of wage

workers, and for the nation as a whole, the number of wage earners for the first time exceeded the number of slaves. Ten years later, according to one estimate, wage laborers outnumbered self-employed members of the labor force. The legal order increasingly served to support the system of wage labor. (p. 59)

In the 100 years following the Civil War, the economic inefficiency of apprenticeship models and a greater faith in formal schooling as the tool to support occupational preparation emerged (Grubb & Lazerson, 2004). During this period, and in many respects today, school-based mechanisms of attainment evolved where the direct effects of family on children's socioeconomic status were less important, relatively speaking, than during the pre-vocational period. Additionally, the effects of schooling are now more powerful. The shift to socioeconomic status attainment through schooling has large implications for serious discussions of public interest research in education. It is clear that in the post–War World II era, learning opportunities across demographic groups in high school, community college, and university-level educational settings expanded significantly. Yet studies of school practice have consistently discovered powerful effects of family background on educational outcomes, much more powerful than the influence of schooling resources (Grubb & Lazerson, 2004; Hedges & Nowell, 1998; Miller, 1995). This finding has generated considerable philosophical debate in the United States. As Popkewitz noted in his chapter, U.S. exceptionalism framed its citizen as the most advanced in the world, and attempted to differentiate and make invisible those who were not part of this Chosen people. He argues that a continuum of values positioned "others" at less advanced stages of development. Thus, their inability to take advantage of the U.S. versions of freedom, democracy, and competition is a functional individual deficiency. This ideal is captured by Grubb and Lazerson' s (2004) meritocratic model of attainment in which the purest form of equality of opportunities are assumed to exist: Individual effort and ability in schooling explain variations in education and SES, and family-background effects are eliminated because the same opportunities are provided to all students. They note that the latter attainment model does not exist in the United States, yet it is part of U.S. Exceptionalism discourse.

Policy aligned with this Exceptionalism discourse is reviewed in several chapters in this volume. In particular, Lipman, Grant, Popkewitz, Hursh, and Cornbleth discuss the No Child Left Behind legislation and the role of assessment and standards in creating opportunity structures for traditionally underserved groups. We learned in these chapters the importance of framing learning problems in schools beyond the rhetoric of individualistic conceptions of attainment. Yet, as described by Apple, Hursh, and Lipman, this is difficult in the contradictory policy environment created by neoliberal policy actors who call for eliminating useless curriculum not connected to the new knowledge economy and neoconservative factions that seek a return to "traditional values" in the school setting. Often at odds, this contradictory conservative movement shares a kind of thinking that

Kennedy (1990) refers to as "colorblind meritocratic fundamentalism." Today's policy environment appears to ignore the historical racial divisions and the bifurcated opportunity structures that exist as a result. This concept is linked to policy formation and implementation in matters related to human development broadly defined (e.g., affirmative action, testing policy, desegregation, and neighborhood patterns). The concept, like other substructures within the history of ideas, is no more than one of many fragments out of which people build their individual perspectives. It is not a function of being left or right of center politically, black or white, male or female. Fundamentalism, according to Kennedy (1990), has a long history within U.S. liberal thought, and within orthodox Marxism, as well as within the conservative movement. It consists of a set of propositions. Each is a slogan with a powerful appeal in the public discourse. The propositions are often presented in isolation, or coupled in a manner that advances a particular argument. They are centered around knowledge about the social worth of individuals and their work. Quality factors of the product, rather the producer, dictate the significance of contributions to knowledge. Additionally, when determining the significance of a product, the race, sex, class, and indeed all the other personal characteristics of the producer are not relevant. These two propositions are associated with the ethos of modern science (Merton, 1968). Further, the scientific ideal is part of an image of how intellectual knowledge is produced. The production of knowledge proceeds from the individual application of talent to inert matter (Kennedy, 1990). Moreover, the value of the effort is a direct function of the quality of the individual talent that developed it, rather than the inert-matter experience of the individual. Context and lived experience are extraneous to this type of fundamentalism. Thus, discrimination is defined in opposition to the assessment of individual merit. Discrimination is simply an unjust condition whereby merit is assessed according to status, rather that according to the value of products. There is no rational reason to link race or any other demographic characteristic to any particular meritorious trait and discrimination on the basis of a race and/or other categorical schemes denies the individual what is due him or her under society's constructed standards of merit. From this logical calculus, the fundamentalist offers the proper role to schools and other academic organizations in general. Academic institutions should seek to maximize the production of valuable knowledge and also to appropriately acknowledge individual merit. Additionally, academic institutions delivering opportunity and allocating honors should do so according to standards blind to race, sex, class, lived experiences, and all other characteristics of the individual except the one characteristic of having produced knowledge of value. This sloganeering is consistent with U.S. Exceptionalism and the ethos of science. It is powerful and blinding in its ability to reframe public discourse about opportunity and policy. However, while aligned with the ethos of science, colorblind meritocratic fundamentalism is inconsistent with sound science about the opportunity structures present in the U.S. context.

Perhaps an example linked to the goals of NCLB legislation will illustrate the point. Recall NCLB was mentioned as part of the public interest perspective of many of the contributors to this book. The stated goal of NCLB is to improve student learning and academic achievement. Throughout this book, sound illustrations have been provided to show that the NCLB strategy is flawed. Additionally, a reasonable amount of evidence existed prior to the passage of NCLB that suggested the NCLB model was a limited change strategy. Additionally, several reports suggest that under some conditions the NCLB testing strategy could actually prove detrimental to student learning and achievement (CSTEEP, 1992; NRC, 1999). What is often ignored in discussions of high-stakes testing and accountability is the evidence and insights gained from studies of student achievement as it relates to intergenerational effects and appropriate policy development. One potential reason is the strength of colorblind fundamentalism in the interpretation of data and the related public discourse about merit.

If student achievement is a priority, why do we ignore the literature? Is this literature designed and driven by statistics and "hard evidence"? Much of what is known about race, learning opportunities, and educational performance in the United States carries an intergenerational and family effect. Phillips, Brooks-Gunn, Duncan, Klebanov, and Crane (1998) analyzed data from the Children of the National Longitudinal Survey of Youth (CNLSY) and additional supplemental data as part of an examination of the contribution of parental education and income on the test-score gap and looked at a range of family environmental indicators. One important finding suggested that it takes at least two generations of changes in parental socioeconomic status to exert their full effect on parent practices. Additionally, Miller (1995) argued that there are three intergenerational factors that should inform the development of policy related to the school achievement of traditionally underserved racial groups:

1. In most cases, differences in academic achievement trends among racial/ethnic groups are indicative of the fact that the variation in family resources is greater than the variation in school resources. Miller's study of achievement patterns and resource allocations demonstrates that most high-SES students are provided several times the resources of most low-SES students, and much of this resource gap is a function of family resources rather than school resources.
2. Demographic group educational attainment is an intergenerational phenomenon. From this viewpoint, education-related family resources are school resources that have amassed over several generations. On average, investments in today's generation of African American, Hispanic, and Native American children in the form of intergenerationally cumulated education-relevant family resources are consequentially less than comparable investments in White and Asian children (see also Shapiro, 2004).

3. Educational attainment is, in large part, a product of the quality of educa-
    tion-relevant opportunity structures over several generations. The pace
    of educational advancement depends on multiple generations of children
    attending good schools (see also Margo, 1990).

Miller's findings complement the work of sociologist Thomas Shapiro (2004)
who conducted a study of the role of race, assets, and opportunity structures in
the United States. Shapiro argued that racial wealth differentials exacerbate social
inequality, transporting advantages from generation to generation. Family wealth
and inheritances negate comparative gains in classrooms, employment, and income distribution. The race to gather more achievement data is off target. Yet, that
is the essence of our current change strategy in the United States. Understand my
point. Evidence is vitally important and sound reporting mechanisms are part of
the U.S. way of governance (Cohen, 1982). However, sound reports do not ensure
improvement. Deputy Secretary of Education Ray Simon (2005) argued:

> Turning around an underperforming school is like rebuilding a damaged home: With-
> out a blueprint to guide us, all the new paint and plaster in the world will make little dif-
> ference. The blueprint is sound, scientific data. The No Child Left Behind Act (NCLB)
> recognizes its importance. Parents are given annual information on school's academic
> performances, so they can make the very best choices for their children. . . . The data
> infrastructure is key to improving instruction. (p. 12A)

What is the theory of improvement undergirding the NCLB model? Is the assumption that better information for parents will help them in the marketplace of
schooling? If this is the theory, sound scientific evidence examining this change
strategy is warranted. This is a place for research in the public interest. How does
this theory operate with parents of different races, socioeconomic status, urban
dwellers, rural inhabitants etc.? This is the scientific evidence required to better
understand the current policy framework. Research that suggests intergenerational efforts influence schooling and learning cannot be ignored, nor can evidence
that indicates that assets and wealth allow some families to buy into more affluent neighborhoods and schools. The solution to this problem will require a more
intensified social problem-solving effort and greater research and development
capacity in the public interest.

CAPACITY AND RESEARCH IN THE PUBLIC INTEREST

Arguably the most important public interest concern in the area of educational
research is capacity. Most of this book's scholars have the kind of infrastructure
associated with research universities. This is indeed significant, yet requires some
rethinking. The capacity to engage in sustained research on important policy-rel-

evant issues, and the ability to share this research with research colleagues and the broader community of practitioners, policymakers, school board members, parents, and other publics, is seriously underdeveloped. The work of Alex Molnar at Arizona State University, as outlined in his chapter and furthered described by Michael Apple, represents an example of a multi-organizational effort wherein numerous scholars and educators engaged in meaningful public interest scholarship and the communication of findings to an array of publics. Yet this example is indeed rare. Generally, education as a research enterprise in university settings is poorly articulated with respect to building sustained programs of research and is certainly not organized around a public interest problem or an area of concern. Even rarer is a university that has a campus-wide effort on a topic of study remotely related to education. Certain problem types are ripe for campus-wide interdisciplinary teams. For example, teams from pediatrics, health policy, education, psychology, audiology and communication sciences, law, social work, criminology, sociology, and business could study the literacy problem in the United States. The nature and scope of the literacy challenge in this country warrants an interdisciplinary team. Literacy is just one example. Topics ranging from school finance to the school environment (physical and social) require ongoing analysis and public communication structures. The list of possible public interest topics in education is long. However long the lists, as noted in the Ayers chapter, universities have at least one important limitation. Today's university is largely a corporate entity governed by corporate leaders who serve as trustees. This is an exclusive club with significant power, means of production, and access to information and information channels. These groups are not neutral, and the notion that universities are disinterested is not realistic. This reality under certain conditions could represent a serious challenge to scholarship in the public interest. Some scholars have argued for nonuniversity settings to assume some portion of the leadership in defining problems and offering solutions to difficult and controversial topics. For example, Shulman (2005) stated:

> I would recommend the formation of a new policy forum to assist in regularly reviewing and evaluating policy-relevant educational research. In some areas, we may need the equivalent of research-review SWAT teams that can be called in on a regular basis to review competing claims and the evidence that supports them. In other cases, the use of "consensus panels" can be quite useful in the face of complex, multiple studies with a range of findings, interpretations, and policy recommendations, though the pace of their efforts can be snail-like. The National Research Council of the National Academies might well take the lead in such an activity, assisted by a range of self-consciously partisan and intentionally nonpartisan bodies. Such forums would organize quick-response review panels and also conduct periodic reviews when serious policy controversies arise. The forum should be nongovernmental, to avoid conflicts of interest with the mission (The current swirl of controversy around the Bush administration's implementation of the No Child Left Behind program exemplifies this problem). (p. 36)

Shulman's ideas are appealing. However, great caution is warranted. In his chapter, Molnar warns of the dishonest examples of think-tank scholars and fellows. It is important not to suggest this is a universal problem. Rather, examples of dishonesty suggest the need for review panels and open access to data as forms of accountability in the public interest. Yet education, like health care and other regulated industries, operates in a world where the manufacturing of uncertainty can be strategically advantageous for private interests. Michaels and Monforton (2005) provide a deadly example that cost the lives of hundreds of children. In 1980, four published studies demonstrated that children with chicken pox or flu who took aspirin were more likely to develop Reye's syndrome. The Centers for Disease Control (CDC) alerted the medical community. However the aspirin industry, with the assistance of the White House's Office of Management and Budget, was able to delay a major government public education program for 2 years, and mandatory labels for 4 years. Despite the four studies and a CDC alert, the industry raised 17 specific concerns about the studies and argued that more reliable studies were needed to establish a causal relationship between aspirin and Reye's syndrome. The aspirin industry maintained their position despite a Federal Advisory Committee's recommendation that children with viral infections should not take aspirin. Ultimately, litigation by the Public Citizens Health Research Group forced the Reagan administration to make the warnings mandatory in 1986.

As Hursh argued in his chapter, and as illustrated by Molnar's center at Arizona State University, it is not enough to have sound scientific studies in journals. The need for legal support, communication strategies, and advocacy groups is vital to the advancement of public interest research. Universities have the resources for this type of activity; however, they are not organized to do this kind of work. Universities that do organize themselves to deal with real policy challenges in the public interest will be invaluable. Additionally, Shulman's recommendation of SWAT teams designed to make sense of the evidentiary base on policy-relevant issues is sound and complements the university role. Why is all of this necessary? Because we live in an era when doubt is an important economic product. Michaels and Monforton (2005) argue that many industries follow a strategic plan developed in the mid-1950s by Hill and Knowlton (H&K) for the tobacco industry. The tobacco industry hired their own scientists and commissioned research to challenge the growing scientific agreement that linked cigarette smoking to chronic health problems. H&K was hired to help control the public discourse emerging from an American Cancer Society Report linking tobacco with lung cancer. The H&K experts focused on communicating three major points. First, no cause-and-effect relationship has been established in any way. Second, the statistical data do not suggest any solutions. Finally, there is a need for much more research. The business of doubt production is powerful, effective, and requires a significant investment of time and resources to counter. Is this strategy possible in education? Is the education community in a position to respond? These are important capacity questions for public interest research. The Data Quality Act (DQA) further complicates the business of educational research.

The DQA, enacted in December 2000, is a two-paragraph provision buried in an appropriations bill. On the surface, the provision appears to be an attempt by some in Congress to ensure that federal agencies use and distribute factually correct information. The DQA requires federal agencies to establish evaluative frameworks to judge quality, utility, objectivity, and integrity of information that they distribute, and to create procedures for affected parties to correct such information.[1] The U.S. Department of Education provides some insights into how they are interpreting these guidelines (NCES, 2003). As per OMB guidelines, they acknowledge that some government information needs to meet a higher-than-basic standard of quality. This level of quality is a function of how the data is to be used. Information that can be described as influential requires a higher level of effort to guarantee its quality and reproducibility. Scientific, financial, and statistical information should be considered influential if the Department of Education deems that it may inform important public policies or private sector decisions. The NCES (2003) report stated:

> Any influential original data files must describe the design, collection, and processing of the data in sufficient detail that an interested third party could understand the specifics of the original data and, if necessary, independently replicate the data collection. In the case of influential analytic results, the mathematical and statistical processes used to produce the report must be described in sufficient detail to allow an independent analyst to substantially reproduce the findings using the original data and identical methods. (p. 9)

There are at least two major concerns related to public interest research in education created by this standard. The first is that the social sciences more broadly defined have not operated in a fashion consistent with the replication goals of the Department of Education. Anderson, Greene, McCullough, and Vinod (2005) found that, with few exceptions, economic researchers provide data and code that fail to reproduce their own results. In theory, economic research is scientific research. How confident can we be of results that change with upgraded versions of software packages, or with two replicators using the original software package yet producing different results? The replication challenge is not limited to economics. It extends into psychology, political science, other social sciences, and the sciences more generally. While there are clearly mechanisms to begin to address this challenge, including how journals deal with data and software codes as part of the publication process, this standard is a barrier, and it could be used to create doubt about important findings and insights. One real concern is that the replication standard can be used as a tool to safeguard government policy or to support a lack of governmental action by eliminating potential studies as lacking in one or more quality factors. Additionally, a host of studies may strongly suggest a particular direction that is inconsistent with administration policy actions.

If the studies are taken as individual sites of learning, they could be eliminated because of replication challenges. Thus cumulative insights from research could be ignored. However, it is very difficult to mount a political argument against this kind of standard.

The Data Quality Act also raises the real concern: What is scholarship in education? As Burkhardt and Schoenfeld (2003) noted, there are three main traditions in educational research. The main traditions or research approaches are referred to as the humanities, science, and engineering. In this discussion, the humanities approach will be central. The main feature of the humanities approach is *critical commentary*, arguably the oldest tradition in educational scholarship. There is no requirement to test theories empirically. Rather, as represented in all of the writings in this book, and argued more directly in the chapters authored by Ayers, Banks, Barone, and Blumenfeld-Jones, critical appraisal concerning plausibility, internal logic, historical context, imagery, possibility, and prevailing wisdom have a serious role in the marketplace of ideas. The ability to understand historical context—and to interpret text broadly defined to include art, written text, religious artifacts, cultural traditions, historical documents, and even statistics—is the heart of being an educated citizen. Yes, understanding and learning from statistics requires hermeneutics. The art and science of interpretation is critical to a public interest research agenda. Moreover, the humanistic perspective, combined with empirical evidence as produced in Gillborn's chapter, provides a hybrid analysis that belongs in the public policy process. His work in England is shocking and meaningful to those working in other locations. The case for understanding the contextual factors related to education more broadly conceived complements statistical modeling and other methodological techniques more aligned with the science and engineering approach than to educational research. Each approach has made important contributions to our understanding of the educational enterprise, and all three approaches have a place in public interest research.

In the 1980s, Romberg and Carpenter (1986) wrote a chapter that provided a synthetic conceptualization of distinct areas of research in mathematics education—research on teaching and research on learning. This chapter was considered a significant advance in the field of mathematics education and beyond. Until then, teaching and learning as research considerations were generally viewed as separate in the minds of many. In the 1990s, Rowan (1995) called for a more transparent research agenda on learning, teaching, and administration. While not seeking grand theories, Rowan argued for mid-range theorizing of moderate scope that incorporated a subfield of administration with a teaching and learning concern. His call represented an important shift in all three areas of teaching, learning, and administration. The authors of this book have challenged the field, and our publics, to think more broadly about research. Teaching, learning, administration, and the social context of human development broadly defined to include political economy represent salient features that should undergird education research in the public interest.

A few words of caution about the public interest research agenda: It is vitally important that public interest research take seriously the intergenerational effects of schooling and the relationship of education to other opportunity structures. Additionally, the subtleties of meritocratic colorblind fundamentalism must be made apparent. Like the example set by John Fisher, the public interest research agenda should be a program of study that helps others see the products and possibilities when men and women look not only to their own interests, but also to the interests of others. Watch your head!

NOTE

1. See http://library.findlaw.com/2003/Jan/14/132464.html. Retrieved November 30, 2005

REFERENCES

Anderson, R., Greene, W. H., McCullough, B. D., & Vinod, H. D. (2005, January). *The role of data/code archives in the future of economic research.* Paper presemted at the annual meeing of the American Economic Association, Philadelphia. Retrieved November 30, 2005, from www.aeaweb.org/annual_mtg_papers/2005/0109_1300_0303.pdf

Ash, M. G. (2005). The uses and usefulness of psychology. *The Annals of the American Academy of Political and Social Science, 600,* 99–114.

Bell, D. A. (2004). *Silent covenants: Brown v.* Board of Education *and the unfulfilled hopes for racial reform.* Oxford, UK: Oxford University Press.

Burawoy, M. (2005). The return of the repressed: Recovering the public face of U.S. sociology, one hundred years on. *The Annals of the American Academy of Political and Social Science, 600,* 68–85.

Burkhardt, H., & Schoenfeld, A. H. (2003). Improving educational research: Toward a more useful, more influential, and better-funded enterprise. *Educational Researcher, 32*(9), 3–14.

Center for the Study of Testing, Evaluation, and Education Policy (CSTEEP). (1992). *The influence of testing on teaching math and science in grades 4–12.* Boston: Boston College.

Cohen, P. C. (1982). *A calculating people: The spread of numeracy in early America.* Chicago: University of Chicago Press.

Foner, E. (1998). *The story of American freedom.* New York: Norton.

Grubb, N. W., & Lazerson, M. (2004). *The education gospel: The economic power of schooling.* Cambridge, MA: Harvard University Press.

Hedges, L. V., & Nowell, A. (1998). Black–White test convergence since 1965. In C. Jencks & M. Phillips (Eds.), *The Black–White test score gap* (pp. 149–181). Washington, DC: Brookings Institution Press.

Kennedy, D. (1990). A cultural pluralist case for affirmative action in legal academia. *Duke Law Review, 4,* 705–757.

Margo, R. A. (1990). *Race and schooling in the South, 1880–1950: An economic history.* Chicago: University of Chicago Press.

Merton, R. K. (1968). *Social theory and social structure.* New York: Free Press.

Michaels, D., & Monforton, C. (2005). Manufacturing uncertainty: Contested science and the protection of the public's health and environment. *American Journal of Public Health, 95,* S39–S44.

Miller, L. S. (1995). *An American imperative: Accelerating minority educational advancement.* New Haven, CT: Yale University Press.

National Center for Education Statistics (NCES). (2003). *Statistical standards* (NCES 2003-601). Washington, DC: U.S. Department of Education.

National Research Council (NRC). (1999). *High stakes: Testing for tracking, promotion, and graduation.* Washington, DC: National Academy Press.

Phillips, M., Brooks-Gunn, J., Duncan, G., Klebanov, P., & Crane, J. (1998). Family background, parenting practices, and the black–white test score gap. In C. Jencks & M. Phillips (Eds.), *The black–white test score gap* (pp. 103–145). Washington, DC: Brookings Institution Press.

Prewitt, K. (2005). Political ideas and a political science for policy. *The Annals of the American Academy of Political and Social Science, 600,* 14–29.

Romberg, T. A., & Carpenter, T. P. (1986). Research on teaching and learning mathematics. In M. C. Whittrock (Ed.), *Handbook of research on teaching* (pp. 850–873). New York: Macmillan.

Rosenburg, A. (1992). *Economics—Mathematical politics or science of diminishing returns?* Chicago: University of Chicago Press.

Rowan, B. (1995). Learning, teaching, and educational administration: Toward a research agenda. *Educational Administration Quarterly, 31*(3), 344–354.

Shapiro, T. M. (2004). *The hidden cost of being African American: How wealth perpetuates inequality.* Oxford, UK: Oxford University Press.

Shulman, L. S. (2005, June 8). Seek simplicity . . . and distrust it. *Education Week, 24*(39), pp. 36, 48.

Simon, R. (2005, November 28). Blueprint for success. *USA TODAY,* p. 12A.

About the Editors
and the Contributors

Jean Anyon is the author of *Radical Possibilities: Public Policy, Urban Education, and a New Social Movement*. She has published widely on the confluence of race, social class, policy, and urban education. She teaches social and educational policy in the Ph.D. Program in Urban Education at the Graduate Center of the City University of New York.

Michael W. Apple is John Bascom Professor of Curriculum and Instruction and Educational Policy Studies at the University of Wisconsin, Madison. A researcher and activist on the relationship between education and differential power, among his recent books are *Official Knowledge; Educating the "Right" Way: Markets, Standards, God, and Inequality; The Subaltern Speak*; and the 25th Anniversary 3rd edition of his classic *Ideology and Curriculum*.

William Ayers is Distinguished Professor of Education and Senior University Scholar at the University of Illinois at Chicago, author or editor of fourteen books on education including *The Good Preschool Teacher: Six Teachers Reflect on Their Lives; A Kind and Just Parent: The Children of Juvenile Court; Teaching Toward Freedom: Moral Commitment and Ethical Action in the Classroom; To Teach: The Journey of a Teacher; On the Side of The Child: Summerhill Revisited;* and *Teaching the Personal and the Political: Essays on Hope and Justice.*

James A. Banks is Russell F. Stark University Professor and Director of the Center for Multicultural Education at the University of Washington, Seattle. As a fifth-grade teacher in Chicago, as a graduate student at Michigan State University, and as a professor at the University of Washington, beginning in 1969, Banks has pursued questions related to education, racial inequality, and social justice in more than 100 articles and 20 books. His most recent books are *Diversity and Citizenship Education: Global Perspectives* (2004); and *Race, Culture, and Education: the Selected Works of James A. Banks* (2006). Banks is a past president of the National Council for the Social Studies (NCSS) and the American Educational Research Association (AERA).

Tom Barone is Professor of Education in the College of Education at Arizona State University where he teaches courses in curriculum studies and qualitative research methods. He is the author of *Touching Eternity: The Enduring Consequences of Teaching* (2001), and *Aesthetics, Politics, and Educational Inquiry* (2000).

Donald Blumenfeld-Jones is the Lincoln Associate Professor for Ethics and Education at Arizona State University, specializing in curriculum studies, arts-based education research, ethics, hermeneutics, and critical social theory. He has published in such journals as the *Journal of Curriculum Theorizing, Educational Theory, Journal of Thought, Journal of Qualitative Studies in Education,* and *Qualitative Inquiry* and has numerous book chapters dealing with curriculum issues, dance curriculum, ethics and curriculum, and arts-based education research.

Catherine Cornbleth is Professor of Education, Graduate School of Education, University at Buffalo, New York. Her work in curriculum studies includes critical examinations of curriculum politics, policymaking, practice, and "reform." Among her books is *Hearing America's Youth: Social Identities in Uncertain Times* (2003). She is currently engaged in a school-based study of "Biography, Social Structures, and Diversity" in the professional preparation of teachers.

David Gillborn is Professor of Education and Head of the School of Educational Foundations & Policy Studies at the Institute of Education, University of London. He is active in antiracist politics and edits the international refereed journal *Race Ethnicity & Education.* His book *Rationing Education* (with Deborah Youdell) was awarded the prize for "best book in the field of educational studies" by the Standing Conference on Studies in Education (SCSE)/Society for Educational Studies (SES).

Carl A. Grant is Hoefs-Bascom Professor of Teacher Education in the Department of Curriculum and Instruction at the University of Washington–Madison. He has written or edited 25 books or monographs in multicultural education and/or teacher education. He has also written more than 135 articles, chapters in books, and reviews. Several of his writings and programs that he directed have received awards. He is a former classroom teacher and administrator. He served as President of the National Association for Multicultural Education (NAME) from 1993–1999; as Editor of *Review of Educational Research* (RER) from 1996–1999; as a member of the National Research Councils Committee on Assessment and Teacher Quality (1999–2001); and is currently the chair of the AERA Publication Committee.

David Hursh is Associate Professor in the Warner Graduate School of Education and Human Development at the University of Rochester. He has helped create several educational and political organizations, including, the Coalition for Common Sense in Education, in Rochester, NY. He is the author of over 45 book chapters and journal articles, some of which have appeared in the *British Educational Research Journal; Policy Futures in Education;* the *Journal for Critical Education Policy Studies; Discourse: Studies in the Cultural Politics of Education;* and *Theory and Research in Social Education.* He co-edited (with E. Wayne Ross) *Democratic Social Education: Social Studies for Social Change.*

Gloria Ladson-Billings is the Kellner Family Chair of Urban Education at the University of Wisconsin–Madison, the 2005–2006 president of the American Educational Research Association, and a member of the National Academy of Education. Her primary research interests are culturally relevant pedagogy and critical race theory applications to education.

Pauline Lipman is Associate Professor of Social and Cultural Foundations of Education at DePaul University. Her research focuses on the political economy of urban education, race and class inequality, and globalization. She is an education activist and the author of *Race, Class, and Power in School Restructuring* (1998) and *High Stakes Education: Inequality, Globalization, and Urban School Reform* (2004), and numerous articles in journals such as *American Educational Research Journal; Race, Ethnicity and Education; Globalization, Societies, and Education; Urban Review;* and *Cultural Studies ↔ Critical Methodologies.*

Alex Molnar is Professor of Education Policy and Director of the Education Policy Studies Laboratory at Arizona State University. Molnar's research focus is privatization and the commercialization of schools. His most recent book is *School Commercialism: From Democratic Ideal to Market Commodity* (2005).

Thomas S. Popkewitz, Professor, the Department of Curriculum and Instruction, The University of Wisconsin–Madison. His studies are concerned with the knowledge or systems of reason that govern educational policy and research in teaching, teacher education, and curriculum. He is currently writing a book that is concerned with the changing cultural theses of school subjects and the child, using the notion of cosmopolitanism to explore how the distinctions and differentiations of the "reason" of schooling produces difference and exclusion.

William F. Tate is the Edward Mallinckrodt Distinguished University Professor in Arts & Sciences and Chair of the Department of Education at Washington University. He served as the 2005–2006 Program Chair for the annual meeting of the American Educational Research Association. His research interests include SMET education and race and urban policy.

Name Index

Abbott, Diane, 184
Abbs, P., 217
Addams, Jane, 123
Airasian, P. W., 208
Alamillo, L., 111
Alexander, E., 83, 97
Alexander, Hanan, 232, 234
Allen, D., 67
Allen, Jeanne, 71
Amrein, A. L., 49
Anderson, Gary L., 243
Anderson, J. D., 5
Anderson, Marian, 147
Anderson, R., 257
Ansley, F. L., 174–175
Anyon, Jean, 5–6, 10, 17–26,
    18, 19, 20, 22, 42, 50–51,
    60, 102, 103, 112, 244–245
    n. 3, 250
Apple, Michael W., 10, 21,
    27–45, 28, 29, 31, 34, 36, 37,
    38, 39, 40, 41, 42, 43 n. 2, 57,
    101, 174, 214, 232, 244–245
    n. 3, 251, 255
Appleby, Joyce, 203
Archer, J., 71
Argyris, Chris, 245 n. 4
Ash, M. G., 249
Atanda, A. K., 111–112
Au, K. H., 143, 149
August, D., 149
Austin, K., 149
Ayers, William, 10, 11, 81–97,
    255, 258

Bachelard, Gaston, 136
Baker, Ella, 25
Baldwin, James, 204
Banks, C. A. M., x, 142, 152,
    153
Banks, James A., ix–xiii, 11,
    141–157, 142, 143, 146–147,
    149, 150, 152, 153, 154 n. 1,
    154 n. 2, 169–170, 258
Barber, B. R., 152
Barone, Thomas, 12, 213–230,
    239, 258
Beady, C., 150
Beane, J. A., 41, 42
Becker, Carol, 224
Bell, Derek A., xii–xiii, 13 n. 1,
    160, 176, 250
Belsey, C., 226

Berdik, C., 68
Berkhofer, R. F., 162
Berliner, David C., 49, 56, 235
Berman, M., 233
Bernays, Edward, 72
Bernstein, B., 32
Bernstein, J., 18, 19
Bertiloot, T., 132
Betancur, J. J., 102
Biddle, B., 235
Blassingame, J. W., 148
Block, A., 234–235
Blumenfeld-Jones, Donald S.,
    12, 231–246, 244 n. 2, 258
Boaler, Jo, 32–33
Boninger, F., 78 n. 5
Boober-Jennings, J., 208–209
Booth, Wayne, 73–74, 227
Bork, Robert, xii
Bourdieu, Pierre, 35, 48, 57,
    134, 243–244
Boushey, H., 18
Bowles, S., 243
Bracey, G. W., 47, 60 n. 2
Bransford, J., 149
Brenner, N., 109
Bridges, Ruby, 4, 162
Brookover, W., 150
Brooks, Gwendolyn, 81–83, 86,
    92, 97
Brooks-Gunn, J., 253
Brown, E., 102, 107
Browne, K., 191 n. 6
Buber, Martin, 233–234,
    239–241
Buchanan, Pat, 39
Bullock, H. A., 162
Buras, K. L., 28, 31, 34
Burawoy, M., 249
Burkhardt, H., 258
Bush, George W., 2, 3, 49, 51–
    52, 54, 99, 100–101, 208
Bush, M. E. L., 174

Cala, William, 58–59
Canizaro, Joseph C., 99
Capellero, C., 56
Carlson, Dennis, 104
Carpenter, T. P., 258
Carver, George Washington, 147
Cary, Joyce, 241
Cashin, Sheryll, 168
Castañeda, A., 142

Cauthen, N., 19
Celimli, L., 102
Cheney, Lynne, 205
Chernow, B. A., xi
Chico, Gery, 52
Cho, M. K., 36, 43
Christiansen, Douglas, 59
Cimbricz, S., 208
Citro, C., 19
Clark, Kenneth B., xii
Clark, M., 104
Clinton, Bill, 100
Cloke, K., 168
Coard, Bernard, 177
Cochran-Smith, M., 144
Code, L., xi, 148
Cohen, I. S., 162
Cohen, P. C., 254
Collins, P. H., 148
Comer, J., 149
Comte, Auguste, 122
Coniff, R., 38, 39
Connolly, P., 188
Cookson, P., 150
Cooley, George Herbert, 127
Cornbleth, Catherine, 12,
    199–212, 203, 205, 206, 210
    n. 2, 249
Cortés, C. E., 152, 153
Costo, R., 162
Counts, George, 121–122
Crabtree, Charlotte, 205
Crane, J., 253
Cruikshank, B., 121
Curry, A. E., ix
Czikszentmihalyi, M., 228

Dale, Roger, 106–107
Dance, L. J., 42
Darling-Hammond, L., 149
Davis, D., 144
de Morales, L., 113 n 1
Delgado, R., 174, 176
Delpit, L., 3, 5, 148
Denzin, N. K., 221, 225
Dewey, John, 10, 31, 46, 72,
    120–122, 124–127, 137 n. 6,
    215, 222, 224, 239
Deyhle, D., 175
Dlamini, S. N., 174
Dobles, R., 31
Dobson, James, 38
Domhoff, William, 22

Dowdy, J. K., 148
Drachsler, J., 142
Dreier, P., 19, 20
Drmacich, Dan, 58–59
DuBois, W. E. B., 87, 91, 148
Dumas, M., 23
Duncan, G., 253

Eaton, S., 5, 48
Eck, Diana L., ix
Edelman, Marian Wright, xi,
   215, 216, 222–223, 228
Edwards, John, 2
Eisenhart, M., 201, 202
Eisenstadt, S. N., 125
Eisner, E., 236
Eldering, L., 142
Elkins, S. M., 148
El Nasser, H., ix
Elson, D., 36

Feagin, J. R., 144
Feldman, D., 228
Felshin, Nina, 220, 229
Feyerabend, Paul, 241
Fine, Michele, 58–59
Finley, Macklin, 220–221
Finley, Susan, 220–221
Finn, C. E., xi
Finn, J., 76
Fisher, John, 247
Flecha, R., 103
Fleishman, Sandra, 163
Flood, P., 150
Foley, D., 58
Foner, E., 250–251
Forrest, K. A., 59
Foster, J., 35
Foster, K. M., 174
Foster, M., 5
Foster, P., 175
Foucault, M., 135–136
Frank, Thomas, 49, 56
Franklin, John Hope, xi–xiii
Freire, Paulo, 35
Frey, W. H., 110
Friedman, T. L., 153
Fries, K., 144
Fuller, Howard, 51–52
Furnival, J. S., 165

Gadamer, H.-G., 238
Galbraith, J. K., 18, 20
Gallagher, Susan, 238, 242
Gallup, A. M., 216–217
Gandara, P., 101, 111
Gandin, L. A., 36, 43
Garcia, D., 67, 78 n. 5
Garcia, E. E., 101, 111
Gardner, Howard, 228
Gaunt, J., 70
Gay, G., 142–143, 147, 148,
   150

Gillborn, David, 11, 12, 49, 55,
   142, 173–195, 175, 177, 179,
   180, 182–183, 188, 189, 190,
   191 n. 6, 258
Gills, D. C., 102
Gintis, H., 243
Gipps, C. V., 179, 188
Giroux, Henry, 234, 244–245
   n. 3
Gitlin, A., 34
Glass, I., 4
Glaude, E., Jr., 125
Goldsmith, J., 168
Gomm, R., 175
Goodman, Nelson, 219
Gootman, J. A., 77
Gore, Jennifer, 244–245 n. 3
Gramsci, Antonio, 28, 84
Grant, Carl A., 11–12, 138 n. 10,
   158–172, 163, 167–168, 251
Greene, M., 213
Greene, W. H., 257
Grubb, N. W., 250, 251
Gustafson, R., 126, 130
Gutstein, R., 33

Habermas, Jurgen, 243
Hack, G., 110
Hahn, C. L., 152, 153
Hakuta, K., 149
Hall, G. Stanley, 121–122
Hall, Stuart, 226
Halpin, D., 54
Hammersley, M., 175
Haney, Walter, 49, 51, 55–56,
   58–59
Haralambos, M., 191 n. 6
Harding, S., xii, 30, 148
Hargreaves, A., 130
Harrington, Michael, 2
Hatcher, R., 43 n. 2
Hatfield, L. D., 204
Hawley, W. D., 150
Hawthorne, Richard, 244 n. 1
Hayden, C., 54–55
Heath, Shirley Brice, 148,
   149
Hechinger, F. M., 145
Hedges, L. V., 251
Henderson, James, 231, 244 n. 1
Henry, J., 162, 180–181
Henry VIII, King, 247
Herrnstein, Richard R., xi–xii,
   147–148, 180
Herzenhorn, D. M., 51, 59
Hess, F. M., 160
Hilliard, A. G., 5
Hirsch, E. D., Jr., 31, 42,
   242–243
Hirshfield, Jane, 83
Holborn, M., 191 n. 6
Holmes, J. J., 40, 105, 111–112
hooks, bell, 173, 219

Horn, S. P., 188
Horowitz, F. D., 149
Horowitz, Louis, 161
Horsman, R., xi
Howard, P. S. S., 174
Howley, C., 76
Hughes, Langston, 83
Hursh, David, 10–11, 46–63, 49,
   58, 60 n. 2, 251, 256
Hurst, M. D., 71
Hutchison, J., 67

Imber, Jonathan B., 161
Imbroscio, D. L., 109
Ingram, H., 215
Irvine, J. J., 5, 150
Iser, Wolfgang, 222, 226

Jackson, Andrew, 165
Jackson, Jesse, 99
Jacoby, Russell, 218
Jaguaribe, B., 126
James, T., 203–204
Jefferson, Thomas, 121
Jenkins, Jerry, 29
Jensen, Arthur R., xi–xii
Joanou, J., 67
Johnson, D. C., 50, 59
Johnson, Lyndon B., 167
Jones, K., 43 n. 2
Joseph, R., 188
Jung, Carl, 95

Kallen, H. M., 142
Kanigel, R., 46
Kant, Immanuel, 232, 234
Kaplan, A., xi
Katznelson, I., 48
Kaufman, D., 71
Kawakami, A. J., 149
Kellner, D., 35
Kelly, G., 169
Kennedy, D., 251–252
Kesson, Kathleen, 244 n. 1
Killeen, K., 55
Kimball, Robert, 56
Kinder, Terry, 69
King, Joyce E., 100, 112, 113,
   204
King, Martin Luther, Jr., 154
Kintz, L., 41
Klebanov, P., 253
Kliebard, H., 46, 125
Kloprogge, J., 142
Kohn, Alfie, 59
Kornhaber, M. L., 188
Kowalczyk, J., 123
Kozol, Jonathan, 48, 164
Kraak, V. I., 77
Kristol, I., 160
Kunitz, Stanley, 95
Kymlicka, W., 142, 151,
   152

Ladson-Billings, Gloria, 1–13,
    42, 52–53, 112, 138 n. 10,
    141, 142–143, 147, 148,
    151, 152, 160, 174, 176, 189,
    231–233, 235, 242
Lafer, G., 18, 20
Lahaye, Tim, 29
Lakoff, George, 210 n. 2
Landsman, Julie, 169
Langley, P., 191 n. 6
Lasch-Quinn, E., 123, 124
Lawn, M., 130
Lawrence, Stephen, 175
Lazerson, M., 250, 251
Lee, C. D., 112, 149
Lee, D. C., 143
Leonardo, Zeus, 174
Lesko, N., 36, 43 n. 3
Levine, D. U., 151
Leys, C., 43
Lezotte, L. W., 151
Lincoln, Y. S., 221, 225
Lindblad, S., 132, 134, 137 n. 9
Linn, R., 60 n. 2
Linn, Susan, 67
Lipman, Pauline, 10, 11, 30, 49,
    52–55, 57, 98–116, 100, 103,
    108–109, 111, 251
Lippmann, Walter, 160
Logan, R. W., 162
Lopez, A., 40, 105
Lortie, Dan, 236
Losen, D., 55
Lowe, R., 42
Lu, H-H., 19
Lukacs, G., 30
Lyotard, Jean-Francois, 215, 221

Mabe, L., 69
Macpherson, W., 175
Madaus, G., 104
Males, M., 217
Mannitz, S., 132
Marcuse, Herbert, 226, 232, 234
Margo, R. A., 254
Marshall, Thurgood, xii
Martin, P., ix
Martina, C. A., 49, 58, 60 n. 2
Martinez, G. M., ix
Marx, Karl, 136
Matthews, D., 179
McCarthy, Cameron, 28
McChesney, R., 35
McCullough, B. D., 257
McCutcheon, G., 232
McEneaney, E., 132
McEvoy, B., 67
McGinnis, J. M., 77
McGirr, L., 21
McIntosh, Peggy, 174
McKenley, J., 173
McLaren, Peter, 174, 189–190,
    244–245 n. 3

McNeil, L., 49, 55, 100, 103
McWalters, Peter, 59
Mead, George Herbert, 127
Meier, Deborah, 42, 48, 49, 57,
    58, 59
Merryfield, M., 152, 153
Merton, R. K., 252
Metcalf, G., 162
Michael, R. S., 6
Michaels, D., 256
Midgley, E., ix
Miguel, E., 70
Miller, D., 102
Miller, L. S., 251, 253, 254
Miller, R., 46–47, 60 n. 1
Mills, C. Wright, 84, 89, 91
Mills, Richard, 58
Miner, B., 42, 52
Mintrop, H., 103
Mirza, Heidi Safia, 175, 181–
    183, 186, 191 n. 6
Mishel, L., 18, 19
Mitchell, W. J. T., 84
Mohl, B., 70
Mollenkopf, J., 19, 20
Molnar, Alex, 10, 11, 34, 64–80,
    67, 73, 74, 75–76, 78 n. 1, 78
    n. 4, 78 n. 5, 255, 256
Monforton, C., 256
Monk, D., 55
Montessori, Maria, 95
Moodley, K. A., 152, 153
Moody, K., 101, 113 n. 3
Morales, J., 34, 67, 73
Moran, R., 101, 111
Moses, Bob, 104–105
Muir, K., 188
Mukherjee, Indrani, 70
Murphy, A., 102
Murphy, M., 127, 128
Murphy-Shigematsu, S., 152,
    153
Murray, Charles R., xi–xii,
    147–148, 180
Mussolini, Benito, 88
Myrdal, Gunnar, 158, 159

Nader, Ralph, 38, 39
Nardo, A. C., 6
Nash, Gary, 205
Nathan, L., 42
Nelson, J., 221
Nieto, S., 150
Noddings, Nel, 244 n. 2
Noguera, P., 112
Nord, Warren, 37
Nowell, A., 251
Nussbaum, M., 153

Oakes, J., 146, 188
Oakley, D., 146
Oliver, A., 36, 43
Olneck, Michael R., 203

Olson, Candy, 56
Olsson, U., 130, 137 n. 8
Orfield, Gary, 5, 21, 48, 55
Orfield, M., 18–19, 20
Osler, A., 152, 153

Paige, Rodney, 51, 54, 56
Palmer, D., 111
Panitch, L., 43
Parenti, Christian, 99, 102, 107,
    108
Park, C., 152, 153
Parker, L., 175
Parker, W. C., 152, 153
Parks, Rosa, 162
Patterson, J., 70
Patterson, O., 141
Pearce, R. H., 162
Perlmutter, P., 160
Peterson, Robert, 6, 42
Petersson, K., 130, 137 n. 8
Petrovich, Janice, 100, 104, 106
Philips, S. U., 143, 148
Phillips, K., 21
Phillips, M., 253
Phillips, Ulrich B., 148
Piestrup, A. M., 143, 149
Pinar, William F., 231, 244–245
    n. 3
Pitts, E. L., 70
Pollock, Jackson, 241–242
Pol Pot, 88
Pope, Denise Clark, 225–226
Popkewitz, Thomas, 11, 119–
    140, 122, 123, 130–132, 134,
    137 n. 8, 137 n. 9, 159, 167,
    244–245 n. 3, 251
Power, S., 54
Prewitt, Kenneth, 248

Quin, D. B., 143

Ramirez, M., III, 142
Ranny, D., 101, 113 n. 3
Ratner, E., 35
Ravitch, Diane, 205, 207
Read, Herbert, 226
Reagan, Ronald, xii, 3, 88, 102,
    256
Reaves, J. A., 67, 73
Reed, Ralph, 39
Reese, W., 125
Reid, W., 232
Reno, Ron, 39
Restori, M., 67
Reuben, J., 122
Revilla, A. T., 111–112
Richardson, R., 183
Riche, M. F., ix
Ricoeur, Paul, 232, 238
Riessman, F., xi–xii
Ringer, B. B., 158, 159, 162,
    165, 166

Rivlin, G., 99
Robert, M., 19
Robertson, S., 49, 54, 106
Rockwell, Norman, 4
Rodgers, D., 123
Rofes, E. E., 105
Rogers, Carl, 95
Romberg, T. A., 258
Roosevelt, Franklin D., 165
Rosaldo, R., 142
Rose, L. C., 216–217
Rose, N., 124
Rosebrock, K., 149
Rosenbaum, J., 6
Rosenburg, A., 249
Rosenstock, L., 42
Ross, Edward, 46
Rothstein, R., 5–6
Rousseau, Jean-Jacques, 31, 160–161
Rowan, B., 258
Roy, Arundhati, 102
Rubinowitz, L., 6
Rusk, D., 18–19, 20
Rust, F., 149
Ryan, Richard, 58–59

Sacks, Peter, 59
Said, Edward, 85–87, 89, 93, 95, 96, 226
St. Pierre, E., 137 n. 2
Saldana, Johnny, 220–221, 226
Salle, Leonard M., 50, 59
Saltman, K. J., 101
Sanchez, R., 73–74
Sanders, W. L., 188
Sanjek, R., 102
Sartre, Jean-Paul, 214, 219–220
Sassen, S., 102, 109
Schlafly, Phyllis, 38, 39
Schmitt, J., 18, 19
Schneider, A., 215
Schoenfeld, A. H., 258
Schonfield, J., 150
Schwab, Joseph, 234–236, 238–239
Schweitzer, J., 150
Scott, Joan T., 40, 105, 129, 136
Seashore, Carl, 126
Segarra, J., 31
Sewell, T., 179
Shakespeare, William, 90
Shapiro, Thomas M., 253, 254
Sheets, R. H., 174
Sherry, A., 78 n. 2
Shore, A. R., 104
Shulman, L. S., 255–256
Siddle-Walker, V., 5
Simmonds, R., 110
Simon, Ray, 254

Sipple, J., 55
Sizer, Ted, 42, 58
Skiba, R. J., 6
Skinner, C., 103
Skocpol, T., 47–48
Sleeter, C. E., 138 n. 10, 163, 167–168, 203, 206, 207
Smith, Anna Deavere, 92–93
Smith, C., 38
Smith, L. C., 232
Smith, Linda Tuhiwai, 34, 142
Smith, Mary Lee, 215, 216
Smith, N., 109
Snedden, David, 46, 53–54
Soja, E. W., 110
Solomon, M., 159
Sowell, J., 146
Soysal, Y., 132
Stampp, K. M., 148
Stanley, Julian C., 180
Stefancic, J., 174
Stein, J., 233
Steinberg, A., 42
Stephan, C. W., 144, 146–147
Stephan, W. G., 144–147, 149, 150
Stephens, S., 75
Sternberg, Robert J., 179–180
Stevens, Rosemary, 161
Stillman, J., 203, 206, 207
Stone, R., 221
Stotsky, S., xi
Stulberg, L. M., 105
Suárez-Orozco, C., 143
Suárez-Orozco, M. M., 143
Sullivan, C., 67
Sung, Y.-K., 36, 43
Swanson, C., 55
Swanstrom, T., 19, 20

Tabb, W., 49
Tate, William F., 12, 104–105, 141, 160, 174, 176, 190, 231–233, 235, 242, 247–260
Tatum, Beverly, 168–169
Tavares, H., 36, 43
Taylor, Frederick Winslow, 46
Taylor, John, 163
Tenorio, Rita, 42
Thatcher, Margaret, 101
Thayer-Bacon, Barbara, 244 n. 2
Theodore, N., 109
Thernstrom, A., 42
Thomas, E., 159, 160
Thorndike, Edward L., 121–122, 124–127, 128
Toch, T., 73
Tocqueville, Alexis de, 158
Towne, L., 201
Trager, H. G., 150
Trump, Donald, 99

Turner, B., 102
Tyack, D. B., 203–204

Urdang, L., 233

Valencia, R. R., 104
Valenzuela, Angela S., 49, 52–53, 57–59, 103
Vallas, Paul, 52
Vallasi, C. A., xi
Van Ausdale, D., 144
Vander Wyst, A., 34, 67
Venkatesh, S. A., 102
Villarreal, B. J., 104
Villenas, S., 175
Vinod, H. D., 257
Viramontes, C., 111
Vogt, W. P., 144, 145, 149

Wald, J., 55
Walker, Decker, 232, 237
Walker, V. S., 202
Wallis, J., 38
Walter, J., 164
Walters, Mike, 170
Walton, Anthony, 81–82
Ward, Lester Frank, 46
Washington, Booker T., 147
Watson, J., 41
Waugh, D., 204–206, 210 n. 2
Weiler, Kathleen, 244–245 n. 3
Wells, Amy Stuart, 4, 40, 100, 105, 111–112
West, Cornel, 9
West, Kanye, 98
Whitty, G., 54
Wildmon, Donald, 38
Wiley, Terry, 67
Williams, P. J., 176
Willis, A. I., 5
Wilson, G., 67
Winerip, M., 56
Wing, A. K., 175
Winter, G., 55
Wirth, A., 46
Wisenbaker, J., 150
Wittrock, B., 125
Wong, T.-H., 36, 43
Wood, A., 183
Wood, E. M., 35
Woodson, Carter G., 142, 148
Woodworth, R. S., 128
Wraga, W., 231
Wright, H. K., 231
Wright, Wayne, 67

Yarrow, M. R., 150
Youdell, Deborah, 49, 55, 177
Young, Iris M., 50

Zinn, Howard, 87, 89–90

Subject Index

Academy for Gifted and Talented Youth (England), 180
Accountability. *See also* Assessment
  contemporary apologists for, 235
  education reform and, 51–60, 100–101, 103
  state-level testing and, 51, 54–56, 100–101, 208–209
  as term, 216
Achievement gap
  challenge of, 145
  increase in, 55
Activist art, 219–225, 228–229
Adequate yearly progress (AYP), 49, 60 n. 2
Advancement Project, 107
African Americans. *See* Blacks
Allen Company, 71
American Dilemma, The (Myrdal), 170–171
American Educational Research Association, 56
American Exceptionalism, 125–126, 248–254
American Family Association, 38
American Indians. *See* Native Americans
Americanization process, 137 n. 6, 146, 204
American Medicine and the Public Interest (Stevens), 161
American Negro Slavery (Phillips), 148
American Psychological Association, Cleary Committee, 180
Antiwar movement, 60
Arizona Education Policy Initiative (AEPI), 34–35, 66–67, 75, 77–78, 255, 256
Arizona State University, 34–35
Art-making, 239–244
  anarchic quality of, 241–242
  freedom in, 236
  hermeneutics and, 234–244
  I-Thou relationship and, 239–241
  limitation and constraint in, 241
  link to research in the public interest, 242–244
  nature of, 236, 237
Arts-based research, 218–229
  activist art and, 219–225, 228–229
  challenges and possibilities of, 227–229
  epistemologically humble, 221–227
  ethnodrama and, 220–225
  nature of, 218
  political interests and, 225–226
  socially engaged, 219–221
Asian Americans
  achievement gap between other minority groups and, 145
  attitudes toward other ethnic groups, 166
ASIPI (Association for Science in the Public Interest), 200
Assessment, 173–191. *See also* Accountability

baseline, in the United Kingdom, 181–189
Foundation Stage Profile (United Kingdom), 184–189, 191 n. 7
high achievement by minority groups, 176–177, 181–189
impact of, 103–105, 208–209
resistance to, 56–60
state-level, 30, 39–40, 51, 54–56, 100–101, 208–209
Assimilation process
  in conception of citizenship, 141–153
  diversity as countermovement of, 204
  role of schools in, 141–153, 204
Association for Science in the Public Interest (ASIPI), 200
Association for Supervision and Curriculum Development (ASCD), 65

Bell Curve, The (Herrnstein & Murray), 147–148, 180
Bilingual Education Act (1968), 165
Bilingual movement, 21, 100, 111, 112, 165
Black Education (King), 100
Black English, 148–149
Black Power, xii
Blacks
  achievement gap between Whites and, 55, 145
  attitudes toward other ethnic groups, 166
  and baseline assessment in the United Kingdom, 181–189
  civil rights movement and, 20–21, 60, 104–105, 141–142, 167
  discrimination against, 20, 99
  double consciousness (DuBois), 87
  dropout rates, 55, 56
  employment problems of, 102
  equity pedagogy and, 148
  foreign-born, increase in U.S., 144
  Freedom Schools, 46–47, 60 n. 1
  gentrification process and, 110
  Hurricane Katrina and, 3–9, 98–100, 159–160
  intergenerational education and, 253–254
  Jim Crow laws and, 162–163, 165
  measures of intellectual ability, xi–xii, 147–148, 177–190
  in the military, 102, 107–109
  multicultural education and, 142
  need for mathematics skills, 104–105
  No Child Left Behind Act (NCLB; 2002) and, 111
  performance on baseline assessments in the United Kingdom, 181–189
  poverty among, 3–9, 18, 19, 98–100, 159–160
  prejudicial attitudes of Whites and, 158
  prisons and, 102, 107–108
  public policies that penalize, 18

red-lining and, 163
settlement house movement and, 123, 127
signifying and, 149
slavery and, 147–148, 162
in special-needs programs, 6
sports and, 164
Blackwell, 99
Brazil, approaches to education in, 35–36
British Academy, 180–181
Brown v. Board of Education of Topeka, xii, 3, 48,
    112, 158, 164, 165, 168

Cable in the Classroom, 71
California
    California State Department of Education, ix, 143,
        207
    culture of materialism and, 225–226
    ethnic minorities in, 143
    History-Social Science Framework and Standards,
        206–207
    state-level curriculum policy in, 204–207
    testing-accountability system, 208–209
Carnegie Report, 235
Censorship, of science, 119–120
Center for Education Policy, Analysis, and Innovation,
    Educational Policy Project, 34–35, 67
Center for the Analysis of Commercialization in
    Education (CACE), University of Wisconsin-
    Milwaukee, 66–67
Center for the Study of Testing, Evaluation, and
    Education Policy (CSTEEP), 253
Centers for Disease Control (CDC), 256
Central Park East School (New York City), 42
Changing Minds (Gardner), 228
Channel One, 38–39, 71
Charter schools, 40–41, 47, 51–53, 74–76, 105–106,
    111
Chicago
    accountability system, 100–101
    Chicago Charter School Foundation, 105–106
    Chicago public schools (CPS), 52–54
    Chicago Teachers for Social Justice, 57
    corporate-center development in, 109–111
    decline in manufacturing jobs, 102–103
    gentrification in, 110
    as global city, 113–114 n. 6
    magnet schools in, 106, 109
    military schools in, 108
    neoliberal foundation for policies in, 57
    New Schools for Chicago, 53
    Renaissance 2010 plan, 53, 57
    school withdrawals from districts, 111
    settlement house movement, 123, 127
    social-justice high schools in, 113
    South Side, 81–82, 93–94
    urban community and child in, 127–128
Children of the National Longitudinal Survey of Youth
    (CNLSY), 253
Children's Defense Fund (CDF), xi
Chosen People, Americans as, 125–126, 251
Citizens for Tax Justice, 18
Citizenship
    assimilationist conception of, challenges to,
        141–153
    challenges to assimilationist conception of, 141–153

education for national and global, 151
    multicultural (Kymlicka), 142, 152–153
Civil Rights Act (1965), 158, 165
Civil rights movement, 20–21, 60, 104–105, 141–142,
    167
Civil War, 250–251
Cleveland, Ohio, voucher program, 73
Coalition for Common Sense in Education (CCSE),
    58, 59
Coca-Cola, 69
Commercial Alert, 38, 67
Commercialism in Education Research Unit (CERU),
    66–78
    Education Policy Studies Lab, 77–78
    formation of, 66–67
    for-profit school management industry and, 73–76
    impact of, 77–78
    recent developments, 76–77
    trends in schoolhouse commercialism, 66, 67–72
Common Core of Data (CCD), 76
Communion, in curriculum research, 233–234
Community of learners, 131–132
Comparable-worth laws, 19–20
Conservative modernization. *See* Neoconservatism
Conspiratorial conversations (Barone), 222
Constructivism, 46–47
Consumer Union, 66–67
Consuming Kids (Linn), 68
Content integration, in multicultural education,
    146–147
CORE Knowledge Curriculum, 106
Corporations
    advertising and, 66, 70, 76–77
    for-profit school management industry, 73–76,
        100–101, 105
    influence on education, 46, 52–54, 99
    lobbying power of, 256
    political-economic reconstruction of cities and,
        109–111
    privatizing public education, 52–55, 71, 73–76
    public relations and, 256
    schoolhouse commercialism and, 64–72
    university boards of trustees and, 89–90
Cosmopolitanism
    cultural theses about unfinished cosmopolitan,
        129–132
    multicultural citizenship (Kymlicka) and, 142,
        152–153
Council on Corporate and School Partnerships, 68
Critical-emancipatory research (Habermas), 243–244
Critical theory
    conservative restructuring and, 28
    critical race theory (CRT), 174–175
    curriculum research and, 232, 234
    practical applications of, 41–42
Cultural democracy, 142
Cultural Politics and Education (Apple), 31
Cultural relevance, 142–143
Curriculum, 199–210. *See also* Curriculum research
    as battleground for conservative restructuring,
        30–34
    impact on students, 147
    research in other countries, 32–33, 35–36
    research on changing, 32–33
    sponsored educational materials (SEM), 65–66, 70

Curriculum research, 231–245. *See also* Curriculum
    art-making and, 236, 239–244
    communion and, 233–234
    education research in the public interest and, 231–
        234, 239, 242–244
    freedom and, 232–234, 237
    hermeneutics of, 236–244
    need for engagement in process of education,
        234–237
    public interest and, 238–244
Curriculum standards, 128–134
    as cultural theses about unfinished cosmopolitan,
        129–132
    as cultural theses about urban child left behind,
        132–134
    developing higher, 203–207
    for mathematics, 131–134, 258
    state-level, 204–207

Dairy Council, 66
Data Quality Act (2000), 256–258
Declaration of Independence, 162, 167, 170
Degenerative politics (Schneider & Ingram), 215
Democracy
    cultural, 142
    Dewey and, 239
    participation in education policy and, 104, 105
    public policy and, 153–154
Democracy Now, 99
Democratic Schools (Apple & Beane), 41
Department for Education & Skills (DfES; England),
    181–182, 185–186, 191 n. 3, 191 n. 7
Design-Based Research Collective, 131
Devolution and Choice in Education (Whitty et al.), 54
Diana v. State Board of Education, 165
Disabilities movement, 21
Distinction (Bourdieu), 243–244
District of Columbia, voucher program, 51–52, 73
Diversity
    balancing unity and, 152
    as countermovement of assimilation, 204
    education and, 145
    increasing, in the world, 143–144
    opportunities and challenges of, 144–145
    public interest and, 153–154
Doing School (Pope), 225–226
Dred Scott case, 161, 165
Dropout rates, 55–56

Eagle Forum, 38
Economic Policy Institute, 18, 20
Edison Schools Inc., 74
Educating the "Right" Way (Apple), 28, 42–43
Educational Policy Project (Center for Education
    Research, Analysis, and Innovation), 34–35, 67
Educational research. *See also* Curriculum research;
    Qualitative inquiry; Scientifically based research
    (SBR)
    American social science project and, 248–250
    Center for Analysis of Commercialism in Education
        (CACE), 66–67
    challenging orthodoxy in, 94–95
    Commercialism in Education Research Unit
        (CERU), 66–78

    conduct of intellectual life and, 85–87
    Data Quality Act (2000) and, 256–258
    humanism and, 82–85, 92–94
    linking consciousness to conduct in, 95–96
    new paradigm of, 21–24
    objectivity and balance in, 89–91
    promise of, 24–25
    qualitative inquiry in. *See* Qualitative inquiry
    role of humanities in, 81–97, 258
    role of public intellectuals in, 64–66
    in service of science, 91–92
    types of research practice, 243–244
    unknown and, 87–89
Educational Sciences Reform Act (2002), 201
Education management organizations (EMOs), 73–76,
    100–101, 105
Education policy
    democratic participation and, 104, 105
    labor stratification and, 102–107
    new paradigm of educational research and, 21–24
Education Policy Studies Laboratory (EPSL), Arizona
    State University, 34–35, 66–67, 75, 77–78, 255,
    256
Education reform, 98–114
    accountability and, 51–60, 100–101, 103
    corporations in. *See* Corporations
    Hurricane Katrina and, 2–3, 5–6, 98–100, 159–160
    inequality and, 112–113
    political economic context of, 101–102
Effective schools, 151
Elementary and Secondary Education Act (1965), 3,
    165
Empirical-analytic research (Habermas), 243–244
Empowerment
    individual, 132
    in multicultural education, 150–151
England, 173–191, 258
    assessment results of Black students, 177–190
    GCSE (General Certificate of Secondary
        Education), 177
    Gifted and Talented programs in, 180
    mathematics curriculum revision in, 32–33
    tiering in London schools, 177–179
English language learners, dropout rates, 55, 56
Environmental movement, 60
Epistemological terrorism (Lyotard), 221
Equity. *See also* Social justice
    assessment and educational inequity, 175–176
    move away from, 100
    pedagogy of, in multicultural education, 148–149
Evidence-based inquiry, 119–138
Exclusion Act (1882), 165
Existentialism, 233

Failures of Integration, The (Cashin), 168
Fair Employment Practice Commission (FEPC), 165
Family
    planning moral life of urban, 124–126
    socialization process in, 127–128
Field Trip Factory, 70
Florida, testing-accountability system, 51
Focus on the Family, 38, 39
Food Marketing to Children and Youth (McGinnes et
    al.), 77

Foundation Stage Profile, 184–189, 191 n. 7
France, systems of recognition and distinction in, 134
Frankfurt School, 232, 234
Fratney Street School (Milwaukee), 42
Freedom
    in art-making, 236
    in curriculum research, 232–234, 237

GCSE (General Certificate of Secondary Education;
    England), 177
General Certificate of Secondary Education (GCSE;
    England), 177
Gentrification, 110
Ghetto Schooling (Anyon), 22
Giant Cement Holding Co., 69
Gifted and Talented programs, 180
Global citizenship
    education for, 151
    global cities in U.S., 113–114 n. 6
Government Accountability Office, 77
Great Depression, 20

Handbook of Research on Multicultural Education
    (Banks & Banks), x, 146
Harvard Center for Civil Rights, 55
Harvard Law School, xii–xiii
Head Start, 21
Hermeneutics, 234–244
    benefits of approach based on, 238–239
    of curriculum research, 236–244
    nature of, 238
High Stakes Education (Lipman), 52–55
Hill and Knowlton (H&K), 256
Hillsborough County (Florida) school district, 69
Hispanic Americans. See Latinos
Historical-hermeneutic research (Habermas), 243–244
Hope
    for inclusive society, 120, 123–128
    as resource in neoconservatism, 42–43
Horse's Mouth, The (Cary), 241
Houston School District, 55–56, 57–58
Humanism, in educational research, 82–85, 92–94
Humanities, in educational research, 81–97, 258
Hurricane Katrina, 1–10
    race and public policy, 3–9, 98–100, 159–160
    relevance to education, 2–3, 5–6, 98–100, 159–160
    responses to, 1–9, 11–12
    September 11, 2001 terrorist attacks versus, 1, 9–10

I and Thou (Buber), 239–241
Immigrants
    education for, 46, 151
    to Europe, 152
    gentrification process and, 110
    multicultural education and, 142
    No Child Left Behind Act (NCLB; 2002) and, 111
    population trends in, ix
    settlement house movement and, 123, 127
    state-level curriculum policy and, 205–207
    wages of, 102
Immigration Act (1924), 165
Immigration Reform Act (1965), 143
Implied reader (Iser), 222, 226
Inclusion and Democracy (Young), 50

Indianapolis, Indiana, Education Resource Centers
    (ERCs), 68–69
Indwelling, The (LaHaye & Jenkins), 29, 43 n. 1
Information Society, 130
Institute of Educational Studies (IES), 201
Intelligence
    measures of, xi–xii, 147–148, 177–190
    psychometric testing, 179–180
    street-wise, of teachers, 133

Jim Crow laws, 162–163, 165
Job training programs, 18
Johns Hopkins University, Center for Talented Youth,
    180–181
Junior Reserve Officer Training Cadets (JROTC), 108

Kitsch, in arts-based research, 223
Knowledge and Human Interests (Habermas), 243
Knowledge construction, in multicultural education,
    147–148

Labeling, 93–94
Labor stratification, 102–107
Language Policy Research Unit (LPRU), 67
Latinos
    achievement gap between Whites and, 55, 145
    attitudes toward other ethnic groups, 166
    discrimination against, 20
    dropout rates, 55, 56
    equity pedagogy and, 148
    Hurricane Katrina and, 99
    intergenerational education and, 253–254
    multicultural education and, 142
    population trends in, ix
    poverty among, 18, 19
    prisons and, 107–108
    public policies that penalize, 18
    red-lining and, 163
Lau v. Nichols, 165
League of United Latin American Citizens (LULAC),
    57–58
Learning as a Political Act (Segarra & Dobles), 31
Learning Society, 130
Lifelong learning, 128–131
Los Angeles
    as global city, 113–114 n. 6
    social-justice high schools in, 113

Magnet schools, 106–107, 109
Manufactured Crisis, The (Berliner & Biddle), 235
Market mechanisms, in education, 53–54, 105–107,
    130–131
Master narratives, in qualitative inquiry, 215–216
Mathematics
    Blacks and skills in, 104–105
    curriculum standards for, 131–134, 258
    research on curriculum change, 32–33
McDonald's, 65–66
Mexican American Legal Defense of Education Fund
    (MALDE), 57–58
Military, 102, 107–109
Milwaukee, Wisconsin, voucher program, 73
Minimum wage, 18, 19–20
Mission Hill School (Boston), 42, 48

Multicultural citizenship (Kymlicka), 142, 152–153
Multicultural education
  defined, x
  dimensions of, 146–151
  goals of, x, 145–146
  plural society and, 166–167
  reason for development of, 142
  state-level curriculum policy and, 205–207
  Whiteness studies and, 174
Multiculturalism
  accommodation toward, 167–170
  racist duality and, 161–164, 168
  resistance to, 161–170
Music education, trends in, 126

National Center for Education Statistics (NCES),
    249, 257
National Commission on Excellence in Education
    (NCEH), 51
National Community Reinvestment Coalition, 163
National Council of Education Providers, 71
National Council of Teachers of Mathematics, 131,
    133–134
National Educational Research Policy and Priorities
    Board, 201
National Endowment for the Humanities (NEH), 205
National Federation of Teachers (NFT), 217
National Law Enforcement and Corrections
    Technology Center, 107–108
National Parent Teacher Association, 71
National Priorities Project, 103
National Research Council (NRC), 19, 201, 210 n.
    1, 253
Nation at Risk, A, 3, 51, 235
Native Americans
  equity pedagogy and, 148
  intergenerational education and, 253–254
  Native Hawaiian "talk stories," 149
NCLB. See No Child Left Behind Act (NCLB; 2002)
Neoconservatism, 27–44
  contradictory school reforms, 30–34
  heretical thinking in, 36–41
  hope as a resource in, 42–43
  learning from other countries, 32–33, 35–36
  making critical educational practices practical,
    41–42
  nature of, 29
  neoliberal-neoconservative alliances and, 38–41
  populist religious groups and, 29, 37–38
  public challenges to, 34–35
  school curriculum as battleground in, 30–34
Neoliberalism, 46–60
  accountability and, 51–60, 100–101, 103
  corporate influence on education and, 47, 52–54
  impact on schools, 101–102
  markets and education policy, 53–54, 105–107,
    130–131
  nature of, 29
  neoliberal-neoconservative alliances and, 38–41
  politics of reversing neoliberal policies, 47–51
  promoting progressive economic and education
    policy, 56–60
  public challenges to neoconservatism, 34–35
  schools as battleground for, 30–34
  standardized testing and, 51–60

New Orleans
  arts-based research in, 220–225
  Hurricane Betsy and, 9
  Hurricane Katrina and, 3–9, 98–100, 159–160
  Mississippi flood of 1927 and, 5, 9
  9th ward, 7–8, 9
  plans to rebuild, 5–6
  scenario for future of, 6–9
  school integration, 4–5
New York City
  corporate-center development in, 109–111
  as global city, 113–114 n. 6
  magnet schools in, 106
New York State
  neoliberal foundation for policies in, 57
  New York Performance Standard Consortium
    (PSC), 57
  Rochester School Without Walls, 58–59
  state-level curriculum policy in, 204–206
  testing-accountability system, 51, 54–55, 208–209
New Zealand, approaches to education in, 36
No Child Left Behind Act (NCLB; 2002)
  accountability and standards and, 100–101, 200,
    208, 235
  adequate yearly progress (AYP), 49, 60 n. 2
  American Exceptionalism and, 251–254
  censorship in, 119–120
  changes in for-profit education industry, 74
  curriculum standards and, 128–134, 135
  described, 3
  disaggregation of data in, 3, 110–111
  Hurricane Katrina and, 11–12
  impact on racial, ethnic, and class tensions, 110–111
  lifelong learning and, 128–131
  origins of name, xi
  progressive critiques of schools and, 29
  race and public policy, 159
  Reading First initiative, 201
  resistance to institutional oppression and, 214–215
  scientifically based research and. See Scientifically
    based research (SBR)
  stated goal of, 253
  testing requirements, 49, 51–52
  theory of improvement as basis of, 254
  zero-tolerance school discipline policies, 107–109

Office for Standards in Education (OFSTED;
    England), 181, 183–184
Office of Educational Research and Improvement
    (OERI), 201
On the Road (Smith), 92–93
Oppositional reader (Hall), 226
Oppression, documenting and describing, 22
Organization of Economic and Cooperative
    Development, 54
"Other," 37–38, 134
Other America, The (Harrington), 2
Outlaw culture (hooks), 219

Pedagogy
  of equity in multicultural education, 148–149
  as politics of schooling, 167–170
People for the American Way, 74
People of color. See Asian Americans; Blacks;
    Immigrants; Latinos

Pepsi-Cola, 69
Performance Standards Consortium (PSC), 58
Phi Delta Kappa/Gallup poll, 216–217
Phrenology, xi
Pizza Hut Book-It program, 70
Plessy v. Ferguson, 161–162, 165
Pluralistic society, defined, 159
Plural society
    defined, 158–159
    multicultural education and, 166–167
    as resistance to multiculturalism, 165–167
Postmodern theory, 219
Poverty
    extent in U.S., 102
    in New Orleans, 7–8, 9, 98–100
    policies to lower, 19–20
    public policy in maintenance of, 18–19
    school desegregation and, 5
Power
    creating in urban communities, 22–23
    knowledge as form of, 89–91
    in postmodern theory, 219
    public intellectuals and, 65
    studying policy elite, 22
    Whiteness and, 174
Prejudice
    intergroup, 166
    reduction of, in multicultural education, 149–150
Primedia Corp., 71
Prison Notebooks (Gramsci), 84
Prison system, 102, 107–108
Privatizing public education, 52–55, 71, 73–76,
    101–102
*Profiles of For-Profit Education Management
    Organizations* (Molnar et al.), 67, 73, 75–76
Progressive reform, 20–21, 123–128, 133, 136
Project for a New American Century, 107
Project Sentry, 107–108
Propaganda, in arts-based research, 223
Psychometric testing, 179–180
Public Citizens Health Research Group, 256
Public intellectuals, 64–78
    Center for Analysis of Commercialism in Education
        (CACE), 66–67
    Commercialism in Education Research Unit
        (CERU), 66–78
    role of, 64–66
Public interest
    capacity and research on, 254–258
    curriculum research and, 238–244
    diversity and, 153–154
    interests of Whites versus, 173–190
    nature of, 160–161
    political economy and, 250–254
Public policy, 17–25. *See also* Education policy
    American Exceptionalism and, 125–126, 248–254
    case for research in the public interest, 199–210
    Data Quality Act (2000) and, 256–258
    democracy and, 153–154
    diversity and, 153–154
    Hurricane Katrina and, 3–9, 98–100, 159–160
    intergenerational factors and, 253–254
    nature of public interest and, 160–161
    need for new, 19–20
    new paradigm of educational research and, 21–24

political-economic reconstruction of cities and
    metro regions, 109–111
political economy and the public interest, 250–254
    on preventing Reye's syndrome, 256
    race and, 158–171
    role in maintaining urban poverty, 18–19
    science in, 119–138
    social movements and, 20–21, 24
    taxes in, 18
Public School Accountability Act (1999; California),
    206

QSP Reader's Digest, 71
Qualifications & Curriculum Authority (QCA;
    England), 184, 191 n. 2
Qualitative inquiry, 213–229
    arts-based research in, 218–229
    challenges and possibilities of, 227–229
    federal government role in education and, 214–215
    master narratives and, 215–216
    public attitude toward public schools and, 216–217
    strategies used in, 217–218

Racism, xi–xii, 173–191
    in New Orleans, 4–5
    racist duality and, 161–164, 168
Radical Possibilities (Anyon), 17–25, 50–51
Reading Excellence Act (1999), 201
Red-lining, 163
Renaissance 2010 (Chicago), 53, 57
Representations of the Intellectual (Said), 85–87
Responsibilization (Rose), 124
Rethinking Schools, 24
Revolutionary reader (Belsey), 226
Reye's syndrome, 256
Rightist movement. *See* Neoconservatism
Rindge School of Technical Arts (Boston area),
    41–42
Robert Wood Johnson Foundation, 76
RPP International, 76

SAGE program (Wisconsin), 34
Sandia National Laboratory, 107–108
Schoolhouse commercialism, 64–72
    impact of, 77–78
    references in the press, 71–72
    trends in, 67–72, 76–77
    types of, 68–71
Schooling in Capitalist America (Bowles & Gintis),
    243
Schools. *See also* Neoconservatism; Neoliberalism
    in assimilation process, 141–153, 204
    characteristics of effective, 151
    as cultural institutions, 28–29
    desegregation of, xii, 3, 4–5, 48, 112, 158, 164,
        165, 168
    militarization and, 102, 107–109, 113
    polls on public attitudes toward, 216–217
    role in changing society by changing people,
        121–123
    social justice-oriented, 112–113
    in transmission of socioeconomic status, 250–254
School Security Technology and Resource Center,
    107–108
School Teacher (Lortie), 236

Scientifically based research (SBR), 119–138, 199–210
  as commitment to public interests, 134–136
  curriculum standards in, 128–134
  development of educational, 201–202
  nature of, 201–202
  Scientific Research in Education (National Research Council), 201–202
Self, concept of, 136
September 11, 2001 terrorist attacks
  Hurricane Katrina versus, 1, 9–10
  other attacks and, 152
Servicemen's Readjustment Act (G.I. Bill), 48
Settlement house movement, 123, 127
Shame of the Nation, The (Kozol), 164
Shortchanged Children of Suburbia, The (Hechinger), 145
Signifying, in Black speech, 149
Simon Property Group, 68
Simon Youth Foundation, 68
Slavery, 147–148, 162
Social Contract, The (Rousseau), 160–161
Social efficiency movement, 46
Socialization
  in classroom, 132
  in family, 127–128
Social justice, 141–154. *See also* Equity
  challenges to assimilationist notion of citizenship, 141–153
  diversity and the public interest and, 153–154
  research on, 88–89
Social movements
  in changing public policy, 20–21, 60, 112–113
  schools as bases for, 24, 112–113
  study of, 23
Social policy
  planning moral life of urban family, 124–126
  urban community and urban child in Chicago, 127–128
Social Question, 120, 123, 135
Social studies, state-level curriculum policy in, 204–207
Socioeconomic status, methods of transmission, 250–254
Sponsored educational materials (SEM), 65–66, 70
Sports, racism and, 164
Standard English, 148–149
Street Rat (Saldana et al.), 220–225
Student activists
  activist art and, 219–225, 228–229
  studying, 23–24
Student-centered approach, impact of, 32–33
Students with disabilities, dropout rates, 55, 56

Tax policies, 18
Teachers
  resistance to institutional oppression, 214–215
  stereotypes applied to, 216
  stereotypes held by White, 178–179
  street-wise intelligence of, 133
  teacher education programs, 128

"Teach-ins," 44 n. 4
Terrorism, 1, 9–10, 152
Testing. *See* Assessment
Texas
  Houston public schools, 55–56, 57–58
  Student Success Initiative (SSI), 208
  testing-accountability system, 51, 55–56, 100–101, 208–209
They Learn What They Live (Trager & Yarrow), 150
Third moment (Denzin & Lincoln), 225
Time Out from Testing, 58
Title I, 3, 100
Title IX, 100
Transformative research, xiii

United Kingdom. *See* England
U.S. Census Bureau, ix, 3–4, 143, 144, 158, 165
U.S. Constitution, 162, 167, 170
U.S. Department of Education, 256–258
U.S. Department of Labor, 103
Universities. See also names of specific universities
  advocacy resources of, 256
  corporate influence on trustees of, 89–90
  endowments of, 247
University of California at Los Angeles
  IDEA center, 113
  National Center for History in the Schools, 205
University of Wisconsin-Milwaukee, 66–67
Urban Academy (New York City), 48

Virtual schools, 74–75
Voting rights legislation, 165, 168
Voucher programs, 37, 40, 51–52, 73–74

WalMart, 103
War on Poverty, 2
What's The Matter with Kansas (Frank), 49
What Works Clearing House, 159
White flight, 163
Whites
  achievement gap between students of color and, 55, 145
  attitudes toward other ethnic groups, 166
  poverty among, 19
  prejudicial attitudes of, 158
  privileges of, 173–175, 189–190
  public interest versus interests of, 173–191
  stereotypes held by teachers, 178–179
White Teacher Talks About Race, A (Landsman), 169
Women
  student-centered approach and, 32–33
  women's movement and, 21
Women's movement, 60
World Trade Center terrorist attacks (9/11/01), 1, 9–10, 152
World Trade Organization (WTO) protests, 38, 44 n. 4
World War II, 20, 143, 165

ZapMe! Corp., 38